PRIME TIME

PRIME TIME
HOW TV PORTRAYS AMERICAN CULTURE

BY

S. ROBERT LICHTER, LINDA S. LICHTER
AND STANLEY ROTHMAN

WITH THE ASSISTANCE OF
DANIEL AMUNDSON

REGNERY PUBLISHING, INC.
WASHINGTON, D.C.

Library of Congress Cataloging-in-Publication Data

Lichter, S. Robert.
Prime time / by S. Robert Lichter, Linda S. Lichter, and Stanley
Rothman : with the assistance of Daniel Amundson.
p. cm.
Includes bibliographical references (p. -) and index.
ISBN 0-89526-491-9 (acid-free paper)
1. Television broadcasting—Social aspects—United States.
2. Television programs—United States—History and criticism.
I. Lichter, Linda S. II. Rothman, Stanley, 1927- . III. Title.
√ PN1992.6.L53 1994
302.23'45'0973—dc20   94-23003
                                                        CIP

Published in the United States by
Regnery Publishing, Inc.
An Eagle Publishing Company
422 First St., SE, Suite 300
Washington, DC 20003

Distributed to the trade by
National Book Network
4720-A Boston Way
Lanham, MD 20706

Printed on acid-free paper.
Manufactured in the United States of America

10 9 8 7 6 5 4 3 2 1

Books are available in quantity for promotional or premium use. Write to Director of Special Sales, Regnery Publishing, Inc., 422 First Street, SE, Suite 300, Washington, DC 20003, for information on discounts and terms or call (202) 546-5005.

CONTENTS

PREFACE

T his book describes how prime-time entertainment has portrayed American society from the 1950s to the 1990s, as television has moved from the sidelines to the front lines of social controversy. To our knowledge, this is the most comprehensive study of life on television that has ever been conducted. Our goal was to depict Hollywood's nightly fantasy version of our society, and to show how it has taken on a life of its own, as a kind of artificial reality. Today, the world of prime time helps define our collective consciousness, as a dream from which we never fully awaken.

In one sense, then, what follows is a self-contained study of popular culture. But it is also one component of a much broader study of leadership and social conflict in contemporary America, which emphasizes the role that mass media play in social change. Thus, this book grew out of a larger study of leadership and social change in America, which was directed by Stanley Rothman. The project was inaugurated by Rothman in 1977 to examine the role of new elites (especially those involved in communications) in producing social and cultural change. In 1978, Robert Lichter joined the project with primary responsibility to conduct a study of the news media and, more generally, to collect and analyze survey data on a wide range of elite groups. In 1979, Linda Lichter completed the research team, as a specialist in content analysis, to conduct the study of television entertainment.

The results of this collaboration are collected in several volumes. In 1986 *The Media Elite* examined the changing social role of the national news media. In 1991 *Watching America* provided a similar analysis of the changing world of television entertainment through the mid-1980s. Currently in preparation is *Elites in Conflict*, of which Rothman is the principal author. That work will present the findings of our entire range of elite and media studies in the context of his theoretical framework. For the past several years, the Lichters have also conducted independent media studies through their Center for Media and Public Affairs (CMPA), while Rothman has pursued his own research agenda through the Center for the Study of Social and Political Change, which he directs at Smith College. (Among his current projects is *Hollywood's America*, a historical content analysis of changing social imagery in motion pictures.)

The current volume grew out of our recognition that television entertainment was undergoing rapid changes in both its program content and its relationship to American society. Once dismissed as a fantasy factory unworthy of serious analysis, it is now widely regarded as a major source of both intentional and inadvertent social commentary. Events such as former Vice-President Quayle's criticism of "Murphy Brown" and congressional efforts to reduce television violence have focused public attention on the medium's impact on individual behavior and societal norms. Public concern has been intensified by larger developments whose impact reaches beyond the broadcast networks. These include the convergence of information and entertainment and the rapid restructuring of the entire communications industry in response to technological change.

To map out the rapidly changing social landscape of prime-time entertainment, we examined every character and socially relevant theme that appeared during the first month of the 1992-93 prime-time season on the four major broadcast networks. This volume presents the results in relation to both the current state of popular culture in America and our historical studies of television entertainment, which first appeared in *Watching America*. The content analysis of television's themes and characters was developed by Linda Lichter. Robert Lichter analyzed the results and wrote the text that follows.

Many individuals and institutions contributed in various ways to the completion of our research on television entertainment. Such a large-scale empirical research project would not have been possible without the generous support of several private foundations. Funding at various stages of the research was provided by the Lynde and Harry Bradley Foundation, the Earhart Foundation, the Philip M. McKenna Foundation, the John M. Olin Foundation, and the Sarah Scaife Foundation.

The project began in 1979 under the auspices of Columbia University's Research Institute for International Change. The early stages were developed as Linda Lichter's doctoral dissertation, which benefited from the invaluable counsel of her advisor, W. Phillips Davison, of Columbia's Sociology Department. The Museum of Broadcasting in New York provided viewing facilities for a pretest of past television programs. From 1980 through 1986 the project was housed at the George Washington University. The 1990s' updating was carried out under the auspices of the CMPA. For the historical component of the study, programs were viewed at the Library of Congress's Motion Picture, Broadcasting and Recorded Sound Division, with the assistance of Barbara Humphreys and Pat Sheehan.

A special note of thanks is due to Dan Amundson, who joined the project as a coder and ended up contributing to every phase of it. As CMPA research director, Dan adapted the content analysis system and supervised its application to 1990s' programming. We have recognized his unique contributions with the credit indicated on the title page. Additional coding was done by Richard Noyes, Fred Dann, Joe Simpich, and Michelle Kelly. Computer assistance was provided by John Williams, Eileen McKeon, and Doug Steinel. Over the course of the study, approximately thirty other student assistants helped us to collect, collate, and type up the data. We thank them all collectively.

PART

I

America Goes Prime Time

PROLOGUE: TV GETS REAL

The answers to life's problems aren't at the bottom of a bottle.
They're on TV!

—Homer Simpson

ake it from Homer, the potted patriarch of America's favorite dysfunctional family. TV sitcoms are no longer a laughing matter. Once dismissed as fluff and fantasy, the lessons that Hollywood teaches are now seen as serious business. The wake-up call was Dan Quayle's much-derided "debate" with Murphy Brown during the 1992 presidential campaign. This exchange smacked of the surreal, as the vice president of the United States criticized the child-rearing techniques of a fictitious television anchorwoman. Yet it inaugurated a serious debate over family values that would not have taken place without the participation of a fantasy character whose recognition factor probably approached Mr. Quayle's, and whose Q-rating was surely higher.

Television entertainment has been making news ever since. Soon "Nightline" was debating Hollywood's influence on Washington, even as Washington debated its own influence over Hollywood. The political debate in the nation's capital ranged from financial syndication rules and cable regulations to parental advisories and violence-zapping "v-chips." Prime-time producers Linda Bloodworth-Thomason and her husband Harry Thomason supervised Bill Clinton's star-studded presidential inauguration. Before the stardust had settled, though, Harry was entangled in an influence-peddling scandal involving the White House travel office. While network executives defended their sweeps month mayhem in hearings on Capitol Hill, the Thomasons defended their ties to the Clintons on "Good Morning America."

Meanwhile, presidential aide George Stephanopolous and actress Jennifer Grey became a gossip column item, as the media continued their endless search for new celebrities. Personality magazines began to profile the moguls alongside the stars, the newsweeklies proclaimed the coming of an information superhighway, and the business press chronicled the creation of a global telecommunications industry. High-definition television became the latest battleground in America's competition with Japan for economic and technological supremacy. And through it all, visions of five hundred channels danced in our heads like virtual-reality sugarplums.

POP GOES THE CULTURE

It is no coincidence that the creators of popular entertainment are becoming newsmakers, even as the content is becoming newsworthy. Social commentators have begun to treat entertainment as seriously as news, and for the same reason: It has become a major voice in America's public discourse. Of course, the sudden prominence of popular culture can be viewed as the culmination of gradual changes. Madison Avenue and Sunset Boulevard have long since displaced classical mythology and the Bible as signposts of our cultural geography. This was already evident in the political catch phrases of the previous decade, when Walter Mondale flung the slogan from a Wendy's commercial at Gary Hart, and Ronald Reagan trumped them all with one-liners from Clint Eastwood films. About the same time, a made-for-TV movie entitled "The Day After" animated the nuclear freeze debate in a manner that foreshadowed the "Murphy Brown" family values flap. We even became accustomed to the bastard genre of news and entertainment known as "infotainment" through a steady stream of tabloid television series and docudramas.

But the 1990s may mark the historical moment when such developments reached critical mass, and the rapid accumulation of quantitative changes produced a qualitative change in the social role of popular culture. Today, the merger of information and entertainment has become so rapid and widespread as to threaten the very distinction between fact and fiction. Journalists and biographers routinely use creative license to put thoughts into the heads and words into the mouths of their subjects, with intuition replacing documentation. Joe McGinniss's notorious Kennedy biography, which was reviled for its use of "imagined" dialogue and motivation, simply recycled the same "new journalism" techniques that had made celebrities of highly regarded journalists from Tom Wolfe and Gay Talese to Bob Woodward and David Halberstam. His mistake was to apply these techniques so blatantly and crudely as to provoke a widespread defense of more traditional methods in book reviews and editorial pages. McGinniss died for Woodward's sins.

For all its de facto deconstructionism, though, the print world runs a poor second to television in recasting reality as mass entertainment. Video verite series like "America's Most Wanted" and "Cops" put competitive pressures on the established networks to introduce tabloid elements into their own magazine shows, which have largely replaced documentary programming on commercial television. It was a short step from the reconstructions and simulations legitimized by this genre to NBC "Dateline"'s decision to rig a crash fire on a General Motors truck, in order to add drama and spectacle to their story. This time NBC News President Michael Gartner died for Rupert Murdoch's sins.

While entertainment values have seeped into the evening news, the prime-time schedule has soaked up the morning headlines. Sitcom characters grapple nightly with sexism and homophobia, dramas take on racism and corporate corruption, and TV movies tackle homelessness and sexual abuse. Reality has become one more ingredient in a pop culture stew that is seasoned to audience taste. These days news events can be tracked in real time by C-SPAN and CNN, relentlessly recapped from "Nightline" to "Newsweek," and then fictionalized for prime time within weeks of their occurrence. News used to be the first rough draft of history. Now it is the first draft of a Hollywood screenplay.

For an example of how this process works, consider the ill-fated confrontation between federal agents and the Branch Davidian cult in Waco, Texas. One month after millions of viewers watched the group's compound become a funeral pyre, an NBC made-for-TV movie reconstructed the early phase of the siege. This quickie docudrama culminated in the initial failure of federal agents to storm the compound. The producers couldn't wait to include the final tragedy, because the film was scheduled to air during the May sweeps period, when audience surveys are used to set advertising rates. Similarly, the murder trial of "Long Island Lolita" Amy Fisher turned into a tabloid takeoff on "Roshomon," as all three networks broadcast their own movie versions of the case. The portrayals of the protagonists varied according to the deals that each cut with the competing production studios.

This sort of material is hardly the exclusive province of the broadcast networks. Major cable companies commission their own original productions, vastly expanding the prime-time pool of fictive "fact-based" drama. A recent example was "Marilyn and Bobby: Her Final Affair," which the USA network labeled as "a fictional account" of an "alleged" romance. In addition to the rumored but unproven Monroe-Kennedy sexual liaison, this pseudo-docudrama peddled such tabloid reconstructions of recent history as a homosexual J. Edgar Hoover and an assassination plot led by Teamster boss Jimmy Hoffa. To capture the full breadth of Hollywood's developing tendencies to rescript recent reality, one would have to include such high profile feature films as "JFK" and "Malcolm X."

But for all the rhetoric about a virtually infinite array of future programming, the broadcast networks remain the centerpiece of television entertainment. To those who dismiss them as dinosaurs ill adapted to a new environment, it is tempting to reply in Hollywood vernacular, "Two words: Jurassic Park." While industry analysts were bemoaning the declining audience share of the major networks, Fox became the first successful addition to this exclusive club in forty years (since ABC supplanted the long-forgotten DuMont network). The frenzied competition between Paramount and Warner Brothers to become the next new member suggests that Fox's success was no fluke. In the latest phase of the information age, empires are being built by those who possess both software and distribution systems. In this case the software is the programming that comes from the Hollywood production studios. And broadcast networks are still the most effective means of delivering those programs to living rooms across the country.

Collectively, the new communications technologies have greatly reduced the networks' domination of television entertainment. Yet no competing entertainment series reaches an audience approaching the numbers attracted to the broadcast networks' prime-time fare. Very few cable series can maintain a weekly audience of a million households. The industry leader, Nickelodeon's "Ren and Stimpy," currently boasts roughly 2 million. By comparison, ABC's top-rated "Home Improvement" reaches about ten times that number. At the other end of the rating scale, the same network's ill-fated "Paula Poundstone Show" ranked one-hundredth in the Nielsen ratings with an audience of "only" 3.5 million households. It was canceled after two episodes. Industry economics rather than sheer numbers made "Ren and Stimpy" a hit and "Paula Poundstone" a flop.

Moreover, many of the most popular shows now appearing via cable are reruns of series that originally aired on the broadcast networks. The cable networks' insatiable appetite for presold products has given today's audiences unprecedented access to the entire history of television entertainment. By recycling the hits of past decades, cable ensures that new viewers will continue to discover the virtues of "Bonanza," "I Love Lucy," and "Hawaii Five-O." In short, cable is building many new byways along the entertainment highway. But the broadcast networks' prime-time schedule remains the royal road to America's fantasy life.

PRIME-TIME POLITICS

All this might amount to very little, if the social significance of TV entertainment were restricted to the occasional docudrama or social advocacy series. Television entertainment's tradition of social commentary extends back to the "golden age" anthologies that produced such hard-hitting dramas as "Patterns" (on the cutthroat corporate world), "Crime in the Streets" (teenage gangs), and "Thunder on Sycamore Street" (a parable of racial prejudice). But television's critics have always shared a far more expansive notion of the politics embedded in prime-time plot lines and portrayals. From the civil rights groups that forced "Amos 'n' Andy" off the airwaves to the religious fundamentalists who organized a boycott of "NYPD Blue," they have seen TV entertainment as an alternate reality whose images can reshape the real world as well as reflect it.

This perception is shared by Hollywood's creative community as well. To hear them tell it, television's content is not solely the product of commercial motives and programming strategies. Many writers and producers insist that they can cater to the audience's tastes without pandering to them. In the words of Leonard Goldberg, whose productions have ranged from "Fantasy Island" and "Starsky and Hutch" to "Something About Amelia," a TV movie about incest, "I think it is the responsibility of television not only to entertain, but present contemporary problems facing our society and to offer some guidance, some hope, and just to make people think about them."[1]

Cop-show specialist Quinn Martin echoes these sentiments: "You must have a point of view, first entertain, then make them think underneath. . . . It doesn't have to be heavy but I do think you can have a little substance in what you're doing as long as you entertain them along the way." Martin provides an example of how this works:

> We start out saying, "Let's do an episode about old people, geriatrics, and how they're treated and what's the right way and the wrong way." Then out of that you say, "How do you do that

story in 'Streets of San Francisco?'" And you do a crime that occurs because of the treatment of old people.[2]

In a similar vein, David Victor talks about his work on medical dramas from "Doctor Kildare" to "Marcus Welby, M.D.": "With varying successes we did the story of a homosexual rape, an unwed father, unwed mothers, abortions, drug addiction, indecent exposure. . . . I'm proud of that. I think I educate as well as entertain."[3] And Earl Hamner of "The Waltons" affirms that "we've always been guided by a sense of responsibility to the audience. . . . Almost without exception, at the end of each story, we have said something, something I hope is of value to the audience."[4]

This is not Norman Lear talking. These are the creators of some of the medium's most popular mainstream shows. Their material is not overtly political, but they are all concerned with social values as well as audience shares. They see themselves as educators, with the tube as their schoolroom. And their success reminds us that the Nielsen ratings don't determine what goes on the air, only what gets taken off. The challenge, as these men see it, is to create stories that will appeal to audiences while simultaneously instructing them.

Some producers even approach this as a kind of game, covering the medicine with a candy coating. Garry Marshall, creator of "Happy Days" and "Mork and Mindy," describes it this way:

> You take it from Pogo better than from a man in a suit. I deal with what society's negative images are, and then try to change them to be positive. . . . The tag on "Mork" is almost like the sermon of the week. But it doesn't look like that. It's very cleverly disguised to look like something else, but that's what it is. . . . Because sitcoms reach so many people, we might as well try to put some issues in them.[5]

Sometimes the disguise is elaborate enough to produce a genuinely covert political statement, with scripts that tackle controversial political issues symbolically or even allegorically. For example, "Daniel Boone" producer Barney Rosenzweig regularly transposed social issues of the

1960s back to the show's eighteenth-century setting. According to media analyst Todd Gitlin, who interviewed Rosenzweig:

> He instructed writers to portray the Revolutionary War by "making it Vietnam, with the colonials as the Vietcong and the English as the Americans." Boone defended civil disobedience. Rosenzweig transposed the black studies controversy, then raging across American campuses, into a story about Red Indian studies in which Boone's son supports a Cherokee chief's son living in Boonesboro who wants to learn about Indian culture. "What's wonderful about it was that I wasn't preaching to the converted. . . . I wasn't preaching to a bunch of liberals in New York or L.A. or Chicago. I was hitting people who never had explored these ideas before. And they were digging it."[6]

Obviously, not all television producers are so concerned to make a full-fledged social "statement" through their work. But their values and preconceptions may be reflected in their productions even when their conscious effort is directed solely at the Nielsen numbers. Audience feedback is poor and incomplete, so that low numbers can be rationalized in terms of whatever explanations best serve a producer or programmer's purposes.[7] One executive told us that the creative community even resists the networks' audience research, because taking it into account would restrict their "artistic creativity."

What remains are the producer's preconceptions about his audience, which may be quite at variance with reality. After Muriel Cantor interviewed eighty producers some years back, she concluded that "some producers who claimed to think of the viewing audience constantly when making decisions actually used their own taste as the yardstick. . . ." When one of them told her, "I think of the audience constantly," she asked how he knew what would appeal to them. He replied, "The only answer I have is that if it appeals to me it will appeal to the audience." Another was even more direct: "I think of myself as the audience. If it pleases me, I always think it is going to please the audience." And a third conveyed a disarmingly ingenuous conception of audience research when asked how he knew that his children's show attracted a partly adult audience:

> I like to think of myself as a rather sophisticated person. I do sophisticated things. I drink booze and go out with girls. I play golf at a very posh club, and I have a friend there; the man is a very sophisticated guy. Drinks more booze than I do. I know he watched my show and did long before he met me.[8]

These musings illustrate how self-conceptions can be projected onto the mass audience as rationales or justifications for program content. Hollywood is a fantasy factory in more ways than one. Thus, the creative community's collective worldview cannot help but influence the world the rest of us view on television, even when that is not the writer or producer's intentions. This insight stands behind Earl Hamner's conviction that "what you see on any television show reflects the morals and the conscience of the people on those shows who have influence."[9]

In this sense television entertainment can be "political" even when it does not deal with the stuff of daily headlines or partisan controversy. Its latent politics lie in the unavoidable portrayal of individuals, groups, and institutions as a backdrop to any story that occupies the foreground. They stretch from Murphy Brown's single motherhood back to Lucy Ricardo's harebrained schemes to break into show business, with their own implicit messages about male authority and women's proper social roles. Whatever the merits of Dan Quayle's argument, he forced millions of viewers to realize what television writers and reviewers have always known: The most innocuous sitcom carries messages about how our society works and how its citizens should behave. Long before Dan and Murphy became the odd couple of the culture wars, sociologist Herbert Gans wrote:

> All cultural content expresses values that can become political or have political consequences. Even the simplest television family comedy, for example, says something about the relations between men and women and parents and children, and

11

insofar as these relations involve values and questions of power, they are political.[10]

Thus, television's portrayals are always political in the sense that Aristotle understood politics, as the set of structures and relationships linking individuals to a community that fulfills their social nature. It is also the sense in which the politics of prime time is too important to be left to the producers. Although this issue has recently attained new urgency, the phenomenon is as old as the medium itself. Its images stay *in* our minds even when they are not *on* our minds. Hollywood actor-essayist Ben Stein observes, "Because [television] shows certain persons, classes, occupations, races, sexes, and situations consistently, it propounds a particular view *of* the world *to* the world continually."[11]

Television has transcended its role as mere entertainment to become a potent force shaping everyday life. The average American now watches over four hours of TV each day, and the average household keeps a set on over seven hours a day. Yet, the full force of television's impact is rarely felt in a single program or even a single season. It is the long-term result of exposure to an artificial reality so pervasive it has become a major part of the social environment. As communications researcher George Comstock concluded from a review of the scholarly literature, "television has become an unavoidable and unremitting factor in shaping what we are and what we will become. . . . Yet it is intricately entwined in the braid of life, so much so that it is easy to mistake it for an entirely passive servant."[12]

There is no shortage of aspirants eager to reveal the mysteries of the magic box. Television critics peruse a few hit shows each season and discover new "trends" that fade away quicker than last week's Nielsen ratings. Scholars count the number of gunshots and fistfights on the tube and reduce the medium's meanings and images to dry statistical tables. Yet, no one has ever before examined fully and systematically the social and political lessons that television teaches. Only when we understand the whole of television's "alternative reality" can we trace its impact on our collective consciousness. That is the purpose of this book.

Our thesis is that television once served as an agent of social control, but it became an agent of social change. The onetime servant of the status quo, it now fosters populist suspicions of traditional mores and institutions. A medium that originally helped legitimize authority today tries to demystify it. Far from always following in the wake of popular tastes, the fictional world of prime time can be sharply at odds with public sentiment. More often, it tries to guide middle American tastes in the direction of intellectual trends emanating from New York and Los Angeles. This process is gaining intensity, as writers and producers become more engaged with social issues and more self-conscious about their educative role.

Today television creates a kind of hyper-reality, a shared fantasy world that merges with and sometimes overshadows the more mundane world of real life for millions of Americans. Political controversies are played out in TV movies as quickly as news stories can be transformed into screenplays. The stars of hit shows spend their nights battling social injustice on the tube and their days testifying before Congress on the issues they dramatize. The writers blend reality with fantasy as quickly as the real world can provide dramatic material. Marx once charged that history is made behind the backs of the individuals who think they are shaping it. In the age of television, we watch history being reshaped before our eyes without noticing it. The goal of this book is to uncover this process by providing the first comprehensive guide to the meanings and messages of prime time.

TV GETS RELEVANT

The history of television is more than a list of dominant program types or hit shows. It is also the playing out of ideas and issues within a very limited format. Usually the ideas remain in the background, tacitly setting the stage for individual behavior and personal relationships. Occasionally they ring out in monologues and fervent displays of oratory. But seen or unseen, in the background or the foreground, prime-time politics are a critical dimension of life on television. The integration of social commentary into entertainment formats is an ongoing storyline in the larger development of episodic television.

The new medium was firmly rooted in the two great forms of mass entertainment that preceded it: vaudeville and radio. From vaudeville came Uncle Miltie with "Texaco Star Theater," Burns and Allen, Jimmy Durante, and all their fast-paced slapstick action. Since the new television networks were run by the major radio networks, radio was an obvious source of programming ideas. Much of early TV programming was, in fact, transplanted versions of popular radio programs. Series as diverse as "Amos 'n' Andy," "Dragnet," and "Gunsmoke" were given visual form and sent out through the magic box.

The decade after World War II was a time of great experimentation in the medium. Television began this period as live entertainment in New York and finished as a filmed product from Hollywood. During the early 1950s, Milton Berle popularized television with the mass audience, and Ernie Kovacs explored the limits of visual comedy. Desi Arnaz pioneered the use of filmed programming, while his wife Lucille Ball showed how slapstick humor could be integrated with family comedy. The major genres of television were formalized during this period—episodic comedy and drama series, anthologies, and variety shows.

Despite all these technical and structural experiments, television's earliest programs featured very little on-screen discussion of ideas and values. This was television's era of the status quo. The heroes of "I Led Three Lives," "The Crusader," and "The Hunter" battled communism on the home front and abroad. "The Untouchables," "The Web," and "Man Against Crime" battled organized crime with the same single-minded fervor. The early comedies were more subtle but just as consistent in upholding current social arrangements. From "I Love Lucy" to "Father Knows Best," traditional values and roles were assumed to be the norm without argument.

During the late 1950s and early 1960s, moreover, adult-oriented Westerns and private eye dramas gradually replaced the dramatic anthologies that had provided what little socially conscious programming there was during the early 1950s. Scripts aired on "Studio One," "Kraft Television Theatre," and the like had occasionally challenged prevailing norms on such volatile topics as racial prejudice, militarism, and business

14

ethics. The status quo remained largely unquestioned in the new dramatic formats. Westerns and police dramas often used crime to reassert traditional ideas of working for your money, walking the straight and narrow, and so forth. All of this gave early TV a conformist profile in its first decade as a national entertainment medium.

In the early 1960s television became dominated by the "idiot" sitcom. Carrying the lighthearted, noncontroversial style of earlier comedies to its logical conclusion, you arrive at the 1962 prime-time schedule. With shows like "Dennis the Menace," "The Real McCoys," "The Beverly Hillbillies," "Mr. Ed," and "McHale's Navy" dominating the ratings, TV seemed determined to prove itself a vast wasteland. To appreciate these comedies you had to believe that social conventions were so ironclad they could not tolerate variation. The scripts assumed that any minute violation of social conventions would lead to a crisis that could be played for comic results.

The few shows that addressed themselves to social issues or political satire were notably short-lived. "East Side, West Side" (social workers battling injustice) and "That Was the Week That Was" (current affairs satire) both survived only one season of head-on competition with "Sing Along with Mitch" and "Petticoat Junction," respectively. It was not until the mid-1960s that shows questioning the status quo gained popularity. As the opening wedge of coming change, a few shows began to stretch the limits of the acceptable. "The Fugitive" used a doctor falsely convicted of murder as its hero. While fleeing the law, this fugitive saw a vast array of corruption, evil, and inequity in "proper" society. Series like "I Spy" and "Mission: Impossible" challenged standard casting by putting blacks in respectable leading roles. Other spy shows like "Honey West" and "The Avengers" presented stronger, more independent women's roles.

What emerged from this stretching of conventions was a changing portrait of American life. This new portrayal was more multifaceted and complex, illustrating a new group of difficult, often intractable problems. Television was searching for a new worldview and found it in sociological analysis. The critical examination of institutions, laws, and social processes provided a wealth of plot lines. Crime was no longer seen as an individual character flaw, but as the result of systemic pressures and inequities. The business world was stripped of its paternalism and repopulated with opportunists in fierce competition. No family remained an island as violence, prejudice, and social injustice invaded more and more happy homes.

Yet, such criticism had to be presented within the narrow formats and codes that governed the medium. These contradictory forces were brought together in a unique group of shows that can be labeled "advocacy" television. Advocacy television got off to a strong start in 1968. In outspoken shows like "Mod Squad" and "Judd for the Defense," and in the social satire of "The Smothers Brothers Show" and "Laugh-In," the status quo came under fire. Over the next few years the cry for change was heard more frequently and stridently in prime time. As shows like "Room 222," "The Senator," "Storefront Lawyers," "The Protectors," "The Young Lawyers," "The Young Rebels," and "The Smith Family" came and went, an ever-widening group of social issues appeared on television.

In earlier series, the heroes and heroines had been forces of the status quo, whose triumphs endorsed longstanding social conventions and moral codes. In advocacy TV, the heroes and heroines were proponents of social change whose work exposed inequities, intolerance, and corruption. The viewer was suddenly shown flaws in institutions that had been praised as virtually infallible. Police could now be seen as corrupt and abusive, the courts could be bought or blinded by rigid procedures, the workplace could be demeaning and discriminatory. Business was treated as an institution corrupted by wealth and power (often illegally procured). Even the family was criticized as potentially abusive or neglectful. It was the job of these second generation heroes to mend the newly unearthed flaws in the system. They were charged with the task of sorting out the bad apples, introducing humanity to the workplace, and saving the children.

Although the advocacy shows never garnered large audiences, they set the stage for a varied and successful group of reformist shows. In 1970 "All in the Family" launched a spate of successful Norman Lear productions. Other Lear series like "Maude," "Good Times," and "The

Jeffersons" leavened the vinegar of social conscience with the honey of laugh lines. No longer railing against every social condition, freed from advocating social policy, these shows tried to chide viewers into remembering their social responsibilities.

Heroes and heroines in this period became less impassioned in advocating change, but they harbored no illusions about the "system's" flaws. There was often a sour undertaste to the humor of the Lear shows, whose protagonists resorted to cynicism and sarcasm in the face of seemingly overwhelming problems. After the advocacy shows failed, TV's politically aware characters were often reduced to keeping their corner of the world intact in a hostile or bewildering social environment.

It was all a matter of context in the postadvocacy shows. Families in a world of turmoil, police moving through cities where they were unwanted, doctors unable to cure disease and clergymen with apathetic flocks were all part of the reformers' world. In series as different as "M*A*S*H," "Kojak," and "Family," the challenge was neither to ignore nor succumb to the pressures of life, but to maintain some control and cohesion in a small piece of the world amid turmoil and change. From this point on, the reformist direction of TV has remained fairly consistent. When TV speaks out on an issue, it is to suggest reform or to point out unfairness, not to advocate radical change. Nonetheless, this is a drastic shift away from the apolitical atmosphere that prevailed until the mid-1960s.

Reform-oriented, controversial shows dominated the ratings up to the mid-1970s, when they were challenged by lighter fare. This new programming trend was furthered by the creation of Family Viewing Time, which stipulated less violent, family oriented programs for the first hour of prime time. ABC raced into this inoffensive zone with a string of titillating fantasy shows. Series like "Happy Days," "Laverne and Shirley," "Fantasy Island," and "Donny and Marie" harked back to earlier days when problems were trivial and personal, isolated from the concerns of a larger world. With enough sex to tease the viewer and enough action to keep things lively, they captured large audiences.

Yet even these insubstantial shows drew on the lessons of advocacy TV when developing plots. Among the banal and vacuous plot lines were incidents of sexual harassment, corrupt politicians and cops, prison abuses, and homophobia. Series like "The Dukes of Hazzard" and "Sheriff Lobo" were built around bumbling, corrupt authority figures. The sun-drenched decks of the "The Love Boat" had to come to terms with homosexuality and discrimination. The trio of voluptuous gumshoes in "Charlie's Angels" were dispatched to expose an exploitative, abusive prison system. The girls of "Three's Company" learned the meaning of sexual harassment through personal experience.

These were the issues of an earlier prime-time era gratuitously thrust into a context where they didn't really matter. Social issues began to function less as causes to be championed than as industry status symbols, which added a patina of quality to series not usually given critical praise. The real champions of social change were the remaining reformist shows like "Quincy," "Lou Grant," and "Archie Bunker's Place."

When these relevance shows and the light and frothy material eventually slid in the ratings, they left two very different program types in their wake. In one direction TV brought its daytime soap operas to prime time, with costlier production values. Lavish productions like "Dynasty," "Dallas," and "Falcon Crest" filled the airwaves with steamy sex and Machiavellian backroom business maneuvering. Moving in the other direction were the new "realist" dramas. Series like "Hill Street Blues," "St. Elsewhere," and "Cagney & Lacey" were the pioneers of this new genre, and the true heirs to the traditions of relevance programming.

These shows were filmed in a gritty pseudodocumentary style from the viewpoint of a wizened veteran of life's travails. Triumph and tragedy ebbed and flowed around the characters as unavoidable parts of life. Sometimes the inequities prodded them to zealous crusades, but more often they could only stand by, powerless to change events. There were just too many people with too many problems demanding help from men and women with too much paperwork to complete. The result was characters who did what they could in the time they had and then moved on to someone else. These shows were the synthesis of advocacy and relevancy television. The characters really wanted to help solve society's problems, but too many things got in the way.

Several other critically acclaimed realist shows met with less popular success, among them "Bay City Blues," "Jessie," "Bronx Zoo," and "Mariah." All these dramas featured lead characters with both virtues and flaws facing decisions in a world without an absolute sense of right and wrong. The rules of the game were unclear, base motives could be hidden behind good intentions, and there was never enough time for the characters to do all they wanted.

This approach began to affect other series that remained rooted in the traditional mainstream of television. Such shows avoided the grittiness and much of the documentary style, but kept their roots in real life experience. Series like "Hooperman," "Slap Maxwell," "Frank's Place," and "thirtysomething" all tried to use more realistic characters facing more common social or personal problems. Most often these shows aimed for personally relevant conflicts, not the cutting edge of social comment.

While realism and soap operas were the newest elements on TV in the 1980s, there remained many throwbacks to status quo TV. In these more traditional shows the characters were mostly isolated from the outside world and its problems. In series like "The Cosby Show," "Family Ties," "Growing Pains," "Who's the Boss," "Webster," "Valerie," "Cheers," "ALF," "The Facts of Life," "Amen," and "Moonlighting," overt politics and social relevance themes were largely absent. When an issue or social concern did appear, it was often in a community bulletin board episode. These episodes were written to provide information on topics like teen pregnancy, drunk driving, fire safety, child abuse, or drug abuse. They were intended less as forums for debate than as community service gestures. Most of the time these shows were just out for a few laughs.

By the current decade, however, the various program formats had begun to converge in ways that altered the relationship between entertainment and social commentary on prime time. The realist spirit worked its way into many sitcoms and soap operas, adding new bite to their shopworn formulas. Simultaneously, the realist dramas learned to add a veneer of soap opera slickness in order to win a wider audience for their social commentary. First, as the lavish adult soaps died off, they were replaced by adolescent versions patterned after "Beverly Hills 90210." These new youth soaps merged the concerns of their daytime cousins with those of the realist tradition by tackling every social issue with a sexual component, including teen pregnancy, condom use, sexual harassment, and date rape.

Meanwhile, the success of "Roseanne" and "Married...With Children" in the late 1980s spawned an antifamily-sitcom format that used sarcasm, cynicism, and real life problems to create a type of in-your-face comedy heretofore unseen on prime time. (The producers' own tongue-in-cheek title for "Married...With Children" was "Not the Cosby Show.") These series and their progeny, like "The Simpsons," "Grace Under Fire," and "Blossom," are the stepchildren of family comedies and realist dramas. They mix sharp commentary on current events and social problems with satirical portraits of life in frequently dysfunctional families. The characters regularly use humor to cope with grim problems ranging from drug and alcohol abuse to racism and domestic violence.

As social pathologies suffused the prime-time schedule, the social relevance tradition won a new lease on life with the success of "L.A. Law." This series combined the social perspective of "Hill Street Blues" with the glitz, sex, and suds of the adult soaps. Personal relationships became more prominent as a means of framing broader issue discussions. The success of this hybrid formula paved the way for a new wave of realist shows in the 1990s, led by police procedurals such as "Law and Order," "Reasonable Doubts," "Civil Wars," and "NYPD Blue." These series attacked flaws in the justice system by counterposing formal rules and bureaucratic procedures against the harsh realities of crime in urban America. They also used their courtroom settings to debate hot button political issues such as abortion, gay rights, race relations, and sexual abuse.

At the opposite end of the spectrum from the big city cop and shyster shows was a new kind of series that looked like the realist tradition seen through Alice's looking glass. Shows like "Twin Peaks," "Northern Exposure," "Picket Fences," and "Beauty and the Beast" played out contemporary social issues in never-never-land settings that ranged from the whimsical to the weird. They used offbeat locales and eccentric characters to provide new vantage points on the same social issues that most other shows were busily integrating into everyday settings.

They also introduced alienating perspectives and New Age ideas that frequently gave a twist to the conventional Hollywood liberalism featured in more straightforward relevancy programming. With a sensibility somewhere between the *Utne Reader* and the "Twilight Zone," these series added a genuinely new mise-en-scène to the homogeneous world of prime time.

Thus, television in the 1990s remains an amalgam of private fantasy and public commentary, as Hollywood vacillates between embracing social change and escaping from it. This represents a major change from the medium's early years, when most prime-time shows either steered well away from social controversy or actively championed traditional values. Contemporary programming has not really retreated from the "relevancy" era. It has incorporated controversial material into more salable formats that make prime-time programs far more involved in the issues of the day than Joe Friday or Ralph Kramden could ever have imagined.

WATCHING TV

Few commentators would question that television has become more open about treating political issues and social controversies as the stuff of entertainment. But the substance and implications of its treatment are hotly disputed. Given the intricacies of sorting out the overt, latent, and even covert values on the small screen, it is not surprising that critics differ sharply on the strength and direction of prime-time politics.

One side of the critical spectrum is represented by Ben Stein, who portrays TV entertainment as a concerted attack on conservative values and traditional institutions. After viewing numerous shows and interviewing their creators, Stein concluded:

> There is, on prime-time television, a unified picture of life in these United States that is an alternate reality. . . . Television land is a world in which the respectable pillars of society turn their daughters out to become prostitutes and heirs kill their mistresses. Businessmen make their real money by turning

sweet-faced youngsters into junkies and barely pubescent girls into depraved hookers. . . . The world of television is peopled by killers wearing three-piece suits, heroin pushers operating behind a facade of civic responsibility, and murderers of go-go dancers sitting behind massive mahogany desks in the corridors of power.[13]

On the other side of the fence stands Todd Gitlin, who concluded on the basis of his own viewing and interviews that television upholds "the values of a business civilization. Capitalism and the consumer society come out largely uncontested."[14] In a collection of like-minded essays edited by Gitlin, Tom Englehart condemns:

. . .a TV-generated vision of Americans as a nation of over-armed, trigger-happy, grasping, anxious, and love-starved people who feel deeply sorry for themselves and beleaguered in the world—something, that is, of a self-portrait of the Reagan era.[15]

This discrepancy may reveal more about the critics' own political principles than those of television. Stein may be the only person who has worked for both Richard Nixon and Norman Lear. Gitlin is a former national president of the radical Students for a Democratic Society (SDS). Their sharp disagreement on this question of fact shows why we need to go beyond such impressionistic generalizations. Inevitably, they are subject to distortions in the eye of the beholder.

A more objective and systematic approach is offered by content analysis, a scientific method of classifying the content of television programs (or other forms of communication) in ways that can be reproduced by other researchers. It does so by dividing material into units, such as character traits or activities, and then noting the frequency with which each occurs. In its simplest form, this method is often used to demonstrate the proportion of television characters who are women, racial minorities, or members of some other group. Characters who possess the required characteristic are simply counted and totaled as a proportion of all characters. In addition, the public debate over TV violence relies on content analysis to compare the number of violent acts that occur each season.

Content analysis is a vast improvement over impressionistic viewing in providing a valid picture of life on television. But such studies have serious limitations. This approach typically sacrifices depth and breadth of analysis in its single-minded search for reliable results. By simply counting the traits of characters, researchers concentrate on television's demographic portrait at the expense of its dramatic structure. As a result, we know a lot about a few aspects of life on television but very little about the big picture. Surely the social messages of television must reflect the themes and plots of its programs as well as the traits and relationships of its characters. Moreover, most existing research dates from the 1970s or later. No study has ever attempted to encompass the whole history of prime-time content except in the most cursory or impressionistic fashion.

Thus, despite a great deal of intensive research into a few topics, we lack a global perspective of how TV entertainment portrays America to itself. There is no lack of critics who claim to know what's wrong with the tube's nightly fare: It's too violent or sexy, or too liberal or conservative, or unfair to women, blacks, gays, Christians, businessmen, or whatever other group finds reason to protest its video image. But scholars have been more reluctant than interest groups to form conclusions, and even those who have studied the parts make few claims to comprehend the whole.

This is where our study comes in. We combined the systematic observation of scientific content analysis with a holistic approach that examines not only individual characters but also plots and themes. Then we charted the results across the history of TV entertainment. Our primary goal was to identify the social and political messages and values that prime-time television conveys, and to chart their changes over time. In short, we sought to produce a scientifically valid overview of life on television as it has evolved since the 1950s. We tried to avoid preconceptions and take television on its own terms, as a medium that seeks above all to entertain, that cannot help but portray many fault lines in American society, and that sometimes chooses to tackle overtly political themes.

The book begins with a portrait of prime time in the 1990s. Chapter 1 explores some of the most controversial aspects of life on television today—violence, sex, race, politics, and (as the promos put it) much, much more. This overview is based on a content analysis of every fictional prime-time entertainment series on the four broadcast networks during the 1992-93 season. Researchers examined the background, appearance, behavior, and motivation of all characters who appeared on the first four episodes of each series—the composite first month of the season. In addition, they analyzed each scene for dialogue and plot developments that addressed social and political themes. The results were computerized, and the tale of the printouts became the basis of the analysis.

The next ten chapters show how the major topics and themes of TV entertainment developed from the 1950s through the 1980s. For this part of the study, we analyzed a randomly based sample of 620 prime-time shows from the Library of Congress video archive. By far the most comprehensive collection of television programs, it contains about twenty thousand listings dating back to the early 1950s. For each of thirty seasons from 1955 through 1986, we first randomly selected twenty different prime-time series, after excluding news and variety programs, game shows, and movies. Then we randomly selected one episode of each series. This procedure gave equal weight to a cross-section of programs spanning more than three decades. The resulting sample provides as near an overview of television's history as we are likely to get, given the disappearance of many old programs.

The researchers took extensive notes, on the order of twenty handwritten pages for each half-hour sitcom, to retain the essentials of plot, character, and thematic development. Then they analyzed the 7,365 characters who appeared, as well as the themes that were treated in each episode. Our research methods are described at greater length in the appendix. In recounting the results, we kept in mind that the statistics are just stand-ins for the characters and plots they represent. Our goal was to recapture the world of television, not just to reduce it to numbers. In the concluding chapter, we summarize these findings and address the chicken-and-egg question that pervades the debate over prime-time politics: Does Hollywood follow the audience's tastes and values, or does it create them?

Thus, this book chronicles television's changing treatment of groups such as businessmen, government officials, law enforcers, and other major occupational, racial, and sexual divisions. It also explores broader concepts such as authority relations in the workplace, the portrayal of institutions, religion and morality, good guys and bad guys. When it comes to those old reliables, sex and violence, we look at what television has to say about them, not just how often they occur. Taken together, our studies provide a systematic analysis of how life on television has changed in the home, at work, and in the public square.

These are the signposts that the road form Sunset Boulevard to Main Street U.S.A. The chapters to come explore the many byways of this alternate reality that has become our cultural common denominator. So take a front row seat for the panorama of life on television as it has been lived night after night in dramas and sitcoms both famous and forgotten. It is a home movie of America's fantasy life, as it flowed from the suburban families and dramatic anthologies of the 1950s, through the cowboys and secret agents of the 1980s, and the New Age dramedies of the 1990s. Along the winding trail of Nielsen ratings that led from Dodge City to Dallas, from the Honeymooners to the Huxtables, and from "I Remember Mama" to "Murphy Brown," we will trace the patterns of social themes, personal relations, and political values schedules. The show to come is America's changing image of itself, refracted through the lens of the American dream machine.

⎯⎯⎯⎯≫●≪⎯⎯⎯⎯

1

A DIFFERENT WORLD

The battle in television has always been to push that envelope so you can grab these networks kicking and screaming into the real world.

—Steven Bochco

It's evening in America. In the Big Apple, an alcoholic cop grabs his crotch and hurls expletives at a female lawyer. Out on the Coast, black honeymooners rediscover racism during the Los Angeles riots. Times are just as tough in the heartland. In Rome, Wisconsin, a serial bather sneaks into the homes of teenage girls and takes baths with their underwear. In Cicely, Alaska, the natives treat Thanksgiving as their Day of the Dead, when they toss ripe tomatoes at whites.

Welcome to the world of prime time in the 1990s. It isn't exactly the real world, but neither is it an escape from reality. There are no more flying nuns, talking horses, or millionaire hillbillies. In their place are divorce courts, station houses, and eccentric small towns, all located a far piece from Mayberry, R.F.D. Instead of providing an escape from the concerns of everyday life, television increasingly incorporates them into its nightly fare. References to social issues and public figures frequently serve as a backdrop that defines characters and anchors their activity in the real world. And sometimes they move to the foreground so as to illuminate social problems by forcing the audience to confront in fiction what it avoids in fact.

During the 1992 fall season, for example, a half dozen series put characters into the midst or aftermath of the riots that had rocked Los Angeles earlier that year. On "A Different World," Dwayne got involved in a confrontation with police. Doogie Howser had to treat both looters and victims who came to the emergency room. "The Fresh Prince of Bel Air" Will Smith helped out with the cleanup. And those were just the sitcoms. The executive producer of "A Different World" announced that the episode was intended to pose the question, "As an American society, can we live together?"[1] This is not what publicists usually mean by the phrase "laugh riot."

Like real-world social problems, real-life political figures are also grist for the prime-time mill. Barbed comments are aimed at politicians far more frequently than in the past. During the first month of the 1992-93 season, we counted ninety jokes aimed at political figures. Not surprisingly, Dan Quayle led the pack with ten, followed by Ross Perot (nine), Bill Clinton (six), Barbara Bush (six), and her husband George (five). But it's a rare sitcom that can go to the well of political satire every week. Only two series, "Murphy Brown" (with twenty-three) and "In Living Color" (twenty-two), accounted for fully half of those jokes. If we add "Love and War," "Hearts Afire," and "The Edge," the joke total rises to sixty-three—over two-thirds of the political humor from the entire prime-time schedule.

Conservatives looking for evidence of partisan bias by the "cultural elite" may note that Republicans were targeted nearly twice as often as Democrats (38 to 20), and the most frequent theme was insensitivity to women and minorities. (Phil to Murphy: "Pat Buchanan's here circulating a petition to change the name of our species to 'heterosapiens.'" Georgie Anne Lahti: "The Republican convention was nothing more than a high-tech lynching of uppity women.") On the other hand, Fox's irreverent "In Living Color" regularly satirizes homosexuals and has skewered such prominent black leaders as Jesse Jackson, Louis Farrakahn, and Al Sharpton.

Even when story lines are not keyed to real-world conflicts, dialogue frequently features references to public figures and political controversies, as a way of setting a scene or establishing character. In this guise, overtly political comments often seem oddly divorced from genuine social controversy. They are banalities uttered in passing rather than expressions of partisan passion. Yuppie couples come and go, talking of Clinton and Perot.

But realism requires more than jokes about political figures and earnest messages about social problems. Prime time still offers a fantasy version of life in America. It's just that Ozzie doesn't live here anymore. In place of the mild domestic spats and clear-cut moral distinctions of yesterday's sitcoms and Westerns, today's characters are forced to confront menopause, sexual harassment, and homosexual suicide. The sex is kinkier, the language earthier, and the problems murkier than they once were. But the plot lines and dialogue still reflect the presumptions and preoccupations of Hollywood, filtered through the timeworn formulas of popular fiction.

To provide a guidebook to this amalgam of fantasy and reality, we analyzed each scene and every character from the first four episodes of all seventy-four fictional series appearing on the ABC, CBS, NBC, and Fox prime-time schedules during the fall 1992 season. The result is a kind of anthropology of America's alternative reality. From this mass of data on its demography and dramaturgy, we culled the patterns of information that bear most directly on recent controversies about the images and messages that television conveys. We shall consider in turn the issues of televised violence, sex and the battle of the sexes, race relations, and the curious phenomenon of the business bad guy, who remains Hollywood's favorite heavy.

LAW AND ORDER

In the current debate over television violence, perhaps the most incongruous comment came from CBS president Howard Stringer. Arguing against overly restrictive standards, he warned, "We don't want to turn the vast wasteland into a dull wasteland."[2] Never mind the apparent admission that television is indeed a wasteland, or the inference that its aridity is relieved by the flow of blood. Stringer should have checked the full text of the famous speech by former FCC Chairman Newton Minow. He called television "a vast wasteland. . . of blood and thunder, mayhem, violence, sadism, murder. . . ."[3] Minow, that is, termed television a vast wasteland partly *because* of the violence that critics were already condemning over thirty years ago, when he delivered his speech to a startled audience of network executives.

Stringer's infelicitous simile reflects the entertainment industry's aggrieved response to the most recent wave of public revulsion and government pressure against media violence. The networks were forced to broadcast parental advisories as a result of numerous congressional calls for more stringent measures. The proposals range from a government-mandated rating system to a computer chip that would allow television owners to prevent their sets from broadcasting violent shows.

All this legislative activity was spurred by an unusually broad social consensus for reform. Polls show not only that three-quarters of the public find TV entertainment too violent, but that an even higher percentage of TV station managers agree.[4] When asked to select measures that would reduce violent crime "a lot," the public chose restrictions on TV violence more frequently than gun control.[5] More ominously for the industry, a majority of Americans believe that the federal government should regulate the amount of violence on television.[6] That polling result appeared less than two weeks after Dick Wolf, a veteran producer of action-adventure shows, told a trade magazine that "nobody wants [antiviolence] legislation except the lunatic fringe."[7]

Network programmers and producers reply that they are being treated as scapegoats for public frustration over real-world crime and violence. Among other things, they argue that prime-time series are less violent than in the past, and that the broadcast network offerings are tame compared to what is available on cable. Our research shows that there is some truth in this, but that the argument is also somewhat misleading and self-serving.

First, it is true that cable fare is far more violent than broadcast programming. In a separate study that examined such major cable channels as USA, HBO, MTV, and Ted Turner's WTBS "SuperStation," we found that the average amount of violence on any *one* cable outlet roughly equalled that on ABC, CBS, and NBC combined. Ironically, though, much of the cable violence appeared on shows that had originally aired on the broadcast networks. It is hardly reassuring to learn that the networks' action-adventure shows just move to new outlets when they can no longer generate the huge audiences necessary to keep them on the prime-time schedule. At least, it is difficult to give the broadcast networks *moral* credit for discarding such shows once they are no longer profitable.

Second, it is undoubtedly true that the current prime-time schedule lacks the kind of high-profile action-adventure fare of the previous decade, such as "The A-Team," "Miami Vice," and "Magnum, P.I." Dick Wolf notes dryly, "I unapologetically produced 'Miami Vice' in the 1980s. The national taste had no problem seeing Colombian drug dealers shot on a weekly basis. That show wouldn't be on today."[8] Nonetheless, there is still plenty of violence to be found during prime time in places that undermine suggestions of industry restraint for any purposes other than purely commercial ones.

Our review of a month of prime-time fictional series episodes found over a thousand scenes involving violence—1,005 to be exact. (We tallied scenes rather than individual acts of violence so that the results would not be distorted by equating a flurry of punches in a single fight scene with a whole evening's worth of aggressive acts. Only intentional acts of physical force counted as violence.) There was little difference among the big three, as the amount of violence ranged only from 264 scenes on NBC to 292 on ABC, with CBS in the middle at 275. Fox was only programming five nights a week but still found time to feature 174 scenes of violence, which projects to 245 across seven nights.

Moreover, this tally probably understates the violent flavor of prime-time programs. Because our study was limited to fictional series, we missed reality shows such as "Cops," which Fox has always featured prominently. Nor was most of this material limited to tame or comic violence of the sort found in "Road Runner" cartoons or "Three Stooges" shorts. One out of five violent scenes (207) involved gunplay, and nearly half (423) included some kind of serious personal assault beyond mere slaps, punches, destruction of property, and the like.

Nor did our sample include a sweeps period, which traditionally includes more sexy and violent material. In fact, it was the gratuitous violence of the May 1993 sweeps that infuriated Congress and fueled the most recent reform efforts. The TV movies that the networks aired that month included such fare as "When Love Kills," "Gunsmoke: The Long Ride," and "Murder in the Heartland," a two-part docudrama on mass murderer Charles Starkweather. The actor who played Starkweather later complained that ABC cut his big sexual mutilation scene.[9] This burst of violent programming followed directly on the heels of hearings in which industry figures had laid on expressions of good will and assurances of diminishing violence.

As these examples illustrate, many memorable or unusually graphic acts of violence are portrayed in one-time events such as miniseries, made-for-TV movies, or theatrical releases that eventually have prime-time showings. None of this material was included in our study. Even apart from these additional factors, our tally shows that weekly fictional series averaged between three and four scenes of violence per episode.

Averages can be deceiving, of course, as we saw in the case of political humor. Over half the episodes had no violence at all. At the other end of the spectrum, the ten most violent series accounted for over 60 percent of all violence shown. About one-quarter of all series contained four-fifths of all violence. The single most violent series, CBS's "The Hat Squad," included over 10 percent of all fictional prime-time violence and over a third of the violence found on CBS's fall schedule. This old-fashioned cop show featured 111 scenes of violence, an average of twenty-eight per episode.

Serious violence was even more concentrated. Ten series accounted for over 70 percent of all murders, shootouts, sexual assaults, and so forth; twenty series accounted for over 90 percent. The leader in serious violence, ABC's "Young Indiana Jones Chronicles," averaged sixteen scenes per episode, nearly one-seventh of the entire prime-time total. To make it into the top ten, a series had to average nine violent scenes or four scenes involving serious violence per episode.

Many of the most violent shows could have been made with few alterations almost anytime in television's history. Whether cop shows or Westerns, in sci-fi and historical settings alike, these action shows use violence in much the same way that episodic television has used it for decades. It provides excitement, keeps the plot moving, and allows the good guys to be placed in jeopardy and then to vanquish the bad guys. Action-adventure entries as diverse as "Covington Cross" (swordplay among medieval knights), "Raven" (martial arts), and "Round Table" (a generic cop show) shared these characteristics with "Young Indiana Jones" and "The Hat Squad."

What is missing from such shows are the massive gun battles and extended chase sequences of a decade ago. The high-body-count SWAT teams and secret agents licensed to kill have given way to a new wave of cop shows that use less violence to greater effect. This developing genre includes such series in our sample as "Law and Order," "In the Heat of the Night," and "Reasonable Doubts," along with lesser known efforts like "Angel Street," "Bodies of Evidence," and "Likely Suspects." Among the more recent entries to attract attention and critical acclaim are "Homicide" and "NYPD Blue." New-wave cop shows often use an initial act of serious violence to set the plot in motion and then follow up with more limited violence in later scenes. They portray violence more realistically than do most other series. They are also more likely to show fear and suffering by the victims of violence and to explore the dramatic and emotional context of individual violent acts.

Consider the hottest new series of the 1993-94 season, Steven Bochco's controversial "NYPD Blue." This is not a particularly violent series as cop shows go. But Bochco intensifies the emotional impact of the violence that does occur, whether by mimicking the feel of a local newscast covering an active crime scene or by using the slow motion and fast-cutting techniques associated with film director Sam Peckinpaugh. The victims of violence clearly suffer pain and anguish, and cops and crooks alike show fear and confusion at the use of violence. For example, during one shootout Detective Kelly (the star) is so unnerved that he repeatedly misses the bad guy, who is so frightened that he drops his gun anyway.

Like other members of this new genre of cop shows, this series clearly intends to associate violence with fear and danger rather than adventure and machismo. Nonetheless, the gritty mise-en-scène and realistic conventions make the violence seem especially intense and exciting. This type of show separates the critics who want to minimize violence per se from those who single out gratuitous violence that is presented cavalierly or used as a dramatic crutch. In any case, the new wave cop shows are the exception rather than the rule in the way that they portray violence.

Our study examined not only the amount of violence but the dramatic context in which it occurs. After all, this is at least partly what separates Shakespearean swordplay from Schwartzenneger and Stallone. So each time violence occurred, we asked whether it was sanctioned and what lasting effects it produced. The results were not encouraging to those who worry about the point of TV violence as well as the prevalence. Across the entire prime-time schedule, acts of violence were committed by good guys more often than bad guys, and they were rarely condemned as illegal or morally wrong. To top it off, violence rarely produced physical damage or even caused characters to behave any differently afterward.

We counted 278 good guy characters who behaved violently toward another person, compared to 212 bad guys. So truth, justice, and the American way were defended by violence more often than they were threatened by it. Another sixty-eight violent characters combined positive and negative traits, along the lines of a Robin Hood clone in "Covington Cross" who stole from the rich and gave to the poor, but kept a tidy carrying charge. A plurality of perpetrators (369 characters) were not clearly identified as either heroes or villains. In percentage terms, 30 percent of those who committed violence were positive characters, only 23 percent were negative, 7 percent played morally mixed roles, and 40 percent were neutral characters without clear-cut virtues or vices. Many of these "neutral" characters were police who appeared in cop shows, chasing or subduing suspects.

Although relatively few acts of violence are committed by bad guys in prime-time series, even fewer are explicitly condemned. Of course, it is usually not defended either. Nine times out of ten, violence just happens.

Whether it seems necessary or uncalled for in terms of the overall narrative, it is not commented upon to bring the message home to viewers. Specifically, no judgment was made about the use of violence 89 percent of the times it occurred during the month of prime time we studied. It was explicitly declared to be necessary or acceptable 2 percent of the time, precisely the percentage of cases that denounced the use of violence.

Thus, scripts actually condoned violence as frequently as they condemned it. But another 7 percent of violent acts were declared illegal, making 9 percent overall that were presented as somehow wrong. Even when gunplay or other serious violence took place, such behavior was presented as bad or unlawful only one time out of eight (12 percent), although verbal defenses of violence dropped to only 1 percent of these extreme cases.

It may seem less surprising that violence is so rarely deemed worthy of comment if we also note how rarely it has any discernible effect on its targets. Fewer than one-quarter of the acts of violence produced any physical injury. Fewer than one-third even caused the victims to alter their behavior in any way. The largest proportion, another one in three, produced no physical or behavioral change whatsoever. When violence is so infrequently presented as hurtful or dangerous, the rationale for denouncing it may seem less compelling.

However much moralists may deplore television's frequently nonjudgmental approach to violence, it might be argued that what the action-adventure audience wants is excitement, not ethical instruction. Moreover, trendsetters like "NYPD Blue" seem to be moving in the direction that the critics urge. For all their differences, however, the old-fashioned shoot-em-ups and the new-wave cop shows in our study had one thing in common besides their portrayal of violence: Most were gone by the end of the season. In fact, seven of the ten most violent series failed to last out the season, as did eight of the ten with the most serious violence. Among the latter, only one new series ("The Commish") and one holdover ("In the Heat of the Night") were still on the air in 1994.

The failure of so many violent series belies Hollywood's claims that it is only giving the public what it wants. Similarly, it undercuts the industry's assertion that calls for reform are coming at a time when the network schedules are less violent than they once were. The absence of conspicuously violent hit shows does not demonstrate the networks' unwillingness to offer such fare. It simply reflects the audience's rejection of the network offerings. Of course, few new series of any sort succeed these days. And if there were really no audience at all for violent entertainment, such shows would quickly cease to be made. But that is quite different from saying that Hollywood is merely responding to audience demand, like Pavlov's dogs barking on cue.

More likely, the industry is programming as it always has, trying a variety of genres (including what is euphemistically termed the "action-adventure" genre) and renewing those that succeed. Network executives like to claim that television works like a democracy, with viewers continuously voting thumbs up or down on each show. But this political system includes only the recall, not the initiative. Audience response doesn't create new shows; it only kills existing ones.[10] Conversely, the networks don't simply respond to demand; they also help to create it. When a new series catches on, it quickly spawns imitators. Stylistic changes are easier to imitate than the talent that originally produced them. That is how programming cycles occur, and the prime-time schedule goes through phases of domination by Westerns, cop shows, family sitcoms, and the like. This season's novelty becomes next season's cliché.

No one, however, knows exactly why a particular series catches the public's fancy. And it is far easier to copy a genre than to reproduce the appeal of a certain style of writing, a particular star or ensemble cast, and so on. Do people watch Steven Bochco's controversial "NYPD Blue" because of the realistic and emotionally gripping violence, the explicit sex and language, the unusually skilled acting, the gritty mise-en-scène, or the male lead's emergence as *TV Guide's* "sex symbol of the season"?[11] Would this series reach an even wider audience if Bochco didn't have to compromise with network censors, or might the audience actually increase if "NYPD Blue" were a little less blue? After all, Bochco's frequently stated intention in creating this series was to confront convention and "push the envelope," not just to maximize audience share.

Obviously, different viewers are attracted to different combinations of such elements, while others are repelled by the same factors. But no one can know the optimal combination that would attract the most viewers and repel the fewest. Even if we could know, an effort to produce the perfect formula would risk stifling the creative spirit that breathes life into a series—that "x-factor" that so often makes imitators or sequels of a hit seem merely formulaic.

The best likelihood is that audiences will be offered more gritty cop shows with heavier doses of sex, violence, and street language next season. If these shows succeed in creating a new program cycle, the networks will shrug that they are only giving people what they want. If they flop, the networks will take credit for forswearing gratuitous violence and foul language, as more benign sitcoms dominate their schedules.

Our study uncovered one other piece of evidence that Hollywood is giving violence the hard sell even though consumers don't seem in a mood to buy. The networks' intentions are revealed by the pitch they make for their programs, as well as by the programs themselves. And minute for minute, the most violent part of the prime-time schedule is not the programs themselves but the advertisements or "promos" that the networks use to attract viewers to upcoming programs. During the month that we viewed, there were actually more violent scenes in the promos for future programming fare than in the series episodes that were the subject matter of the rest of the study. The promos contained 1,313 violent scenes, compared to the 1,005 that we tallied during three hundred half-hour and hour-long programs.

The comparison isn't quite fair, because we counted promos for movies as well as series episodes, and it is movies that are most heavily promoted. For example, our study picked up thirteen airings of promos for the Steven Segal action flick "Under Siege," which totaled seventy-two scenes of violence. On the other hand, the promos themselves were extremely brief, typically lasting either fifteen or thirty seconds. Frequently inserted as teasers between the credits of the previous program and the start of the next one, they typically pulled together the most violent moments of a show in rat-tat-tat fashion, rather like armed NFL highlight films.

Ironically, these repeated doses of concentrated violence probably gave ammunition to critics by making the program schedule seem more violent than it actually was. The promos for some heavily promoted programs added nearly as much violence to prime time as the shows themselves contained, since they showed the same violent acts over and over again. So when programmers claim that they are just feeding the audience's taste for violent fare, it is well to remember how they choose to whet that appetite.

HEARTS AFIRE

For all the recent furor over video violence, foreplay has surpassed gunplay as prime time's favorite pastime. The tube has become so saturated with sex that documenting its incidence seems redundant. Still, one intrepid team of researchers recently tallied a sexual act or reference every four minutes during prime time.[12] Sexual activities and allusions are so pervasive that even married couples are getting into the act. In the premiere episode of "Mad About You," sex-starved newlyweds sated their appetites on the kitchen table, while their guests went hungry in the dining room. The network president congratulated the producers for "celebrating a loving marriage."[13]

Of course, television's unmarried couples still have more fun. They just have it a lot sooner these days. Sample first date come-on, from Jack to Wally in "Love and War": "Your condom or mine?" (We were unable to find a statement from a network executive praising this episode for promoting safe sex, but one doubtless exists at the bottom of someone's pile of press releases.) They also have it a lot earlier. From Doogie Howser to the Beverly Hills high school crowd, very young lovers joined the roster of once-closeted groups from lesbian couples to single mothers whose causes television has, so to speak, embraced.

Searching for new corners of the envelope to push, "Picket Fences" recently featured the first prime-time series episode on teenage lesbianism. The producer noted the educational benefits of dealing with "a complicated issue for adolescents . . . with a tremendous sense of responsibility."[14] In another episode, the same teenage character precipitated a discussion of heterosexual teen sex by being caught in bed with her boyfriend. Meanwhile, her younger brother reached puberty, which led to plot developments involving sexual fantasies and wet dreams.

Actually, teen sex is just about the only sex whose propriety is debated on television anymore. It's not that people don't talk about whether to have sex, just that the answer is always the same. As *New York Times* television critic John O'Connor writes, "To do it or not to do it has long been the titillating question on prime-time entertainment. Today it's merely rhetorical."[15]

We lacked the stamina of those researchers who tabulated every one of the myriad sexual references that suffuse the prime-time schedule. Instead we limited our tally to actual sexual activity. Given the conventions of network television, most couples were shown just before or just after having sex. Every season the emphasis shifts slightly more toward coitus and away from interruptus. We noted every scene that involved characters either having sex or deciding whether it would be appropriate. In the 220 scenes that dealt with sex between unmarried partners, fewer than one in ten (9 percent) concluded that having sex would be wrong or inappropriate for any reason. In over two out of three scenes (69 percent), the script endorsed the desirability of having sexual relations. In the remaining 22 percent of all sex scenes, no judgment was rendered either way.

Of course, it didn't take a lecture from Dr. Ruth for a script to endorse a sexual relationship. Usually sex was just portrayed as a positive experience for both parties. For example, in the premiere episode of "Flying Blind," Alicia tells Neil: "God, I would love to sleep with you." Neil replies, "I would very much like to be slept with." When Alicia insists that "I need to know that this means something, that I'm not just some sort of trophy," Neil suggests that they try it once and then wait awhile to see how each feels about a repeat performance. A few scenes later, Alicia decides that they've waited long enough and arrives at Neil's house unannounced. Standard sitcom hijinks ensue from their efforts to find a trysting place while avoiding Neil's visiting relatives.

Neil and Alicia are typical of television's current version of a fun couple—just two happily consenting adults. Only one script in twenty raised any objections against unmarried adults having sex. Over three out of four (76 percent) endorsed their intentions; almost one in five (19 percent) passed no judgment. Yet this represents a remarkable change in television's previously ambivalent attitude toward sex outside marriage. Even during the tremendous surge of sexual activity on prime time that began in the late 1970s, as chapter 2 recounts, only a minority of all consenting sexual relationships were sanctioned as appropriate. Today it is the rejection of sex that is deviant. Indeed, "L.A. Law" made news when a fundamentalist Christian character rejected Arnold Becker's advances by defending her decision to remain a virgin until marriage.

Even among teenagers, scripts were more likely to endorse sexual relations than to condemn them. It is a measure of how quickly prime-time standards have changed that one out of every five scenes involving premarital sex concerned teenagers. (Teen sex almost never occurred on prime-time series before the 1990s.) A plurality of these scripts (42 percent) endorsed premarital sex among teenagers, compared to only 25 percent that criticized it. And one time in three, young love was consummated without eliciting any judgment.

Fox's trend-setting teen soap "Beverly Hills 90210" derived a publicity bonanza from Brenda's continuing ambivalence about going to bed with her boyfriend Dylan. In one episode Brenda took the radical step of listening to her father's advice to wait. (She eventually submitted to Dylan's advances, though not without later regrets.) However, in "Roseanne," daughter Becky acted more typically for a prime-time teen when she asked her mother for birth control pills only after beginning a sexual relationship.

Although television frequently finds humor in parents' misgivings about their children's sex lives, it does not write off the older generation as dinosaurs. On the other hand, the clearest rejection of teen sex in our sample did come from dinosaurs. An episode of the ABC animated sitcom by that name dealt with teenaged dinosaur Robbie's sudden urge to do the mating dance. After Robbie tries to relieve the tension with a mating dance-hall girl, he accepts his mother's advice that "the mating dance is most appropriate within the confines of a loving monogamous relationship—preferably marriage." Moreover, no one suggests that this is why dinosaurs became extinct.

For adults on prime time, the question is no longer whether to have sex but which kind of sex to try next. Today television leaves no stone unturned in its quest to educate the viewing public in the varieties of human sexual experience. The prevalence of sexual references is exceeded only by their diversity. Little more than a decade after "Charlie's Angels" jiggled their way to a number one Nielsen rating, interested viewers can hear about masturbation, fetishes and fantasies, group sex, bondage and discipline, sadomasochism, and uses for jello that the cookbook doesn't mention. How do I love thee on TV? Let us count the ways.

Sex on television is usually an interpersonal activity. But scripts are increasingly playing adult variations on a "Home Alone" theme. The best known treatment of masturbation occurred in an episode of "Seinfeld." Jerry and his friends stage a contest to see who can go the longest without masturbating. Much of the humor grows out of their efforts to find unembarrassing ways to talk about this activity. They settle on the code phrase, "Are you still master of your domain?" This term has remained the euphemism of choice when the same topic was mentioned in later episodes.

A 1993 episode of "Roseanne" ventured into similar territory. When young DJ reaches puberty, his parents uncover his stash of pornographic magazines. They try to explain to him that his feelings are normal, and he thereupon feels free to talk with them. The humor derives from the contrast between DJ's blasé acceptance of his own normality and the parents' embarrassment and revulsion over discussing the topic. "Married . . . With Children" has made a running joke of a similar situation. Over the years Bud Bundy has undergone repeated teasing about how masturbation is his only outlet for romance. His sister Kelly hasn't had that problem.

Not to be outdone, "Picket Fences" featured twin sisters who were psychically connected, so that each felt the other's intense emotions and

41

sensations. When one twin is locked in a passionate embrace with her boyfriend in front of a cozy fire, the other becomes so aroused that she pulls her car over to the side of the road and begins to masturbate. This experiences leads the twins to decide that the boyfriend is such a good lover that they should share him.

For some characters, sex is all in the head. In fact, that is the high concept premise of "Herman's Head," as Herman's id keeps generating fantasies that his superego won't tolerate. In the wet dream episode of "Picket Fences," Matthew Brock's erotic dreams are played out. In one fantasy a family friend who excited his attraction shows up in a bikini and offers him chocolate cake, Nintendo, and herself. Naturally, viewers of "Married. . .With Children" have been treated to Al Bundy's erotic dreams of scantily clad women, and to Bud's sex life with blow-up dolls. Nor are sexual fantasies and fetishes limited entirely to sitcoms. "The Commish" broke up a prostitution ring that specialized in acting out customers' fantasies. During the episode one hooker dons a police uniform to play cops and robbers.

Of course two can play this game and frequently do, although the game sometimes gets rough. One cast member of the aptly titled "Going to Extremes" was a female doctor whose practice included bondage and discipline. Viewers got to observe the bedside manner of this dominatrix, as well as her technique of confining a patient to bed. An episode of "Designing Women" dealt with the unusual interior design challenge of a dungeon-like s-m playroom decorated with an array of hardware and a large wheel to which playmates can be fastened and spun around. Painful pleasures are not all fun and games. On "Law & Order" an s&m triangle ended with a masochist's murder, as the game got out of hand. And "Reasonable Doubts" featured a pornography and sex tools shop whose inventory included gags, shackles, and restraints.

Is any sexual topic taboo on television anymore? Producers who seek the cutting edge recall Tom Wolfe's image of test pilot Chuck Yeager confronting the space age in *The Right Stuff*: When the envelope is ripped wide open, there is nothing left to push against.[16] In 1991 Linda Bloodworth-Thomason was reduced to proclaiming that a new plot development in "Designing Women" would be "the first time incest has been featured *in a situation comedy*"(emphasis added).[17] A 1992 *New York Times* article entitled "What's a Network TV Censor to Do?" suggested that oral sex remains one of prime time's few remaining taboo topics.[18] Later that year our sample included a postcoital scene from "Flying Blind" in which Neil complains to Alicia that his tongue "feels like it's been lifting an Oldsmobile."

In the face of this lusty litany, yesterday's eye-opener becomes today's yawn and tomorrow's snooze. The cutting edge material of the 1980s is commonplace in the 1990s. For example, the word "condom" was first uttered in a prime-time series in 1986. Today's series score points for social responsibility by writing in references to rubbers. Strippers were once a rarity; now they may be the girl next door. "Beverly Hills 90210" and "Thea" featured strip artists who were working their way through college. A stripper who files a sexual harassment suit in "Civil Wars" is just a struggling working girl who needs the money. Although Al Bundy and Jefferson Darcy are not quite the boys next door, both tried dancing as male strippers.

Television's changing treatment of homosexuality is somewhat more complicated. A decade ago producers flaunted their progressive credentials by getting on the gay rights bandwagon. Dramatic series condemned social prejudice against the latest oppressed minority, while sitcoms lampooned homophobic ignorance. Hollywood's sentiments have not changed, but the shows have become less strident. Today's characters can combine abstract tolerance with personal discomfort toward homosexuality without being condemned as bigots.

Scripts implicitly send up this ambivalence without explicitly denouncing it. For example, after a newspaper article refers to Jerry Seinfeld's friend George as his "longtime companion," Jerry's friends and parents call to ask if he is really gay. Although their tone is one of shock, they invariably add, "not that there's anything wrong with that." The tension between their cognitive and emotional reactions becomes a running joke. And on "Hearts Afire," John struggles with his emotions after learning that his ex-wife has moved in with their female marriage counselor: "I have absolutely nothing against gay people. It's just a little

43

difficult for me to conceptualize my ex-wife slow dancing with some-one named Ruth!"

Television's low-key pitch for tolerance is also illustrated by "Roseanne," one of the few current shows whose cast includes open-ly gay characters. When Roseanne goes to work in a cafeteria, her new boss turns out to be gay. The other characters express surprise but accept his sexual orientation without real concern. Later Roseanne's married friend Nancy gets a divorce and announces that she is a lesbian. Once the other characters get over their shock, they take it in stride. The effect is to treat homosexuality as a fact of life that shouldn't determine anyone's evaluation of another human being.

The didactic approach has not entirely died out. Typical of the old school is a "Law & Order" episode about the shooting of a cop in the line of duty. Suspicions arise that he did not get adequate back-up because he was gay. Predictably, an investigation reveals bigotry within the police department, and suggests that some fellow officers deliberately delayed in coming to his assistance.

Similarly, an episode of "Picket Fences" intertwines homosexu-ality with transsexualism when the school board dismisses a postop-erative transsexual teacher as a dangerous deviant. Of course she is a wonderful teacher and a beautiful human being. Not only does a judge dismiss their objections as bigotry, but the schoolchildren stage a protest to denounce their parents' intolerance: "The children of Rome do hereby reject the prejudice of their parents. . . we reject your fear and narrow-mindedness." Apart from such exceptions (and the occasional TV movie about heroic AIDS victims), prime time's pitch for gay rights is shorter on sermonizing than it used to be.

It is not quite true that anything goes on prime time. Mirror-ing well-publicized developments on college campuses, television combines a laissez-faire attitude toward consensual sexual relations with a heightened sensitivity toward coercion. Date rapes took place in episodes of "Reasonable Doubts" and "Life Goes On," while stu-dents fended off unwanted advances or assaults by teachers in "Class of '96" and "Beverly Hills 90210."

But the ambiguities still present in such issues can be illustrated by the heavily hyped "Northern Exposure" episode in which Joel and Maggie's love-hate relationship is finally consummated with a literal roll in the hay. The sex is unplanned, unsafe, unwanted, and unsurpassed. Afterward Maggie is so appalled by her own behavior that she suffers an attack of amnesia. Eventually she has to admit that her conscious judgment was no match for the forces of unconscious passion and sheer carnal attraction. CBS's promo for this episode featured a clip of the attractive Maggie telling the camera with increasing conviction, "Sex is good . . . . Sex is great!" That might serve as television's current motto.

Love and War

The relationship between "Northern Exposure"'s Dr. Joel Fleischman and Maggie O'Connell illustrates more than the tendency of today's Tracy-Hepburn wannabees to leave less to the imagination. It also shows how television's current preoccupations extend beyond sexual relations to relations between the sexes. In fact, the battle of the sexes seems to occupy prime-time producers more than anything other than sex itself. Shows debate the treatment of women, the adequacy of traditional gender roles, and the traits alleged to typify each sex. More than one out of every three episodes in our sample contained some treatment of whether men or women are more caring and clever in handling their relationships. More pointedly, one out of five episodes deplored the unequal treatment of women, and one in twelve specifically made a case for women's rights.

Gender stereotypes are a staple of popular culture, and television long ago discovered "women's lib," as chapter 3 relates. What distinguishes the 1990s is the frequency with which shows use this material to structure settings and develop characters rather than just to advance the plot. For example, "Northern Exposure" intertwines the relationships of three couples to produce a running critique on the benign battle of the sexes. Providing variations on Joel and Maggie's fractious folie à deux are the sexagenarian Hollis and his teen squeeze Shelley, along with the Neanderthal master chef Adam and his hypochondriac wife Eve.

Just as the names of the latter couple express a certain elemental quality in gender relations, the pairing of Joel and Maggie provides a comic variation on the Jungian animus and anima. (If this sounds far-fetched, consider that both Jung and Freud have made appearances as characters on this series.)   An earthbound internist and a flighty bush pilot, complementary personalities, are doomed both to attract and repel each other, because neither understands the forces animating the opposite sex.

In one episode Maggie's anger at Joel produces a tirade about the male approach to sex: "Men, it's all unfocused, impersonal lust. . . men will go to bed with just about anybody, even women they're indifferent to." In another she complains about male dominance, "Men have been running things for thousands of years, and what do we have to show for it? War, pollution, the S & L thing. . . ." When Shelley tells her not to get so upset, Maggie replies grandly, "This isn't upset, this is empowered!"

This series is set in Cicely, Alaska, a New Age Brigadoon named after one member of the lesbian couple Cicely and Roslyn, who founded it as a refuge from the ravages of male chauvinism. (When a female resident asks Roslyn's advice on a problem of the heart, she recommends "the love of a good woman.") In a witty flashback episode, viewers learn how the two women exerted a civilizing feminist influence on the no-holds-barred turn-of-the-century boom town. They created a utopian artist's colony, turning the residents from their base instincts toward nobler pursuits, before succumbing to a counterattack by the town's unregenerate phallocentrists.

If "Northern Exposure" is sui generis, "Home Improvement" is the very model of a modern mainstream sitcom. As such, it illustrates how traditional prime-time formats can be built around gender issues. Lead character Tim Taylor is the host of a TV home improvement show (à la "This Old House") and a big fan of power tools, hot rods, and other traditionally masculine pursuits. He promotes a philosophy of "masculinism," which holds that the answer to any problem is more power. He is also very concerned that his sons avoid any effeminate activities.

In his efforts to uphold his masculine ideals, along with his inevitable failures to play handyman in his own household, Tim's character satirizes male attitudes toward women and life in general. In an episode that we viewed, for example, Tim recommends that his son keep from fumbling footballs by putting diluted glue on his hands. When the boy notes that the label warns against contact with the skin, Tim replies that they mean "pretty little pink girl skin; we got man skin—callouses, warts, open wounds."

The well-meaning but bumbling Tim is regularly chided by his forbearing wife Jill, who clearly has the brains in the family. Tim frequently seeks advice on male-female relations from his neighbor Wilson, a Robert Bly knockoff who dispenses quasi-mystical wisdom involving concepts such as collective memory. In the same episode, Tim is caught looking at another woman with lust in his heart. After a friend of Jill's accuses him of being "your typical American male, no self-control," Tim talks to Wilson about his problem. Wilson attributes it to "ancient man's primal fantasy to seek out women," while "a woman's primal fantasy [is] a meaningful relationship with just one man."

These examples show how contemporary sitcoms use individual relationships to comment more generally on gender issues, but also how they soften the sharp edges to keep the dialogue from getting tendentious. Maggie's diatribes against men come across as an expression of her own emotionalism, allowing traditionalists to laugh at her as feminists laugh with her. And chauvinist Tim is clearly good-hearted and educable. Still, women tend to get the better of these arguments. For example, an episode of "Full House" dealt with Jesse's discomfort at finding his twin sons playing with a doll. He takes it away and brings home more gender-appropriate toys, such as a football and boxing gloves. But his wife Rebecca intercedes and argues that the boys should "have a full range of experiences and grow up to be well-rounded human beings. . . . A boy who plays with dolls. . . just might grow up to be a terrific father." Jesse eventually concedes the point. He not only gives back the doll but uses it to show the boys how to hold a baby.

This outcome was typical of the benign battle of the sexes, as our statistical analysis revealed. In situations involving issues of conscience or compassion in family or other close personal relationships, women were more than twice as likely as men to display sensitivity toward the emotional needs of others. Moreover, women were not only portrayed as the sensitive sex; they were also seen as more sensible. When the plot or dialogue presented one partner as more capable, competent, or cool-headed than the other, women proved wiser than men three times out of four. On prime time today, Mother knows best.

Finally, when characters generalized about the traits that distinguish the sexes, the comparison favored women three times out of five. The generalization heard most frequently was that men are philanderers or sex fiends. Eight shows featured some variation of Maggie's complaint about male promiscuity. For example, during her first date with Jack in "Love and War," Wally already understands his primal motivation: "He's a man! I know how they think. 'Wake up, have sex. Brush teeth, have sex. Rebuild transmission, have sex.'" The most frequent generalization about women was that they are overly emotional, a complaint aired in six shows.

If prime-time sex shows the medium taking on once-taboo topics, TV's gender relations treat an old topic in a new way. Chapter 3 details the past discrepancy between television's endorsement of women's lib and the mostly unliberated individual women who populated prime time. Today the schedule is filled with strong and independent female characters fighting for their rights. However, the major battleground has shifted from social injustices to domestic disputes. As family sitcoms have displaced issue-oriented dramas from the prime-time lineup, television's new woman is less concerned with changing the world than with getting her boss to take her seriously and her husband to help with the kids.

This is no retreat into traditional sex roles; quite the reverse. Arguments for sexual equality are being grounded in the travails of ordinary life and everyday relationships. In a standard sitcom plot device, an overly aggressive man disregards a woman's advice and soon regrets it, or a blustery know-it-all male exaggerates his abilities and is shown up by a quietly competent female. In a previous era Lucy Ricardo would get in over her head in complications from some wild scheme. In the 1990s, such pratfalls are the province of Tim Taylor, Al Bundy, or Homer Simpson.

Similarly, series that portray young males on the make frequently treat them as blustery buffoons or immature clowns. Swinging bachelors and successful ladies' men have been glamorized throughout television's history, from the suave photographer Bob Collins on "The Bob Cummings Show" through the country hunks Luke and Bo Duke on "The Dukes of Hazzard." More recently, would-be lotharios like Joey Emerson on "Roc," Vidal Thomas on "Out All Night," and Charley on "Empty Nest" are targets of derision whose lover boy antics fall flat. Nowadays a well-practiced pickup line is frequently a prelude to a feminist putdown.

The battle of the sexes is not always shown benignly or played for laughs. Ugly scenes of domestic violence and sexual abuse have become a specialty of made-for-TV movies, whose plot lines cover the spectrum from standard "women in jep" (i.e., jeopardy) fare to "Thelma and Louise" revenge fantasies. Similarly, "NYPD Blue" and "In the Heat of the Night" have run episodes about women who kill their harasser or abuser. In "Civil Wars" a female lawyer was forced to pull a gun on an obnoxious suitor who cornered her in a stalled elevator. And the famous Clarence Thomas episode of "Designing Women" created a brief flurry of prime-time denunciations of sexual harassment.

More interesting are series in which domestic violence turns up as a biographical detail designed to help establish a strong female character who has overcome a background of male subjugation. This is the case for both "Roseanne" and "Grace Under Fire," in which the star's personal biography is written into the show. The link is clearest for the character of Grace Kelly, who is nobody's princess. She rarely lets an episode go by without making a cutting remark about her no-good abusive ex-husband. These wisecracks identify her as a tough cookie who has learned not to let any male take advantage of her. The Thanksgiving episode included a plot line in which Grace helps a co-worker whom she thinks was beaten by her husband.

The linkage is less evident in "Roseanne," where it is referenced in occasional jokes about Roseanne Conner's past. However, the series featured one segment in which Roseanne discovers that her sister Jackie was beaten by her live-in boyfriend. When Jackie tries to cover it up and make excuses for his behavior, Roseanne reminds her of the childhood abuse they both suffered. She eventually convinces her sister to move out and also warns the boyfriend to keep away from her.

Traditional issue-oriented treatments of women's rights are more rare. But they contribute to our overall finding that twenty-four episodes made some argument for women's rights, and fifty-seven contained an objection to the unequal treatment of women (only four episodes were tolerant toward gender discrimination). In "Picket Fences," for example, Maxine is passed over for promotion after the male interviewers ask about her personal life, including her plans to start a family. A judge later criticizes this behavior and orders that she be reconsidered. In "L.A. Law" a female judge denounces the chauvinism of a lawyer, after he attacks the credibility of a witness going through mood swings associated with menopause.

Such courtroom set pieces have a certain dated quality when compared to the more integrative approach currently in vogue. And several series in the sample that pushed hard for women's rights disappeared after finding few viewers of either gender. For example, a shrill sitcom called "Frannie's Turn" was built around a middle-aged seamstress who asserts her need for independence against a reactionary macho husband. Their relationship is so one-sided that Frannie has to fight even to see the family bank book, much less manage the money. The equally tendentious "Angel Street" featured two female homicide detectives who seemed to spend as much time fighting racist and sexist male cops as they did fighting crime.

Two other failed series anachronistically transposed feminist perspectives and concerns to earlier time periods. ABC gave up on "Homefront," a low-rated socially conscious soap set in 1945 but with an up-to-the-minute sensibility that led one critic to comment, "all that's missing . . . is a reference to date rape."[19] "Covington Cross" got an even shorter run out of a longer step back in time. The cast of this medieval Western included a tomboyish teenager who rejected traditional female roles (which were quite traditional indeed in the fourteenth century) and a widow who managed her late husband's estates and insisted on being treated as an equal. For a time when women were considered chattel, these were very independent-minded chattel.

There are two linked reasons for the pervasiveness of prime-time feminism: To an unprecedented degree, series are being produced by women and for women. Television programming has long been tilted toward female audiences. Advertisers value women for being more frequent and loyal viewers than men (channel surfing is practiced mainly by males), as well as for their influence over household purchases. Recent trends have only intensified gender differences in viewing habits. Cable channels peel away male viewers of sports, sleaze, and shoot-em-ups, leaving a more heavily female broadcast audience. Equally important, men and women are increasingly watching different prime-time series. As this is written, ten series are on the Nielsen top twenty list for either men or women but not both.[20] A recent study found that the audiences of five different prime-time series were at least 65 percent female, while no fictional series had even a 55 percent male viewership. [21]

The importance of female viewers helps to explain the prevalence of sitcoms and soapy dramas built around personal relationships, but it does not fully account for the feminist perspectives that these shows express. The other component is the newfound prominence of female writers and producers in Hollywood. Many of these women are strong feminists, who express their commitments through organizations such as the Hollywood Women's Political Caucus.

Chapter 3 chronicles the first wave of feminist influence on prime time during the 1980s. Their ranks included such hitmakers and trendsetters as Diane English ("Murphy Brown"), Linda Bloodworth-Thomason ("Designing Women"), Susan Harris ("Golden Girls"), and Barbara Corday ("Cagney & Lacey"). This rising tide has carried a flood of female talent into the current prime-time schedule, including Roseanne Arnold ("Roseanne"), Beth Sullivan ("Dr. Quinn, Medicine Woman"), Carmen Finestra ("Home Improvement"), Fran Drescher ("The Nanny"), and Marcy Carsey and Caryn Mandabach ("A Different World"). These creators and producers are joined by a host of lesser-known writers, whose prevalence is most pronounced on sitcoms.

This rapid influx has reached the point of critical mass. Ten years ago women had barely begun to challenge the tone of prime-time gender relations; now they are starting to set it.

Our own 1982 survey found that women made up only 1 percent of the Hollywood "creative community."[22] Only eight years later, another academic survey of Hollywood opinion leaders found that the proportion of women had jumped to over one in four (26 percent). The researchers found these women to be "even more liberal than the men" in this heavily liberal subculture (see chapter 12). They concluded, "If women continue . . . moving into Hollywood power centers . . . we can expect that its already dominant liberal tone will only intensify."[23] For example, at a time when 41 percent of the general public favored more restrictive abortion laws, among the Hollywood sample 11 percent took this position, while every female "strongly opposed" restrictions on abortion.

In the past, the mostly liberal males who created prime-time entertainment were willing to put occasional expressions of support for women's rights into their scripts. Yet these abstractions did not prevent them from portraying individual women in more traditional terms. It took the recent influx of socially conscious women into the creative community to produce the ground-level critique of gender relations that suffuses television today. This change reflects a more visceral feminism that is grounded in the life experiences of the industry's female vanguard and expressed in the everyday behavior of the characters they create. As Hollywood becomes less of a man's world, prime-time perspectives on gender are increasingly refracted through a feminist prism.

IN LIVING COLOR

The portrayal of race on prime time has changed as much as that of gender in recent years, and for some of the same reasons. But the nature of these changes has been quite different. To begin with, any discussion of race on television today is mainly a discussion of blacks on television. Major roles for Asians, Hispanics, and other minorities are almost nonexistent. All minority groups apart from blacks totaled only 5 percent of the characters in our sample. By contrast, after many years during which black characters were seen roughly in proportion to their actual numbers in the population, the presence of blacks on prime-time shows has increased sharply.

A Different World

During the 1970s and 1980s roughly one prime-time character in ten was black, a period when census data show the actual proportion of black Americans rising gradually from 10 to 12 percent of the population. Throughout these decades blacks were seen mainly in all-black series created by white producers or in supporting roles in series otherwise populated by whites. Norman Lear and his protégés created the first all-black shows since "Amos 'n' Andy" in a series of family sitcoms that included "The Jeffersons," "Good Times," and "Sanford and Son." Black characters were also featured regularly in urban cop shows like "Starsky and Hutch" and "Baretta," as members of "salt and pepper" police teams, informants, and criminals.

A new era began with the 1984 premiere of "The Cosby Show," the first series for which the creative team as well as the cast were mainly black. Since Bill Cosby's pioneering efforts (and owing partly to his continuing influence), not only have the number of black characters and black-oriented series increased, but the formative influence of blacks has grown apace. In our sample from the 1992-93 season, nearly one out of every five characters (18 percent) was black, while just over three out of four (77 percent) were white. For the first time, the artificial world of prime time contains proportionately more blacks and fewer whites than the real world does. (One could not, however, call television more racially diverse than the real world, given the paucity of other minority characters. No other racial group made up more than 1 percent of the prime-time populace.)

The major source of this increased African-American presence is a growing number of black-oriented sitcoms and variety shows. Unlike the first wave of black sitcoms during the 1970s, most of the current crop has been shaped substantially by black talent. Many of these shows were built around a bankable celebrity with demonstrated audience appeal. They include singers such as Patti LaBelle ("Out All Night") and rappers Will Smith ("Fresh Prince") and Queen Latifah ("Living Single"). More common, though, are shows developed from the work of successful stand-up comedians. This was the path taken by Cosby himself, and followed more recently by Doug E. Doug in "Where I Live," Mark Curry in

"Hangin' with Mr. Cooper," Martin Lawrence in "Martin," Sinbad in "The Sinbad Show," filmmaker Robert Townsend ("Townsend Television"), and Keenan Ivory Wayans, who created "In Living Color."

Creative influence has been exerted in more traditional fashion by producers such as Erich von Lowe ("Roc," "Where I Live") and Oprah Winfrey ("Brewster Place"). But blacks have lagged behind women in gaining entrance to the executive suite in this as in other industries. The key entry point to date has involved the lateral movement of black entertainers into television. Whereas most prime-time series are first created and then cast, several of these stars have been involved in the creative process. High ratings provide a further opportunity for creative control, following the model of socially conscious actors turned producers like Cosby and Roseanne Arnold.

The flip side of this development is the concentration of black characters in relatively few series and a lack of diversity in their roles. During fall 1992, we found that twelve series contained 65 percent of all appearances by blacks. This means that fewer than one-sixth of the shows contained two-thirds of the black characters. Continuing characters were even more concentrated; eleven series accounted for just under 70 percent of all recurring black roles. The clustering of black characters in a few shows is not new, but it is noteworthy that the overall increase in black roles has not produced more integrated programming.

More disturbing is the fragmentation of the audience along racial lines. A segmented audience translates into segregated airwaves. Thus, trends in television viewing habits appear to reflect the increasing self-segregation of American life. Indeed, the differences that we found in the viewing tastes of men and women pale before the split screen that separates black and white viewers. Ironically, the expansion of black creative influence, by facilitating series more closely linked to the black experience and presold to the black audience, may have helped to create a kind of viewership ghetto for the new black-oriented shows.

This result was by no means preordained. The first wave of Lear-inspired ethnic sitcoms won a vast and diverse audience. "Sanford and Son" stayed in the Nielsen top ten list for five consecutive seasons.

During the 1974-75 season four of the top seven series featured minority leads: "Sanford" ranked second, "Chico and the Man" was fourth, "The Jeffersons" fifth, and "Good Times" seventh. Their viewership ranged from about 25 to 30 percent of the audience. Nor did the potential for crossover shows disappear during the 1980s. "The Cosby Show" stayed at or near the top of the ratings for most of its prime-time run from 1984 through 1992. At its peak "Cosby" generated the highest ratings of any series since "Bonanza." Yet none of the current black-oriented shows rank in the top ten, only one ("Fresh Prince") is in the top twenty, and just one other ("Hangin' with Mr. Cooper") is among the fifty most frequently watched series. Even "Fresh Prince" is seen by fewer than half the number of households that watched "Sanford" or "Cosby" in their heydays.

The source of this audience dropoff is clear. Blacks are watching the new black-oriented shows; whites are not. A study of the 1992 fall season found that eleven of the twelve top-rated series in black households revolved around black lifestyles and culture.[24] (The only exception was "Married. . . With Children," which ranked tenth.) Among that group only "Hangin' with Mr. Cooper" made the top twenty list for nonblack households; it tied for twentieth place. Three of the black top ten— "Roc," "Out All Night," and "In Living Color"—finished one-hundredth or lower in the nonblack rankings. Conversely, blacks are not watching many of the shows that are most popular with white audiences. Among the top ten series in all households for fall 1992, only the number one rated "Roseanne" even made the top twenty list for black households, coming in at fifteenth. Other top ten hits watched by few blacks included "Home Improvement" (forty-seventh among black households), "Murphy Brown" (sixty-fourth), and "Love and War" (seventy-sixth).

Thus, the new prominence of black-oriented shows does not stem from their popularity with white audiences. Instead, it reflects advertisers' increased interest in targeting audiences demographically, as well as heavier TV viewing by blacks than whites. The average black household watches television seventy hours a week, compared to forty-seven hours for nonblack households. But advertisers are not just buying a black audience by placing commercials on these shows. They are also going after the more affluent young white urbanites who watch black-oriented shows to keep abreast of the latest styles and trends. This is a key element of Fox's programming strategy. As the president of Fox Entertainment puts it, "We use black shows to hook the hip white audience. That's one reason we've become the cutting edge network."[25]

Of course, all "black" shows are not the same in format, viewpoint, or audience appeal. In our 1992 sample, series oriented toward the black experience fell into three groups: variety shows, family comedies, and what we called "man-about-town" sitcoms. The variety format had languished for years on prime time until it was revitalized by comedian Keenan Ivory Wayans' creation "In Living Color." An irreverent and risqué collection of skits and sketches punctuated by rap music and street dancing, the show is closely attuned to the black community. But it is definitely not a black "Ed Sullivan Show." A typical episode contains something to offend almost everyone. One satirical setpiece, "Men on Film," features flamboyantly gay critics reviewing films "from a men's perspective." Running gags make fun of black entertainers like Arsenio Hall, and various skits have satirized Spike Lee, Al Sharpton, Jesse Jackson, and Lewis Farrakahn. "Townsend Television" was another experimental and highly individual variety show (created by filmmaker Robert Townsend), which tried unsuccessfully to emulate "ILC'"s popularity with the street-smart set.

Less innovative but far more widespread are the family comedies, which apply the "Cosby" approach to family relations in more downscale settings. Series such as "Family Matters," "Thea," "Roc," and the failed "Tall Hopes" come closest to the ideal espoused by many critics of black images on television. They remain rooted in the black experience and are not shy about critizing social institutions, but their outlook on life is rather traditional. Most families are portrayed as intact and stable, with parents who are flexible enough to maintain their authority while accommodating their children's concerns. The scripts often uphold such old-fashioned virtues as hard work, commitment, and responsibility. Attempted shortcuts and get-rich-quick schemes end in disaster and teach the characters some valuable lesson about life.

At the opposite end of the image spectrum are the "man-about-town" shows. A specialty of the Fox network, they feature slick operators. They are on the make and make no bones about it. The most blatant of these portrayals is "Martin," a shoot-from-the-hipster radio talk show host whose flamboyance and overt sexism recall George Jefferson. Martin revels in his outrageous opinions and considers himself a macho ladies man. Sample come-on: "Girl, gimme some of the wet mouth." "Hangin' with Mr. Cooper" features a toned-down version of this character type as a black Jack Tripper in a "Three's Company" setting. (Horny young man has two female housemates, drools over the sexy one, pratfalls ensue.) "Living Single" reverses the roles but retains the stereotypes. This time it's four young women on the make, who look at men with a mixture of lust and disgust.

These shows are marked by an atmosphere of acquisitiveness. The characters know what they want out of life, and their short list includes sex, money, and consumer goods. They yearn to display the symbols of material success—the coolest clothes, hottest cars, biggest TVs, and best-looking partners. Unlike the wealth and status seekers of the upscale white-oriented soaps, however, these characters are rootless ne'er-do-wells who talk the talk but can't walk the walk. They are always looking for the winning lottery number, the perfect pick-up line, or the short line for a cushy job. Though they rarely fail to make a dash for the flash, it usually ends up as a flash in the pan.

Finally, several shows combine elements of both sitcom genres by putting young hipsters together with more traditional family members and playing off the conflicts that arise between them. The most popular is "Fresh Prince," in which young Will uses his Philadelphia street smarts to loosen up his uptight Bel Air relatives. "Where I Live" features a hard-working inner-city Jamaican cabdriver and his wife, who try to steer their son away from his natural instinct to con his way to fat city. "Sinbad" and "George" also incorporate similar value conflicts into generation gap sitcom formats.

The man-about-town shows glamorize loud, brassy, and very hip characters who thumb their noses at mainstream culture and middle-class sensibilities. The shows are typically laden with sexual innuendo, and the leads revel in sexist attitudes. For example, when Will Smith's prep school goes coed, the guys hold up score cards as attractive girls go by. This episode also satirizes the moment of truth—the articulation of some lesson learned—beloved of family sitcoms. To the strains of "The Battle Hymn of the Republic," Will anguishes, "Am I as superficial as all those [other] guys?. . . Might I not be able to look deeper and to cherish women as full and complete and complex individuals, and with this new understanding to finally find and keep this true love that eludes so many of us? . . . Nah!!!" With that he runs off in pursuit of an attractive girl who just walked by.

Not surprisingly, such portrayals sometimes draw the wrath of black leaders for playing to racist and sexist stereotypes. For example, Bill Cosby has condemned the portrayal of African-Americans as "living cartoons." Similarly, outspoken actor Frank Reid complains that "by depicting African-American culture solely through the hip-hop generation, Fox is making a tiny segment of us drive our entire TV image."[26] It is easy to sympathize with such sentiments. The behavior and lifestyles that these shows portray are neither ennobling nor conducive to social mobility.

On the other hand, these are not mere minstrel shows that lampoon black stereotypes for white amusement. They pride themselves on their fresh-from-the-street flavor and irreverent attitudes, which clearly strike a chord with their heavily young, urban, and black audience. They are intended to offend middle-class and middle-aged sensibilities regardless of race, just as many adolescents prefer music that their elders find unlistenable. Their affectionate send-ups of recognizable (if somewhat disreputable) character types may simply connect with a sizable segment of the audience, just as Norman Lear's blue-collar white ethnics once did, despite the critics who found them too rude and crude.

Moreover, one person's reality can be another's stereotype. The widely admired "The Cosby Show" was itself attacked from the Left for promoting an inauthentic deracinated version of black life based on middle-class white norms. The *Village Voice* assailed Cosby as an Uncle Tom for creating a black family whose "whole context of reference is that of

American Caucasians."[27] Academic critics went further, complaining that the Huxtable household represented a false ideal that legitimized a spurious ideology: "'The Cosby Show,' by incorporating a black family into the American dream. . . symbolizes the fairness of the American system. . . . It is part of a belief system that allows people in the United States to disregard the inequities that generate this nation's appalling record . . . on poverty, crime, health, homelessness, and education."[28] In this case, one person's positive role model was another's false consciousness.

The new face of black life on television has also shaped its portrayal of race relations. As with gender relations, the discussion is no longer so much about restrictions and inequities as it is about attitude. In the case of race, however, this takes on a double meaning. Scripts expose residual bias in white attitudes, while black characters display "attitude" with sassy putdowns of square white cultural styles. We noted every discussion that alleged racial discrimination by social institutions, as well as biased attitudes and actions by individuals.

Fifteen shows dealt with allegations of unfair treatment by institutions, of which twelve (80 percent) affirmed that whites were treated better than blacks. Most of these occurred in socially conscious dramas in the realist mode. For example, "I'll Fly Away" dealt with segregation in the pre-civil rights era South. In one episode a black child exiled to the "colored" balcony in a theater complains to her white companion, "It's not fair you get all the good seats." She retaliates by throwing candy down on the whites seated below. More up-to-date was the "L.A. Law" Los Angeles riot episode, which featured a black nationalist leader who tells an enthusiastic crowd, "The jury in Los Angeles delivered a clear message. Black people are on their own. No justice, except what we do for ourselves. No prosperity except what we create with our own hands. . . ." At the end of this speech he is murdered, apparently by a white assassin.

Discussions of individual bias were more common. Out of thirty-two shows that contained such material, about two-thirds (63 percent) affirmed the existence of discriminatory beliefs or behavior, while the remainder exonerated individual whites of bias. (There were also four discussions of bias among blacks, only one of which was affirmed.) Most but not all of these concerned black-white relations. For example, in a scene from "Crossroads," the male leads are sitting in a bar eating with their friend Virgil Little Eagle, when a drunk begins to berate Indians: "We should have finished you guys off when we had the chance. Now we have to give them free medical care, free schooling, free housing, and they don't even pay taxes." An effort to defuse the situation by buying every-one a drink brings the response, "We don't want nothin' from no Indian lovers." The exchange eventually ends in a fistfight.

Most instances of bias were presented more subtly. In "Home-front," it was expressed in the condescending tone the wealthy white Sloans took toward their black cook and driver, Gloria and Abe John-son. After treating them like children, the Sloans couldn't understand why the couple finally quit to start their own business. Criticism of white bias could also be played out in a single scene or exchange of dia-logue. For example, in an episode of "Love and War," the gang at the Blue Shamrock decide to go to a big sale at a New York department store. The waitress is afraid to go, because she shoplifted from the store years ago as part of a sorority initiation. The black bartender reassures her that it's a ritzy uptown store, so every security guard will be follow-ing him. This recalls a scene from "A Different World," in which a white store clerk treats the wealthy Whitley Gilbert like a welfare recip-ient simply because she is black.

As these examples suggest, few Archie Bunkerisms are voiced on prime time these days. White racism is most frequently portrayed as insidious, even unconscious, rather than overt and intentional. Thus, TV typically tries to uproot the preconceptions and apprehensions that whites bring to their everyday dealings with blacks. Sometimes, though, these relatively minor affronts to dignity become more serious. Some of the most pointed criticisms concern the way the criminal justice system treats African-Americans. Thus, in "Fresh Prince" Will is picked up by the police after he accidentally sets off a car alarm in Bel Air. This echoes an episode of "L.A. Law" in which a young black attorney takes the police to court after they stop him simply for jogging through a mostly white neighborhood. Among the shows in our sample, the harshest criticism along these lines occurred in an episode of "Roc." Two overzealous policemen arrest Roc Emerson on suspicion of breaking and entering. After six hours in a cell without getting his phone call or being told what the charges are, the furious Roc lashes out:

> I'm a citizen. I go to work. I pay my taxes. I'm the guy they're supposed to be protecting. But when they look at me they don't see that. All they see is another nigger. Some crackhead who is going to steal their money and rape their women. It doesn't matter what we do, 'cause just when you think things might be getting better and we don't have to put up with this stuff anymore, they whack you over the head to remind you that nothing's changed.

It is worth noting how thoroughly this portrayal of race relations contradicts the notion that commercial television reinforces popular prejudices or stereotypes. If anything, writers and producers challenge white preconceptions through their portrayals of minority individuals victimized by passive bias and active discrimination. Further, these overt themes dealing with race relations are reinforced by the portrayals of black characters. As noted, most complaints about negative stereotyping ironically target a program genre that is heavily influenced by African-American creative talent and watched by mainly black audiences. But any discussion of stereotypes should also consider what Sherlock Holmes called the dog that didn't bark—the absence of images that would reinforce white apprehension or condescension toward blacks.

It is no coincidence that several shows addressed the anger of African-Americans over being treated as criminals because of their color. The association of race and crime is probably as widespread and as central to racial stereotypes among whites today as fears of interracial sex were a generation ago.[29] Yet television does not play to popular fears. Indeed, the degree to which prime-time portrayals avoid reinforcing these images is quite striking.

Unhappily, blacks account for over one-third of all Americans arrested for serious crimes, nearly half of those arrested for violent crimes, and a majority of those arrested for murder. On prime time, by contrast, our study found that only 8 percent of criminals were black. In fact, whites committed crimes against blacks twice as frequently as blacks committed crimes against whites. (Most prime-time crimes, however, were committed by whites against other whites.) As a result, blacks appeared as crime victims half again as often as they appeared as perpetrators.

Similarly, television did not reinforce presumptions of white superiority by showing blacks primarily in subservient or inferior social positions. African-American characters accounted for over one-third of the teachers and professors portrayed on prime time, one in four police officers, one in five business owners, one in eight lawyers, and one in ten doctors. The roster of regular characters included a lawyer on "L.A. Law," a doctor on "Going to Extremes," teachers on "Hangin' with Mr. Cooper," successful restaurant owners on "Homefront," "Evening Shade," and "Family Matters," assorted educated professionals on "A Different World," and a network vice-president on "Murphy Brown."

African-Americans rarely appeared in some high-status positions, such as corporate executive or psychiatrist. But overall, black characters were seen in business, managerial, and professional occupations more frequently than as blue-collar or clerical workers or as unemployed persons. They accounted for one out of six characters in the former categories and one out of seven in the latter.

Thus, the prime-time images in our sample did not legitimize racial inequality, either overtly or by inference. Although blacks and whites are often shown separately, they are certainly portrayed as equals. In fact, there is one context in which African-American life is shown as separate but superior. In its treatment of cultural styles, television portrays black culture as urbane, vibrant, and vital. This perspective is often implicit in the black-oriented series that celebrate urban hip-hop styles and send up whites or black "oreos" as hopelessly unhip.

This viewpoint appears explicitly when a cool character pokes fun at someone who either just doesn't get it or can't get with it. For example, in an episode of "Hangin' with Mr. Cooper," Mark repeatedly tries to teach Robin's incredibly square date how to clap in time with the music, before giving up in disgust. In "Fresh Prince," the butt of Will's jokes is his very preppy schoolmate Carlton. The impossibly uncool Carlton is Will's age, but he is hopelessly middle-aged in hip-hop terms. For instance, he loves argyles and khaki pants, which represent the epitome of nerdish attire in these shows.

To a great degree this is the flip side of the same old racial stereotyping. It's the "white men can't jump" approach—the point isn't that blacks have rhythm but that whites can't dance. The underlying comparison remains, but its target is reversed. These shows get laughs out of having white characters butcher the pronunciation of black rappers' names or incorrectly use the latest street slang. If some black critics are not amused, well, this is also a way of illustrating the generation gap. It's not just a black thing; the same shows use this motif in exchanges between hip kids and their out-of-it elders. Nonetheless, hipness is seen as a kind of validation of blackness that is off-limits to whites.

One series in the sample made this culture clash into a "high-concept" plot device. In "Rhythm & Blues" a black radio station hires a new DJ named Bobby Soul without realizing that he is white. Bobby has a great on-air persona and wide knowledge of black musical styles, from the blues to rap and hip-hop. Nonetheless, many of his co-workers refer to him derogatorily as "Opie" and "cracker" and try to get him fired. Eventually he wins their respect by boosting the station's ratings with its black audience and demonstrating his genuine love for the music. This NBC sitcom did not survive its first season. Perhaps the premise of a white man trying to make it in a black world resonated with too few viewers of either race. But *TV Guide* raised a question about this series that will not disappear so quickly: "What makes a show built on white jokes better than a show built on black jokes?"[30]

AMERICA'S MOST WANTED

In the rapidly changing world of prime time, it is comforting to know that some things remain constant. The sex may get bolder, the women stronger, and the streets meaner, but the bad guy businessman is forever. When we first reported over a decade ago that TV treated its business characters as "crooks, conmen, and clowns," it was big news.[31] Since then the evil executive has become a Hollywood cliché, as characters like J.R. Ewing and Gordon Gekko entered the pop culture pantheon of villainy. Yet the notion of business as Hollywood's favorite heavy still retains its original man-bites-dog quality. The networks nightly bite the corporate hand that feeds them, by turning real world capitalists into video villains.

This state of affairs not only seems contrary to common sense, it is also considered counterintuitive by many scholars. Academic communications theorists tend to treat popular culture as an instrument of social control, which serves the interests of business elites by lulling the mass audience into becoming passive consumers. In a post-Marxist world, they see television as the new opiate of the masses.[32] So it is worth revisiting this unlikely phenomenon, if only to understand how entertainment images can take on the powers that hold the purse strings. Along the way, we will also explore recent trends that may take some of the sting out of television's negative portrayal of business, while providing broader insights into prime time's changing character types.

In our sample, about one out of every nine characters with a known occupation came from the world of business. But if this was a populous group, it was not a popular one. Business characters were twice as likely to be bad guys and three times as likely to commit crimes as were characters in other occupations. No other prime-time profession attained even half the proportion of criminals that business produced. Businessmen and women were also at their worst when they were shown actually engaging in business, rather than purely personal pursuits. Thus, most of their criminal conduct was directly related to their business activities.

The bad behavior of these business characters ranged from low-level avarice and garden-variety venality to such serious villainy as kidnapping and murder. On "Home Improvement," the president of the tool company that underwrites Tim's show tries to get Tim to plug the company's new saw. When Tim balks because of the product's poor construction and performance, the boss threatens to cancel the show. On "Law & Order," a jewelry store owner is apparently forced to kill a robber in self-defense. The police eventually discover that he hunted the robber down and shot him in cold blood. On "Raven," a martial arts crime drama, a corrupt businessman who patronizes a high-priced call girl service ends up committing a murder.

Of course, no discussion of contemporary corporate villains would be complete without a nod to Montgomery Burns, the nuclear plant owner on "The Simpsons," who has replaced J.R. Ewing as the prime-time businessman audiences love to hate. Burns is the archetype of the comically evil entrepreneur, whose character at once embodies and parodies the greedy corporate chieftain. Our sample found him tricking the terminally gullible Homer Simpson out of suing over a radiation leak that left Homer sterile. Our favorite Burns ploy, though, had him illegally dumping radioactive waste in the neighborhood park. He had to stop dumping it in the playground, he observes, because "all those bald-headed children are beginning to attract attention."

What is most interesting about "The Simpsons"'s portrayal of business, however, is that Burns is just beginning. All the business characters wear black hats, from Smithers, Burns' sycophantic assistant, to Moe, the coarse and sarcastic bar owner, to Apu, the price-gouging convenience store owner, and Krusty, the rapacious clown. In another episode in our sample, the Simpson kids go off to Kamp Krusty, a summer camp owned by their favorite TV clown. But Krusty turns out to be an absentee owner who spends the summer sipping champagne at Wimbledon, while the corrupt manager and thuggish counselors turn the campers into slave laborers. An angry Bart decides he's had enough: "I've got a rapid heartbeat from his Krusty brand vitamins. My Krusty calculator didn't have a seven or an eight. And Krusty's autobiography was self-serving and full of glaring omissions. But this time he's gone too far!" When Bart confronts Krusty with his misdeeds and demands an explanation, the repentant clown replies, "They drove a dump truck full of money up to my door. I'm not made of stone."

Television's jaundiced view of business was not confined to the personal qualities of individual characters. Over three out of four shows that contained discussions of business dealings treated corporate or entrepreneurial activity as corrupt or unethical. These were not isolated instances; one out of every eight episodes in the sample (thirty-five in all) contained some thematic treatment of business. And that total doesn't include eleven instances of favoritism or preferential treatment (such as nepotism in hiring and promotion practices), which we tallied separately.

For example, another episode of "Law & Order" concerns a faulty pacemaker that causes a fatal heart attack. It turns out that the greedy manufacturer cut costs by using wire leads that were corroded. He remains unrepentant after the truth comes out, defending his right to place his company's health above that of his customers. On "Murder, She Wrote," a Manhattan-based tycoon who owns a baseball team keeps his fortune intact through shady business dealings, which he covers up through bribery, intimidation, and murder. He also uses philanthropy and a carefully crafted media image to keep the public in the dark about his true nature, which rules out George Steinbrenner as a model. In a milder vein, an episode of "Full House" illustrated favoritism with a sequence in which the boss adds his wife to the staff of Joey's kiddie show. When Joey finds the woman impossible to work with, he gives his boss an ultmatum. Guess which one gets the boot? And in an episode of "Wings," when Joe is angered by the small settlement he receives after a plane crash, his brother Brian tries to defraud the insurance company. At one point, Brian argues that they are fighting "for all the victims, all the little people who ever got stiffed by big companies."

On the surface, the 1990s looks like business as usual for TV's treatment of its favorite targets. Throughout the history of prime time, as chapter 6 recounts, the statistical portrait of business bad guys looks remarkably similar to the results from our 1992 study. In a nutshell, from the 1950s through the 1980s business characters proved twice as villainous and three times as criminal as everyone else, they were at their worst when actually doing business, and this character portrait was backed up by thematic treatments that depicted business as dishonest or corrupt four times out of five. No other aspect of television in the 1990s showed as much continuity with previous trends as the behavior of businessmen.

Yet, this is not the whole story. The statistical patterns mask some genuine improvements in television's most recent portrayal of business. We also found that business characters in the 1990s behaved less badly, on the whole, than their counterparts from earlier decades. For example, over the previous three decades studied, one out of seven business characters committed a crime. In our most recent study, the proportion dropped to one in sixteen. How can this be, in light of the striking similarities over time that we just enumerated? The short answer is that it is all relative. The number of criminals and other evildoers has dropped among *all* prime-time characters. That means that the number of business bad guys could drop, while remaining proportionately higher than in other occupations, because other occupational groups also contain fewer bad guys than in the past. Thus, there is less business villainy on the tube in absolute terms, but not in relative terms.

This answer is hardly a full explanation. It raises the further question of why the proportion of heroes and villains should change over time, as well as what this means in concrete terms for understanding the place of businessmen in television's group portrait of American life. A fuller answer to the first question involves both the periodic changes in programming styles that are a familiar feature of television's history, and more recent and novel developments in the way prime time presents business characters.

The image of business on television has always been partly a function of the reigning program genres. The last time most businessmen wore white hats, the prime-time schedule was dominated by Westerns that frequently featured good guy ranchers and storekeepers, along with family sitcoms that rarely ventured into the office. Early cop shows like "The Untouchables" often used professional gangsters as their bad guys. Of course, such settings can accommodate a wide range of occupational portrayals and ideological expressions, as more recent "revisionist" Westerns have amply demonstrated. Nonetheless, the opportunities to present businessmen as formulaic villains vary with the mix of roles to be cast, which in turn depends upon the relative popularity of various program formats.

As chapters 8 and 9 relate, the rise of swinging detective and secret agent shows in the mid-1960s and the urban cop shows of the 1970s brought with them a rash of evil industrialists and power-hungry tycoons who could provide formidable opponents for the good guys to defeat. The changing Zeitgeist also played a role, as Hollywood sought out evil in high places to expose, and television's creative community began to project its social and political sensibilities more directly into its products. Thus, when television discovered a new sitcom format that made the workplace into a surrogate family, the bumbling boss took the place of dear old dad. The benevolent Jim Anderson of "Father Knows Best" gave way to the unctuous Louie DiPalma of "Taxi," who rarely knew best for anyone but himself. If big business was criminal, small business became the butt of the joke. The corporate image continued to slide before bottoming out in the 1980s, as the prime-time soaps provided a host of new opportunities for double-dealing in high places.

In recent years, however, the pendulum has swung back in the direction of the family sitcom, at the expense of the soaps and shoot-em-ups. For the 1983-84 season, the top ten rated fictional series included four soaps (led by "Dallas"), five action-adventure series or cop shows ("The A-Team," "Magnum, P.I."), and only one sitcom ("Kate & Allie"). A decade later eight of the top ten are sitcoms; the only exceptions are "Murder, She Wrote" and "NYPD Blue." Fewer plot lines can accommodate all those scheming financiers and mendacious moguls from past seasons.

Equally important, numerous sitcoms are built around stars or ensemble casts set in mom-and-pop enterprises that provide partly or wholly positive business roles. The many current series with such settings include the charter airline in "Wings," the Barbecue Villa in "Evening Shade," the Brick and Ruth Ann's general store in "Northern Exposure," the construction company and beauty shop owned by the entrepreneurial Fosters in "Step by Step," and Tom and Roseanne Connor's efforts to open first a motorcycle shop and then a diner. Recent seasons have also featured popular entrepreneurs like those on "Designing Women" (who owned Sugarbaker's interior design firm) and well-known establishments like the Boston bar "where everybody knows your name."

Business characters in the current crop of workplace sitcoms tend to be either good guys with foibles or lovable jerks who are basically good-hearted. They rarely include comic book bad guys like Montgomery Burns or Superman's nemesis Lex Luthor, who is cast as an international business tycoon on "Lois and Clark." Instead, as more shows deal with small businesses going about routine operations, more plot developments have focused on relatively realistic day-to-day business activities. Several black family sitcoms, such as "George" and "Where I Live," have even featured episodes about kids going into business to try to earn money the old-fashioned way instead of through get-rich-quick schemes.

In the past, businesses were frequently confronted by crusading outsiders who prevented them from harming the social fabric. Today business (at least small business) is more likely to be seen through the eyes of insiders. Their business decisions are more frequently presented as understandable, if not always desirable. Even the bad guys are not as vicious as they used to be. Instead of kidnapping competitors, stealing state secrets, and bumping off business associates, today's corporate villains are more likely to practice sexual harassment or put the bottom line ahead of their employees' interests. Although television still gives business the business more often than not, the bottom line no longer looks quite so bleak for the long-suffering TV businessman.

THE WONDER YEARS

The 1990s mark the fifth decade of America's romance with prime-time entertainment. But the marriage of the broadcast networks and the mass audience is facing fresh challenges from younger suitors like cable and computer games. So the networks are trying to renew their vows with something old (bad guys in high places), something new (programming by and for women and blacks), something borrowed ("realistic" violence that looks more like the movies), and something blue (and getting bluer every season). Whether or not this union survives its golden anniversary, the prime-time landscape is changing rapidly in response to unprecedented levels of experimentation.

This chapter has examined some of the most controversial aspects of television in the 1990s. In the process it has chronicled some of the major changes that have swept over the artificial world of prime time in the recent past. Since we completed our original survey of episodic television in the late 1980s, hip-hop has replaced the Huxtables, sex has moved from the bedroom to the kitchen table, and the battle of the sexes has heated up almost as much as the sex itself. More generally, fictional series have become more firmly anchored in the social conditions and controversies of the real world. These days prime time provides few havens for those who think the world is too much with us. Even its version of small-town Americana now includes resident shamans ("Northern Exposure"), nuclear waste ("The Simpsons"), and serial mercy killers ("Picket Fences").

The intended social relevance of TV entertainment should not be overstated. The themes and series that define TV trends for the critics often draw yawns from the audience. Experimental shows, even when critically praised, frequently struggle to find an audience. Thus, such diverse representatives of recent innovation as "Tribeca," "Cop Rock," "Sirens," "Bakersfield P.D.," and "Townsend Television" all flopped. "Picket Fences" has won an Emmy and a national critics' poll as television's best dramatic series, but it has yet to break into the top fifty shows in the Nielsen ratings.

Further, the most controversial episodes draw so much attention precisely because they break conventions. Defenses of abortion or single motherhood as a "lifestyle choice" remain the exception rather than the rule in prime time's portrayal of family life. Such controversial images as "Roseanne"'s lesbian kisses and graphic violence like "Wild Palm'"s eye-gouging scene are even rarer. On the other hand, it is far easier to break a taboo the second time than the first. Producers push the envelope of acceptability as much to benefit their next show as their current one. Once-forbidden material has a way of moving gradually from the controversial to the commonplace.

It was partly to avoid overemphasizing the exceptional that we based our analysis on a systematic content analysis of the entire prime-time schedule. By applying the same techniques across many seasons, the rest of this book provides a moving trendline that tracks the long-term changes in prime-time's landscape across the past four decades. Another reason for this approach was to avoid imposing our own selective perceptions and expectations onto the material, by submitting our interpretations to the discipline imposed by scientific methods. But this method carries its own limitations. Part of the price that must be paid for scientific rigor is an emphasis on the parts rather than the whole, and the substance of social messages rather than the form that they take. It is necessary to address these pieces of the puzzle as well, in order to appreciate how much television's picture of the world has changed in recent years.

After viewing a random sample of prime-time shows stretching back to the 1950s, it became obvious how much television had improved in many respects. Fond memories of a "golden age" of past programs tend to be colored by nostalgia that diminishes with critical viewing. The hackwork that comprises much of the schedule was always stupefyingly banal and remains so today. And every era has its standout performers whose work would grace any season, from Sid Caesar through Mary Tyler Moore to Bill Cosby. Among the better shows, however, the writing, the characterizations, and the production values seem generally higher than their counterparts from previous decades, while program formats have evolved to accommodate the requirements of the medium.

We noted earlier the convergence of formats that permits current series to combine elements from sitcoms, soaps, and social issues dramas. It is now common for prime-time series to use elements of both comedy and drama in multiple plotlines that overlap several episodes. They feature more psychologically complex characters who are becoming far harder to categorize as good or bad guys. The largest number of characters in our 1992 sample were neither clear-cut heroes nor villains. Rather, they combined positive and negative traits in ways that made them more complicated and less one-dimensional.

The prevalence of ambiguous or double-edged characters in the current prime-time schedule represents a distinct departure from the more clear-cut portrayals that we found in earlier seasons. The proportion of such characters is over twice as high as in earlier decades. Nor is it always easy to discern the "message" of a show that deals with some social controversy.

Instead, a variety of perspectives may be explored through the views of various characters, without a clear resolution beyond an appreciation of the complexity or ambiguity involved.

To be sure, there are still traditional social advocacy shows that drive home a position with all the subtlety of Murphy Brown's closing soliloquy on single motherhood and family values, in the episode that rebutted Dan Quayle's attack. But strident advocacy looks curiously old-fashioned on the current prime-time schedule. The favored formats for social statements these days are one-shot events such as docudramas and miniseries, which are are television's Sunday sermons. Audiences will sit through these exercises in uplift on occasion but not every night of the week.

Overt advocacy series from the old school have fared poorly in recent seasons. Shows that wear their social conscience on their sleeves usually prove too strident or earnest to find a mass audience. Recent efforts like "Against the Law" and "E.A.R.T.H. Force" were early casualties of their own preachiness. When Robin Givens' continually angry character in the short-lived cop show "Angel Street" expressed opinions like "blacks killing blacks is viewed by whites as inexpensive population control," black and white viewers across America united in changing the channel. And when a fictionalized civics lesson like "I'll Fly Away" ends up on PBS, it probably belonged there in the first place.

More interesting, and more representative of recent trends, are shows like the 1993 Christmas episode of "Picket Fences," in which a courtroom battle over an alleged virgin birth provides opportunities for various characters to grapple with their own religious (or secular) convictions, and their willingness to apply abstract beliefs and principles to everyday life. Various positions are expressed in a way that defines the characters through their beliefs without passing judgment on the beliefs themselves.

It is difficult to imagine a more potentially volatile premise for a Christmas show, and nearly as difficult to imagine this script airing in prime time until recently. Yet, this socially liberal series managed to do a theme show on the meaning of Christmas that took Christianity seriously. Consider how this approach contrasts with the didactic Christmastime TV movies that annually lambaste American society for failing to help the homeless. A recent representative of this genre moved *Washington Post* television critic Tom Shales to suggest retitling it "A Hollywood Liberal's Christmas."

There are also sitcoms that present a politically correct attitude through witty lines delivered by sympathetic characters, while putting the incorrect attitude in the mouth of a stooge whom the rest of the cast doesn't take seriously. The former typically represents the "progressive" position on whatever cause is currently trendy in Hollywood, while the latter is given to an old-fashioned, dim-witted, or flamboyantly conservative character. Among the many recent variations on the latter are Corky in "Murphy Brown," Maurice in "Northern Exposure," and Senator Smithers in "Hearts Afire."

But comedy series are also evolving in their treatment of social controversy. For example, a scene in "Northern Exposure" began with Chris using his radio show to broadcast a paean to erotic imagery in Whitman's poetry. This incenses Maurice, the homophobic owner of the station. He throws Chris out and announces to listeners that he will replace this sleazy material with good old-fashioned clean-cut fare—a recording of show tunes by Cole Porter. This sequence conveyed the gay rights sentiments that are standard on prime time, but it did so in a lighter and more sophisticated fashion than the Lear-style insult humor and double-takes common to past sitcoms. Similarly, "The John Larroquette Show" made its point about racial stereotyping through John's incredulity that the African-American owner of a bus station snack bar not only was familiar with Thomas Pynchon's *Gravity's Rainbow* but actually knew Pynchon himself.

By the same token, however, this low-key approach may limit the impact of the material. Esoteric references and subtle messages are best appreciated by the already enlightened audience members who can congratulate themselves on being in on the joke. Thomas Pynchon is not exactly a household name, and not everyone is aware that Walt Whitman and Cole Porter were both gay. To some extent the more "progressive" shows are pitched at would-be intellectuals who watch partly to validate their own sophistication. They may be less preachy than past sitcom sermons, but only the converted can hear the homily.

Thus, even as prime-time politics have become more pervasive, they are growing more closely integrated into character and plot development, and their expression is getting less predictable and more difficult to measure. Increasingly, political and social issues are introduced not only to comment on real-world controversies, but also to identify characters and to provide intellectual cachet. In this way social advocacy and entertainment are mutating into a kind of "advotainment" that integrates social commentary into entertainment packages in a more sophisticated and complex fashion than either Dan Quayle or Norman Lear ever imagined.

So why are neither critics nor viewers cheering over television's new artistic maturity? Perhaps it is because these changes in the form of television series have been accompanied by changes in their substance, which are not so clearly improvements. All the advances in production values and storytelling techniques serve to showcase material that gets sleazier and more sordid every season. Thus, Steven Bochco devoted his considerable talents and energies to ensuring that characters could say "asshole" on prime time. And "Picket Fences"'s Christmas episode notwithstanding, virgins seem almost as rare as virgin births in Rome, Wisconsin. More typical of this series was a plotline that had a high school teacher impregnating his female student while his wife was having an affair with the student's father.

These are the products of the industry's leading lights. How the hacks use their new "artistic freedom" troubles even producers themselves. Diane English recently complained, "TV has the responsibility to pull itself out of the gutter. The shows that are filled with dirty jokes that serve no purpose ruin it for the rest of us."[33] Unfortunately, viewers may find it difficult to tell where television's titillation leaves off and its artistic elevation begins. For instance, it was Ms. English's creation "Love and War" that included the snappy come-on, "Your condom or mine?"

The most striking feature of the current prime-time landscape is the sheer incongruity of earnest social criticism juxtaposed against crude dialogue and sleazy storylines. As one reviewer recently wrote, "There are few oxymorons as delightful as a Hollywood producer on a moral crusade."[34] Yet, television's tendency to appeal to both high-mindedness and base instincts is not really contradictory. It partly reflects the tension between preachiness and profit-seeking that brings so much derision down on Hollywood. But it also expresses the moral sensibility that Lionel Trilling termed egalitarian hedonism. Prime-time programs champion personal fulfillment, self-expression, and sensory gratification against institutional restrictions and traditional restraints.

As we shall see, this sensibility represents the culmination of several long-term trends in prime time's portrayal of American society. However, the current combination of moralism and libertinism that dominates prime time virtually guarantees continuing tensions between the producers and consumers of prime-time images. While the producers ponder what television should say to America, the public worries about what television may do to America. In order to know where television is going, however, we need to understand where it is coming from. That is the topic to which we now turn—the evolution of prime-time images of private life and public issues, in the first half century of the video age.

PART

II

Private Lives

2

TV'S SEX LIFE

In olden days a glimpse of stocking
Was looked on as something shocking
Now heaven knows
Anything goes

—Cole Porter

I n the opening credits of "Cagney & Lacey," the two intrepid police-women are confronted by a flasher who opens his trenchcoat to reveal himself. They wave nonchalantly and continue on their way. In the opening credits of "Spenser: For Hire," Spenser and his girlfriend share a passionate kiss while taking a shower together. And that's just for openers.

Flip the dial and sample "The Sex Tapes Scandal," a TV movie about a deluxe prostitution ring specializing in sadomasochism, replete with tools of the Marquis's trade. Or try "Favorite Son," featuring a vice-presidential hopeful whose private life would make Gary Hart blush. Bondage and a ménage à trois are among NBC's inducements to presumably panting viewers. (In one scene an ambitious lobbyist drops her robe, picks up a satin ribbon, and begs her lover, "Tie me up. Come on. Tie me up.")

Welcome to the steamy world of prime time in the late 1980s. Television now offers a little something for the voyeur in every viewer, from the opening credits, through the heavy breathing plot turns to the, well, climax. It invites us to embrace a potpourri of tangled love affairs, kinky vices, and erotic experiments utterly unknown in the medium's earlier days.

Just how sexy has television become? A 1987 study by the Planned Parenthood Federation concluded that 65,000 sexual references a year are broadcast during the prime afternoon and evening hours.[1] That includes hourly averages of ten sexual innuendos and between one and two references to intercourse and "deviant or discouraged sexual practices." The study concluded that the average American television viewer now sees nearly 14,000 instances of sexual material every year.

The tube wasn't always so titillating, of course. Just as the movies used to give married couples separate beds, the small screen steered around overt mentions or portrayals of sex prior to the jiggle shows and Lear-ing comic style of the 1970s. Much of the change reflects the loosening sexual mores of the broader society, or at least its trendsetting elements in the coastal urban centers. Indeed, television's treatment of sex is paradigmatic of how the medium serves as an instant trendmaker carrying changes in tastes and standards from cosmopolitan centers across middle America. Television followed the intellectual and social vanguard, as well as other media of popular culture (like novels and films) in treating varieties of sexual experience as appropriate subject matter. But it has lately played a leading role in questioning traditional moral standards before a vast national audience.

Beyond simply reflecting our changing sexual mores, television has endorsed the changes, and may have accelerated their acceptance. The impact is probably strongest on young people, whose initial understanding of sexual expression increasingly comes from prime-time players rather than parents or peers. As a National Institute for Mental Health report recently concluded, "entertainment television has become an important sex educator."[2] Meanwhile, in challenging onetime taboos from extramarital sex to homosexuality, television entertainment increasingly transmits Hollywood's perspectives rather than middle America's.

TV's Sexual Awakening

In its infancy, TV (like any child) seemed to know little of sex. Early television was dominated by the slapstick routines, sight gags, and comic parodies of the flagship variety shows. "Texaco Star Theater" with Milton Berle, "Your Show of Shows" with Sid Caesar, and "All Star Review" with Jimmy Durante had little need and no place for sexual innuendo. These programs cleaned up the vaudeville tradition for family consumption. Meanwhile, family comedies like "The Life of Riley," "The Adventures of Ozzie and Harriet," "Make Room for Daddy," and "Father Knows Best" had a place for sex but no opportunity with all those precocious kids around.

The occasional discreet references to sexual relationships were left to the dramas. Prestige shows like "Playhouse 90," "Screen Director's Playhouse," "Studio One," and "Alfred Hitchcock Presents" dominated early on. These early dramatic anthologies pulled in a rich variety of material, but stayed away from explicit sexual references. Any rumor of impropriety was scandalous. No wife was ever seen leaving her lover's apartment. It was merely hinted that she was often seen alone with a certain man. A man was never seen in an unmarried woman's bedroom. He would simply be referred to as a womanizer or playboy.

This began to change as TV dramas of the 1960s became more action packed. The "swinging detective" series like "77 Sunset Strip," "Peter Gunn," and "Surfside Six" featured sexy leads and even sexier guest stars. Women in these shows could be vamps, though they were still a long way from tramps. Men could be suave and openly seductive. With a sultry saxophone playing a seductive phrase, these beautiful people begin to flirt and proposition each other before the camera. Promiscuous sex was still frowned on, but an active social life was no longer a sin.

Tod and Buzz, the young nomads of "Route 66," got to date attractive women, but they always behaved with gentlemanly courtesy and no onscreen action. In one episode Buzz even turned down the advances of a young model because she was married. And none of these leading men would be caught dead without his shirt on.

This reticence regarding sex continued into the late 1960s with only minor changes. Some married couples, like the Stevenses in "Bewitched" or the Douglases in "Green Acres," could share a bed, but discretion was still the guiding principle. Viewers could only guess if Mrs. Peel was more than just a colleague to "The Avengers'" Mr. Steed. Napoleon Solo, of "The Man from U.N.C.L.E.," and lawyer Paul Bryan in "Run for Your Life" were direct descendants of "The Thin Man"'s suave Nick Charles. They spent much of their time with beautiful women, but never in compromising positions.

In 1969 several shows in the fall schedule were destined to change the image and place of sex on television. "Rowan and Martin's Laugh-In," "Love, American Style," and "The Brady Bunch" brought some new elements to TV's treatment of sex. "Laugh-In" gave audiences gyrating bikini-clad beauties, sexual innuendo, and double entendres. A fast-paced, youth-oriented melange presented sexually oriented material with pioneering casualness. Ruth Buzzi's little old woman pummeling the dirty old man on a park bench made TV's aversion to such material seem stodgy and passé.

"Love, American Style" was an early forerunner of the titillation to come. This series never seemed to run out of embarrassing situations from the dating scene. The problems were usually solved amidst a great deal of blushing and nervous stuttering. Racy items like nudity, striptease, honeymoon protocols, premarital sex, and adultery received comic mention. That same season, "The Brady Bunch" showed audiences that two single parents could date, get married, share a bed, and engage in a good number of passionate embraces. "The Brady Bunch" and "Bewitched" presented married couples who kissed and touched each other in a less wooden manner than earlier spouses had displayed.

These shows mark a rough transition point for TV's entrance into the bedroom. Throughout the 1970s the medium would increasingly include sexual material in comedy situations and bring sexual behavior to the screen. This was not an abrupt change, since many more traditional shows remained popular. "My Three Sons," "That Girl," "Bewitched," "Green Acres," "The Beverly Hillbillies," and "Gunsmoke" all continued to exercise discretion in mentioning sex.

In the 1972 season, sex came out into the open in new series like "M*A*S*H," "All in the Family," "The Sonny and Cher Comedy Hour," and "Maude." Not only were innuendoes and double entendres plentiful, but more detailed discussions of impotence, bad sex, abortion, premarital sex, and adultery also became common. The act of sex was still taboo, however, as the producers of "The New Dick Van Dyke Show" found out. In one episode, Dick and his wife Jenny were shown in bed making love when their young daughter walked in. Despite the script's sensitive handling of the situation, such behavior still lay beyond the limits of the network broadcast standards department. The episode was never broadcast.

Throughout the rest of the 1970s almost anything could happen in the willy-nilly race for new frontiers of titillation. Maude had an abortion and went through menopause, while her husband Walter suffered a bout of impotence. Hawkeye Pierce perennially searched for a new sexual encounter while reading nude-volleyball magazines. "M*A*S*H" also gave us a guest appearance by Colonel Baldwin, who wore a hood and leather pajamas in his sexual adventures. There were countless hookers and pornographers in cop shows like "Kojak," "Police Story," "Joe Forrester," "Baretta," and "Starsky and Hutch."

In the late 1970s "Family" served up an adulterous husband and an unwed mother. "One Day At A Time" led viewers through debates on teenage sex and affairs between the elderly. "Charlie's Angels" carried on the titillating style established by "Love, American Style." In "Barney Miller" Sergeant Wojohowicz had an affair with a policewoman and later chose a prostitute as his live-in girlfriend. Despite all this he was suspected of being a homosexual. Finally he disclosed that he was sterile. Meanwhile, across the squad room, Sergeant Harris was producing a blue movie to help the department catch pornographers. In "Soap," Chester and Jessica appeared to be waging an infidelity contest. A nudist caused a scene on the deck of "The Love Boat." And the beat goes on.

The speed of this raunchy race can be measured by comparing the amount of sexual activity in a week of prime time during 1975, 1977, and 1978. One study found that:

contextually implied intercourse increased from no weekly occurrences in 1975 to 15 in 1977 and 24 in 1978; sexual innuendos increased in frequency from about one reference per hour in 1975 to 7 in 1977 and to almost 11 in 1978. Most dramatically, direct verbal references to intercourse increased from 2 occurrences in 1975 to 6 references in 1977 and 53(!) in 1978... allusions to prostitution increased more than four-fold and allusions to aggressive sexual contacts increased three-fold from 1977 to 1978.[3]

The fantasy shows of the late 1970s approached sex with giggling false modesty. The "Three's Company" crowd forever protested that no sex was going on, and "Laverne and Shirley" took offense whenever their virtue was brought into question. This approach continued to tease viewers in the romantic comedy/dramas of the 1980s. In "Moonlighting" Maddie Hayes launched a fierce defense at any suggestion of impropriety or promiscuity on her part (until the final season, when even passion unleashed could not save the show). In "Scarecrow and Mrs. King," a remake of "The Avengers" with an inexperienced version of Mrs. Peel, the question perennially surrounding Amanda King and Lee Stetson was not "Do they or don't they?" but "When will they?" In a segment of "Remington Steele," investigator Laura Holt is shocked when retouched nude photos of her show up in a porn magazine. Despite her liberated attitudes, attractive appearance, and complete innocence of posing for the pictures, she is embarrassed and afraid of scandal. Eventually her innocence is proven and the photos are confiscated.

While some shows still feature this blush-and-stammer element, today's television usually ranges far afield in its search for new thrills. Recent seasons have offered viewers incest, child prostitution, kiddie porn, a variety of fetishes, transvestites, sadomasochism, and bestiality. For example, a 1985 episode of "Hill Street Blues" featured a vignette about a man and a sheep. The man is found dead in his room with only his pet sheep as witness. The cause of death is at first obscure. Gradually it dawns on the officers that the man may have died from a heart attack while having sex.

As for his partner, well, the only potential witness isn't talking. Agatha Christie never thought of that one.

"Hill Street"'s venture into bestiality never attracted much attention, but the same can't be said of NBC's excursion into incest. The network gave the full treatment to "Something About Amelia," a made for TV movie with tie-in discussions on network news shows. Polish Director Roman Polanski once explained that he introduced the theme of incest into his 1974 film, "Chinatown," because it was the only thing left to shock jaded American sensibilities. A mere decade later it had made its way into millions of living rooms.

Meanwhile, TV's recent trend-setting series have decided that innuendo and racy dialogue are a mark of sophistication. When "Moonlighting"'s David Addison sees Maddie on her hands and knees, he asks, "You looking for something or have you finally come to your senses?" The "St. Elsewhere" writers tried to name a character "Connie Lingus" but NBC censors force them to call her "Constance." NBC executive Perry Simon explains that risqué dialogue "is a reflection of the quality of the programs. I think [it] makes the audience feel it is witty and clever." In addition, he argues, "Certain of these adult lines can be . . . the most memorable or character-revealing moments in the whole show." As an example, he cites a joke "L.A. Law"'s Arnie Becker makes about oral sex. Along the same lines, "Moonlighting"'s creator Glen Gordon Caron boasts, "We're double-entendre city. And you have to be of a certain age to get them, and a certain sophistication. . . . Shakespeare used them all the time."[4] To make this point, one episode sent up "Taming of the Shrew," "Moonlighting"'s thematic ancestor. Unfortunately, the writers kept more of the bawd than the bard. Sample riposte, Maddie (Kate) to David (Petruchio): "Try-est to plow this acre and thy blade might get broken." When TV writers confuse sophistication with titillation, they find that the flesh is willing but the artistic spirit is weak.

It's hard to say where we go from here. Sex acts are still simulated under the sheets, and frontal nudity remains a no-no, though bare backsides are gaining ground. Fundamentalist critics notwithstanding, even the raciest prime-time shows still rate an "R" rather than an "X." Yet, that represents an enormous shift from the "PG" world of seasons past. Today the presence of sex is pervasive, and prudery has become the scriptwriter's new taboo.

This chapter will sample the various courses on television's erotic menu, which range from premarital sex and adultery to pornography and prostitution. We will explore not only what television shows but how it deals with the sexual issues it raises. Television stories come with morals, no less so when morality itself is the subject matter.

Modern Romance

Few topics on television have undergone such a thorough transformation over the years as extramarital sex. During the 1950s and 1960s it was rarely portrayed at all; even more rarely was it presented as justified.

In the early years, viewers mostly learned about sexual affairs through references in the dialogue, while the action discreetly took place offstage. Men and women had to keep a tight rein on their actions, since even small transgressions destroyed reputations. Recreational sex or looking for "a little action" was rarely condoned. After all, a woman's virtue was at stake. Thus, in a 1963 episode of "Stoney Burke," an attractive young woman picks up a man in a bar, setting off a fight between two of her suitors. Stoney tells her sternly she has to choose between being "a playgirl or a working girl." When she fails to change her wanton ways, he confronts her with virtue's demands: "You owe . . . decent behavior and responsibility or you get slapped down." In short, the lady is a tramp.

A decade later the camera had entered the bedroom, and the scriptwriters liked what they found there. Affairs became such a commonplace plot device that they were often treated as part of the emotional scenery. Since then, extramarital sex has rarely been condemned. Instead it is usually portrayed as an acceptable form of recreation.

A 1975 episode of "Baretta" epitomizes the new perspective. The free-wheeling detective Tony Baretta is lured into a trap. He's knocked unconscious, stripped naked, and put into bed with a nude woman (under the bed sheets) who poses to create blackmail photos. Awakening, Baretta struggles but is held down. Finally he sizes up the situation, asks some-one to turn out the lights, and commands, "Let the good times roll!" At this point the camera's sense of discretion reasserts itself, but a good time is apparently had by all. No attempt at blackmail is ever made, presum-ably since Baretta has nothing to be ashamed of.

But the change in extramarital sex on television is more than just an abandonment of discretion. TV now includes far more recreational sex in its nightly bill of fare. Prior to 1969, we coded fewer than one instance of extramarital sex in every thirty shows. During the early 1970s, extramari-tal sex cropped up on about one out of every eight shows. Since the mid-1970s, the ratio has dropped to one in six, and it continues to narrow.

One team of researchers studied one episode of each series during the 1976-77 season. In the fifty-eight programs they watched, they counted forty-one instances of extramarital sexual intercourse and only six instances of sexual intercourse between married couples, a ratio of almost seven to one.[5]

There is more to TV's treatment of extramarital sex than sheer numbers. Standards of sexual morality have changed just as dramatical-ly. Prior to 1970, 38 percent of the shows we coded presented extramar-ital sex as wrong. The proportion dropped to only 7 percent after 1970. Before that year, none of the shows we coded ever portrayed recreational sex as acceptable without qualification. In prime time's passionate world of the 1970s and 1980s, 41 percent of the shows we coded viewed recre-ational sex as acceptable without qualification, and 33 percent made no moral judgment.

Prior to 1970, any shows that justified extramarital affairs did so by stressing the characters' love for one another, as in a 1963 episode of "East Side, West Side." On this early "social problems" series, twenty-one-year-old John wants to marry seventeen-year-old Alice, but her father objects. A police detective from the old school, he decides to press charges of statutory rape against the "punk" who defiled his daughter. The audience knows, however, that the daughter initiated the incident and took proper precautions. The stiff-necked father perseveres against various voices of reason, including the show's social worker heroes, and John is placed on probation. But the show sides with the lovers against the rigid parent. Their behavior is justified by their love and their intention to marry.

This show is highly unusual in pointing out some negative consequences of extramarital sex. Here they are legal and emotional, not biological, but painful repercussions do exist. On the TV screen, sex is usually without consequence, without worry, and with rarely a bad experience. Worry-free sex became ever more common as TV latched onto the sexual revolution. Increasingly, P.I.s, cops, lawyers, and just plain folks hopped in the sack. Such passion plays most commonly received little or no comment. Not all shows, however, expressed such a cavalier attitude. A minority (18 percent) of shows coded since 1970 continued to justify extramarital sex through the characters' love for one another.

Meanwhile, the theme of old fogies holding to outworn sexual mores never entirely disappeared from prime time. The rigid traditionalist who would deny romance its natural physical expression has become something of a stock villain. A 1978 episode of "Little House On the Prairie" is notable for projecting this conflict between enlightened and shopworn sexual attitudes back into the nineteenth century. (It's also worth noting that "Little House" was a nostalgic series aimed at middle America rather than urban sophisticates.) In this segment a young woman falls in love, has a sexual relationship, and becomes pregnant. She tries to hide her condition from her father, a religious fanatic who even rejects marriage based on physical attraction. Father to daughter: "You would marry him for the flesh, like your mother did. Then steal off into the night with another." The daughter eventually has her baby and, with the Ingalls family's help, is reunited with her lover.

This show suggests that Victorian mores weren't appropriate even in Victorian times. The father is the only character who can't accept sex before marriage between two people in love. His opposition is so zealous that he sometimes appears mentally unbalanced. The message is that repressive restrictions and oppressive moralism are roadblocks to personal happiness.

These days, however, the authorities themselves often weigh in on the side of romance rather than repression. Throughout the 1970s, various exemplars of law and order were called upon to engage in sex and seduction in the line of duty. The roster included scantily clad crime fighters like Charlie's voluptuous angels and Angie Dickinson's "Police Woman," whose idea of undercover operations left little to the imagination.

By the 1980s very little short of forcible rape seemed to threaten a woman's virtue. In a 1985 episode of "Cheers," Sam's latest love interest, a waitress, quits upon finding out that he's also been sleeping with her sister. The general reaction to this situation is best summarized by Carla, Sam's only other waitress. Upset at having to cover all the tables herself, she tells Sam not to "boink" another waitress unless it's she (Carla).

A notable shift in recent years is to treat extramarital sex more as a fact of life. In the late 1960s and early 1970s, "progressive" scripts tended to make a point of its acceptability. Since then it's been taken for granted as a form of recreation with no moral or even emotional consequences.

The old school approach is typified by a 1965 segment of "Then Came Bronson." It concerns a Catholic ex-priest who is guilt-ridden over getting his lover pregnant. One exchange of dialogue serves to illustrate the superheated atmosphere.

He: "My rituals were a farce, too much flesh to contain, and all those pretentious rituals, too vivid a will for sensationalism , and good deeds to cover up all of the evil thoughts. They were all liars, so I did the only honest thing I could do." (What he did was leave the priesthood).

She: "I love you, enough to settle for being your sin. If that's all I can give you, so be it."

Eventually they come to see that their physical relationship is not sinful. Their love makes the affair acceptable in the eyes of the producers, if not the Pope.

Such talk of guilt and sin are worlds removed from television's current standards of sexual behavior. In political scientist Michael Robinson's pithy summary, the pattern is now "lots of sex, very little remorse."[6] For example, a 1985 episode of "Stingray" presents a one-night stand as therapeutic. After losing a patient, a young woman doctor invites the hero back to her place for a romantic dinner. Suitably coiffed and gowned, she greets him with a bottle of wine in hand. As they talk, he asks about the patient she lost. She replies, "You and the bottle of wine were supposed to help me forget." A painless form of therapy, and cheaper than analysis.

In 1982, when Christine Cagney (of "Cagney & Lacey") has an affair, neither her partner Marybeth Lacey nor anyone else views it as a question of morals. The same nonjudgmental assumption underlines a recent scene from "Golden Girls," in which Blanche recounts her retaliation against a onetime beau who dumped her: "I slept with his brother." In 1985 this is a laugh line, with Blanche's advanced age presumably adding a touch of titillation to the humor. Fifteen years ago it would have been daring for television to wring a laugh out of an older woman's sex life. But that was before Dr. Ruth hit the talk show circuit.

TV also adds some racy variations to its depictions of extramarital sex. Davenport and Furillo shared a hot tub and a bubble bath as well as a bed in the closing scenes of various "Hill Street Blues" episodes. Cathy Martin, a young resident in "St. Elsewhere," enjoyed sex on a slab in the hospital morgue. Sergeant Esterhaus and Grace Gardner could be counted on to add body painting and edible massage lotions to "Hill Street" plots. The sergeant's exotic tastes eventually caught up with him. In a 1983 segment he died of a heart attack during sex with Grace. But that's about the closest thing to an objection TV raises against sexual encounters these days. Extramarital sex has become a matter of morale rather than morals.

LOVE AND MARRIAGE

Adultery was one of the first issues of sexual morality that TV added to spice up plot lines. Early dramas like "Alfred Hitchcock Presents," "Perry Mason," and "Route 66," often had plot lines featuring an unfaithful spouse. The actual infidelity took place offscreen since, as with premarital sex, rumor and innuendo sufficed to destroy reputations.

Like other extramarital sex, televised adultery became more common over time. "Doctor Kildare," "Peyton Place," "The Fugitive," and

"Mannix" all allowed viewers a glimpse into the lives of adulterers, but the indiscretions remained out of sight. Not until the 1970s, as soap operas moved into prime time, did adultery come out in the open. In a typical episode of "Dallas" in our sample, J.R. barely has time to leer at an airline stewardess he has brought to his hotel room before the camera cuts to his wife, dressed in her negligee, hopping out of another man's bed.

Adultery is now more common, more open, and more humorous than ever before in prime time. The controversial comedy "Soap" kept the nation laughing at the philandering Chester and his equally unfaithful wife Jessica. Such infidelity would have been unthinkable as a source of comedy in the golden years of television. Of course, that was the point of "Soap"'s parody of contemporary steamy soap operas.

Television's nonjudgmental view of extramarital sex applies surprisingly often to married as well as single individuals. The sheer incidence of adultery on television is up sharply in recent years. We coded more instances in the decade since the mid-1970s then in the two previous decades combined. Across the entire thirty-year period, however, shows condemning adultery have consistently been outnumbered by those that treat it as understandable, a fact of life, or something that doesn't require comment. Overall, 63 percent of the shows coded for adulterous characters rendered no moral judgment. The remainder treated the behavior as morally wrong, although some of these shows expressed sympathy for the characters involved.

Unlike sex among singles, adultery is rarely presented as justified. It just occurs without comment in many scripts. For example, in a 1979 segment of "Kate Loves a Mystery," crime solver Kate is trying to clear a husband suspected of murdering his wife. She discovers that the wife, Ida, was apparently having an affair with Ed, a married man. When she confronts Ed, he explains that it wasn't exactly a love affair. He was paying Ida $100 an hour for her time. Kate is shocked that Ida, a suburban housewife, was a part-time hooker. The element of adultery, however, elicits neither shock nor condemnation from Kate. It's just one of those things.

A comic version of this facts-of-life approach occurs in a 1973 showing of "All in the Family." Archie Bunker, feeling depressed about

91

getting old, has a drink with an old friend named Bill. The bartender comments that Bill looks fifteen years younger than Archie, though they're actually the same age. Bill explains that he "thinks young and acts young," which includes liaisons with a young woman. Although he's married, he explains, "I figure I'm doing my wife a favor by staying young for her." When Archie meets Bill's lover, he's initially impressed that his friend has landed such a young and pretty woman. Then he finds out that this looker is also a hooker. When Archie realizes that Bill's friend is attracted by his wallet rather than his savoir faire, he becomes more reconciled to growing old. It's not Bill's adultery that turns him off, though, only the futility of trying to recapture one's lost youth.

Negative judgments about adultery do appear, in both comedy and dramatic formats. In a 1981 sitcom called "Making a Living," a baseball player picks up a waitress and leads her on until she discovers that he's married. When she confronts him, he tries the worldly approach: "Come on, babe, we had a few laughs, now let's have a drink on me." Taking the invitation literally, she dumps a bottle of wine on his head. A decade earlier, "Night Gallery" took an even more judgmental approach. In one segment of this series, which specialized in the occult, the protagonist's affair with another man's wife ends with her suicide. Later he is confronted and condemned by the devil himself. The show ends with his electrocution, apparently engineered by the prince of darkness. Now that's what we call judgmental!

Yet these are the exceptions. Much closer to the prevailing norm is the laissez-faire attitude expressed by a number of characters in a 1977 cops and robbers show called "Rosetti and Ryan." The adulterous relationships in this show are seen as natural by-products of loveless marriages. Clarice, who is unhappily married to Ted, has affairs with both Eddie and Jim. Asked about the latter, she replies, "Eddie was very understanding about Jim and I. I loved Jim." Ted takes all this in stride: "Eddie once made a play for Clarice, but what else is new?" Later, Jim is killed, and his widow is asked about the affair with Clarice. She responds, "There could have been another woman, but it could be a lot worse—I could still love him."

If all this sounds reminiscent of "Bob and Carol and Ted and Alice," it differs in one important respect. The Paul Mazursky film concerned the difficulties that even trendy would-be spouse swappers encounter in overcoming old-fashioned ideas of marital fidelity. Television's Ted and Clarice and Jim and Helen are more worldly. They take infidelity for granted.

OUT OF THE CLOSET AND ON TV

Homosexuals are the beneficiaries of perhaps the single most dramatic change in television's depiction of sexuality. It also offers the most fully documented case of when and how the shift occurred. Until the early 1970s, there was a virtual blackout on any mention of homosexuality. The breakthrough came, typically, in a TV movie. In 1972 "That Certain Summer" cautiously explored a son's discovery that his divorced father was living with another man. In each of the next two seasons, "Marcus Welby" episodes featured male homosexuals who were portrayed as psychologically deviant. One show concerned a high school teacher who molested a fourteen-year-old boy. In the other, Dr. Welby assured a worried patient that he could be "cured" of his inclinations with proper treatment.

Programs like these sparked a major lobbying effort by gay activists. Their efforts proved so successful that, as *TV Guide* reports, "by the mid-70s, half the sitcoms on television had done a positive ('prosocial') gay show that often made its point—and garnered laughs—by having a particularly macho character announce his homosexuality."[7] By 1976, gays had made a transition "from invisibility to saturation," as popular sitcoms like "Alice" and "Barney Miller" introduced recurring homosexual characters. Equally important, most scripts on gay themes were reviewed by the Gay Media Task Force, which sought to eliminate negative stereotypes such as effeminate mannerisms. Another group, the Alliance for Gay Artists, began giving out awards for "sensitive and honest" depictions of gays and lesbians.[8] But this new openness contained its own seed of closed-mindedness. According to screen writer Ernest Kinoy, who wrote "Roots," "You can handle homosexuality—as long as you handle it in a lovely, tolerant fashion that will not upset the gay liberation lobby."[9]

The results have been obvious and lasting. Our pilot study of two hundred shows from the 1979-80 season included seven that dealt with homosexual themes. Every show portrayed homosexual characters sympathetically, as decent and compassionate people. All emphasized that sexual preference has no bearing on an individual's job performance or personal qualities. For example, episodes from two different series portrayed beleaguered gay fathers battling for custody or visitation rights with their children from previous marriages. Finally, none of the characters displayed any mannerisms of the opposite sex. The sentiments of these shows are best summarized by a scene from "The Last Resort," in which a young attractive lesbian gently breaks the news of her sexual preference to her best (female) friend. After the predictably shocked reaction, they are able to recapture their warm relationship. As she tells her friend, "I'm the same girl I've always been."

Michael Robinson found a very similar pattern in his study of the 1978 season. He concluded that prime time's favorite "innocent victim. . .was clearly the misunderstood, harassed homosexual."[10] As examples he cites an excellent high school teacher on "Family" whose career is threatened by homophobic bigots, and a police detective whose murder leads his tough guy colleagues Starsky and Hutch to express newfound empathy for the plight of homosexuals.

This remarkable turnaround does have its limits. They were demonstrated in 1981, when NBC presented "Love, Sidney," the first series built around a homosexual lead (who is, however, middle aged and sexually inactive). Sidney lives with a young woman who is raising an illegitimate child, the product of her affair with a married man. The premise of this plot generated bitter protests from a fundamentalist Christian group, the Coalition for Better Television, which had previously threatened to boycott the sponsors of shows they deemed too sexually explicit. The nervous network responded by quashing any mention of Sidney's sexual orientation in episodes that followed the pilot (which itself contained only two indirect references). Nonetheless, series star Tony Randall received an award from the Alliance for Gay Artists for portraying "episodic TV's first homosexual hero."[11]

To date, Sidney is also episodic TV's last homosexual hero, at least among main characters. Perhaps chastened by Randall's experience, more recent series have quietly introduced positive homosexual characters in continuing but nonstarring roles. For example, "Hooperman"'s Rick Solardi is a San Francisco policeman who is a consummate professional well liked by his peers. Attractive to women, he frequently has to turn aside come-ons from his female partner. In one episode, Rick resolves his estrangement from his brother, who finally comes to terms with his sibling's sexual preference. And ABC's 1988 medical drama "Heartbeat" features nurse practitioner Marilyn McGrath as prime time's first continuing lesbian character, described by actress Gail Strickland as "a loving, warm professional who cares about her daughter and has been in a good [lesbian] relationship for four years."[12] Writer Sara Davidson's description typifies television's socially conscious approach: "We wanted people to see her as a terrific person first, then to find out she has a private life that at its core is no different from anyone else's."

If television's gays are rarely heroes, they are often shown as victims brutalized by homophobic bigotry or traumatized by social convention. Our study included eight portrayals of homosexuals, all since 1973, only one of whom was portrayed negatively. Several shows stressed the theme of victimization. For example, a 1977 episode of "All in the Family" revolves around the brutal murder of Edith's friend Beverly, a female impersonator who is beaten to death by a gang of thugs "because he was different." This gives Archie the opportunity to observe that "fags in New York are an endangered species." We know that Beverly is a good person, because he saves the life of Archie's son-in-law, Michael, during the attack. With similar subtlety, the script tells us that he's a homosexual by having him sing "now we don our gay apparel, fa la la la la. . ." when he changes into women's clothing.

More often, the stress is on minimizing the external vestiges of sexual preference. For example, when Chris Cagney's father discovers that her attractive male neighbor is gay, he comments, "I thought he was a regular guy." She answers, "He is." A 1985 "Love Boat" episode makes the same point in a less succinct fashion. Doc is visited by Buzz, his old college roommate. Not realizing that Buzz is gay, Doc puts him through a rigorous routine of girl chasing. When Buzz eventually breaks down and tells him, Doc apologizes for acting stupidly. The theme of the show is that homosexuals are no different from anyone else except in one respect, and they have a right to their own sexual preference. As Doc tells Buzz, "You found yourself and you're happy. . . We all have to do what is right for us, as long as it doesn't hurt others."

What a difference a decade makes. In 1972 ABC censors insisted that the lead character of "That Certain Summer" tell his son, "A lot of people think it's wrong. They say it's a sickness. . . .If I had a choice, it's not something I'd pick for myself." In 1981 network censors objected to the script of a TV movie about a woman who had a lesbian affair but eventually went back to her husband, telling him, "It's good to be home again." The censor's complaint: "Don't you realize this will offend every lesbian in America?"[13]

PRISONERS OF SEX

Like homosexuals, prostitutes came out of the video closet in the mid-1970s. They quickly became a regular feature of the urban landscape, providing backdrops to the action on police shows from "Kojak" and "Starsky and Hutch" to "Hill Street Blues." Routine roundups of hookers are one feature of the realistic ambiance that shows modelled after "Hill Street" try to project. Prostitutes also play a more central role as informants to police and private eyes. For example, a P.I. on "Moonlighting" gets advance information on upcoming crimes from a call girl. It seems that her regular client, a major mob figure, talks in his sleep. Both "Miami Vice" and "Hunter" featured female cops who impersonated hookers while working undercover, so to speak. These women spent so much time portraying prostitutes that it was easy to forget they were really cops.

Since the late 1970s, prostitutes have tended to leave TV's mean streets (except for shows like "Hill Street Blues" and "Cagney & Lacey"). They now show up in more unlikely places. We mentioned the 1979 segment of "Kate Loves a Mystery," which features a prostitution ring running out of a local bar. The hookers are unexpectedly attractive, suburban housewives who turn tricks for extra cash. In a 1985 episode of "Airwolf," an ingenious fellow buys army surplus helicopters and uses them to airlift call girls to all-male fishing trips. The girls show up in evening gowns and are picked up the next morning.

In a "Miami Vice" segment that same season, Crockett and Tubbs come across an art deco whorehouse specializing in unusual practices and fetishes. They eventually use one of the prostitutes to uncover a major drug dealer. The 1985 season also offered viewers a "Spenser: For Hire" segment where teenage girls are given drugs to feed their habit in return for sex and posing in porn films. This operation is very exclusive, catering to wealthy middle-aged men.

The nature and genesis of prostitution has also emerged as a regular theme. Prior to 1965, not a single show in the sample dealt with prostitution. In the next decade, four shows addressed this titillating topic. In the most recent decade, the number nearly tripled, to eleven. That projects to four or five shows every week in the prime-time schedule. Scripts take up the theme of prostitution not to condemn but to understand. The women tend to be portrayed as confused or abused, the victims of drug problems, abusive ex-husbands or boyfriends, and uncaring or even sexually abusive parents. They are downtrodden or emotionally scarred people trying to survive in a hostile world.

One recurring plot device concerns the naive young woman on the verge of being thrown into what was once called a life of sin. On a 1973 "Adam's Rib," lawyer-heroine Amanda Bonner defends a young girl arrested for soliciting. Amanda shows that the girl was down on her luck, and when a man approached her and offered her $20 to have sex, she accepted. She had never done this before and accepted this time only as a last resort. In a notable aside, Ms. Bonner criticizes the police for focusing their antiprostitution efforts on "working women" instead of organized crime, the real villain.

A similarly woebegone figure appeared on a 1985 episode of "Hill Street Blues." An eighteen-year-old picked up for solicitation explains to her public defender that she'd never done this before and was desperately trying to raise money to get away from her father, who'd been forcing her to have sex since she was twelve. Lest we conclude that television deals only with first offenders in this realm, the same episode provides a less sympathetic portrayal of Rhonda, a seasoned pro. When arrested, she bares her chest to a police lieutenant and promises more if he lets her go. The ploy fails and she pays a fine. Later the same day, however, she's arrested again. This time the lieutenant has her released, saying he'll "take care of" the charges. Unlike the sweet young things discussed above, Rhonda has no hard luck story and makes no apologies for her profession. The script neither condones nor condemns her activities. Her appearance typifies "Hill Street"'s tendency to present the seamy side of everyday police work with minimal editorial comment.

This portrayal of a casual relationship between police and prostitutes was carried a step forward on "Joe Bash," a 1985 comedy by the team that created the better-known "Barney Miller." Joe is a middle-aged cop on the beat who has long been a regular customer of Lorna. One night his sex life is unexpectedly complicated by Lorna's desire to make the relationship "more than a business deal." Flustered, Joe calls the idea "unethical" and asks, "Don't you girls have rules or something?" Lorna persists, telling him the price of future sex will be for him to come over for dinner, send her flowers, and telephone just to chat. Joe ends up reluctantly sending her flowers, without being happy about the new arrangement. The comic spirit of this vignette derives from the cop's resistance to turning illegal sex into an ordinary extramarital affair.

Only occasionally are prostitutes portrayed as genuine evildoers. A 1976 episode of "Police Woman" features a madame who blackmails a gubernatorial candidate by taking pictures during his visits to her salons. It seems he isn't a "normal" customer but is into "s-m." This script is also memorable for its explanation of the politician's masochistic proclivities. He explains that he used to get beaten at boarding school and withstood it by transforming the pain into "an act of immense pleasure."

Prostitutes are also seen as the victims of crime, as in a 1972 segment of "The Streets of San Francisco." Beverly, the woman in question, is placed in protective custody after she's threatened by a psychopath. In one scene she draws a parallel between her profession and that of the policeman guarding her: "We're a lot alike, the hooker and the cop. Nobody likes us but they can't live without us. We work the same lousy hours, meet the same crummy people, and get the same stares if people happen to know what we really do. Somebody's got to do it, so here we are." She goes on to say that she survives, and "that's what it's all about." Here the familiar theme of the downtrodden prostitute struggling to survive is coupled with the intriguing argument that prostitutes, like the police, serve a necessary social function. To borrow a refrain from Gilbert and Sullivan, the prostitute's lot, like the policeman's, is not a happy one.

Thus television has dispensed with one hoary stereotype, the hooker with a heart of gold, only to replace it with another, the hooker as sympathetic victim. Prime time's prostitutes are not victims of bigotry, like gays, or of prudery, like the parade of misunderstood young lovers who discover the joy of sex. They are society's victims all the same, prisoners of their unhappy upbringings or unlucky circumstances. Television tells us not to condemn but to sympathize with them. They're mostly ordinary people down on their luck, just trying to survive.

DIRTY BOOKS, CLEAN MINDS

Pornographic material is another relatively recent ingredient in TV's sexual stew. We found only one show dealing with alleged or outright pornography before 1974, but eight episodes since. Most treat sexually explicit material as less than completely acceptable, but few make the case for outright censorship. In fact, two out of three make the point that the material in question is constitutionally protected.

This argument is most fully presented in the earliest show in our sample to raise the issue, a 1963 episode of "The Defenders." The idealistic lawyer-heroes defend an eminent author who is arrested in a small town for selling an allegedly obscene book that he wrote. The arrest is carefully orchestrated to catch him actually accepting money for the book. Later we see the local judge arguing about the case at home with his wife and father-in-law. Their exchange illuminates the terms of debate as the script presents it:

Judge: How do you know [it's obscene]?
Wife: I know they arrested him for writing it.
Judge: Yes, Petronius had the same trouble in his day.
Wife: There you go quoting Greeks to me. . . .What difference
does it make, quoting people dead two thousand years, as
though they could teach us anything about living today?
Judge: Jesus has been dead almost that long.

At this point, the father-in-law weighs in with a more substantive argument, and the debate shifts:

Wife: Isn't it time the law stopped protecting only perverted
readers and paid attention to normal, decent people?. .
We've got rights too, haven't we?
Judge: You've got a right not to read the book if you don't
want to. . . .There has been no crime committed here.
James Henry David is one of our country's leading authors.
Wife: He wrote a dirty book.
Judge: No cultural policeman is going to solve that question.

Most of the community seems to favor the father-in-law's stance, although the judge's position gets support from the local newspaper editor. He tells a hostile city council, "If we are going to ban everything that might create the wrong kind of desire in young people, we ought to go the whole way. We ought to ban cosmetics and perfume and popular music and bathing suits."

During a recess in the trial, the author confronts his chief accuser and suggests that pornography is in the eye of the beholder: "We are both writer and reader. A book is a two-way mirror. It shows not only the writer's soul but the reader's also." In his summation, the defense counsel takes the high road of art and enlightenment: "Don't pass laws against dirty books. That ruins literature, that ruins art with a great big capital 'A'." The district attorney argues less eloquently that the community has the right to protect itself.

Finally, it's the judge's turn. He tells the jury:

It may be there are some questions which no jury composed of ordinary laymen should decide. . . . We all belong to a free society, distinguished by the absence of governmental restrictions. We are all free to contribute whatever we can, a small mosaic to a great pattern. James Henry David has contributed a book. And what people think of it is bound to differ because of different backgrounds and tastes, but as Judge Learned Hand has said, truth and beauty are too precious to society at large to be mutilated by any law. . . .

Case dismissed.

We have paid special attention to this single episode for two reasons. First, it presents the classic liberal defense of protecting allegedly obscene material. The program signals its sympathies both in the arguments presented and the characters who make them. The debate is between free expression and community standards, and free expression wins hands down. Moreover, the defenders of freedom are an eminent author, a wise judge, and a thoughtful editor. Their opponents are portrayed as small-town know-nothings or hard-hat types willing to sacrifice art and freedom for sexual repression and stifling conformity.

Second, this episode is distinctive for *not* being representative of episodic television's portrayal of sex-related controversies. It's that rarity, an issue-oriented show that seeks to inform as well as persuade. If it were broadcast today, it would be a TV movie. The didactic and preachy style, which presents social controversy as a conflict between enlightened and repressive forces, is perfect for the genre.

Equally unrepresentative is "The Defenders"'s active endorsement of a "racy" book's artistic merit. More typical is the view that pornography is an unavoidable evil, but a constitutionally protected one. For instance, a 1976 police show called "Joe Forrester" deals with the mob's effort to peddle hard-core movies and magazines. When a kindly old news dealer refuses to stock the magazine, thugs beat him up. Joe, the cop on the beat, organizes a neighborhood crusade to oust the smut peddlers. Joe's sergeant, however, tells him that pornography is a constitutionally protected means of free expression. Joe replies that pornography is one thing, but people getting beat up is another. Thus this program distinguishes between pornography as constitutionally protected and the evil pornographers who should be locked up on other grounds.

Finally, some shows present pornography as a social evil with no mention of its protected status. On a 1981 episode of "B. J. and the Bear," B. J. discovers that a candidate for governor is accepting payoffs to protect a porno film operation. This is viewed as so disgusting that even the film director attempts to quit rather than use young "teeny-boppers" in the films. No questions are raised about legality; in the end, the police break up the operation. As for moral issues, the politician reminds the film director, "You gave up your morality long ago." Again, however, this get-tough approach is the exception. More often than not, television reminds viewers that allegedly obscene material is legally protected, if not the art with a capital "A" that "The Defenders" guard against narrow-minded censors.

One theme first raised in "The Defenders" does recur. It is the notion that pornography is in the eye of the beholder. This notion is addressed most topically in an episode of "WKRP in Cincinnati." In this segment an evangelical minister, who bears an uncanny resemblance to Jerry Falwell, presents the radio station with a list of songs he and his supporters consider obscene. Over the objections of his program director and disk jockey, the station manager, Mr. Carlson, agrees not to play the songs. A short time later the reverend arrives with another list, this time including songs the station hasn't played. Carlson asks how the reverend and his small group can dictate what gets played. He replies that the air waves are public and that only a few program directors and station managers control them now. The program director tries to argue that declining ratings will indicate what they should play. The reverend responds that his group is exercising its rights in a democracy.

Carlson hesitantly agrees not to play the songs with allegedly obscene lyrics. Not much later a third list arrives, this one including songs whose lyrics are clearly not obscene. Carlson confronts the reverend with the fact that the songs express ideas, not obscenity. He responds that the ideas are immoral and godless. Carlson says he won't censor the music, and the reverend threatens to boycott WKRP advertisers. The station begins to lose advertisers, but Carlson stands firm. He even warns the would-be censor that broadcasters who give in easily to pressure will also be the first to desert the reverend's cause. The show seems to agree that some material may be in bad taste or even obscene, but it also parodies New Right censors and warns that their targets extend beyond obscenity. Give 'em an inch and they'll take the First Amendment.

This message is presented with a lighter touch in a 1978 'Little House On the Praire" episode, in which the prim and proper Harriet Oleson catches her son Willie looking at corset ads in a mail order catalogue. Her more easygoing husband refuses to discipline the boy, saying Willie was just curious. With a look of disgust, Harriet responds, "How horrible." But we're clearly meant to side with the husband's understanding approach and against Harriet's prudishness.

That same season, "Welcome Back, Kotter" provided a variation on this theme by defending sex education against prudish objections. When high school administrator Julie Kotter approves a sex education film for student viewing, some outraged parents protest. When Julie meets with them, she has the following exchange with the aptly named Mrs. Ugler:

Mrs. Ugler: You're not going to show any disgusting sex films!
Julie: We're trying to show our children that sex is not disgusting.
Mrs. Ugler: I've been married twenty-seven years; don't tell me what's disgusting.
Julie: We don't tell our children that they have to drive cars, but they're going to do it, so we offer driver's education.
Mrs. Ugler: So they can go to drive-ins and fool around.

At this point, echoing a similar exchange in "The Defenders," the know-nothing objections of Mrs. Ugler give way to a more substantive question from another parent: "Isn't there a chance that your program gives children ideas? Wouldn't they get along fine if you just left them alone?" Julie is ready for this one. "They don't get along fine. Do you know the teenage pregnancy or teenage V.D. rate in this country?" At that, Mrs. Ugler intercedes, "If you're going to talk dirty, I'm leaving." After that laugh line, the meeting breaks up, with the parents agreeing to see the film before judging it.

Then an intriguing plot twist occurs. Through an accident, Julie's sex education film is switched with a porn film some students intended to watch. Thus the parents get an unexpected chance to see what real pornography looks like. Predictably enraged, they demand Julie's resignation. But she explains (while covering for the students):

> I wanted to prove a point: to show you the difference between sex education and true pornography. Too many of our kids get their sexual knowledge from films like you saw yesterday. . . If [we] all work together, we can arm our kids with the truth, so that movies like this won't mislead them.

Julie's good will and enlightened attitude carry the day.

This show, too, has a point to make, and a viewpoint reminiscent of "The Defenders," though couched in less didactic fashion. The forces of enlightenment are pitted against counterproductive prudery. The issue is posed in black-and-white terms. Exposure to new ideas and information is good; repressive sexual attitudes are dangerous or self-defeating. "Kotter" adds the coda that overzealous restrictions on sexual information will only drive impressionable young minds to real pornography.

The viewer can't gauge the difference, since we never see either Julie's sex education film or the students' blue movie. But the argument is crystal clear. We can tell the good guys from the bad guys, and the right from the wrong position. If there are intelligent arguments on the other side, they are never presented. Nor do other series dramatize the opposing side. For example, a conservative script might present policeman Joe Forrester's dilemma as the result of efforts by misguided do-gooders like those on "The Defenders." But this seems to be outside the boundary of television's approach to pornography. The perspective is certainly not pro-pornography; it is anticensorship. But that is about as far as the debate gets. On prime time, the middle ground is that pornography may be bad, but efforts to prohibit it are worse.

What Next?

Abortion is one of the few sexually related issues that television still treats gingerly. It combines minimal titillation with maximal controversy, not a happy combination for sponsors and program executives. But since over 95 percent of Hollywood is pro-choice (as we have seen), it has begun to attract occasional crusading producers and writers. The most noteworthy result was "Roe v. Wade," a docudrama of the landmark Supreme Court case that legalized abortion. The show aired in May 1989, as the Court heard arguments on a major challenge to its earlier decision. Abortion foes called for a viewer boycott, and several nervous advertisers withdrew their sponsorship. The writer complained that NBC executives ordered seventeen major script changes to add "balance" to the debate.[14] The result was to portray the "Roe" character as a troubled individual, while giving the righteous pronouncements to her lawyer ("The law doesn't stop abortions; it just makes them dangerous"). The "Wade" side's arguments are sometimes less incisive. For example, the male district attorney attempts to establish his empathy by wisecracking, "I may not have a uterus, but I was definitely a baby." *New York Times* critic Walter Goodman summed up the balance of dramatic forces: "Although the play's sympathies are plainly with Roe . . . the network may deserve some credit for making 'Roe v. Wade' a less doctrinaire show."[15]

What happens when someone on the production end is personally opposed to abortion? Audiences found out during a 1985 episode of "Spenser: For Hire," when Spenser's girlfriend Susan wrestles with the decision to have an abortion. "Spenser" star Robert Urich felt the pro-life arguments were not strong enough. He also had enough clout to get the script rewritten to strengthen the pro-life material.

Thus, when Susan tells Spenser that she doesn't want a baby, because of her need for independence, Spenser replies that he is ready for the responsibility, and the child has a right to live. Susan asks, "What if I don't think of it as a baby?" When Spenser remains silent, she says it must be easy for him since he's so sure. He asks, "Do you think the highest point of mankind is when we are all independent individuals?" Despite his objections, Susan eventually has the abortion. In the closing scene, Spenser goes to see her in the clinic. His voice-over leaves the debate unresolved: "Susan and I had gone to war. We were both committed to our beliefs and we were arguing over the biggest dilemma. Susan and I had gone to war, but under it all we still love each other. Love, maybe that's the route to peace." He gives her flowers and they sit silently looking at each other.

It is too early to say whether such shows portend a breakthrough in episodic television's reluctance to take on the abortion issue. Until now, the passions this topic stirs have helped make it one of the few sexually related topics that the networks still find too hot to handle. Thus, our study turned up only four widely spaced shows dealing with abortion, and none took a clear position on the issue.

Less controversial forms of population control also get short shrift on prime time. Birth control is very rarely mentioned in prime time, and then only in passing. For example, on a 1979 segment of "The Ropers," we learn that Helen Roper's sister Hilda has five children even though she's on the pill. Hilda says it happens because she forgets to go to the drugstore. Helen and sister Edith wish that Hilda weren't so forgetful, because they think she should stop having children. Similarly, on a 1981 segment of "Nurse," a patient asks a nurse if the operation she had to have her tubes tied was permanent. After being assured that it was, the woman expresses relief because, she says, she and her husband don't have very much self-control.

The assumption on such shows is that birth control is appropriate and sometimes necessary. But the message is low-key and the theme peripheral to the main plot line. We found no equivalent to the plot development in Philip Roth's "Goodbye Columbus," when a romance is disrupted by a mother's discovery of her daughter's diaphragm. Not until 1986 did "St. Elsewhere," that bellwether of anatomical frankness, have one lover tell another, "I use a diaphragm." (Network censors changed the line from "I wear a diaphragm.") It appears that the only aspect of sex that television still avoids is its biological consequences. The Planned

Parenthood study cited earlier found that only one in every eighty-five sexual references on television concerned sex education, birth control, abortion, or sexually transmitted diseases. Ironically, television is now willing to integrate sex into almost every aspect of life except marriage and children.

Under the shadow of AIDS, this oasis of squeamishness may soon disappear. Even as stations debated the propriety of condom advertisements, programs like "Cagney & Lacey," "Kate & Allie," and (appropriately) "The Facts of Life" began to include references to the need for birth control among teenagers. During the 1986-87 season Marybeth Lacey first uttered the word "condom" on prime time, and Valerie Harper actually beheld one. Two seasons later Allie's teen-aged son Chip was embarrassed by his mother's discovery of a condom in his pants pocket. According to a writer of "Daddy," a TV movie about unintended teen-aged pregnancy, "ABC wanted to. . . stretch the boundaries of television. . . . The kids talk with as much candor as possible. . .about abortion, about condoms and diaphragms, about orgasm and ejaculation."[16]

This is in line with press reports that Hollywood's growing concern about AIDS may lead to less promiscuity but even more sexual explicitness on prime time. "Cagney & Lacey" producer Barney Rosenzweig decided that Chris should become "relatively monogamous" because, "When the series began, we wanted to dispel the myths about women's lack of sexual curiosity. But now we think it's important to show that she lives in the real world of New York City where she has to be concerned about AIDS."[17] At the same time, he is concerned not only that having her "practice abstinence. . .is not really a practical message," but also that "we [don't] want to create any more of the homophobic hysteria that already exists."[18] On the other hand, a "Falcon Crest" producer argues that the market for voyeurism will rise as real-life promiscuity declines: "As sexual behavior becomes more dangerous in real life, we might tend to do more of it on the show."[19] Our own instinct, after analyzing three decades of programming, is never to bet against more sex on television.

THE JOY OF SEX

What are we to make of this potpourri of seething passions and sexual victims? First, the portrayal of sex on television has increased dramatically over the past fifteen years, and the rise in sexual themes and explicitness shows no sign of abating. Unrequited passions are increasingly passé, the love that dared not speak its name now shouts it from the rooftops, and onetime taboo topics like incest, sado-masochism, and bestiality have become so much grist for the prime-time mill.

Twenty years ago sexual activity was rarely hinted at, much less headlined, and extramarital sex was often condemned. Today most forms of sexual behavior are either taken for granted or treated as legitimate choices of personal lifestyle. Extramarital sex, adultery, homosexuality, pornography, and prostitution have all lost their taboo status.

Everyone knows the basic reason for this transformation of life on television. Sex sells. It sells audiences to advertisers, and it ultimately sells their products back to the audience. As the network and production companies discovered that they were titillating more viewers than they outraged, they gradually increased the sales potential of their product by permitting more and more taboos to be broken in ever more explicit fashion.

Yet this sexual explosion is not simply a cynical competition to whet the tastes of an increasingly jaded public. Television also presents a point of view about sex, which roughly parallels the "progressive" approach to sexual diversity and enlightenment. The attitude is not quite that of the 1960s credo, "If it feels good, do it." It is less libertine than libertarian—do whatever you want, so long as you don't hurt anybody. Adultery, prostitution, and pornography are bad when they result in emotional harm. In general, though, sexual expressiveness and frankness are good. Indeed they are a great advance over repressiveness and prudery, those barriers against happiness and human fulfillment. Even if a program uses sex mainly to attract an audience, the script can also strike a blow for sexual (and even human) liberation.

In 1983 Marlo Thomas wrote a *TV Guide* piece plugging her latest new comedy special. She chose to highlight the difference between her current character and Ann Marie, the young woman she portrayed fifteen years earlier on the popular sitcom "That Girl": "Ann Marie never slept with her boyfriend. . . .And in this show, the woman I play gaily offers that, in her opinion, sex may well be 70 percent of a relationship." She uses this comparison not to shock, but to make a point: "It seems astonishing to me how television has grown up. . .since the days of Ann Marie."[20] Ms. Thomas means both that television is handling more "mature" (i.e., sexual) material and that it is handling sexual themes in a more mature way. "Nobody ever said the word 'sex' on 'That Girl,' ever," she writes.

Today television is willing both to talk about sex and to tell the truth about it as the Hollywood community sees it. That truth is roughly that sex is important, it needs to be dealt with in all its diverse expressions, and those who would suppress it from popular entertainment are doing the mass audience a disservice. Indeed the real villains on programs that deal with sexual issues are the Mrs. Grundys and Moral Majoritarians who would deny romance its natural physical expression, restrict free expression and much needed information, or condemn as "deviant" social victims like gays and prostitutes, who are no different from the rest of us except in one minor regard—their sex lives. As for extramarital sex, it's a fact of life, which popular entertainment would be foolish either to ignore or treat moralistically according to outmoded standards.

The point should not be overdrawn. Television rarely says that adultery or prostitution or homosexuality or abortion are wise options that should be applauded. Instead it criticizes censorship, homophobia, and puritanism, while treating the victims of these evils in a generally sympathetic light. Television's perspective on sex is not revolutionary; it is an expression of social liberalism. In this regard TV's sex life typifies the medium's approach to social relations. As a leading form of mass entertainment, television rarely mounts the barricades. Instead it breaks down barriers one by one, gradually extending the limits of social acceptability. Whether this is a positive or negative development depends on the viewer's own perspective. But it is, as television tells us so often about sex, a fact of life. Even in the face of AIDS, an "L.A. Law" producer muses, "We may be heading for a new repression, a new 'Father Knows Best' era. I hope not. For television, married or celibate characters aren't as much fun."[21]

—————⟫⟪—————

3

FROM LUCY TO LACEY

I feel like June Cleaver on acid.

—Murphy Brown

I magine a world in which television programs are made by media moguls like Frieda Silverman, Norma Lear, and "Granny" Tinker. Hard to imagine? Maybe it's because television's creative community has always been a male preserve. Our survey of that group, described in chapter 12, found only one woman out of 106 people interviewed. How would a change of gender at the studio and network boardrooms affect the fantasy world of television entertainment? We can't know for sure, and such a feminist fantasy is unlikely to come to fruition anytime soon. But there is one way to examine the relevance of gender for prime-time programming. We can look at how the mostly male creative community has portrayed the other half of humanity on the small screen.

SUGAR AND SPICE

In the beginning there was Lucy. Television's first female archetype was a zany housewife whose madcap machinations bedeviled her loving but long-suffering husband. In her original incarnation, Lucy Ricardo and her friend Ethel Mertz were constantly getting into scrapes stemming from their efforts to get around some rule or prohibition announced by their husbands. They often ended up causing trouble for themselves and their spouses alike. Devotees relish the time Lucy finagled her way onto Ricky's TV show to do a cough syrup commercial, then got drunk on camera from sampling the highly alcoholic product. Another escapade involved Lucy's efforts to crash Ricky's nightclub act by impersonating a clown. The emphasis was on the women's ability to manipulate their men, despite the limited amount of actual power they possessed. And audiences loved it. "I Love Lucy" was the number one show with audiences for four different seasons. Along with "Here's Lucy" and "The Lucy Show," Miss Ball's vehicles landed in the Nielsen top ten for an incredible fifteen years.

Lucy Ricardo/Carmichael/Carter played in prime time from 1951 through 1974. Her most lasting influence, though, has been the many characters modeled on Lucy lines, defined largely by their frantic efforts to manipulate husbands, boyfriends, bosses, or other figures of male authority. A year after Lucy premiered on CBS, another wacky housewife was making trouble for her husband, a staid judge, on NBC's "I Married Joan." The cycle soon included working women who complicated the lives of their male bosses, like Gale Storm's Susannah Pomeroy, the social director of a luxury liner on "The Gail Storm Show" (a.k.a. "Oh Susannah"), and Ann Sothern's Susie McNamara, who was a "Private Secretary" to a talent agent. When such characters weren't married, they spent much of their time and energy hunting for men, as did Susie and her friend Sylvia, along with Eileen Sherwood, a.k.a. "My Sister Eileen," Connie Brooks of "Our Miss Brooks," and many others.

This type of irrepressible character was carried through the 1960s in various new incarnations. There were perky· teenagers like "Gidget," "Tammy," Patty and Cathy Lane of "The Patty Duke Show," and the

Bradley sisters (Billie Jo, Betty Jo, and Bobby Jo) on "Petticoat Junction." The harebrained housewife routine was reprised by Phyllis Diller on "The Pruitts of Southampton" and Eva Gabor on "Green Acres." The indomitable illogic that undercut rational male authority even found its apotheosis in the supernatural powers of a beautiful witch on "Bewitched" and a glamorous genie on "I Dream of Jeannie." Both these series derived much of their comedy from the often futile attempts of hapless males to retain control over their households in the presence of such powerful female magic.

In the 1970s and 1980s, the tradition of slapstick comedy by lovable screwballs was upheld by characters like the 1950s-era friends "Laverne and Shirley" and the more contemporary Janet and Chrissy, lucky Jack's roommates on "Three's Company." Other variations on this theme were played by Mary Richards' busybody landlady "Phyllis" and Tina, the flaky housekeeper to a chauvinistic Japanese inventor on "Mr. T and Tina." The use of settings like the 1950s or male-oriented Japanese society suggest that social change may have caught up with the Lucy formula. One wellspring of such comedy is the conflict between a socially subordinate female and a theoretically dominant male authority figure, who gets manipulated by guile, charm, or the sheer lunatic inspiration of some nutty scheme. But the upsetting of male domination through feminine wiles presupposes that audiences accept the premise of male dominance in household, workplace, and love relationships. As that premise changes, the descendants of Lucy Ricardo may follow the giddy heiresses of 1930s screwball comedies into broadcast history.

Another enduring prime-time comedy type is the warm and loving housewife or mother figure. These women were often the female counterparts of their sage and tolerant husbands in happy middle-class households. They were more likely to work with their husband in solving family problems than to work around him, although the man remained primus inter pares in their partnership. If father knew best, mother was usually there backing him up. Unlike the frenetic physical comedy that was Lucy's forte, these family comedies were slower paced and aimed more at smiles than belly laughs.

Television's archetypal comic mother figure came from a show titled, appropriately, "I Remember Mama." From 1949 through 1956 "Mama" Marta Hansen, along with "Papa" Lars, presided over a Norwegian-American family of five around the turn of the century. Each episode was introduced by daughter Katrin, seen turning pages in the family album, and telling viewers, "Most of all I remember Mama." This prototype for the family comedy genre is less familiar to today's viewers because it was broadcast live and thus denied the immortality of syndication. A similar fate befell most episodes of "The Goldbergs," which featured Molly Goldberg as everyone's favorite Jewish mother from 1949 through 1954.

The wholesome housewife persona was firmly established by such long-running mother figures as Margaret Anderson of "Father Knows Best," Ozzie's wife and helpmate Harriet, and Beaver's understanding mother June Cleaver. A prime repository of television nostalgia is the rec-ollection of watching the children in these shows grow up. Less memorable, perhaps, but cut from the same mold were characters like Donna Stone, Dr. Alex Stone's wife on "The Donna Reed Show," Danny Williams' wife Margaret on "Make Room for Daddy," and even Alice Mitchell, the hapless mother of "Dennis the Menace." All these shows carried the tradition of family comedy relatively unchanged into the 1960s.

The new decade also saw some variations on the original model. A surrogate for the traditional housewife-mother appeared in Mayberry, North Carolina, where the lovably befuddled Aunt Bea helped Sheriff Andy Taylor, a widower, raise his young son Opie. Her younger counter-part in Washington, D.C., was Katy Holstrum, the Swedish "Farmer's Daughter" who became governess of Congressman Glen Morley's two sons (and eventually became Mrs. Morley). About the same time, this character type was sent up by Jean Nash, the unconventional housewife in "Please Don't Eat the Daisies." She wrote a newspaper column, slept till noon, and could not care less what her proper suburban neighbors thought about her lifestyle. Nonetheless, she managed to raise a tradi-tional family that included four boys and a sheepdog.

Notwithstanding this effort to break the mold, the warm and wise mother figure was carried into the 1970s by the matriarchs of two popular clans, "The Brady Bunch" and "The Partridge Family." The former numbered six children, a cat, and a dog, who were looked after by housewife Carol Brady and her architect husband Mike. The latter included five kids and a dog, along with their sound-recording equipment (the whole family became pop stars). The tradition continued through the latter 1970s with "Eight is Enough," in which first Joan and then Abby Bradford helped her journalist husband raise their brood of eight.

More recent family comedies are likely to give mom an occupation aside from child-rearing, but the scripts rarely stray far from domestic situations. Thus Elyse Keaton may have been an architect, but the real question was how this former flower child got along with her conservative children on "Family Ties." Clair Huxtable on the "The Cosby Show" is a practicing attorney, but we usually see her practicing the art of child-rearing on her five children. Whatever the changes in the American family structure, "Mama" appears in no danger of being displaced as a timeless comic figure.

One significant spinoff from this form deserves mention for merging the traditional warm but gentle mother figure with a very different environment. "The Mary Tyler Moore Show" essentially shifted this character to a work setting as the "mother" to a family of co-workers. This series made a breakthrough in portraying a happy, successful, single professional woman. But Miss Moore's character was worlds away from Faye Dunaway's dragon lady television executive in "Network." Mary Richards, the assistant producer to a local television news show, provided an island of warmth and good sense in the midst of chaos. Around her swirled emotional storms induced by grown-up children like Ted Baxter, the blustering, egotistical anchorman, Phyllis Lyndstrom, the busybody landlady, and Sue Ann Nivens, the catty and man-hungry "happy homemaker."

Executive producer Allan Burns later recalled, "On 'The Mary Tyler Moore Show' we were feeling our way. Mary was a character who was breaking out of her shell, emerging as a woman with a little authority."[1] Thus television managed to finesse a major shift in the occupational role of women by accommodating the new social situation to the older archetype. As women moved into the workplace, "mom" went to the office, surrounded by her temperamental but loving brood of fellow workers.

If Mary Tyler Moore poured old wine into new bottles, producer Norman Lear introduced a new kind of heroine who carried a hundred-proof kick. The Lear lady combine Lucy's zaniness and "Mama's" sagacity with a dollop of sharp-tongued sarcasm all her own. Most earlier comediennes portrayed middle- or upper-middle-class women whose problems revolved around family squabbles or simple failures of communication. Suddenly, in the 1970s, struggling working mothers and even welfare mothers were finding biting humor in such unlikely sitcom situations as rape, drug abuse, poverty, racism, and alcoholism. It all started when Archie Bunker's wife Edith evolved from a slow-witted "dingbat" to a more fully rounded, mature, and sometimes troubled character.

The more typical Lear woman, however, evolved from Bunker acquaintances like next-door neighbor Louise Jefferson and cousin Maude Findlay. Maude was as loud and shrill in her liberal litany as Archie was in his hard-hat conservatism. When Maude wasn't battling Archie, Louise was deflating her self-important husband George, a black version of Archie. Their interactions helped develop a style of topical, political, and ethnic comic repartee that owed considerably more to Don Rickles than Noël Coward.

A remarkable number of spin-off series established this format as the dominant comedic style of the 1970s. A stock character was the woman whose strident insults and sarcastic wit undermined male bluster. These characters included the Jeffersons' maid Florence, Maude's maid Florida Evans, Archie's housekeeper and cook, Aunt Esther of "Sanford and Son," and Della Rogers of "Chico and the Man." Most were poor blacks or white ethnics, and the problems they dealt with had rarely been encountered in the sunny middle-class world of previous sitcoms. In her own spin-off, "Good Times," Florida Evans struggled with poverty while raising three children in a Chicago housing project. In "One Day At A Time," divorced mother Ann Romano had to deal with her daughter's ventures into premarital sex, her own dating problems, sexual harassment on her job, child support and alimony, and eventually a collapse from exhaustion (little wonder!). The triumph of low-life "realism" in the lives of sitcom women inspired this bit of doggerel from one critic: "Maude has been married and married/Phyllis's husband dropped dead/Florida's boyfriend has cancer/Joe's moved from sweet Rhoda's bed./Mary must find new employment/Alice is still slinging hash/It's assembly line work for Shirley and Laverne/The Sanfords collect people's trash."[2]

Less remarked upon, but equally dramatic, was their new relationship to men. The women of seventies' sitcoms were not afraid to go it on their own. Maude and Ann Romano were divorcees, as was Maude's daughter, and Rhoda untied the knot in the course of her series. Even more significantly, they regularly stood up to men, cheerfully trading insults with husbands, boyfriends, and employers. The longtime comic formula has not changed in some respects, however. Women are still upending men who attempt to stand on their authority. But instead of working around or subtly manipulating their men, the women slug it out toe to toe. It's a feminist version of the blue-collar fantasy, telling off the boss as an equal. "9 to 5," in which the office secretaries run roughshod over their inept sexist boss, was the culmination of a decade of change that began when Mary Richards joined WJM-TV News and Edith Bunker became an equal partner in her marriage.

The history of female stars in dramatic series is somewhat more truncated. Throughout the entire first decade of our study, there were none. Anthology hostesses like Loretta Young and Jane Wyman often starred in episodes of the shows they introduced, but they did not create continuing characters. It was not until the 1965-66 season that viewers were introduced to strong female characters who took top billing or at least shared it with a male. Ironically, one of the first pioneers was actually a British import. Mrs. Emma Peel (Diana Rigg), the cool and supremely competent secret agent on "The Avengers," was more likely to rescue her partner John Steed than to be protected by him. Another female James Bond that season was the title character in "Honey West," a tough private eye in a fetching trenchcoat.

Meanwhile, the Western genre produced a less glamorous but no less authoritative female lead. On "The Big Valley," Barbara Stanwyck portrayed Victoria Barkley, the no-nonsense matriarch of the Barkley ranch. The next few years brought such diverse but equally independent women as Julie Barnes, the "Mod Squad"'s hippie cop, and "Julia," a widowed black working mother. Such roles were strong on substance if short on the realistic situations faced by Mary Richards' circle of friends, not to mention the travails of Norman Lear's characters.

Beginning in the mid-1970s, though, female stars started getting more exposure in a different sense. Under pressure to tone down the violence of cop shows, the networks found an alternative audience grabber in a genre most succinctly described as "T & A TV." The trendsetters were "Charlie's Angels," an interchangeable team of pin-up detectives peddling soft-core suggestiveness. The new sex imagery soon ranged from "Buck Rogers'" Lycra-clad helpmate Wilma Deering to the immaculate but revealing haute couture of "Moonlighting"'s Maddie Hayes. Not coincidentally, when "The New Avengers" appeared in 1978, Mrs. Peel was replaced by sex kitten Tara King, who was much more the voluptuous damsel in distress.

Perhaps the best microcosm of the shift in female dramatic roles was the detective drama "Remington Steele." The series opened in 1982 featuring Laura Holt, a brilliant private eye, who couldn't attract business because she was a woman in a man's profession. So she created an imaginary boss named Remington Steele. The ruse was a success, and business boomed for this staunchly independent self-employed crime-fighter. When clients kept wanting to meet the elusive Steele, she hired a front man to play the part. Well into the series' second season, Steele was portrayed as a charming bumbler who knew more about old Bogart movies than actual crime-solving procedures. Laura remained very much the senior partner. Gradually, however, Steele became more polished, less naive, and more successful. At the same time, Laura began wearing fewer tweed suits and more evening gowns. In the show's final seasons, Steele became a worldly man about town, often rescuing Laura from danger. Meanwhile, Laura grew less independent and more concerned about her relationship to Steele and their future together. This role reversal ended only with the series' demise in 1986.

In the 1980s this trend was carried by the prime-time soaps, with their emphasis on heavy-breathing themes, lightweight characters, and low-cut necklines. On shows like "Dallas," most women existed primarily to provide sexual conquests for various male Ewings. Competing series created female J.R.s like "Dynasty's" glitzy Alexis Carrington Colby Dexter and "Knots Landing's" Abby Cunningham, a worthy heiress to the Ewing tradition into which she married. In Harlequin romance fashion, these women lusted for sex and power in equal measure and attained enough of both to keep the supermarket tabloids buzzing.

Thus, today's TV sex symbols are often career women whose characters revolve more around their sexual needs than their professional achievements. Yet this is not the whole story. The 1980s also found a niche for women whose sexual presence was matched by their career competence. Such characters ranged from female police detectives "Cagney & Lacey" and public defender Joyce Davenport of "Hill Street Blues," to the unlikely secret agent Amanda King of "Scarecrow and Mrs. King" and psychologist Susan Silverman, detective Spenser's girlfriend in "Spenser: For Hire." Most prominently, the co-workers in "Designing Women" combined professional success with Mae West dialogue. There have also been occasional authoritative characters who don't need to depend on their sex appeal. The most popular is Jessica Fletcher, the middle-aged amateur detective played by Angela Lansbury. Secondary characters who exercised strong authority independent of sex included Mrs. Pynchon, the newspaper publisher on "Lou Grant," and Amanda Harding, the tough politician on "Fortune Dane." To date, the heirs of Diana Rigg and Barbara Stanwyck have managed to endure, if not prevail against, the Farrah Fawcett clones.

GROUP PORTRAIT

The popular image of women on television usually begins and ends with memorable characters from hit shows. This can be misleading, though, because most female characters are neither stars nor even continuing characters. TV's women include a parade of long-forgotten housewives, secretaries, and damsels in distress whose roles never outlast a single episode. Only a systematic content analysis can chronicle the comings and goings of *all* female characters. So we catalogued the distribution, social background, and personal traits of the 2,060 women we encountered across thirty-one seasons.

In the artificial world of prime time, how do women rate? In general, a clear second to men. Female characters are less in evidence than males and, in many ways, they are portrayed as the weaker sex. They are less likely to be mature adults, are less well educated, and hold lower-status jobs. Their activities tend to represent the private realm of home, personal relations, and sexuality, while men represent the public realm of work and social relations. Moreover, despite television's discovery of social relevance in the late 1960s, this pattern has changed surprisingly little over the years.

The most basic finding is that men have always outnumbered women by hefty margins on prime-time shows. Since 1955, 72 percent of all characters have been male, although the gap has gradually narrowed over the years. Prior to 1965, only 22 percent of all characters coded were female. From 1965 through 1974, the proportion of women increased to 28 percent. Since then women have accounted for one-third of television's prime-time population. That represents a 50 percent increase over television's early days, but it means that two out of every three characters are still male.

Nor do women make up in credentials what they lack in sheer numbers. Among characters whose level of education was known, men have accounted for 85 percent of the college graduates and 89 percent of those with postgraduate training. The education gap has receded only slightly over the years. For example, in the first decade of our study, women made up a minuscule 6 percent of the characters with advanced degrees. In the most recent decade, their proportion has risen to 16 percent, or about one highly educated female character for every five males.

On television, a viewer's knowledge of someone's education is usually a function of that character's occupation. The audience rarely hears about a housewife's schooling, whereas we can assume that a lawyer holds a J.D. and a doctor an M.D. So the best test of social standing and authority is usually the type of job the script assigns a character.

THE GIRLS IN THE OFFICE

In the world of work, women are usually found wanting. Nine out of every ten highly educated professionals on prime-time television have been male. Since 1955 men have portrayed 93 percent of all doctors, 87 percent of lawyers and 93 percent of judges, 86 percent of corporate executives, and 87 percent of college professors. Part of the reason women represent such a small proportion of high-status jobs, of course, is their sheer lack of numbers. However, women have provided a majority of schoolteachers and low-status white-collar occupations such as clerks, typists, and secretaries, as well as most of the models and nurses. In addition, almost two women in five (39 percent) have been portrayed either as housewives or without any other identifiable occupation.

Just as notable is how little television's employment picture has changed over the years. The proportion of women in many occupations has remained constantly at very low levels. Most significant is the medical profession, always a popular setting for TV drama. Women accounted for 6 percent of the doctors throughout the 1950s and 1960s, and their numbers have increased to only 8 percent since 1975. Similarly, the proportion of female politicians went from 4 percent before 1965 to 5 percent since 1975. And throughout the entire study we coded no female engineers.

The number of women portrayed in many other professions has increased since the 1950s, but the change is usually modest, with the only real jump taking place since the mid-1970s. Prior to 1965, for example, only 2 percent of all lawyers were played by women. During the next decade the proportion increased only slightly, to 8 percent of the total. Since 1975, however, one lawyer in four has been female. The number of judges has moved in tandem, increasing from none at all before 1965 to 7 percent and then 20 percent during the next two decades, respectively. Female corporate executives have increased more gradually, from 6 to 12 and then 18 percent of the total across the three ten-year intervals. Similarly, women constituted none of the police officers during the first decade, 5 percent during the second, and 10 percent during the third.

Note, however, that part of these shifts are due to a gradual increase in the total number of women on prime time over the years.

Moreover, while women have been filtering into some high-status occupations in recent years, their portrayals of low-status employees have also increased. From 1955 through 1964, women played only a minority (42 percent) of the low-level white-collar workers—clerks, typists, receptionists, and the like. Their proportion increased to exactly half of this occupational group during the next decade. Since 1975, women have taken a big jump ahead into television's pink-collar ghetto, accounting for two out of three low-status white-collar jobs.

A very similar trend is evident among unskilled blue-collar and service workers, a category that includes casual laborers, some factory workers, taxi drivers, waiters and waitresses, and domestic workers. During the 1950s and early 1960s, women made up only one in six unskilled workers shown on television. Their numbers grew slightly, from 16 to 19 percent, during the following decade. Since 1975, however, it has increased to 36 percent. Thus, even as female characters have moved into some high-status jobs recently, the proportion of low-status female workers has more than kept pace.

How do these numbers translate into the actual characters who arrive and depart from new series each fall season? Until the mid-1960s, women had little opportunity to establish characters with a strong occupational focus, since there were no female dramatic leads, and the dominant sitcoms were homebound. Most working women in continuing roles had low-status or sexually stereotyped jobs, like beautician Esmerelda Nugent on "The Gale Storm Show" or the various nurses on medical shows like "Hennessy," "Ben Casey," and "Doctor Kildare." An exception was Dr. Maggie Graham, who always seemed to be a potential love interest for tall, dark, and handsome Dr. Casey.

Most women climbed no higher on the occupational ladder than the occasional social service job, held by characters like schoolteacher Helen Crump on "The Andy Griffith Show" or Frieda Hechlinger, the head of a welfare agency on "East Side, West Side." Otherwise, women exercised authority mainly as the boss's assistant or "girl Friday." The best known characters in this mold were Perry Mason's assistant Della Street, photographer Bob Cummings' assistant Schultzy, and Suzy McNamara, Ann Sothern's title role in "Private Secretary."

The role of working women during these years was best epitomized by the advent of the action-adventure format. This formula was introduced in 1958 by "77 Sunset Strip," the office address for a glamorous private detective duo who were assisted by Suzanne, their ravishing French switchboard operator. The success of this show quickly spawned imitators with the same mix of characters, which was wryly dubbed "two parts private eye, one part cutie pie."[3] Among the contenders: "Bourbon Street Beat" featured two New Orleans-based private detectives and their gorgeous secretary, Melody Mercer. "The Alaskans," set in the 1890s' Yukon gold rush, presented two prospectors who teamed up with a beautiful saloon entertainer named Rocky Shaw. "Hawaiian Eye" substituted palms for pines but stuck with the usual two detectives, who were assisted by photographer/nightclub singer Cricket Blake, played by real-life singer Connie Stevens. It would be several years before women began to portray private eyes or other law enforcers themselves. For now they were stuck in supporting roles, holding down jobs that depended on their looks or office skills.

By the mid-1960s, women started to move into other occupations, although the largest proportion remained in more traditional settings. The advent of secret agent shows created some glamorous roles like those of Cinnamon Carter on the "Mission: Impossible" team and April Dancer, the "The Girl From U.N.C.L.E.," in addition to Honey West and Mrs. Peel. For the first time, women also began to portray police officers, such as Eve Whitfield and Fran Belding of "Ironside" and "Mod Squad"'s Julie Barnes. (ABC's promos identified the mod squad team as "one black, one white, and one blond".) There was even the first female lawyer in a lead role, Patricia Marshall of "The Jean Arthur Show." Characters in business-related professions ranged from rancher Victoria Barkley to "Petticoat Junction"'s hotel owner Kate Bradley.

These inroads into new job opportunities must be viewed against a backdrop of traditional women's work. Lucy Carmichael continued to work as a secretary, and "Gilligan's Island" carried on the sexy starlet stereotype with Ginger Grant. Housekeepers were also well represented, including the Baxter family's "Hazel," Mrs. Livingston on "TheCourtship of Eddie's Father," and Alice of "The Brady Bunch." Even social relevance shows, like "Room 222" and "Julia," which provided the first starring role for a black woman, placed their female characters in traditional roles like teaching and nursing.

The contemporary career woman got off to a rocky start on television with Marlo Thomas's portrayal of "That Girl" from 1966 through 1971. The title character, Ann Marie, was a spunky young actress trying to make it alone in the big city. She bounced from one odd job to another while awaiting her big break in show biz. The scripts mostly ignored the potential for portraying a determined working woman, concentrating instead on physical humor and Ann Marie's Lucy-like lovable dizziness.

As we noted earlier, the breakthrough series in this sphere was "The Mary Tyler Moore Show," which premiered in 1970, just as "That Girl" was fading toward cancellation. Like Ann Marie, Mary Richards was a small-town girl building a career in the big city. There the resemblance ended. Mary had a regular job at a local TV station as a news producer, and her fellow workers accepted her as a skilled professional. As Harry Castleman and Walter Podrazik write:

> Mary's image as an unmarried career woman with a responsible job other than a secretary or a teacher was a major break from television tradition. She was not a widow, had no children, and was working because she wanted to build her own life and career. . . the program presented, without fanfare, women as being capable of interests beyond housework, marriage, and crazy sitcom schemes."[4]

Moore's portrayal quickly became the prototype for career woman sitcom settings. For example, when Mary Richards' friend Rhoda got her own spin-off series, she quickly left her job as a department store window dresser to start her own business. Equally instructive were changes in "The Doris Day Show" format to accommodate the MTM influence.

When the show began in 1968, lead character Doris Martin was a widow with two children, who had moved from the big city back to the family ranch. The next season she took a job at "Today's World" magazine—as a secretary. In 1971, however, after the success of "Mary Tyler Moore," the entire supporting cast was changed and Doris became a single staff writer for "Today's World."

On other fronts, Amanda Bonner appeared as a crusading lawyer on "Adam's Rib," and Dr. Anne Jamison teamed with her father Sean as pediatricians who ran a free clinic on "The Little People" (later renamed "The Brian Keith Show"). Even in a more traditional occupation, Major "Hot Lips" Houlihan of "M*A*S*H" was very much the head nurse, providing a sharp contrast from the docile nurse Martha Hale of "Hennessey" days.

The trend toward working women in middle-class jobs has accelerated since the late 1970s and shows no sign of abating. In 1975 the first female lawyer in a dramatic lead role appeared in the person of "Kate McShane." Medical shows began to supplement nurses with female doctors as regular characters, such as "St. Elsewhere"'s Drs. Annie Cavanero, Cathy Martin, and Wendy Armstrong, and "Trauma Center"'s Dr. Brigitte Blaine. Women even graduated to the role of hospital administrator, in the person of "House Calls" character Ann Anderson and, later, Jane Jeffries.

Female law enforcers proliferated on cops 'n' robbers shows. They ranged from sexy supercops like "LAPD's" Christie Love, "Policewoman" Pepper Anderson, and "Bionic Woman" Jaime Sommers, to more realistic police officers like "Barney Miller"'s officers Whitworth and Baptista, "Chippies" Bonnie Clark and Sindy Carhill, and Robin Tataglia and Lucy Bates of "Hill Street Station." The shortlived "MacGruder and Loud" even offered a husband-and-wife team of California cops who must hide their marriage from the department so they can remain partners on the job.

Women also began to acquire business savvy as executives and even owners of businesses. At radio station "WKRP in Cincinnati," the staff was very much under the thumb of owner Lillian Carlson. Nor did "Los Angeles Tribune" publisher Margaret Pynchon brook any nonsense from staffers, not even crusty city editor Lou Grant. In the 1980s, the evening soaps offered tough businesswomen who acquired new properties and new husbands almost interchangeably, like "Dallas"'s Pamela Barnes Ewing Grayson, "Dynasty"'s Alexis Carrington Colby Dexter, and Abby Cunningham Ewing of "Knots Landing."

Even the journalistic profession, long a male preserve in prime time as in reality, began to acquire female representatives. Following in Mary Richards' footsteps were Jennifer Barnes, news anchor of Boston's WYN-TV on "Goodnight, Beantown"; hard-driving reporters Carla Mardigian and then Billie Newman on Lou Grant's staff; and even Mindy McConnell, who worked for KTNS-TV when she wasn't dealing with the alien Mork from planet Ork. Finally, "Murphy Brown" represents TV's current feminist ideal as a TV newswoman who is intensely career-oriented and independent, bulldozing her way into interviews and all-male social clubs with equal comic ferocity.

All the while, despite these genuinely new opportunities, television has continued to provide many more traditional portrayals. The 1970s began with banker Milburn Drysdale depending on his trusty girl Friday, Miss Jane, on "The Beverly Hillbillies," and English nanny Phoebe Figalilly taking equally good care of her math teacher employer on "Nanny and the Professor." Throughout the decade various male series stars relied on their female secretaries. They ranged from detective "Mannix"'s Peggy Fair, a Della Street clone, and attorney "Owen Marshall"'s legal secretary Frieda Krause, to the brash and breezy Carol, psychologist Bob Hartley's receptionist on "The Bob Newhart Show."

On the medical shows, meanwhile, the occasional female doctor continued to be eclipsed by far more numerous nurses. Even in the 1980s, shows like "Trapper John, M.D." preferred to focus on hoary stereotypes like loyal nurse-assistant "Starch" Willoughby and sexy young nurse "Ripples" Brancusi. The short-lived 1989 series "Nightingales" traded on the nurse-as-sex-kitten stereotype to a degree that brought protests from the nursing profession and hastened the show's cancellation. The 1980s also brought a profusion of female schoolteachers, who populated the faculty of New York's High School for the Performing Arts on "Fame," as well as mythical schools like "Fast Times at Ridgemont High" and "Square Pegs'" Weemawee High School. College teachers, however, remained mostly male.

The early 1980s also witnessed a profusion of cooks and waitresses, as a kind of déclassé version of the happy homemaker of yore. "Archie Bunker's Place" was staffed by Veronica Rooney, the sharp-tongued Irish cook, and Archie's niece-turned-waitress, Billie Bunker. On "Alice," Mel's Diner was worked by title character Alice, fun-loving Flo, and the more demure Vera, as well as later replacements Belle and Jolene. "It's a Living" featured a more upscale setting in a Los Angeles restaurant, but waiting tables was still the main order of business for a crew that included Lois, Dot, Vicki, and Cassie. Thus, even as new doors began to open for some female characters in recent years, others walked through them right back into the kitchen.

Female upward mobility on television was epitomized by Ann Romano of "One Day At A Time." She was a divorced mother trying to support two teen-aged daughters by working as a secretary. When one of her daughters entered college, Ann decided to go as well. (She had married and begun to raise her family right after high school.) After some travail, she eventually got a degree and began a career in advertising, ending up as a partner in a new agency. Thus Ann began the series with little education or occupational status and gradually worked her way into the upper middle class.

As a counterpoint to Ann Romano, consider the long but traditional career of the ubiquitous Lucy. During the 1950s Lucy Ricardo of "I Love Lucy" mainly wanted to raise her family, though she did have aspirations to break into show business, which husband Ricky regularly thwarted. During the 1960s, on "The Lucy Show," Lucy Carmichael was cast as a widow trying to snare a new husband. Partly to meet more eligible men, she went to work as a secretary in a bank. Throughout the 1970s, on "Here's Lucy," widow Lucy Carter worked for the Unique Employment Agency, which was owned by her brother-in-law. Lucille Ball finally moved up to ownership status when she inherited half of her husband's hardware store (which she shared with old nemesis Gale Gordon) in the short-lived 1986 flop "Life With Lucy." Lucy the career woman turned out to be a not-ready-for-prime-time player.

MAKE ROOM FOR MOMMY

Women not only hold lower-status jobs on television, they also tend to have a weaker occupational identity than men. Female characters are less likely than males either to hold a job or to be shown working at one. Only three out of five women have been identified as holding a paying job throughout television's history. Despite the rise of the TV career woman since Mary Richards joined WJM, the totals have been surprisingly consistent over the years. In the era of the sitcom homemaker prior to 1965, 43 percent of all female characters were either identified as housewives or had no known occupation outside the home. From 1965 through 1974, the breakthrough period for working women in lead roles, the proportion declined only to 40 percent. Since 1975, this figure again dropped slightly, to 37 percent. Overall, that makes an increase of only 6 percent across three decades in the proportion of working women on television.

Some of the difference stems from the persistence of housewives on television. The little woman who cleans house and takes care of the children is usually associated with television's early days. The enduring image of the aproned housewife as a bedrock of stability was established by a wide range of sitcoms. In many ways, TV's housewives seemed interchangeable during the 1950s. They spent their days dealing with children (Wally and Beaver, Ricky and David; Princess, Bud, and Kitten) and neighbors (the Mertzes and Nortons), while waiting for their sometimes bumbling husbands (from Ralph Kramden to Herbert Gillis) to come home. Through it all they represented domestic tranquility and provided a homey simplicity.

The 1960s featured some variations on the theme of sitcom housewives. There were rural comedy wives like Lisa Douglas of "Green Acres," who knew not a whit about cooking and housework. And there were positively unearthly housewives like Samantha Stevens of "Bewitched" and Morticia Frump Addams from that ghoulish family. In

"Gentle Ben," Ellen Wedloe kept up a household in the Florida Everglades that included a 650-lb. black bear as an honorary member. And Maureen Robinson showed that the nuclear family could survive in the Alpha Centauri star system in "Lost in Space."

Lily Munster and Morticia Addams notwithstanding, these housewives were for the most part more attractive and alluring than their earlier counterparts. Their careful coiffures and stylish attire helped them avoid the dowdy appearance previously deemed appropriate for television housewives. Their successors in the 1970s continued to keep up appearances. Carol Brady and Shirley Partridge kept up with fashion trends, as did young brides like Carrie Bratter on TV's all-black version of "Barefoot in the Park" and Nancy Smith, the president's daughter, on "Nancy." Sally McMillan of "McMillan and Wife" was young and gorgeous and dressed the part, as did Bridget Fitzgerald of "Bridget Loves Bernie" and Emily Hartley on "The Bob Newhart Show."

Some of these women, like Bridget and Emily, held jobs, but the audience usually saw them in their wifely roles. Nonetheless, they were neither the kindly nurturers of the 1950s family shows nor the zany wives of the far-out 1960s sitcoms. Many were childless, which eliminated the frenetic pacing of earlier shows. They were calmer, more together, with more time to be involved in activities outside the household. They were sometimes called upon to deal with real social issues, such as inflation, minorities' and women's rights, drug abuse, and runaway children. They also began to have serious problems of their own, like Maude's abortion, Edith's attempted rape, Bridget's Jewish in-laws, and woes that ranged from an adulterous husband to breast cancer on "Family."

The 1980s brought a continuation of these trends, except that outside careers have become much more obvious. In fact the "pure" housewife, whose life was circumscribed by home and family, has largely disappeared from prime time. Thus, Pam Davidson Hinkley portrayed a top-notch lawyer and loving wife on "The Greatest American Hero," as did Claire Huxtable on "The Cosby Show." Muriel Rush, a band singer before her marriage, became a successful free-lance photographer while looking after her college-aged daughters on "Too Close for Comfort." Home and work activities were often integrated in the plot. On "Newhart," Joanna Loudon helps husband Dick run a country inn, and police officer Marybeth Lacey was assisted by a very understanding husband. On "My Sister Sam," Samantha (Sam) Russell acted as a mother surrogate to sister Patti while running a successful photography business out of her apartment. And the inimitable "Roseanne" races back and forth between home and job trying to stay a step ahead of both the household chores and her work quotas at the plastics factory. It has been a long haul from Lucy to Lacey, but television seems to be making the transition to two-career families.

There is another, less obvious reason why women only rarely establish authoritative job identities on television. Even when their characters are assigned occupations, they are less likely to be shown actually working at their jobs than are males. Thus, a majority of plot lines involving women concern their personal or private lives rather than their work activities. Just under 60 percent of the female characters are shown in a purely personal context. That's nearly double the 33 percent of males whose roles don't concern their occupational activities. This ratio has narrowed somewhat over the years as the proportion of men shown at work has remained stable, while the proportion of working women has risen. Even since 1975, however, a majority (54 percent) of female roles has nothing to do with their occupations, compared to one in three male characters.

As noted, the best-known female leads of the 1950s and early 1960s rarely ventured beyond home and hearth. They were balanced somewhat by the nurses, librarians, teachers, and secretaries who appeared in shows with mainly male stars (excepting the occasional Gale Storm or Ann Sothern). Even as a new crop of working women entered prime time with the private eyes and superspies of the mid-1960s, other series began to show women balancing their careers and personal lives. "That Girl" Ann Marie was forever juggling her acting and modeling activities to make time for Donald, her boyfriend. Lawyer Patricia Marshall likewise balanced her law practice with an active social life. Even Lucy Carmichael/Carter was shown trying to meet the often competing demands of her children and her boss. "The Mary Tyler Moore Show" is often remembered in this context. It also marked a sharp contrast to the earlier "Dick Van Dyke Show," a prototype home-and-office comedy in which Miss Moore's character, housewife Laura Petrie, was confined to the home front.

Throughout the 1970s women continued to move slowly into shows that actually showed them at work. Ironically, this is one area in which the Lear women sounded a traditional note. Edith and Maude were both housewives without outside careers. Florida Evans' life also centered on her home and family. Louise Jefferson and Helen Willis were housewives whose only outside activities involved volunteer work. The female characters in "Chico and the Man" and "Sanford and Son" were usually involved in personal rather than work-related activities. Ann Romano, with her simultaneous concerns over career advancement, social life, and parental responsibilities, was the exception rather than the rule among this group.

Elsewhere the proliferating law enforcement shows offered increasing opportunities for writers to show both the personal and occupational aspects of female characters' lives. Such diverse shows as "Get Christie Love!," "The Bionic Woman," "Policewoman," "Charlie's Angels," "Kate McShane," and "Barney Miller" all featured women who worked at solving crimes while remaining open to personal (often romantic) involvements. In fact these women differed from the single-minded male crime fighter stereotype precisely in their openness to personal involvement. There were no female equivalents to "Hawaii Five-O"'s Steve McGarrett or Bumper Morgan of "The Blue Knight," not to mention earlier crime-fighting machines like Joe Friday and Elliot Ness. Thus, even when they leave the household, women are shown as more open to the personal side of life.

The past decade has actually seen something of a resurgence in popular shows that place women mainly in a personal context. The women in series like "Laverne and Shirley," "Three's Company," and "Eight is Enough" often had jobs but were rarely seen at work. The focus was on their family or social lives. The same is true of such recent trendsetting shows as "Family Ties," "Silver Spoons," "The Cosby Show," and "Kate & Allie." Even working women aren't as fully integrated as men into their careers, at least in the world of prime time.

PRISONERS OF SEX

Why are women less linked to the workaday world? One major reason is their traditional function of providing a romantic interest. In recent years, as scripts have become increasingly desublimated, romance has given way to sex, with no apologies offered for presenting women as overt sex objects. Throughout television's history, however, female characters have been defined in terms of their sexual identity to a greater degree than males. This is shown indirectly by the use of attractive young women who often function as window dressing in shows dominated by older, more authoritative male characters.

The typical female character has always been younger than her male counterpart. Women are about twice as likely as men to be portrayed as young adults between the ages of eighteen and twenty-nine. Thirty-five percent of all women fall into this category, compared to 18 percent of men. We found the opposite trend among mature adults, the thirty through fifty-nine age bracket, when characters tend to be most authoritative. By this definition, only a minority of women (49 percent) are portrayed as mature adults, compared to 70 percent of men. Since most characters are male, that means just over one out of five mature adults on television are women. These differences have remained almost unchanged over the years, with shifts of less than 5 percent in any age category across three decades.

Even a cursory review makes clear that Hollywood favors young women for just one reason. Although kindly mothers were the most memorable female characters of television's early years, there were plenty of pretty young things even then. There was photographer Bob Collins, who chose his dates from a bevy of beautiful models on "The Bob Cummings Show." In fact Bob referred to his workplace as "the harem." An equally successful ladies' man was "Bachelor Father," a Hollywood attorney who squired a succession of glamorous starlets. The sexiest girlfriend of the period was probably Edie Hart, the sultry jazz singer at Mother's, where Peter Gunn used to hang out.

A major infusion of young beauties was provided by the wave of action adventure shows pioneered by "77 Sunset Strip." Not only was the "cutie pie" series regular an essential part of the formula; each episode also brought with it a newly minted damsel in distress. You can't be a glamorous detective without an endless procession of fair maids to rescue. Beginning in the mid-1960s there was a profusion of pulchritude in continuing roles, ranging from Ginger and Mary Ann on "Gilligan's Island," to backwoods beauties like Elly May of the "Beverly Hillbillies" and the Bradley sisters on "Petticoat Junction," to dashing secret agents like Mrs. Peel and April Dancer.

All this was nothing compared to the cheesecake boom that began in the mid-1970s and has yet to abate. In addition to outright "jiggle shows" like "Charlie's Angels" and "Three's Company," the ogle quotient rose across the board. There were sexy sitcoms like "The Love Boat" and "Operation Petticoat," dramas like "Fantasy Island," and rural comedy/adventure series like "B.J. and the Bear" and "The Dukes of Hazzard," which provided their Li'l Abner heroes with plenty of Daisie Maes. In the 1980s this pattern began to change as the nighttime soaps discovered the allure of middle-aged sexpots. In addition to the requisite quota of sweet (and not so sweet) young things, viewers could choose from such fortyish and even fiftyish sex symbols as Alexis and Krystle of "Dynasty," Sable Colby of "The Colbys," and Valene and Abby Ewing and Karen MacKenzie of "Knots Landing." Even in its so-called decade of the older woman, television wasn't about to give up on women as sex objects. It just found a way to stretch the age limit.

Women on television behave as sexual creatures in more overt and directly measurable ways as well. Take TV's answer to Freud's famous question: What do women want? By a margin of 32 to 18 percent, women are more likely than men to act out of a desire for sex, romance, or marriage. On the other hand, men are more likely to be motivated by political concerns or ideological principles. Here the margin is nearly four to one, 27 to 7 percent. Thus, television's dichotomy between the public and private spheres influences men and women's behavior as well as their backgrounds.

A similar split is evident from the methods characters use to get what they want. Men are over twice as likely as women to rely on their authority and on violent means, while women are twice as likely to depend on the help of "champions" and seven times as likely to use sex appeal or romantic charm. As usual, there has been little change in these sex-typed ends and means over the years. So while men tend to exert either force or forcefulness, women depend on romantic charm and the kindness of strangers.

The games women play have changed somewhat over the years. Flibbertigibbets like "Petticoat Junction"'s Bradley sisters and hard-core manhunters like the girls in the office on "Private Secretary" have lately given way to cool independent singles like Christine Cagney and Kate McArdle. But the name of the game is still the same—to catch or hold a man, whether as a long-term provider or (lately) a one-night stand. The single woman on the prowl for a husband is a sitcom caricature dating back to Eve Arden's high school English teacher in "Our Miss Brooks," forever frustrated in her efforts to land the shy biology teacher Mr. Boynton. Other representatives of the genre range from comedy writer Sally Rogers on "The Dick Van Dyke Show" to Mary Richards' friend Rhoda Morganstern. In fact, when wedding bells finally rang for Rhoda in her own spin-off series, the husband-hunting activity shifted to her younger sister Brenda, in a kind of Rhoda redux role.

Another perennial theme concerns the complications that arise from women's fickleness, jealousies, or romantic strivings. A typical example comes from "I Dream of Jeannie." The title character is a genuine genie, remarkably well preserved for her two thousand years, who develops a crush on Tony Nelson, the astronaut who finds her in a bottle. In a 1969 segment we coded, Jeannie thinks Tony is cheating on her because his companion on a mission is a sergeant named Marion. She shows up on their plane and causes pandemonium by using her magic powers to switch the top-secret film he's carrying. When Jeannie discovers that Marion is a male, she changes the film back again. Jeannie was actually one of the more successful husband hunters in TV history. In her first season she made life so difficult for Tony's fiancee Melissa that the poor woman disappeared from the series. Then, after four years of being chased by a jealous genie, Tony finally let himself be caught.

This vein is by no means confined to comedy. Consider that hardy perennial, the fool for love, which popped up on a very serious "Playhouse 90" telecast. In this 1956 story, the widow of a shipping magnate takes a cruise on one of the ships she now controls. Also on board is a Latin American revolutionary being extradited for trial. The woman falls in love with him and tries to convince the captain to release him before they reach port. He refuses, on principle, even after she offers to give him title to the vessel. Then, as his boss, she orders him to release the rebel. Again he refuses, on the ground that she has no authority over a ship's captain at sea. Readers will recall that women do have difficulty exercising authority on television.

In recent years the motives of marriage and romance have been joined by less sublimated forms of desire. Sometimes this is sanctioned by marital relations. Thus, one episode of "Eight is Enough" avails itself of that old chestnut, the husband and wife whose kids never let them, well, have time to themselves. Tom and Abby Bradford employ various stratagems too clichéd to recount in order to get rid of the children. Meanwhile, Abby flirts and acts seductively to keep her husband's interest up. Alas, they never do find the opportunity to be alone together. After all, this is the family hour time slot.

No such constraints have ever hampered the intrepid Christine Cagney, who epitomizes television's portrayal of the sexually active single woman. In a 1982 episode we coded, Chris is attracted to a defense lawyer she's dating. She grows increasingly disappointed and troubled, however, when he fails to make a pass at her. Finally, after dinner at her apartment, she takes the bull by the horns. She tells him, "by now we should be getting a little more familiar." Reminding him that his parking space is valid only until 6:00 A.M., she hands him the keys and asks, "We don't want to wake up that early, do we?" It turns out that her friend can take a hint. Imagine Cagney's surprise the next morning, though, when she finds out the fellow was having qualms because he's married. Sometimes you just can't win.

TV's women are not only more likely to want romance, they are also more likely to use sex to get what they want. Given the constraints of network censors, this usually means the promise of sex, offered in somewhat oblique fashion. Back in 1960, an attractive young wife on "Route 66" in effect declares her intentions by walking in on her husband's business meeting while wearing only a swimsuit. She wants Buzz to take her away from all this, but her method of enlisting him is made clear less from the dialogue than from a sultry saxophone playing on the soundtrack. These days the pitch is likely to be more direct. In a 1979 episode of "Alice," the lusty waitress Flo gets the show business bug. She decides to network in time-honored fashion by getting to know a country singer she meets as a guest on the "The Dinah Shore Show." She tells him, "Here is a matchbook from Peppy Siesta's Motor Court. Call that number and you won't be 'Lonesome Larry' no more."

The most proficient practitioners of sexual promises are the female detectives and secret agents who routinely use their charms to lead the bad guys on to their doom. Charlie's angels made this approach to crimefighting into something of an art form, but it goes back at least to Honey West, the female James Bond who lasted one season in the mid-1960s. Among the shows in our study, a typical femme fatale was a U.S. agent on "I Spy" named Melanie. She flirts and teases her way into the villain's lair, stretches out seductively in his bedroom, fends him off "since things might get out of hand," and emerges with both the top-secret microfilm and her virtue intact. Apparently this stratagem is unlikely to grow stale with overuse. In an episode of "Buck Rogers," a glamorous agent of the Earth Defense Directorate lures a crime syndicate boss to her room, where she gets the drop on him. Television writers are apparently confident that bad guys will be suckers for a sexy come-on at least until the twenty-fifth century.

Rounding out this portrait of woman as the more sexually oriented gender are those characters for whom sex serves as both ends and means, both what they want and how they try to get it. One example will suffice, drawn from a "Dick Van Dyke Show" episode we sampled. The character in question (and her character is in question throughout) is a young dancer named Joan. When scriptwriters Rob and Buddy decide to put her in the Allen Brady show, she kisses Rob and tells him that she loves him. Naturally, Rob's wife Laura walks in at this point, and the plot is off and running. After Joan does some more heavy-duty flirting with Rob, Laura tells him to chase Joan to scare her off, "but don't, under any circumstances, catch her." Rob unfortunately does just that, and Joan agrees to run off to Mexico with him. Of course, she first calls her boyfriend, Ernie, to inform him of this slight change of plan. Ernie arrives and slugs Rob, to Joan's delight, since her real motive was to win Ernie's devotion by making him jealous. So Joan gets Ernie, Laura gets Rob back, and Rob gets a shiner and a new appreciation of the sexual wiles of women.

From "Mama" to Maude

Television's treatment of women is more than the sum of its individual characters. It is also reflected in story themes and plot lines that deal with women's role in American society. Our study detected fifty-four instances where scripts address issues of women's rights or equality between the sexes. Despite all the sex-role stereotyping of female characters, most shows that raise such issues have come out foursquare for women's rights: 71 percent support feminist arguments, while only 7 percent reject them, with the rest taking no position. There was also a clear shift over time. Prior to 1965, 22 percent of the episodes coded rejected the feminist position. Thereafter not a single episode derided notions of sexual equality.

Perhaps the most common theme is that women's abilities should not be underestimated. They can accomplish as much as males if given a fair opportunity. An episode of "Eight is Enough" raised this point in the context of a family camping trip. The men of the family, Tom Bradford and his four sons, plan to go off alone without the women. But his wife and four daughters get wind of this plan and protest their exclusion. They insist they can hold their own in the wilds and argue that the men are being insensitive. Eventually they win the argument, and the whole family goes together.

More often this theme comes up in the context of women's work aspirations. Although job opportunities for female characters were quite limited before the mid-1970s, this theme has recurred in various program formats throughout television's history. The earliest version we observed came in a 1956 segment of Loretta Young's dramatic anthology. In this

137

episode Miss Young plays a young woman struggling to meet the mort-gage payment on her small farm. The bank officers are skeptical about trusting a woman to run a farm alone, but she charms them into granting an extension on her loan. When the loan finally comes due, after many travails, it appears at first that she can't come up with the payment. The bank president opines that they shouldn't trust "young ladies" with such responsibilities. The woman demurs and, in the end, she prevails. Throughout, the struggle of a small farmer is also presented as a woman's struggle to prove her worth against male skepticism.

A decade later virtually the same theme was played out in a Western setting on "The Road West." When a small-town doctor dies, his daugh-ter tries to fill in for him. Early in the show she is forced to fend off the repeated unwanted advances of a male patient. Later she decides to go to the aid of a farmer who needs her help. The liveryman is reluctant to give a team of horses to a woman, but she insists. During the trip, her inde-pendence is underscored by an encounter with a farmer and his wife. The farmer is a brute who orders his terrified wife to do his bidding. The con-trast of this wretched cowering woman with the self-sufficient heroine could hardly be more obvious.

About the same time, "The Jean Arthur Show" applied a lighter touch to the notion that a woman can more than hold her own in a man's world. The star plays Patricia Marshall, a vivacious fortyish widow who is the best defense attorney in town. In the episode we coded, however, she is asked to teach manners and sophistication to a mobster so that he will be able to find a good woman. Of course, her protégé falls for her and is about to pop the question when she is called to work on a fast-moving case. Her breakneck pace quickly proves too much for a mere man to handle, and the pupil is ready to drop from exhaustion while Patricia is still going strong. Eventually Patricia explains that she enjoys his company but can't give up her freedom and fast-paced lifestyle to become his wife. They agree that she needs to remain free to live her active life without apron strings attached. Quite a trick for the 1966 sea-son, when "That Girl"'s dizzy young actress Ann Marie represented the TV sitcom's idea of a working woman.

Bringing this motif up to date was a recent episode of "Hardcastle and McCormick," on which a young female clerk at the police department discovers an undercover operation that has run amok. She falls for McCormick, who is helping her uncover the scheme, but she nonetheless insists that he treat her as an equal. A leitmotif of the script concerns McCormick's repeated efforts to leave her behind and relegate her to unimportant tasks, to ensure her safety while he goes off to fight the bad guys. The script, however, opts for equality over chivalry. She insists on being involved and, in the end, proves a useful partner to the intrepid detective.

Thus, despite its depiction of women as the weaker sex in many ways, television has also presented object lessons of women proving themselves men's equals through pluck and determination. The clear lesson is that, whatever their traditional status, women possess the potential to compete effectively in supposedly male pursuits. An even more basic lesson, also observed repeatedly, is that women are independent beings and not men's chattel. For example, a 1965 segment of "Chrysler Theatre" concerned an overly possessive husband in the old West. At one point he accuses his wife of planning to leave him for a rival named Paxton and threatens to shoot them both. She asks, "Do you think I'm some piece of property. . . you can kill a man for?" He responds, "Yes, I do [kissing her]. . . your body. . .[passionate kisses] I own. . . If you turn my property over to Paxton I'll do a little shooting to get it back." Angered, his wife breaks away from him and leaves. Later he realizes that she really loves him, and that his possessive and domineering approach threatens their marriage. He makes peace with himself and promises to show more respect and understanding for his wife.

A 1963 segment of "East Side, West Side" gave a Freudian twist to the theme. This time the problem is a father's domination of his daughter. He tries to keep her cloistered from the outside world and especially the boyfriend she loves. He also tries to keep her away from the show's social worker protagonists, who attempt to intercede. At one point he argues that he has a right to make decisions for "his kid." A social worker asks tartly whether she's his kid or his maid. But the program's main point is delivered by Frieda, the head of the welfare agency. She accuses him of a vision of life in which "boys are hoods and grabbers who take what they can. . . .You are the father of a child who stopped being a child and became a woman. That is what is shining in your eyes, not the love of law and order."

In the 1970s television began to supplement these general expressions of support for women's rights with more contemporary themes. A leader in this area was Norman Lear's "Maude." Many of the plots in this series revolved around Maude Findlay's frequently comic but always serious efforts to assert both her own independence and the rights of modern women. In one episode in our sample, Maude is directing a 1975 bicentennial celebration. She decides that its theme should be famous women in history. Her husband Walter and the other men involved disagree; they're afraid no one will come. Maude comes under considerable pressure to change her mind, and she wavers briefly. Then she remembers what the show is all about. In her own words, "the show was supposed to inspire women to strive and struggle for their place in life." Taking heart from her own principles, she decides to stick it out: "The whole point of the show is not quitting but persevering for one's rights." Impressed, her husband rallies to her side, and the show is a huge success.

Less well remembered but no less in the forefront of feminist scripting was the 1973 sitcom "Adam's Rib," named after the Tracy-Hepburn film about dueling husband-and-wife lawyers. Half the show's writers were women, and many of the scripts tackled women's rights themes. In the episode in our study, defense attorney Amanda Bonner becomes outraged at the legal double standard that subjects women (but not men) to arrest for sexual solicitation. To prove her point, she goes to a bar and deliberately gets herself arrested for picking up an undercover cop staked out there. She explains to her district attorney husband (and the audience) that she did it to show up the legal system's hypocrisy, since she neither mentioned money nor promised any sexual activity. Her husband takes on her defense and, in court, says the case will show how women are denied rights that men enjoy. Eventually the charges against her are dropped, and, to drive the point home, the arresting officer is reprimanded.

It was not only high-profile feminist-oriented shows that began endorsing more activist forms of women's liberation. But the less socially committed shows tended to have things both ways, first taking potshots at "libbers" and then piously putting down the traditionalists. An example comes from "The Jimmy Stewart Show," a short-lived early seventies sitcom featuring the star as James Howard, an avuncular anthropology professor. In one scene we learn that James' wife Martha has joined a consciousness-raising and civic action organization with the acronym "WAG," for Women's Action Group. James cracks that it really stands for Women Against Gentlemen. Their young son complains that "they're always having meetings and causing trouble," and James chimes in, "kind of like Congress in skirts." Martha has the last word, however, explaining that "we WAG women are trying to make this man-made world a better place." The show clearly endorses this unexceptionable sentiment, thereby having its chauvinism and berating it too.

Still, a decade earlier the script might well have denied Martha her rebuttal. For television has not always applauded such sentiments. A case in point comes from the aptly titled 1950s sitcom "My Favorite Husband." The main characters are George and Liz Cooper, a bank executive and his scatterbrained wife. In one episode Liz, a typical suburban housewife, decides there must be more to life than just cooking and cleaning. She decides to write a play that will express her disaffection with the traditional homemaker's role. George decides that he shouldn't stifle his wife's needs and arranges for her to go to a cabin in the mountains where she can concentrate on her play. As she struggles to write, without much success, George bumbles around at home trying to handle the household chores. Finally George begs her to come home, though he tells her he has no right to ask her to give up her new life and admits, "I stifled you into being a scullery maid." If this show were being done today, Liz would accept his apology and return with assurances that her career needs would be accommodated. But this is 1956. In the actual script, she replies, "Well, then, that is what being a woman means, George. I accepted those terms when I married you. You have a right to ask me to come home. . . .I'd rather be your wife than anyone else on earth." Liz returns home with renewed dedication to her role as a happy homemaker.

A few years later, the question of appropriate sex roles was raised in quite different fashion on "Ensign O'Toole," a typical service comedy set aboard a destroyer. In this episode an attractive Russian ballerina named Anya defects by swimming out to the ship and requesting asylum. When the ship is ordered to bring her to the United States, she demands to be treated as an equal and sets about scrubbing, swabbing decks, and taking KP duty. Then O'Toole convinces the ship's executive officer that it's a mistake to treat her as "one of the men." He argues that her desire for equal treatment "stems from Russian thinking. . . . We don't want her to arrive on the shores of America proud of her treatment as a man. . . . We want her to arrive proud of our treatment of her as a woman." The change in treatment is a success, and Anya becomes kittenish and seductive or, as an officer puts it, "a beautiful testimony to freedom." The only problem arises when she's scheduled to hold a press conference on arrival. She refuses to come out because she just doesn't have a thing to wear.

This show is interesting for the way it turns a feminist argument on its head. Its premise is that sex roles are indeed socially determined, but traditional roles are the American way. The desire for equal treatment, by contrast, is the product of communist indoctrination! The theme echoes "Ninotchka," without the Lubitsch touch—inside every female commissar lurks an all-American desire for silk stockings.

To round out these examples of the way we were, consider how a 1963 "Ben Casey" segment presents a modern career woman. Dr. Casey is treating a young female lawyer (incidentally, the earliest female lawyer to appear in our study). An unpleasant and embittered person, she went on an alcoholic binge and tried to kill herself. Later she reveals the reason behind her unhappiness and self-destructive behavior. Her mother died when she was a child, and her father, a prominent judge, tried to make her into his ersatz son. He forced her to compete first in sports and then in the law. Once, she tells the earnest Dr. Casey, she bought a doll and tried to hide it. But her single-minded father found it and threw it away. Eventually the pressure to succeed in male fields drove her to drink. A cautionary tale, indeed, and not one you would be likely to see a quarter century later.

TWO FACES OF EVE

Television has shown that it can tell both feminist and traditionalist tales about women's place in American society. The dominant message has always supported woman's rights and rejected sex role stereotyping. An undercurrent of traditionalist sentiment remained until the mid-1960s, when it virtually disappeared as a plot motif. By the 1970s themes of sexual equality became more timely, often including references to the rapidly growing women's movement and its focus on discrimination and consciousness-raising. In the 1980s, it was less of an issue and more of a given, with women's equality taken for granted. When a character in "The Cosby Show" incautiously voices the sentiment that women's place is in the home, the entire Huxtable family ridicules the notion. There's hardly a conflict; it's more a matter of correcting an embarrassing anachronism.

The upshot is that television sends mixed messages about women. The roles played by female characters provide some powerful reinforcement for traditional ideas about women's proper place. Throughout television's history viewers have been exposed to female characters with lower status and less authority than males. The concerns of women on television tend to revolve around either home or "him." The edges have softened somewhat in recent years, so that this portrait is not so sharply etched as it once was. The proportion of working women and divorcees is certainly rising, and "December Bride" is a distant memory. But television still balances Kate with Allie, just as Edith Bunker used to follow Mary Richards on CBS's Saturday night lineup.

Many of these traits have been documented before. During the 1970s scholars began to study the traits of television's female characters. Their conclusions are very similar to ours, although the measures are sometimes different. The results were summarized in a 1982 National Institute for Mental Health report: Men greatly outnumber women; they are older and hold higher prestige jobs; they are more authoritative and represent the public realm of politics and work, while women occupy the private realm of home and family.[5] Our study traces these characteristics back to the early years of television and shows how slowly they have changed.

At the same time, our study reveals a longstanding dichotomy between the portrayals of individual characters and the themes addressed by the scripts. This thematic analysis is a critical component of any effort to understand television's worldview, because programs are more than the sum of their characters. The plots and scripts present conflicts, provide options, and drive home morals that create a framework of meaning for the characters. The demographics and behavior of female characters are important to know, but no less so than the overt messages the program proffers about the proper place of women in society.

Thus, the theme of women's rights has always been prominent in prime time, and characters who deride women's abilities are now invariably shot down by the script. This facet of the study fails to support feminist critics who charge television with nothing less than the "symbolic annihilation" of women.[6] The overall picture is more ambiguous. What television says about women in general is often quite different from what it shows about particular women.

This discrepancy probably reflects the inevitable compromises between social conscience and commercial incentive among creators of mass entertainment. The writers and producers we surveyed present themselves as progressive on feminist issues, but they are hardly radical. For example, they overwhelmingly believe feminists should have greater influence and reject the notion that a woman's place is in the home, but most also reject preferential hiring treatment for women. Moreover, since virtually all are male, their shows may reflect a discrepancy between their conscious "ideological" sentiments and the unquestioned assumptions that shape their female characters.

Finally, the success of a series depends on its appeal to popular tastes, which tend toward the traditional almost by definition. Thus, "Cagney & Lacey" began as an avowedly feminist show that concentrated on breaking down stereotypes as the heroines broke up crime rings. But when initial ratings were poor, CBS executives decided the show was "too harshly women's lib. . . too tough, too hard, and not feminine." An unnamed network source told *TV Guide* that "The American public doesn't respond to the bra burners, the fighters. . . .We perceived them as dykes."[7] As a result, Cagney was recast with a softer, more "feminine" actress in the part, although the character remained socially and sexually "liberated."

For all that, the mid-1980s featured a breakthrough in depicting stronger and more professionally competent women. The watershed year was 1984, which saw the first screenings of "Cagney & Lacey," "Kate & Allie," Angela Lansbury as a mystery writer detective in "Murder, She Wrote," a male-female cop team in "Hunter," and two popular series that reversed the traditional homemaker-breadwinner roles—"Who's The Boss" and "Charles in Charge." Another change has been the introduction of female "buddy" shows like "Cagney," "Kate," "Golden Girls," and "Designing Women." According to CBS executive Harvey Shepherd, "There is nothing coincidental about the trend. Traditionally, if you used women in prominent roles. . . they had to be in nonthreatening roles. But there is really a sociological change going on. . . .There is a growing acceptance of the more liberated role of women. Our schedule reflects that."[8]

One source of this shift is audience demographics. The networks' audience is becoming more heavily female, as males are drained off by the "spice and slice" sex and violent action programming available on cable channels. Further, women are most likely to purchase many of the products, such as cosmetics and household goods, that are advertised heavily on prime-time shows.[9] But pressure for change is coming from the supply side as well as the demand side. The new shows reflect the personal perspectives and social commitments of the first generation of successful female writers and producers. Those working in the comedy genre include Diane English ("My Sister Sam," "Foley Square," "Murphy Brown"), Linda Bloodworth-Thomason ("Designing Women"), and Susan Harris ("Soap," "Golden Girls," "Empty Nest"). Among their counterparts in drama are Barbara Corday ("Cagney & Lacey"), Terry Louise Fisher ("L.A. Law," "Hooperman") and Esther Shapiro ("Dynasty," "The Women's Room").

All these women received their first major writing or producing credits in the past ten years, most within the past five. Each created or developed concepts for female-centered shows that have been hits with audiences and critics. Their shows have featured strong-willed and sharp-tongued professionally successful women, who often function within a wider circle of female "types." A common device is to contrast the powerhouse character with traditional foils like a scatterbrained friend, a sex kitten, or a June Cleaver-style mother figure. The strong character sometimes serves as a mentor or role model for the others.

Like many contemporary TV characters, the tube's liberated women share a tentative, ambivalent view of life. They want a "relationship," but only on terms they can live with. They want family ties, but are wary of the commitment and bother, or the effect on their self-image. They want career success, but wonder about the cost to their personal development. Characters like hard-driving Murphy Brown reflect Diane English's own perspective on the changing social persona of women: "Nice and sweet are out. TV's new women aren't trying to please other people. . . . Not being afraid of what people think of you is in." Similarly, comedienne Roseanne Arnold so resisted what she considered stereotypical aspects of her character in "Roseanne" that she forced the departure of the show's (male) executive producer.[10]

As television enters the 1990s, Ben Stein writes, "A medium once studded with manly men and shrinking women is now peopled with strong, aggressive women—women who kill, women bossing around men, and women without men."[11] Yet Stein's description is composed of equal parts wit and hyperbole. The change is undeniable, but it still takes place against a backdrop of traditional mothers, sex symbols, and unthreatening comediennes. Women's place in television may be undergoing a decisive shift at the hands of Hollywood's newly empowered feminists. But, despite the more rapid change in recent years, television's portrayal of women has long included some progressive flourishes that stand out against a more traditional landscape.

This mixed bag reflects the conflicting tendencies that feed into scripts and storylines. The fantasy world of prime time is neither a pure reflection of popular taste nor the product of a consistent ideological agenda. Television's view of women is influenced partly by what its creators think the audience wants, partly by what they think it needs, and partly by the stereotypes and assumptions they inadvertently project onto their creations. Put it all together and you get a curiously ambivalent view of women that runs from Alice to Allie, from Edith to Maude, from Lucy to Lacey. According to television, woman is man's equal, but women are still the second sex.

―――――⇒>●<⇐―――――

4

ALL IN THE FAMILY

And there ain't no nothin' we can't love each other through
What will we do, baby, without us?
                    —"Family Ties" theme song
My husband complained that he needed more space. . . .So I
locked him out.
                    —Roseanne Arnold

O ne wintry week in 1953, America held a family reunion, courtesy of the newest mass medium. On January 20, millions of viewers saw Dwight D. Eisenhower sworn in as the nation's president and symbolic father-figure for the 1950s. It was the first coast-to-coast broadcast of a presidential inauguration, an early hint of television's ability to create a national town meeting. But millions more were still recovering from the really big show of the night before. After happily suffering through Lucy's cravings for papaya milk shakes and Ricky's sympathetic morning sickness, the largest audience in television's brief history was there to congratulate Lucy Ricardo on the birth of Little Ricky. Lucille Ball was unable to attend the celebration. She was busy giving birth to Desiderio Alberto Arnez IV that same night.

Little Ricky's birth was only the first of many life transitions that TV viewers have vicariously celebrated or mourned. There were the children who grew up and went off to college, from Betty Anderson ("Father

149

Knows Best") to Denise Huxtable ("The Cosby Show"), or who left home to get married, like "Ozzie and Harriet"'s sons David and Ricky. More recently, TV marriages began to end in divorce, like those of Rhoda Morgenstern or Lionel and Jenny Jefferson. There were also tragedies, like the deaths of Edith Bunker and Col. Henry Blake of "M*A*S*H." And there have been difficult moral decisions, like Maude Findlay's abortion. Through good times and bad, America's families have never wavered in their lasting love affair with their video counterparts.

THOSE WERE THE DAYS

In the early years family comedies were a major force in television, as series like "The Adventures of Ozzie and Harriet," "Make Room for Daddy," "Father Knows Best," "Leave It to Beaver," and "The Many Loves of Dobie Gillis" came to dominate the world of television comedy. In shows like these, families lived in harmony and were seemingly undisturbed by major problems. Parents faced minor family strife with gentleness and easy humor. Impetuous, curious children suffered through relatively benign childhood traumas that could always be resolved in a half hour. It was a golden age of innocence and inconsequence.

The late 1950s presented the first deviation from the standard two-parent family as the stars of television comedy. This was the introduction of single-parent households. In series like "Buckskin," "The Eve Arden Show," "The Farmer's Daughter," "The Rifleman," "The Virginian," "Bonanza," "Bachelor Father," "My Three Sons," "The Beverly Hillbillies," and "The Andy Griffith Show" widows or widowers headed up households that appeared very much like their two-parent counterparts. If these parents encountered any unique problems in raising children alone, they were almost never mentioned. For single moms or dads the problems of parenthood could be dealt with through sage advice and gentle humor. These adults became superparents who played both mother and father to their children.

Television turned increasingly to silly or farfetched premises in the family comedies of the 1960s. The popular rural comedies like "The Real

McCoys," "The Beverly Hillbillies," and "Petticoat Junction" used cultural clashes as the main source of humor. In "Bewitched" it was the magical powers of Samantha the witch (and the rest of her family) that presented challenges for husband Darren. David Crabtree discovered that his dead mother had been reincarnated as an old car in "My Mother the Car." Patty and Cathy Lane were identical cousins whose identity changes were played for laughs in "The Patty Duke Show." Despite the unusual situations and bizarre circumstances, there were no insoluble problems in these families. In fact, few serious problems were ever confronted.

Families were central in some dramas during this time as well. "Bonanza," "The Rifleman," and "The Virginian" continued to present families confronting the trials and tribulations of the Old West. These problems tended to be more significant than anything in the comedies, but they were not beyond solution by these tight-knit clans. Family problems remained philosophical battles between good and evil. They still avoided the topical issues that would arise in the late 1960s.

RELEVANCE AND ESCAPISM

The family-based dramas of the late 1960s and early 1970s were marked not so much by a change in family structure as a change in the types of issues raised. The featured families were among the first continuing characters to move into social relevancy. This was the period when "relevance" became a campus catchword. It meant outspoken criticism and broad-ranging, pontifical statements on the nature of the world, mankind, and the "system." Issues were addressed as ideological battles over policy choices, not as philosophical battles of good vs. bad or right vs. wrong. Almost any argument could turn into a debate about how to deal with current social ills. The draft, the war in Vietnam, racial violence and discrimination, Indian rights, sex and age discrimination were all thrown into family discussions and arguments.

Yet, even as dramatic series moved into social commentary, the family comedies remained as silly as ever. Shows like "I Love Lucy," "Petticoat Junction," "The Doris Day Show," "The Brady Bunch," and "Bewitched" continued to present frenetic or farfetched comedy. In a more sedate vein "Family Affair" and "Mayberry, R.F.D." maintained the thread of nonthreatening humor so popular in 1950s comedies. None of these shows, however, touched on the issues of the day or presented any serious problems for the starring families. This was laughter for laughter's sake, an escape route from the problems of reality.

Television did make two forays into social relevance with family comedies of the late 1960s, but both were rather low key and proceeded without controversy. In "Julia," Diahann Carroll played a widowed black nurse trying to raise a young son. She faced problems and obstacles on several fronts, none of them insurmountable. She handled her problems with the dignity, warmth, and gentleness found in most family comedies of an earlier era. In the process she taught her young son lessons in tolerance and decency. Overall this was a show structured as a social comment (a black mother, widowed by the war in Vietnam, living in an integrated building) but without much topical content.

A similar approach was taken by "The Courtship of Eddie's Father." Tom Corbett was managing editor of a newsmagazine as well as a widowed single parent. Tom and his son were very close, and lessons were presented in a kind, loving manner. The theme song said it best: "People, let me tell you 'bout my best friend. . . . Whether we're talking man to man or we're talking dad to son. . . ." Together this pair learned about discrimination, national differences, greed, politics, and other issues of the day. With subtle coaxing and reassurance, Tom directed his son's curiosity, helping him to learn the lessons of life.

KING LEAR

In 1971 a family comedy premiered that would become one of the most controversial and widely watched shows in the history of television. "All in the Family" was the first in a string of hits produced by Norman Lear and his associates. These shows provided a different kind of social commentary from that seen in the late 1960s. The Lear comedies ("All

152

in the Family," "Maude," "Good Times," "The Jeffersons," "One Day At A Time," "Sanford and Son," "Chico and the Man," "Mary Hartman, Mary Hartman") charted the course of parents and children through tough social and personal problems while trying to keep the family together. The world of these families was full of problems and hazards, but each was approached in relation to one particular family. In their lives, inflation was not an abstraction debated by economists; it was what made Edith buy Archie a cheaper brand of beer. Discrimination wasn't some inherent evil of a racist or sexist system; it was what made it hard for the black Lionel Jefferson to find an apartment or Ann Romano to find a job. All topical discussions had a direct relationship to the family. Solutions to problems were practical and specific, not sweeping reforms that changed laws and social practices.

In many respects these series were the family comedies of the 1950s turned on their heads. "Father Knows Best," "Ozzie and Harriet," and "Make Room for Daddy" became "All in the Family," "The Jeffersons," and "Good Times." "Bachelor Father" became "One Day At A Time" and "Sanford and Son." Family life moved from homes where life was peaceful, with only simple problems, to homes where life was in an uproar and the problems often divisive. In place of gentle humor came coarse insults. Homespun warmth was replaced by vigorous tongue-lashings. Lucy Ricardo, Harriet Nelson, and Margaret Anderson would have been shocked to see their Lear counterparts Ann Romano, Maude Findlay, and Mary Hartman. No one would confuse Archie Bunker with Bill Anderson or, for that matter, Mike "Meathead" Stivic with Bud Anderson. As carefully as the family comedies of the 1950s had avoided issues, the Lear families sought out conflict.

These families found themselves facing a broad range of problems. There were Maude's divorces and abortion. Divorced mother Ann Romano tried to reenter the dating scene while dealing with teenage drinking, premarital sex, and sexism. Archie and Edith had to deal with an attempted rape, the murder of a friend, and the slow decline of their neighborhood. The Evans family ("Good Times") lived in poverty in an urban housing project, threatened by crime, drug abuse, and landlord abuses.

In the 1970s real world problems would invade the lives of more than just the Lear families. For Alice Hyatt, the star of "Alice," family problems included explaining homosexuality to her son, teenage drinking, and dealing with new sexual mores when returning to the dating scene after widowhood. Mrs. Thomas, the divorced mother of two in "What's Happening!" faced a different set of problems raising two children in a large city. There was the always short money supply, a conniving conman for an ex-husband, and the threat of crime. "Hello Larry" featured Larry Alder as a divorced father trying to raise two teenage daughters on his own. Appropriately, by the 1980s even the once perfect life of little Theodore "the Beaver" Cleaver turned sour. A 1983 made-for-TV movie ("Still the Beaver") reunited most of the Cleaver family, only to find the Beav unemployed and facing divorce. Even TV's one-time archetype of the ideal childhood had to grow up to meet the harsh world of the contemporary sitcom.

THE FAMILY HOUR

In the fall of 1975 the three networks, under pressure on several fronts, finally acted on longstanding complaints about television violence and sexual content. They agreed to "sanitize" their early evening programming and created what was called the Family Viewing Time. Family Viewing Time prohibited "programming inappropriate for viewing by a general family audience" from eight to nine o'clock every night.[1] What were the implications of this decision for family life on television?

There were relatively few effects in the world of comedy. Some of the potentially offensive shows were simply moved to later time slots. Content was not suddenly changed, since the controversial Lear comedies were ensconced among the most popular programming on the air. These early evening time slots were filled with some of the safer Lear shows, spinoffs of "The Mary Tyler Moore Show," several variety shows, and reincarnations of the silly, implausible, frenetic humor pioneered in shows like "The Beverly Hillbillies," "I Dream of Jeannie," and "My Mother the Car." This structure was recast in the popular series "Happy Days" and lesser known series like "Mr. T and Tina," "Apple Pie," "That's My Mama," and "A New Kind of Family." The shows tried to keep the laughs rolling through a string of contrived or unlikely situations. The families faced no serious problems and held no real opinions. They were in a world without substance, always aiming for one more joke. But their time was past. With the exception of "Happy Days," none of the "don't worry be happy" family comedies lasted long.

Dramatic programming changed more significantly, since the family hour encouraged the production of less controversial material. Family dramas turned to homey, deeply caring, nurturing family situations as a new context for social commentary. As in the Lear comedies, they provided commentary rooted in specific situations rather than sweeping statements on the nature of the world. Some of these shows, like "The Waltons," "Little House On the Prairie," "Apple's Way," "The New Land," and "Family Holvak," were set in rural communities and drew heavily on small-town stereotypes. Others, like "Eight is Enough," "Harris and Company," and "Joe and Sons," were urban and contemporary. The problems confronting these families were difficult but rarely controversial. For the Walton family, it was the Depression followed by World War II, punctuated with a host of personal traumas including severe illness and antisemitism. The cast of "Little House On the Prairie" had to deal with natural disasters, the problems and stigmas of blindness, and economic hardships.

Out of this cycle of dramas, only "The Waltons," "Little House," and "Eight is Enough" enjoyed any popularity or longevity. The real future of dramatic television was in the dramas presented in late evening. It was shows like "Skag," "Family," and "James at 15" that showed families confronting truly daunting issues. These were often the toughest problems facing society, and they posed real threats to family stability. In "Skag" a steelworker's family faced economic hardship, teenage sex, unemployment, prostitution, and impotence. The Lawrence clan of "Family" confronted adultery, blindness, alcoholism, sexism, and terminal illness. The fifteen-year-old James Hunter would lose his virginity in the most controversial episode of "James at 15," while his family dealt with other premarital affairs, venereal disease, and alcoholism. These families, unlike their predecessors, saw every human weakness, flaw, and social problem as they tried to stay together and care for each other. These series laid the groundwork for the realist dramas that would come in the 1980s.

The onset of the 1980s meant more changes in family life on TV. Prime-time soap operas had replaced many of the earlier socially relevant dramas. The Lear families were beginning to fade, to be replaced by less caustic families. The fantasy shows of the late 1970s were dead or dying. The "jiggles and giggles" era of teasing sex was waning, making it once again acceptable for series to be based on married stars with children. All this led to new uses of dramatic families and a bit of experimentation with the family in television comedy.

SOAPS AND SOCIAL WORK

Family dramas of the 1980s fell into three main groups—prime-time soap operas, "realist" dramas, and baby boomer settings. The prime-time soaps featured plots filled with infidelity, deception, and backstabbing. Most focused on the actions and intrigues of wealthy, powerful families. Their protagonists were usually extended families that included miscellaneous ex-wives, illegitimate children, and mysterious relatives. These wide-ranging extended families allowed for the complex interwoven plots associated with the genre. In "Dallas" it was the ongoing feud between the Ewing and Barnes families over the oil business. In "Dynasty" it was the Carrington and Colby families who were sometimes allies and sometimes adversaries. There were other shorter-lived examples of the genre, like "The Secrets of Midland Heights," "The Yellow Rose," and "For Love and Honor," which presented families with similar sets of improprieties.

All these families were deeply scarred by strife and personal traumas, but none of this reflected the larger issues of the day. Family members encountered all types of human flaws and weaknesses (alcoholism, adultery, drug addiction, nervous breakdowns, terminal illness) but there was apparently no larger world around the family worthy of comment.

The realist dramas, on the other hand, said a great deal about the wider world. This is a genre best known for "Cagney & Lacey," "Hill Street Blues," and "St. Elsewhere," but other lesser-known look-alikes have also surfaced for brief periods. These shows cast a jaundiced eye on the depressing, tragic, or horrifying aspects of life. There were few winners, since even good guys came out looking flawed.

While Alexis Colby Dexter was finding out that her grown daughter Amanda was having an adulterous affair with her new husband "Dex" Dexter on "Dynasty," Father Milton C. Hardstep uncovered a far sadder family trauma on "Hell Town." He had to deal with a father sexually abusing his young daughter while intimidating her to keep her from reporting it. In this episode, Hardstep continues to look into the girl's problems despite the father's opposition. Eventually he forcibly takes the girl away from her father while gathering evidence of abuse. The father is so enraged that he comes to kill Hardstep, who manages to convince him that he needs help and that his daughter needs some time away from him.

While the Ewings of "Dallas" tried to decide who was the real father of Kristen's baby, Marybeth Lacey of "Cagney & Lacey" faced a more difficult dilemma. Her father, who abandoned her family thirty years earlier, returns and wants to patch things up. She reluctantly goes to see him, but refuses to forgive him or let him become a part of her life. As she puts it, "Family isn't what you're born into, it's what you make of it." Family life is also seen outside the Lacey household. There is Chris Cagney's rocky relationship with her alcoholic father and her lengthy estrangement from her brother. Several families have also made one-time appearances on this series to present a full range of social problems. One episode involved a tragic case of spouse and child abuse so severe that it ended in the death of one of the children. The suspicious death of an elderly invalid turned out to be a homicide by a young grandson. He could no longer stand to see her in pain or to hear his family fighting over what to do with the old woman, so he ended the problem.

"St. Elsewhere," another realist drama, presented several continuing families with significant problems. Dr. Donald Westphall was a widowed father raising an autistic son and a teenage daughter. Several doctors have been divorced, and one lost his young wife in a car crash. There were also single-appearance families who arrived at the hospital in need of help. In one segment a husband and children watched helplessly as their wife and mother dies of a degenerative brain disease. In another, a young couple tried every medical technique to have a baby to no avail, while another mother decided to have her retarded daughter's fetus aborted. Thus, the dramatic families of the 1980s faced more tragedy and a stronger sense of limitations than families of earlier times. Many had their triumphs, but they were almost always seen against a backdrop of suffering and tragedy.

Perhaps in response to all this grimness, the late 1980s brought a new wave of young yuppie families whose problems and outlooks were those of the baby boom generation. The most successful and influential of these was "thirtysomething," an introspective look at life through baby boomer eyes. The problems faced by the Steadman family and their friends were usually domestic, reflecting a privatized milieu that is rarely linked to broader social concerns. In this sense the series was a throwback to earlier genres of family drama. But a notable element of the series was the running comparison between the Steadmans' lifestyles and the models their parents provided them. In some segments the old-school approach was shown up as delusory. In others the characters recognized the timeless truths that underlay their parents' lectures, often wishing they could return to those simpler times of simple virtues.

A less successful (but critically applauded) snapshot of modern yuppiedom was "Almost Grown." This series melded past experiences (seen through flashbacks) with current behavior to dramatize the choices and events that shaped the Foley family's lives. The generational theme permitted the writers to reexamine sixties' issues like draft-dodging and selling out to the establishment, as well as premarital sex, divorce, and drug abuse. "The Wonder Years" took another approach to bridging the gap between childhood and adulthood for the "thirtysomething" generation. Set in 1969, the series moved through the typical middle-class suburban adolescence of Kevin Arnold, described through the offscreen narration of the adult Kevin. Some of his experiences are hardy perennials—first date, school bullies, piano lessons. Others are unique to his generation—

dealing with a hippie sister, organizing an antiwar protest, consoling a friend whose brother is killed in Vietnam. "The Wonder Years" is a mixture of bittersweet memories that formed the character of the grownups seen in "thirtysomething" and "Almost Grown." Its air of nostalgia and ambivalence are typical of the genre and may be a harbinger of future family series from the rising generation of TV scriptwriters.

YOU CAN CHOOSE YOUR RELATIVES

The family comedies of the 1980s were characterized not so much by strong social comment as a redesigned family structure. The comedies of the late 1950s first presented widows and widowers as single parents in starring roles. The sitcoms of the 1970s introduced divorced parents heading households. By the 1980s, however, widowed and divorced parents by themselves were becoming old hat. The new strategy was to twist family structures into new shapes. The most unusual version was the so-called accidental family. Formed from characters who are not all blood relatives, these families became a demographic and psychological cross-section. Though the structure was not new (it was seen earlier in "Bachelor Father," "Accidental Family," and "Family Affair"), three versions of it from the 1980s are worth noting.

The premise of "Diff'rent Strokes" had wealthy white widower Phil Drummond adopt two brothers orphaned by the death of his black housekeeper. Phil, daughter Kimberly, and the two brothers set up a happy Park Avenue household. In later years Phil remarried and added a stepson to his family.

In "Punky Brewster," the seven-year-old title character came into the life of bachelor Henry Warnimont rather inauspiciously. She was illegally living in a vacant apartment when Henry, the building manager, discovered her. Henry was determined to turn her over to the juvenile authorities, but she was such a cute kid he couldn't do it. He persuaded the authorities to let Punky stay with him for a while. Together they started a new life and began to learn from each other.

Life for seven-year-old Webster Long of "Webster" was not much better at the start. Orphaned when a car crash killed his parents, he was left in the custody of his godfather George Papadapolis and his wife Katherine. As if this adjustment were not enough, his new parents added their own idiosyncracies. George was a burly ex-football player and Katherine a socialite who knew nothing of homemaking. They had met on a Greek cruise, decided to get married on the spur of the moment, and returned home to find Webster waiting. The three of them all got down to the business of creating a family.

These three shows were very much like the family comedies of the 1950s, except that the lessons to be learned were more obvious and more topical. The moral of the story was often underscored by the presence of an important guest star. First Lady Nancy Reagan made an appearance on "Diff'rent Strokes" to underscore the point of stamping out drug abuse. Other segments of the show dealt with child abuse, physical handicaps, and discrimination. "Punky Brewster" taught viewers about the dangers of running away from home. A segment of "Webster" taught kids how to cut down on crime in schools.

TV revived another old structure when it found a new group of indispensable housekeepers to throw into wacky family situations. "Mr. Belvedere" starred a butler in a two-career family trying to keep the household running smoothly. Nell Carter played a sharp-tongued black housekeeper to a widowed white police chief and his three daughters in "Gimme a Break." A young college student worked for room and board as a live-in male governess to the children of a busy working couple in "Charles in Charge."

"Kate & Allie" and "Who's the Boss" resemble the structure of accidental families but are really unique portrayals of divorced parents. In "Kate & Allie" two divorced mothers lived together for mutual support and to save money. Their different roles were structured to make this combination seem even more like a family. One was a career woman out in the world of work, while the other remained at home and pursued her college degree. The premise of "Who's the Boss" is a bit more unusual. In this comedy, Tony Micelli takes a job as a live-in housekeeper for Angela Bower so that he and his daughter can live in a wealthy suburb.

The structure works out well for both. Angela supplies a woman's touch for Tony's daughter, and Tony serves as a father figure for Angela's son.

TV in the 1980s reassembled several other artificial families for comic results. "Silver Spoons" presented Edward Stratton as a wealthy toymaker who had never really grown up, until his estranged twelve-year-old son invited himself into the household. The two began the difficult process of growing up and building a family. Edward's lovestruck secretary Kate was an informal mother figure at first, but later married Edward, completing the symmetry.

Seven years after Henry Willows and his wife were divorced, Henry opened the door to find his teenage son Matt coming to move in and kick off the series "You, Again." The two found they had little in common but a great deal of resentment. Despite this they settled down to try to live with each other. In the opening episode of "All Is Forgiven," Paula marries widower Matt Russell and gets a teenage daughter named Sonia. But no one asked Sonia if she wanted a new mother, and she goes out of her way to make clear that the answer would have been no.

The past decade has also seen a return of more traditional two-parent families with young children. "The Cosby Show," "Family Ties," "Charlie and Co.," "227," and "Growing Pains" use two-parent families with only slight twists. Most notably, all except "227" feature two-career families. These families are in other respects like those discussed above. They offer simple lessons about life, touch only lightly on most social issues, and present a strong, positive image of family life.

In the mid-eighties a group of stable two-parent traditional family shows climbed to the top of the Nielsen charts. "Cosby" led the ratings surge, followed by similar show like "Family Ties," "Growing Pains," and "227." All these shows focus on baby boom generation families, and they reflect the families the boomers watched on TV in the 1950s and 1960s. Most of them feature two-career families. Unlike TV families of the 1950s, mom is an equal partner in the marriage, but she still conforms to the traditional nurturing image of motherhood.

Lessons on these "new traditional" family shows were usually taught with love and kindness and a minimum of Lear-style sarcasm. The late

1980s, however, seemed to portend another shift to a more freewheeling, sassier comic style that sends up the saccharine-sweet TV family. In 1988 "Roseanne" dislodged "Cosby" from the number one spot with a sharp-tongued, sarcastic portrait of blue-collar domestic chaos. About the same time, the new Fox network attracted notice with a comedy that self-consciously tried to shatter the conventions of television's domestic bliss. "Married. . .With Children" is known on the set as "Not the Cosby Show." The Bundy family is sarcastic, insulting, cruel to one another, and even nastier toward outsiders. It features a sex-starved wife and sex-aversive husband and their two children, who include the school "easy girl." Much of the comedy concerns—guess what? Sample exchange: Wife: "If you had what other men have, I wouldn't need batteries." Husband: "So that's what happened to my Die-Hard." Of course, "Married... " is to family comedy what "Mary Hartman. . ." was to soap opera—a satire whose humor depends upon the popularity of the conventions being satirized. And unlike the milder "Roseanne," this series posed no ratings threat to "Cosby." The future television family is less likely to reflect the neurotic Bundy household than Garrison Keillor's mythic Lake Wobegon, where "the women are strong, the men are good-looking, and all the children are above average."

WHO WEARS THE PANTS?

Television has taken a fairly traditional approach to family authority, consistently portraying parents in firm control of their children. In our study, control of the family was indicated by making plans for the family that were carried out and having the general ability to direct family actions. In the first decade of our sample, parents were in control of the family 83 percent of the time, while children had control of the family less than 7 percent of the time. In the remaining instances control was shared between the two generations. Most often these cases involved older children still living at home. Parental control was usually exercised with ease and little or no opposition from children. Parental control in this early period often meant simply setting rules and limits for children.

A 1958 segment of "Bachelor Father" reveals just how easily parental control was exercised in this tranquil period. Kelly wants to go on a date and asks her guardian Bentley's permission. After asking various questions about who she is going with, who is chaperoning, and where they are going, he grants permission. He also sets a curfew for her. She readily agrees to all this without any real discussion. She happily goes off on her date while Bentley worries. He goes out for a time and misses her early return from a dull date. When she doesn't arrive by curfew time, he begins a frantic search for her, only to find she has been safely asleep all along. His control is never questioned, even if he appears overprotective and slightly foolish.

Parental control did not always mean that parents controlled events throughout the show, or that they were portrayed as totally virtuous. An episode of "The Tall Man," an early Western, shows that even failing parents can redeem themselves and regain control over their children. In one segment young Jody Latimer despises his drunkard father and looks up to Billy the Kid as a hero and role model. Jody's father Clint appeals to the sheriff to do something about Billy's influence over Jody, but the sheriff's efforts fail. Clint decides that he has to do something to save his son from the influences of an outlaw. He proceeds to sober up, clean himself up, and practice with his gun. When he is back up to his old fast draw he goes to challenge Billy. At the sheriff's insistence, however, Billy walks away from the fight. Clint, through his show of courage, wins Jody's respect. Clint is now firmly back in control, and he has saved his son from criminal influences.

In this case Clint knew what was best for Jody, but knowing what was best was not always necessary for parents to assert control over their offspring. "East Side, West Side" offers a case where the parent is very firmly in control, but (in the opinion of the show) has the wrong attitude. In the episode coded, John and Alice engage in premarital sex at her urging. The two want to marry, but Alice is underage and her father won't give his consent. Alice's father finds out about the illicit affair and presses statutory rape charges against John. Both young people, John's parents, and the social workers brought into the case try to persuade Alice's father that what the couple did was not wrong. They try to explain that it was an expression of love, but the father remains adamant that his daughter was defiled and the "punk" must pay for it. John is eventually convicted of statutory rape and sentenced to probation. The father has won his battle and, with the force of law behind him, maintained control over his daughter. Alice, however, tells him what the future holds: "...for the next six months and fourteen days, I'll do everything you say. Then it's my birthday, and I'll be of age."

Alice may have envisioned a breaking of parental control, but the picture for most of TV's families changed little over the next decade. Parents maintained control in almost four-fifths (79 percent) of the family situations where authority in the family was raised as an issue. The most recent decade has emphasized parental control more than any other. Parents now control nearly nine-tenths (89 percent) of family situations where authority is an issue, while situations where children control the family have dropped below 3 percent.

The circumstances of parental control do change over time, as broader social issues enter into the equation. A 1971 "All in the Family" episode presents a clear example of this trend. Archie and son-in-law Mike first argue over what to watch on television. Mike wants to see an environmental special critical of pollution. Archie wants to watch football. After dismissing Mike's arguments, Archie watches his game.

Peace reigns until Archie's daughter Gloria returns home from shopping with a bag of health foods. Mike and Gloria are both concerned about chemicals and pollutants in foods. Archie just wants his regular food. Another argument ensues as Mike and Gloria start to criticize the way companies pollute the world and abuse the consumer by not warning people of dangerous products. Archie replies that they are always tearing down the country and talking about how bad everything is. Then Archie is outraged to learn that Mike has written President Nixon complaining about all these issues. He seizes the letter and says that it's not going out of his house until he can write a positive letter to cancel out Mike's complaints. Archie writes his letter in praise of the president and the country, with a great deal of hyperbole.

When he is finished he agrees to mail both letters at once, so that they will arrive at the same time.

The issues raised here reach beyond the Bunker household, touching on topical social concerns. The larger argument, however, serves only to underscore Archie's hard-hat attitudes, not to undermine his control. Even though his daughter and her husband are adults, Archie can dictate what goes on in his house. For the Bunker family Archie, is king of the castle, and there is little they can do to change it.

A segment of "Family Ties" introduces the idea of negotiation into parental control of the family. Alex, the Keaton's oldest child, is about to turn eighteen. He decides that he is now an adult and can do what he wants. He and two friends make plans to drive from their Ohio homes to a wild West Virginia bar. His mother, meanwhile, makes reservations for a family dinner to celebrate. Alex sweeps these plans aside and goes out with his friends on his birthday. Undaunted, his mother drives to West Virginia and finds him at the bar, where he is trying to impress some girls. She takes him aside and tells him to come home with her. He argues that he is an adult now and has every right to stay. She says he's wrong and threatens to stay there all night if she has to.

The two finally go home, and the real argument ensues. Alex tells his mother she embarrassed him in front of his friends. She replies sarcastically that it's her job as a parent to do so. He says he's heard the line "as long as you live under my roof, I make the rules," but he's an adult now and can do as he pleases. She argues that a parent sets up rules, and it's the child's job to negotiate within those rules and create exceptions. Moreover, she continues, he never considered her feelings and the fact that she would be hurt by his insensitive actions. Alex realizes that he was unfeeling but still believes she has to cut the apron strings. The tensions ease as his mother recalls that they have had this argument all his life, that even in kindergarten he wanted to do things on his own. She remembers that she let him walk to school alone but followed to watch out for him. Alex agrees that he should have discussed his plans with her. Mrs. Keaton realizes that she will have to allow him more freedom. But this freedom is to be won through negotiation of her rules. She maintains control, but its limits are negotiable.

A recent "Cosby Show" episode reveals that, even today, TV's older forms of parental control are not dead. In this scenario daughter Vanessa wants to have a Halloween party for her friends. The parents agree to this and set up a few ground rules. They then proceed to offer constructive suggestions on costumes and other elements of the party. Vanessa uses these suggestions to throw a very successful party. On the night of the event, Mrs. Huxtable appears in costume to help serve the guests, while Dr. Huxtable takes the younger children out trick or treating. Before leaving with them he sets down some rules of behavior and explains that they will have two bags. One bag is for treats they get from people they know, the other is for treats from people they don't know. He says their parents will have to check the candy that they get from strangers. Parental control is asserted in a sensitive, concerned manner not unlike Bentley Gregg's approach almost thirty years earlier.

Parental control of families has been a constant in television from the days when Ward Cleaver gently guided Wally and the Beaver over the ups and downs of childhood, through the socially conscious, issue-laden family discussions of the late 1960s, up to the often sarcastic, divorced duo "Kate & Allie." Over the years families have faced new issues with wide-ranging social and political consequences, but their internal distribution of power has changed little.

DOES FATHER KNOW BEST?

We have seen that parental control is not always synonymous with being wiser or holding the right attitudes. So we asked which generation is portrayed as being in the right when family conflicts arise. Television has often been labeled a youth-oriented medium. The fascination with youth has definitely influenced casting and programming choices, but it has had little impact on the way families are portrayed. Our study found that in family situations, television has reinforced traditional images of the older generation as a source of wisdom. When television questions who in the family "knows best" or shows common sense, it most often points to the older generation.

Surprisingly, the older generation is presented as being wiser or knowing what is best more often as time goes on. In the first decade of the study, only a narrow majority (53 percent) of the cases portrayed the older generation as the fount of wisdom. In the most recent decade, parents were wiser in 63 percent of all conflicts. The number of cases in which the younger generation appears wiser is small and has remained stable across all time periods. Thus, the social movements of the late 1960s and early 1970s did not create a revolution within television families.

The real change over time does not concern whether parents or their children are in the right. Rather it comes in the circumstances and contexts surrounding presentations of parental wisdom. It is the issues under discussion that change over time, not the dynamics of the parent-child relationship. Larger social issues begin to enter into family discussions and situations, requiring new parental solutions and new areas of knowledge. TV parents have not become old fogies in recent seasons. They are given progressive, forward-looking opinions tempered only by a sense of caution. Rarely were they left lagging behind as the last promoters of some archaic notion.

A 1973 segment of "Sanford and Son" introduced the larger issue of racial heritage into a family argument in which the younger generation eventually accepts the common-sense wisdom of the older. Fred Sanford wants his son Lamont to buy him cable TV. Lamont doesn't want to discuss it. He has decided to reach back to his true African roots and live as an African, "not as the white man says they should." Lamont changes his diet, giving up pork and other items that contradict the proper African lifestyle.

Lamont then invites a Nigerian woman from one of his classes home for dinner. He hopes to impress her with this new-found awareness of his roots. Once she arrives, Fred tells her he doesn't know or care much about African culture. He says everyone and everything he knows is American. Lamont is angry with Fred for expressing such parochial attitudes, since he was trying to impress this woman. Lamont and Fred begin to fight, and Lamont tries to send Fred to bed. Then the woman tells Lamont that she is disgusted with his behavior. She explains that in

Africa he would be beaten for showing such disrespect to an elder. After she leaves, Lamont decides to give up the African nativist idea altogether. He reluctantly agrees with Fred that they are Americans and really know nothing about being African. Fred may be sharp-tongued and nagging in this episode, but his realistic, practical views clearly win out. He is the one who realizes they are no longer in Africa, and those traditional ways lack meaning in America.

The following season, "Apple's Way" debated the very survival of the family as a meaningful institution. In this segment, teenager Paul Apple and his grandfather argue over the meaning of family. Paul asks, "Are we all bound to one another with hoops of steel?" Grandpa replies, "We're bound because we're family, family is a sacred thing." Paul retorts, "Not anymore it isn't. That kind of family is obsolete. Grandpa, you've locked yourself into a lifestyle that went out with the butter churn. . . .Families stay together for economic reasons. We'll all be going our own ways soon."

Grandpa remains angry, but an approaching tornado preempts their argument. The family is separated as the father and part of the family hide in the storm cellar, while Grandpa and Mom search for a missing son. Everyone survives the tornado, and Paul tells his father he can see them years from now talking about the tornado of '74. Paul admits that he was wrong about families not being important and even adds, "Sometimes I don't know what I'm talking about!" To underscore the wisdom of age and the value of old ways, Grandpa uses a horse to remove debris and free the family members stuck in the storm cellar. Clearly the older generation's concept of family is not obsolete and proves useful in times of crisis.

Problems facing modern parents on television are often more complex than these last two examples indicate. Parents are now called upon to deal with premarital sex, teenage drinking, crime in schools, family violence, incest and sexual abuse, divorce, and illegal drugs. Today's prime-time parents need to make more complex decisions more frequently and with a greater degree of uncertainty than their predecessors. Yet they continue to show wisdom and good sense when doing so.

For example, in a 1987 segment of "Heart of the City," a teenaged boy tells his father he had sex with his date the night before. Momentarily speechless, the father recovers to remind his son that it's important to respect the girl and not take advantage of her, and that sex should be part of a loving relationship. Times have changed since the Beaver's day, as have social mores, but the lines of communication are still open.

DON'T TRUST ANYONE OVER THIRTY

Since family structures and authority patterns have remained fairly stable over time, it is not surprising that television has only rarely dealt with open rebellion in the family. When it has presented incidents of rebellion, however, it has generally viewed them as acceptable. Our sample contained only a few cases where rebellion appeared as an issue in the family. Among those instances, though, more than three out of four were viewed as acceptable. This was never presented as a pleasant event for anyone in the family. Typically it was seen as a stage parents must live with as their children become adults.

In the late 1960s rebellion became a way of introducing conflicting ideologies. These conflicts also illustrated television's view of the generation gap. This is again a theme that television only rarely touches upon, but when it does the outcome is consistent. Even in the first decade, two-thirds of the cases made the generation gap an argument between ideological opposites. The second decade (1965-1974) almost doubled the number of times the generation gap was inserted into family life. During this period, four out of five shows viewed the generation gap as a battle between ideologies. In the most recent decade, the issue dropped in frequency to its earlier level. When the gap exists, however, it is always an ideological split. Ideological differences and a structure amenable to rebellion form a perfect platform for the debate of topical issues.

For example, a segment of the Western "High Chapparal" uses two families to illustrate different views of racial relations. In the starring Cannon family, the white John Cannon is married to a beautiful Mexican woman named Victoria. They are a loving supportive couple who have encountered few problems in mixing their different ethnic heritages. The Stoner family, a widower and his teenage son, are scalphunters who kill Indians for a living. Since they do not think of the Indians as people, they are willing to kill them for the mine owners. Young Chad is injured in an Indian fight and spends a few days with the integrated Cannon family. In this short time he comes to see that the Apaches are people and not animals. Jacob wants his son to come back and join the scalping raids, but Chad feels that he can no longer kill innocent Apaches. They argue heatedly over the morality of slaughtering Indians and the equality of all people, but an Apache attack cuts their argument short. They want Jacob Stoner to die to avenge the deaths of their brothers he has killed. Jacob decides that to save his son and others, he will sacrifice himself. Racist attitudes are thus eliminated with the death of an unregenerate racist of the older generation, and more tolerant views are endorsed by the show.

In a "Bold Ones" episode of the early 1970s the issue of generational rebellion was even more topical. In the opening scene of the segment, the audience hears a young boy talking on a radio call-in show. He says his brother is serving in Vietnam. The boy adds that his brother enlisted when he was drafted, but many of his brother's friends went to Canada. He reports, "My father looks the other way when he sees their parents on the street. He says if you live in this country you ought to be willing to fight for it." The show goes on to explore generational differences over the war, the draft, and draft dodgers. The parents represent the more traditional view outlined above, while the younger generation is typified by confusion and ambivalence. The ideological split very neatly conforms to the generational split as well. Both sides make broad statements on the issue at hand as this show moves towards its tragic ending in the suicide of a young deserter.

Thus, when rebellion or the generation gap are addressed, they are most often used to set up a topical debate on some controversial social problem within the setting of a family drama. Such presentations also emphasize television's view that families need not be repressive or narrowminded, and that the younger generation can bring renewal and relevancy to this institution.

CAN WE TALK?

For television families, the answer to Joan Rivers' perennial question is a definite yes. Throughout the thirty years of our study, television has repeatedly stressed that the generations can communicate. In the early years, discussions between parents and children were a given. Parents were a source of wisdom and valuable assistance in a child's life.

In the 1955-1964 period, eight out of ten cases where intergenerational communication was an issue concluded that communication was indeed possible. The second decade, perhaps surprisingly, raised the issue less frequently than the first. Nevertheless, 93 percent of the cases during television's "radical period" voiced the opinion that the generations could communicate across the generation gap. But the most recent decade presents more situations where intergenerational communication is an issue than the previous two decades combined. Since 1975, seven scripts out of eight (88 percent) have endorsed intergenerational communication.

The contexts of communication in the family and the issues under discussion have changed over time. Communication between parents and children in the early years was simply a matter of course. Television parents of the 1950s and early 1960s were not usually like the repressive father discussed earlier on "East Side, West Side."

Parents commonly talked to their children about a variety of personal problems. Thus, a "Dick Van Dyke Show" episode revolves around parents Rob and Laura talking to their son Ritchie about the facts of life. Rob had earlier talked to Ritchie about "the birds and the bees" in a straightforward, honest manner. One day they get a call from Ritchie's principal informing them that Ritchie has been telling other kids where babies come from. It seems that Ritchie has told the kids that parents pick out the baby they want from under a cabbage leaf. When they meet with the principal, his complaint is not that Ritchie shouldn't know about such things or talk about them. Rather, he thinks it is irresponsible of Rob and Laura to tell Ritchie false stories about sex. Rob and Laura both assure the principal that, to the contrary, they were very honest in their talk with Ritchie. They go home and have another talk with Ritchie and

171

tell him not to tell other kids the cabbage patch story. A few days later they get another call from the principal saying that now Ritchie has been saying that the stork brings babies. When Ritchie gets home they ask him why he has been telling kids stories he knows are false. He says he likes to make up stories "just like Daddy" (Rob is a TV writer). He says the kids like to hear his stories, and the stories Daddy makes up aren't true. Rob and Laura are relieved when they finally get the whole account. The show's message is that, even with an often embarrassing topic like sex, parents and kids can communicate. In this case, continued communication solves the problem and puts a positive light on a potentially bad situation.

Since major social issues were not yet included in most shows, discussions of major social issues between the generations did not occur before the late 1960s. Even as such issues crept into family dialogues, the generations continued to communicate. They did not always agree, nor did each understand completely the motivations of the other. They could, however, maintain an open, often mutually informative dialogue.

A segment of the short-lived series "The Smith Family" used just such an approach to the generation gap in discussing the problems of teenage runaways. The runaway in question is a rich girl who seems to "have it all" but is ignored by her parents. She disappears after complaining to her friend Cindy Smith that her parents never listen to her. Cindy's father, a police detective, sets out to find her. He has little success until he turns to his own kids for advice. They suggest looking for her at a concert and running ads in an underground newspaper widely read by runaways. Sergeant Smith tries both and almost catches up with her at the concert. He continues looking for her and eventually finds out she is at a group house. Before going to get the girl, he swings by his daughter's college and takes her along to help. He sends Cindy in first to convince the girl to go home. This strategy works and she goes home. When she returns, however, she finds out that her parents have decided to ignore the fact that she ran away. They want to make pleasant conversation as if it never happened. She runs away again, and this time Mr. Smith tells the parents that he doubts the police will ever find her. He

says she has learned more about running away than he knows about finding her. In the closing scene he tells his own daughter never to stop asking them questions, demanding answers, and talking about what is going
on in her life. He never wants to lose contact with her as the other family did with its daughter.

The unmistakable message here is that parents and kids need each
other. Communication is not always easy, nor will the discussion always
be enjoyable, but it can and must be done. There are no easy answers to
the problem in this show and no clear winners.

In recent years, many shows have dealt with bridging the generation
gap, but the conflict is without the broader social implications seen in the
shows of the late 1960s and early 1970s. One of television's realist dramas, "St. Elsewhere," even recast an old storyline from "Father Knows
Best." In several episodes there is a minor plot line in which Dr. Donald
Westphall tries to convince his daughter Lizzie to go to Vassar. She wants
to go to Boston College, so that she can live at home and take care of her
father and autistic brother. Donald thinks she should leave home to be
on her own. They finally agree that she will go to Vassar for a year and,
if she still wants to move back, she can transfer to Boston College. After
the year is up, Lizzie returns home and decides to stay. Donald makes one
last attempt to have her return to Vassar. He tells her he wants her to have
time to be a kid and to fool around. He says he's been worried that he
forced her to grow up too quickly after her mother died and put too much
of a burden on her in raising her brother. Lizzie responds that she
doesn't mind, and they need her to take care of things. They agree that
she'll live at home while she goes to B.C., and peace returns to the house.

Not unlike Jim and Margaret Anderson thirty years earlier, Donald
Westphall realizes he must let his daughter make up her own mind. Like
her predecessor Betty Anderson, Lizzie is successful in convincing her
father that it's her life, and she must make decisions for herself. The contexts change and the concerns of the two young women are different, but
the theme of successful communication is the same.

Television has always told us that the generations can talk. Parents
and children may have legitimate disagreements, but they can usually

compromise. In both past and present series, there are repressive parents who keep their children too tightly reined in, but the majority use a lighter touch. Appeals to reason, family loyalty, or a sense of decorum are far more common than harsh edicts, strict rules, and corporal punishment as tools for television parents.

Thus, television legitimates a relatively egalitarian family structure both through its critical portraits of authoritarian parents and its admiring portrayals of "progressive" ones. The message is liberal rather than radical; parents typically retain their authority by not abusing it. They earn their children's respect by emphasizing self-development over conformity, communication over authority, and compromise over obedience.

TELEVISION'S SPECIAL FAMILIES

Television has presented many examples of nontraditional families. Departures from the two-parent family structure have included single, widowed, and divorced parents, parents with an unknown marital status, foster homes, guardianships, and a few two-parent families created by blending two single-parent families. There are also many variations on these forms, such as the inclusion of other relatives or servants in the family structure.

We were curious to find out if television sought to make any special points about such families. Our coders looked at two aspects of the portrayal of nontraditional families. The first was the types of problems they face, and their ability to solve them.

Coders first determined the nature of the problem facing the family. Some were presented as unique to nontraditional families, such as a divorced mother trying to explain to her children why her last night's date is at breakfast the next morning. Others were presented as common to all types of families, like concerns over teenage dating or curfews.

During the first twenty years studied, television did not treat nontraditional families in any unique way. Less than a third (32 percent) of the problems they encountered were presented as different from those of other families. For example, in "Bachelor Father," Bentley Gregg worries about his niece (and ward) when she is out on a date, but Ozzie Nelson also worries when David is out on a date in a similar episode. These families faced relatively few problems, and most were simple difficulties that could be used to teach a gentle lesson. During the first two decades of our sample, almost nine-tenths (88 percent) of the problem situations could be solved by these families. Even when problems were seen as unique to nontraditional families, they were solved four times out of five. The fact that most problems were viewed as soluble corresponds to television's portrayal of parents controlling the family and acting wisely. All this serves to underscore the similarities between nontraditional families and their more traditional counterparts.

In the most recent decade studied, however, there has been a marked shift in the types of problems these families face. From 1975 to 1986, over half the problems confronting these families were presented as unique to their structure. They often served as a vehicle for the introduction of controversial ideas or situations. For example, there is the battle between Anne Romano and her daughter Julie in "One Day At A Time." Julie is dating an older man who is only a few years younger than her mother. Anne does not think this is a good dating situation for Julie. She tries to convince her daughter that he is just taking advantage of her. Julie refuses to listen, so Ann confronts Julie and her date. There is a heated argument that resolves nothing. Ann eventually goes to see the man by herself. They are attracted to each other and he makes a pass at her. Just at that moment Julie walks in and says she understands now why her mother wanted her to break it off. She accuses Ann of wanting him for herself, and asks if there aren't enough men so she has to steal Julie's. Julie runs out, and Ann's efforts to explain fail. Finally the man breaks off seeing both Julie and Ann. Once they have both been cast aside, they find some common ground and slowly and painfully patch up their relationship. Having a divorced mother out in the dating world certainly makes problems for Julie that are unique to single-parent families.

By the 1980s these problems were becoming somewhat less controversial than intergenerational sexual competition. We came across the troubles children have dealing with divorce, the economic hardships of widowhood, and the difficulties of reentering the singles scene. These

contemporary single parents were not daunted, however, by the tribulations in their lives. In this most recent decade, parents solved the problems they encountered in almost 95 percent of the family situations where
a problem existed. Some were fairly simple solutions, as in the "Kate &
Allie" segment in which Allie has to console Chip and assure him that the
birth of a stepbrother or sister will not make his father stop loving him.
Others were more difficult solutions to more complex confrontations,
such as a parent kidnapping the children after losing a custody battle, or
failing to make child support payments.

Television's nontraditional families act like their traditional counterparts in terms of authority in the family, wisdom, and communication.
What has changed for this group is the infusion of new problems into their
lives. The number of unique problems facing these families in the most
recent decade was more than double that in any previous decade. Despite
this onslaught of difficulties, these families still manage to solve most of
their problems and flourish in the contemporary prime-time world. As
"Kate & Allie" producer Bill Persky puts it, "Any group of people that cares
about one another and protects one another is a family."[2]

HAVEN IN A HEARTLESS WORLD

Television has stretched, bent, and reshaped its fictional families to
fit a changing world. In the process it has affected the habits and lives of
real-world families. In 1953, when millions watched Lucy Ricardo have
a baby boy, only half of all American homes owned a television. Now the
medium reaches into 98 percent of our homes. Over 85 million homes
can tune in to watch the machinations of the Ewing family or hear the
low-key humor of Cliff Huxtable. Recent studies indicate that families
spend one-quarter of their leisure time together in front of the set. It is
now one of the most popular forms of family recreation.[3] America's thirst
for fictional families continues as each new season adds new creations to
entertain viewers.

Each of these new families is much like its predecessors. For the
most part we have seen families where wise, tolerant, and communica-

tive parents stay firmly in control by offering gentle guidance to inquis-
itive and quick-witted children. There are few tyrants, buffoons, or
prudes in the ranks of television parents. Few children are wild rebels,
denouncing the traditions and shared understandings of mainstream
America.

As each new season premieres, critics and reviewers attempt to come
up with one phrase that encapsulates the themes of family life in the new
shows. Each season thus becomes "the season of. . . " with a new catch-
phrase each year. At various times there have been so-called seasons of
rebellion, seasons of the younger generation, seasons of rekindled
warmth, and so on. These generalizations are often based on the plot
lines of a few well-known shows or incidents in a few preview tapes,
ignoring all the other families that will appear in all types of shows. Our
more systematic results point out just how superficial such judgments can
be. The television family has been a fairly stable institution. Its cast of
characters and their familial relationships may change, but the basic distribution of power and wisdom remain unaffected.

The broad generalizations made by critics do not point to real
changes in family dynamics on television, but rather the increasing complexity of the issues they must deal with. Simple advice about study
habits, dates, clothes, and such was the staple of earlier generations of parents. More contemporary parents may have to debate the nuclear arms
race, the pros and cons of premarital sex, or teenage drinking. They may
come home to be told their unwed daughter is pregnant, or their son is a
heroin addict. When asking their child what happened in school today,
they may learn that he or she was molested by a teacher, offered drugs, or
assaulted by a gang of thugs.

Moreover, the values passed on from one generation to another have
changed with the times (and Hollywood trends). As television critic
Martha Bayles notes:

> The older family sitcoms contained frequent didactic refer-
> ences to homely virtues such as honesty, loyalty, bravery,
> decency—words we don't hear on TV nowadays. Instead, we

hear messages about the sort of "social" values that survived the
'60s: tolerance, equality, self-esteem.[4]

All this can make the show more controversial, or seemingly radical,
but when the shouting is over and the tears have dried, what often
remains is an old familiar pattern. The parents still control the family,
they have helped to solve the problem, and they have often gained a new
appreciation of their children. Children, meanwhile, have learned from
the situation and become more open with their parents. The internal
dynamics of the family have successfully passed a test, and in the process
commentary was offered on a current issue.

Scenes like these have tended to be more emotional and topical over
the years, as the family has become a platform for social comment. The
tide of social commentary has picked the family up and moved it along.
Progressive or open-minded parents have found new answers to new
problems and thus preserved older patterns of family interaction. Unlike
other authority figures, parents are rarely seen as reactionaries, buffoons,
or the proponents of outmoded values.

There may be debates on the worth of certain values in the modern
world, but the form that debate takes and its eventual resolution will very
likely follow an old pattern. Parents will compromise after being convinced to do so by their children. The basic dynamics of parental control
and judgment will be followed, however, so that it is the parent who must
validate any changes in the rules.

These days egalitarian parenting styles preserve family harmony by
accommodating modern mores, and progressive parents stay in charge by
meeting their young charges halfway. Thus, while television has turned
permissive on sexual matters and sends mixed messags on feminist concerns, it takes a more traditional approach to family ties. But even this
traditional institution is pulled along by the tides of modern times.

————>✈<————

PART

III

The Working World

5

9 TO 5

Workin' nine to five
What a way to make a livin'
Barely gets you by
It's all takin' and no givin'

—"9 to 5" theme song

W hat does television have to do with work? At first the answer was as little as possible. The tube was supposed to help you forget the office, not bring it into your living room. Only gradually did producers and writers realize that the workaday world could be a source of nightly entertainment. The subsequent increase in occupational themes was a major development in television's life cycle. This chapter examines prime time's gradual discovery of life from 9 to 5. The following chapters discuss the occupations that provide Hollywood with its favorite heroes (educated professionals) and heavies (businessmen).

In the 1950s ordinary people rarely seemed to have ordinary jobs on television. TV's "golden age" was dominated by the domestic sitcom, in which the husband went off to work but the camera stayed at home. Jim Anderson, Ward Cleaver, and Ozzie Nelson all supposedly pursued middle-class professions, but they were rarely seen at work. These early TV icons are fondly remembered as loving husbands and fathers, not as an insurance agent, an accountant, and a producer.

To be sure, the fantasy world of prime time always included some workers. But television's occupational life was largely restricted to fantasy settings far from the humdrum offices and factories that employed most Americans. Many of these settings quickly evolved into established genres—cop shows, Westerns, medical and courtroom dramas—whose conventions were borrowed from radio or the movies. In 1955 "Gunsmoke" introduced the first wave of what quickly became a flood of cowhands riding the range and tending their herds of cattle. The Westerns also presented legions of sheriffs and marshals standing up against gunslingers and other threats to law and order. Meanwhile more contemporary cops like Elliot Ness fought similar battles against gangsters and other assorted lawbreakers. Private eyes like Peter Gunn and crimesolving lawyers like Perry Mason picked up where the police left off.

Television has always been top-heavy with law enforcers. Teachers and doctors were also allowed to pursue their noble professions on screen, and viewers quickly became familiar with the make-believe dramas that went on in courtrooms, classrooms, and operating rooms. The pattern in almost all these shows was to present the characters in either a work setting or a personal setting, but not both. For most of the characters who were shown at work, your job was your life. Laconic Sergeant Friday had no home outside the squad room, just as the young Doctor Kildare had no personal life until the mid-1960s.

TV GOES TO WORK

A few early shows began to break out of this pattern in their handling of the work world. Comedienne Ann Sothern's "Private Secretary" and "The Ann Sothern Show" featured more common business and clerical jobs. Both shows also solidified lasting stereotypes of the girl Friday who works diligently to keep her boss's private life, as well as his business life, in order. Such women were at times indispensable to their male bosses. At other times they made nuisances of themselves and only exacerbated his problems. In such shows the players' personal and professional lives often intruded into one another or overlapped. The star's best friends were other women at work, and any men entering her life were met through work. "The Bob Cummings Show" (a.k.a. "Love That Bob") soon established another common theme for workplace settings. As a plain-Jane photographer's assistant, poor Schultzy loved that Bob but could never win his affection. So she had to watch him go from one beautiful model to the next. This pattern would be repeated through a steady stream of shows in which the faithful girl Friday was doomed to love from afar.

Into the early 1960s, television continued its preference for showing people at work mainly in unusual or glamorous occupations. Entertainers, writers, and investigative reporters were added to the small list of those who plied their trades on screen. A few continuing characters also began to appear with garden-variety jobs. There were Floyd the barber and Howard the county clerk on "The Andy Griffith Show." There was Herbert Gillis, a small grocery store owner, in "The Many Loves of Dobie Gillis." Though the workplace was not the main focus of their activities, they were much more down to earth than most of their predecessors on the job.

Then, in 1961, TV made a significant move into the workplace as a setting for entertainment. The actual work activities of the cast became a part of the plot on "The Dick Van Dyke Show." Rob Petrie and his writing staff were actually shown earning a living by writing comedy routines. They were also among a small group of characters who could have both a home life and a professional life in the same episode. This was soon followed by "The Lucy Show," in which Lucille Ball combined the girl Friday image of Ann Sothern with her own brand of wild foul-ups. Lucy, like the characters in "Dick Van Dyke," had a personal life that often affected her work habits.

The world of work that emerged in both these shows was dominated by a stuffy, pompous boss who was unable to control his staff. In "Dick Van Dyke" it was producer Mel Cooley who could do little to rein in the writers. In "The Lucy Show" it was Mr. Mooney who could never succeed in regimenting Lucy's behavior. Like the girl Friday, the inept boss soon became a fixture of TV entertainment.

Despite the popularity of these shows, television did not make any more substantial forays into the workplace for several years. More characters were said to have jobs, but their work activities remained largely unseen. In "The Beverly Hillbillies," Mr. Drysdale and Miss Jane clearly worked at a bank. They never seemed to do any banking, though, aside from occasionally handling the Clampetts' finances. In "Petticoat Junction" Kate Bradley ran the Shady Rest Hotel, but little of her activity actually involved the hotel business.

There continued to be a few exceptions to prime time's general avoidance of the workplace. For instance, in "Mickey," much of the comedy centered on the problems of running a hotel. These problems were magnified by a desk clerk who was always cooking up ways to make money on the side, while ignoring his real duties. In "Bewitched" the world of advertising provided many script ideas, but the actual production of ads got short shrift. Most of the comedy emerged from family involvement in Darren's work or from the buffoonery of his glory-seeking boss. Overall, such shows presented only a thin slice of the work world, and even that derived from the personal lives of the characters. These characters did not hold very glamorous jobs, however, and this followed the pattern of TV moving into ordinary occupations.

The majority of series continued to present only action-packed or high-status jobs. Most shows also continued to separate the world of work from the personal world, usually by limiting settings to one area or the other in each episode. In those cases where TV did present workplace settings, the emphasis was on what the characters did for a living, not how they did it. For most TV businessmen and professionals (not to mention cops and private eyes) there was no workplace routine, and the office was just a place to collect messages.

The 1970 premiere of "The Mary Tyler Moore Show" marked a watershed in television's image of the working world. Expanding on the formula developed for "Dick Van Dyke," characters in this show were seen not just at work but doing work. These characters' jobs, including their relationships with co-workers, spilled over into their personal lives. "Mary Tyler Moore" laid the groundwork for a profusion of shows that would follow as TV moved into the workplace with increasing gusto.

In the 1970s the number of shows focusing on the work world proliferated, and work activities became more prominent. "Alice" used a diner as a backdrop. "Needles and Pins" used the clothing business. In "Calucci's Department" a government office served to set up situations for comedy. "Rhoda," a spin-off of "Mary Tyler Moore," followed its pattern of mixing personal and professional activities. "WKRP in Cincinnati," "Taxi," and "Lou Grant" (another MTM spin-off) all used workplace settings as a backdrop. More important than their use of occupational settings, however, was the way those workplaces appeared to function.

Beginning with "Dick Van Dyke" there was a tendency to treat co-workers as an ad hoc family. This relationship was evident between Rob Petrie and his immediate co-workers, but not with his superiors. In "Mary Tyler Moore" and the shows that followed it, this trend became more central to plot lines and character development. The WJM newsroom was usually a friendly, mutually supportive place, where everyone was part of the family. The staff confided personal problems and fears, sought advice, and, in general, performed many family roles. The popular ensemble comedy format of the 1970s was based on this pattern. In hit shows like "Taxi," "WKRP in Cincinnati," and "Barney Miller" the family roles were emphasized by the cast actually describing themselves as a family or saying they should work together as a family. In dramatic programming a similar pattern developed in "Mod Squad," "Charlie's Angels," and "Lou Grant."

Most of these comedies and dramas featured a superior who was only grudgingly accepted by other "family" members. This character was the thorn that pricked an otherwise cozy, peaceful arrangement and sparked conflicts. These bosses were not quite the comic buffoons of earlier eras. One group had good intentions but was too inexperienced or naive to realize the full implications of its actions. Such blundering bosses included Mr. Carlson of "WKRP" and Inspector Lugar on "Barney Miller." Another group of people was very shrewd, often miserly, and viewed employees only as assets to be bought and sold. These superiors realized the bad effect they had on staff morale, but they didn't care. This group of Scrooges included Mrs. Carlson on "WKRP," Louie DePalma of "Taxi," and Mel Sharples in "Alice."

Even in the 1980s the workplace tended to be shown mainly in more glamorous or exciting jobs (at least in TV's version) like police work or the law. Shows of the eighties that focused on other office settings were rare, with "9 to 5" and "One Day At A Time" the best known. Routine office work remains very much in the background of most TV shows, and factory work is nearly invisible. But the office routine does increasingly intrude on the work of the more glamorous occupations. More and more frequently, police officers are shown working on a pile of paperwork, and doctors are seen subjected to onerous routines and schedules. But that's another story. First let's bring to center stage the working stiffs that TV usually consigns to the sidelines.

HOW THE OTHER HALF WORKS

The relative lack of office and factory workers, in contrast to the surfeit of wealthy businessmen and professionals, suggests an obvious imbalance in the TV workplace. The world of prime time has always been weighted toward the upper middle classes. Doctors, lawyers, and other professionals, not to mention business executives, are much more populous on TV than in real life. By contrast, our study counted only one out of four characters in low-status occupations. That included 8 percent in white-collar jobs like low-level office workers, supervisory staff in factories, telephone operators, and cashiers; and 17 percent in blue-collar or unskilled jobs ranging from skilled workers like carpenters, plumbers, and electricians to farm and ranch hands, domestic staffs, and food service workers.

Even though these sectors of the economy are underpopulated compared to their real-world counterparts, they still constitute a sizable block of characters, including a good many memorable ones. The importance of these little guy or gal Friday roles is attested by the number of characters with whom millions of Americans were on a first-name basis, from Archie and Alice to Lucy and Hazel. Despite many individual exceptions, however, the bulk of TV's working stiffs have always formed a kind of support staff for the more glamorous, high-status stars. These groups contain by far the highest proportion of characters who serve neutral plot functions—nearly half (48 percent) of the white-collar workers and 43 percent of the blue-collar group. Such characters are usually relegated to the sidelines of the story.

Even those who play a more active role are portrayed less positively than most other groups (businessmen always excepted). Overall, television uses many more positive than negative characters. Over the thirty seasons we studied, among all the characters with identifiable census-coded occupations, good guys outnumbered bad guys by nearly a two-to-one margin (45 to 25 percent).[1] The remaining 30 percent played neutral roles. Subtracting the negative percentage from the positive one yields a margin of +20 percent, as a simple index of how positively a group is portrayed. By comparison, 30 percent of white-collar workers are positive and 22 percent negative characters, a positive index of +8. The blue-collar group is not much better—34 percent positive and 22 percent negative, for a +12 margin.

These figures haven't changed much over the years. The white- and blue-collar groups both generated positive margins of +9 before 1965; +4 from 1965 to 1975; +13 thereafter. About the only noticeable change in their plot functions is a tendency toward more central roles, especially for the blue-collar and unskilled workers. The proportion of neutral characters in that group fell gradually from 48 percent before 1965 to 36 percent since 1975, still higher than the 28 percent average for all census-coded occupations. The change reflects an increasing use of domestic workers (like "Benson"), and waitresses (like "Alice"), and the like in continuing roles.

Low status white-collar jobs are mainly the province of TV's women and one of its most memorable groups of people. Since we discussed many of these characters in chapter 3, a brief reprise should suffice here. They include the secretaries in an endless number of offices in comedies and dramas. For comic relief in the office there was Lucy Carmichael/Carter, Katy O'Connor, Schultzy on "The Bob Cummings

Show," Julie Marshall of "My Hero," and "My Sister Eileen"'s sibling Ruth Sherwood. In the dramas legal secretaries like Perry Mason's Della Street or Marsha Spear of "The Law and Mr. Jones" were the good right arms of the stars. Later would come Miss Jane in the "The Beverly Hillbillies," Peggy Fair in "Mannix," and Tina Rickles of "The Courtship of Eddie's Father." The 1970s presented Carol Kester on "The Bob Newhart Show," Frieda Krause on "Owen Marshall," and Maggie on "Switch." The 1980s offered Jennifer Marlowe in "WKRP in Cincinnati," Kate Summers, who eventually marries her boss Edward Stratton on "Silver Spoons," Agnes DePesto, the rhyming secretary on "Moonlighting," and Mildred Krebs of "Remington Steele."

These women are usually helpful, although many are slightly off-center. They often manipulate the boss for his own good. In other shows like "9 to 5," they manipulate a pompous, overbearing boss to a comic downfall. These characters have a strong sense of right and wrong. They usually possess a great deal of common sense and serve to stabilize the world around them.

Skilled blue-collar occupations are relatively rare on TV, especially in dramatic settings. Since very little ordinary work activity goes on, there is no need for skilled workers or tradesmen. A few cop shows of the 1970s might have used a tailor or a jeweler as a witness to a crime, but even these were often artisans who owned their own businesses. Thus, this category consists almost exclusively of single-appearance characters who usually did little and were coded as neutral.

Any attempt to break this dreary mold would probably founder on the fate of "Skag," NBC's highly touted 1980 dramatic portrait of working-class life. Skag was Pete Skagska, a middle-aged union foreman at a Pittsburgh steel mill, portrayed by Karl Malden. Considering the problems the scriptwriters gave him, they might as well have named him "Job." While recuperating from a stroke, Skag had to deal with an aging and infirm father, a promiscuous teenage daughter, a Jewish second wife trying to fit into his Catholic household, and a job that might not be waiting for him when he could return to it. There was a great deal of talent involved in the series, from title character Karl Malden to producer Abby

Mann, not to mention literate scripts, a big publicity budget, and general critical acclaim. All it lacked was an audience. This realistic portrayal of a troubled steelworker was apparently just too downbeat for viewers looking to Hollywood's fantasy factory for relief from their own problems. "Skag" lasted less than two months.

Unskilled workers are another story entirely. In TV's version of the proletariat, this category included countless cowboys, numerous taxi drivers, a host of waiters and waitresses, and more than a few bossy maids. Many were single-appearance characters serving mainly as background, but a fair number have been stars. Perhaps the most memorable and lovable blue-collar heroes were Ralph Kramden and Ed Norton from "The Honeymooners." Ralph the bus driver and Ed the sewer repairman represented an early picture of the working man shorn of Hollywood glitter but not of humanity. Of course, we didn't actually see them at work (mercifully, perhaps, in Norton's case). The single studio set was almost always the main room of the Kramdens' low-rent Brooklyn apartment. It contained a table and chairs, a chest of drawers, and a stove and ice box. Ralph usually appeared in his bus driver's uniform, Norton in a tee shirt. Yet their life was anything but grim, despite script references to money problems and get-rich-quick schemes. The boys' resilience and optimism provided the perfect counterpoint to the drab setting. It allowed audiences to identify with them without being depressed by their all-too-realistic environment.

These days prime time's favorite working-class hero is actually a heroine. "Roseanne" is a brassy working-class housewife who works long hours in a plastics factory to supplement the income of her husband, a none-too-successful self-employed contractor. Roseanne Connor can match Ralph Kramden's tirades as well as his girth. But the show displays a sarcastic and sometimes bitter tone that cuts more deeply than "The Honeymooners." Despite its alienated perspective, however, the view of American life is more one of frustration than rejection.

More generally, humor has provided the sweetener that attracted audiences to television's working-class characters. No television series has ever featured a realistic portrayal of the lives of domestic workers. But maids, butlers, and valets have enlivened the tube ever since Rochester resigned himself to Mr. Benny's stinginess in 1950. His successors have been as varied as a comic strip character named Hazel, the Norman Lear heroine Florida Evans, and Benson DuBois, the butler on "Soap" who rose to become a state budget director on his own series. Longtime viewers will remember Rochester's contemporary "Beulah," the popular black maid who straightened out the affairs of the Henderson family, and Hop Sing, who made a housekeeper unnecessary in the all-male Cartwright household on "Bonanza."

Housekeepers who picked up after exasperating employers included Florence of "The Jeffersons," Tina Kelly employed by the inscrutable Mr. T, and Mrs. Naugatuck on "Maude." Then there were the very proper butlers who made their employers feel like slobs. But who wouldn't leave their domestic affairs in the capable hands of "Mr. Belvedere," Brentwood ("The Two of Us"), or Mr. French ("Family Affair")? An inevitable 1980s' addition to the cast of characters was Mickey McKenzie, the sexy but efficient maid to two urban bachelors on "We've Got It Made." And that yuppie labor-saving device, the au pair, could be seen on "Growing Pains" and (briefly) "Designing Women."

Prime time's working class is hardly exhausted by butlers and maids. Other feature characters have ranged from the waitresses on "Cheers," "It's a Living," and "Alice" to the ambitious but klutzy janitors on "Working Stiffs," the frontier loggers on "Here Come the Brides," and the cabbies of "Taxi." Archie Bunker also did a stint behind the wheel of a taxi after he left his original job as a dock foreman for a tool-and-die company. Laverne and Shirley kept the bottle caps coming at the Schotz Brewery. In 1986 ABC even ventured briefly into the world of auto assembly line workers in "Gung Ho." Overall, however, unionized workers are a rare breed in prime time. A 1981 study counted "44 attorneys for every plumber; nine advertising executives for every electrician; 14 congressmen for every garbage collector; five times as many foreign spies as meat cutters; twice as many pimps as firemen; 16 times more prostitutes than mineworkers."[2]

For the most part these low-status characters are decent people, though they can be bumblers. In some cases, they provide a source of wisdom and common sense, while in others they are comical foul-ups. The domestic workers tend to deflate pompous and overbearing bosses. The blue-collar factory workers are mostly well intentioned but coarse and lacking in social graces. Waitresses are usually spirited, sharp-tongued experts at wisecracking repartee. In general these characters have considerable control over events, even if they lack structural authority. Thus "working stiff" comedies often play on blue-collar fantasies of control over a world in which real-life events are usually determined from above. But that raises the question of just what television's fantasy workplace is like.

WHO'S THE BOSS

So far we have looked at the prime-time images of various occupations. But what about the world of work itself? The way particular groups are portrayed doesn't tell us much about the relationships between bosses and workers or professionals and their clients. Just as prime-time portrayals of different professions have evolved over the years, so too has the structure of authority in the workplace. This is a more slippery question, since it involves situations and relationships rather than individual characters. So we looked at the themes that emerge when a show deals with the interaction between bosses and their underlings.

Several stock situations define the quality of life in television's workplace. They range from personal conflicts between supervisors and their subordinates to competing loyalties between institutions and personal conscience, and conflicts between upholding the rules and demanding changes.

Although these situations may sound abstract, television presents them in very concrete ways: A worker ridicules the boss to his face. Is this backtalk tolerated or rebuked? An employee breaks the rules to get the job done more efficiently. Is he reprimanded or praised for his initiative? A worker's vigorous pursuit of his goals brings him into conflict with an outsider, who pressures his superiors to call him off. Does the boss support him or knuckle under to the outside pressure? A boss and underling quarrel over how to get the job done. Who wins? Taken together, such questions define television's portrait of authority in the workplace, in settings that stretch from The Love Boat to the *Starship Enterprise*. Who's in charge, and how do things get done, when TV scriptwriters rather than the marketplace or government regulators govern the world of work?

This aspect of life on television has changed dramatically over the years. In the early days, bosses remained firmly in control and won praise for good management. After 1965, however, some drastic changes occurred. Subordinates who stood up to their superiors began to have a nearly even chance of prevailing. At the same time, those in charge increasingly became adversaries rather than supporters of their underlings. Finally, especially in recent years, bosses were less likely to have a heart, and subordinates increasingly had to act as the conscience of the workplace.

Conflicts of authority are a prime-time commonplace and an enduring source of dramatic conflict. We coded 162 such clashes, better than one in every fourth programs studied. Viewers can undoubtedly recall many bosses who were firmly in control. Crimebuster Elliot Ness's team of "Untouchables" never questioned his orders. Nor did James Phelps have to worry that his "Mission: Impossible" team might choose *not* to accept their mission. Anyone who questioned Ben Cartwright's authority as patriarch of the Ponderosa soon thought better of it. And Sheriff Andy Taylor rarely had to raise his voice to keep his excitable deputy Barney Fife from going off half-cocked.

On the other hand, the subordinate who successfully controls or manipulates his superiors is also much older than TV entertainment. On prime time, this type goes back to Sgt. Bilko, who could pull the wool over the hapless Colonel Hall's eyes without breaking a sweat. Nor was there any question about who was in charge in the Baxter family. George Baxter, a successful corporate lawyer in the outside world, knew better than to challenge his maid's authority at home. "Hazel" may have been his employee, but in her bailiwick, George marched to her tune. In a dramatic context, deputy Sam McCloud brought his Western methods of police work to New York City, regularly bypassing and frustrating precinct chief Clifford, his ostensible superior. And Gabe Kotter never let administrative regulations or vice principals come between him and his sweathogs.

So there are numerous well-known characters on both sides of the equation. Moreover, there have been uncounted conflicts between characters who appeared in only one episode or in some long-forgotten series that quickly failed. Our study was designed to uncover the overall pattern of victories and defeats in this ongoing struggle between chiefs and Indians. When push comes to shove, we found, the boss is more likely to come out on top. But his position is more precarious today than it ever was. In fact, the mid-1960s brought a lasting change in television's view of authority at work. Prior to 1965, exactly three out of four such conflicts were resolved in favor of the superior. During the next ten years, the boss's winning margin dropped to 55 percent. In the most recent decade studied, it declined slightly, to 53 percent, while subordinates prevailed 47 percent of the time.

These figures encompass a wide range of situations and story lines. For example, the principle of authority was upheld in the setting of a cattle drive on a 1965 "Rawhide" that we coded. In this episode trail boss Rowdy Yates creates dissension by shooting an army officer who tried to requisition his cattle. The cook, Wishbone, worries that "you shoot the U.S. army and the army shoots back." Colby, his second-in-command, complains, "Mark this down for yourself, they'll make you eat that gun." He also tells Rowdy that he's quitting at the end of the drive. But when another cowboy suggests a mutiny, Colby orders him to shut up. Eventually, they discover that their antagonists were really cattle rustlers impersonating soldiers, and Rowdy is vindicated in his men's eyes. Even back then, it didn't pay to question Clint Eastwood's authority.

More recently, the chain of command was upheld in a familiar medical drama conflict of youth vs. experience. In a 1976 episode of "Medical Center," a young Soviet sailor is brought to the hospital. Because he's the son of an important diplomat, his superiors want a Soviet doctor. Dr. Gannon refuses to accept this and wants to help the boy himself. But chief of surgery Paul Lochner steps in and orders him to acquiesce in the Soviet doctor's treatment. In this conflict Gannon's effort to place his patient's welfare above politics (another familiar theme) must bow to his superior's cool professionalism and diplomatic sensitivity.

On the other side of the coin, a 1962 episode of "Saints and Sinners" featured a beaten-down subordinate who finally discovers his backbone. The plot concerns Colby, a self-centered and immature movie star who depends on a bookkeeper and flunky he calls the Baron to get him out of scrapes. As the Baron tries to smooth over an accidental shooting, he takes a stream of verbal abuse from his boss. Sample: "You listen to me, you lousy kraut. You don't tell me when to rehearse. You just stay funny and keep the books." At the climax of the show, the mild-mannered minion suddenly draws himself together and announces that he's had enough: "No more bailing you out of dames, hit and runs, and all the rest." Realizing he's gone too far, Colby apologizes, but to no avail. As his employee prepares to walk out for good, he calls after him pleadingly, "Baron." The reply: "I'm not a baron. I'm *Mr.* Kessler."

More recently, it has become common to grant series stars a certain prima-donna status vis-à-vis their superiors. Authority seems increasingly nominal in these shows. It can only be exercised with the subordinate's assent. For example, a 1979 segment of "Kate Loves a Mystery" starts with newspaper publisher Josh Allen having lunch with reporter Kate Callahan. He tries to convince her to cover a labor dispute between the city and its garbage collectors. She refuses and tells him that buying her lunch won't change her decision. Later Kate finds a murder story more to her liking. Real-world journalists would envy the premise that she covers only the stories that interest her.

This approach was institutionalized on "Quincy M.E.." The crusading medical examiner was forever manipulating his boss, Dr. Astin, into endorsing his hunches and unconventional methods. In a 1977 episode we came across, Quincy finds a human bone at a construction site. He promptly closes the site to look for further evidence of a possible crime. Apparently under pressure from the construction company and the police, Astin finally reopens the site. Undeterred, Quincy furtively continues the investigation and manages to switch Astin's schedule to get him out of the way at a crucial moment. Overall, Astin ranges from malleable to ineffectual in his exercise of authority. His primary function is to provide obstacles for his quick-witted subordinate to overcome.

Quincy's difficulties with Astin are part of a broader trend in which superiors increasingly fail to support their employees in conflict situations. This is seen most clearly when the conflict concerns a third party. Even as the boss's authority slides away, it seems, he increasingly becomes an antagonist rather than a source of support for his own people. Before 1965, a subordinate could depend on his superior backing him up in this situation over two-thirds (69 percent) of the time. Since then, support has been forthcoming only 40 percent of the time, a figure that has remained steady across the past two decades.

A classic supportive boss appeared in a 1962 oater called "Empire." In the episode we coded, a foreman sticks up for a ranchhand accused of murder. In the face of strenuous opposition, the foreman hires a lawyer for his employee, bucks him up with visits in prison, and continues to stick by him after a jury's verdict of innocent proves unpopular. When his unbending stand alienates the other cowboys, he even offers to quit, saying, "Integrity and principles fall in the category of luxury items. If you can't afford them yourself, don't expect anyone else to foot the bill." Adherence to principle underlies all his actions and translates into unyielding support for an unpopular employee. He's just that kind of boss.

His kind began to disappear after the mid-1960s, however, ushering in the era of the nonsupportive superior. For example, the premise of "Kolchak: The Night Stalker" was to contrast the weird occurrences unearthed by reporter Carl Kolchak with the unbending skepticism of his editor, Tony Vincenzo. In a 1974 episode, Kolchak is investigating strange disappearances and even gets pictures and autopsy reports of the missing people. Then some government agents intervene and pressure Vincenzo into spiking the story. He tells Kolchak to mind his own business, stay away from kooky stories, and leave him alone.

Just as typical of the abuse our heroes now take from above was a confrontation between Drs. Gannon and Lochner in a 1969 "Medical Center." The setting is a medical complex attached to a large university. The ever-concerned Gannon wants a star player for the school's football team to stay on the bench until his health can be checked out. In the midst of his efforts, he inadvertently conveys his concerns to a reporter in the locker room, whom he mistakes for a coach. After a newspaper story appears, Lochner dresses him down. As head of the medical center, he points out the facts of life. He tells Gannon that the player is the key to the game, and the university needs a full stadium. Lochner also calls Gannon's tentative diagnosis a "way-out" suspicion. He warns that if Gannon keeps the player from competing, the blame will fall on the hospital. "So what was an incident becomes a crisis, and those few ordinary words you said yesterday become a breach of medical ethics and may be actionable at law." Despite this dressing down, Gannon sticks to his guns. He eventually discovers and removes a dangerous tumor, no thanks to his superior.

In light of the increased tendency for workers to confront their superiors, it comes as no surprise that television enjoys baiting the boss. In fact, TV's subordinates have always gotten away with ridiculing the people in charge. In this fantasy workplace, giving the boss the raspberry rarely brings a pink slip. Up through 1974, workers could subject their bosses to ridicule without adverse consequences nearly two-thirds (64 percent) of the time. Since then, the rate of risk-free ridicule has risen even higher, all the way up to 78 percent.

This tradition goes back to prime time's first regular foray into the white-collar world, "The Dick Van Dyke Show." Buddy, a comedy writer on the fictitious "Allen Brady Show," regularly skewered his nominal superior Mel, the show's producer. A 1962 episode we watched provided some typical repartee. When Mel says he has to go do some work, Buddy responds, "Good luck cleaning the ashtrays." The put-upon Mel calls Buddy a trained ape, provoking Buddy's inevitable topper that he, at least, is trained. It may not be Dorothy Parker, but the gist is clear. The repartee goes on endlessly in this vein at no risk to Buddy's job.

This kind of byplay didn't become institutionalized, however, until insult humor became entrenched in the late 1970s sitcoms. Feisty characters like "The Jeffersons'" maid Florence, the cabbies in "Taxi," and the waitresses in "Alice" spent much of their time flinging barbs at pompous or incompetent bosses. For example, in a 1981 segment of "Alice," the waitresses taunt Mel for not being able to think and work at the same time. When the bald Mel tells a lie, one waitress warns him his nose will grow, and another chimes in, "Too bad lying doesn't grow hair." "The Slap Maxwell Story" even featured a running joke in which sportswriter Slap harasses his editor Nelson, by trying to convince the staff that Nelson has some fictitious handicap like a glass eye or a wooden leg.

Ridicule isn't always risk-free. A 1966 episode of "The Monkees" concerned an automation-minded general manager who scoffs at the traditional methods of the company's owner and taunts him for inheriting the firm and lacking ambition. When their conflict comes to a head, he snaps, "Do you really think you—an indecisive jellyfish—can stand up to the march of machines?" That remark snaps his boss's backbone into place, and the G.M. is quickly out on the street. This show inverts the formula in the "Saints and Sinners" episode cited above, in which a pleasant but spineless individual suddenly stands up to his tormentor. The difference is that this time it's the boss who overcomes his wimpiness. It's much more common, though, for the boss to reply in kind without punishing the employee. Moreover, the underling usually gets the better of the exchange. On television, bosses tend to take their punishment and come back for more.

THE MAVERICKS

Perhaps the most characteristic change in television's workplace is the degree to which the underling, rather than the boss, has come to represent the conscience of the workplace. Once upon a time it was the person in charge who showed empathy or compassion. It might be Mr. Garlund calling off an overzealous employee in order to deal magnanimously with an opponent, detective Muldoon showing patience and compassion in one of the 8 million stories in "The Naked City," or Frieda Hechlinger protecting the clients of her social welfare agency on "East Side, West Side."

Of course, the boss with a heart has hardly disappeared from the screen in recent years. He lived on in benevolent characters ranging from the 27th precinct's Captain Barney Miller to "The Love Boat"'s Captain Steubing. Especially since the mid-1970s, though, the hero has been a maverick who has to challenge or circumvent his superiors in order to pursue truth, justice, and the American way. Examples of the new nonorganization man (or woman) include such unorthodox cops as Theo Kojak, Tony Baretta, and Marybeth Lacey, unflappable professionals like Hawkeye Pierce from the "M*A*S*H" crew, and various earnest crusaders like Quincy, the indomitable pathologist.

The numbers bear out this trend. Until 1965, superiors played the role of institutional conscience in a majority (55 percent) of shows that raised this theme. From 1965 through 1974, that role shifted toward subordinates by 54 to 46 percent. Since 1975, the idealistic underling has himself become something of an institution. In the most recent decade, the subordinates have held the moral high ground three times out of four (75 to 25 percent). The new format of underlings fighting for the underdog was perhaps best symbolized by the two-hour pilot for "Kojak," which goes by its TV movie title, "The Marcus-Nelson Murders." Based on an actual case, it pitted Lieutenant Kojak against the D.A. and various higher-ups who were out to nail a poor black ghetto youth for a murder he didn't commit. Throughout the show, the justice system was shown as an insensitive and even malevolent force, with the exception of the maverick crusader Kojak. As the series developed, Kojak was given great latitude by his mild-mannered superior Captain Frank McNeal.

Quincy was probably the best-known crusader from within the system during the late 1970s. Whatever the injustice he discovered, his response was predictable. The hard-charging Quincy would have either to enlist his reluctant superior Astin to the cause or else work around him. That was also Hawkeye Pierce's approach, more or less, in dealing with his commanding officers. Indeed, the whole premise of "M*A*S*H" was that an inhumane situation (war) and social structure (the military) could only be humanized by irreverent mavericks who do the right thing instead of just following orders.

This type of situation has become widely diffused throughout television drama in recent years. For instance, we coded a 1984 episode of "AfterM*A*S*H" on the plight of injured war veterans. Hospital administrator Mike D'Angelo, a callow and insensitive bureaucrat, is puzzled by the appearance of holes in the wall. Then he discovers that a hospitalized vet has been taking out his pent-up frustrations by punching the walls out. When D'Angelo officiously orders the man to stop, he knocks out the hapless administrator. The empathetic Dr. Peter Boyer, who witnesses this, hustles the vet out and tells him he'll cover for him. Boyer tells the man he understands how he feels, gives him his card, and tells him to get in touch if he wants to talk. Here it's not a matter of a subordinate upholding a grand principle or fighting the establishment. Boyer is just showing the empathy and human feeling so lacking at the top in TV's workplace.

By no means did all these shows carry anti-establishment or anti-authority messages. What they had in common were scripts that placed the banner of justice in the hands of a middle-level employee, whether the setting was the U.S. army, the New York City Police Department, or the Los Angeles County Coroner's Office. These days the Lone Ranger has to fight the bureaucrats as well as the black hats. In fact, this formula has become so pervasive that it's necessary to emphasize its recent vintage. A quarter century ago, our figures show, this type of character was still in the minority.

The heartless bosses and callow administrators who populate the screen today can be contrasted with the type of superior we encountered in a 1966 segment of "The FBI." It concerns a pharmaceutical company employee named Ed Leonard. He sells a company secret to a criminal who intends to pass it on to an unfriendly foreign power. Ed thinks the formula is for a hand lotion. Actually, it's a deadly virus for germ warfare. Despite this horrendous error, Ed's superior Harry Keeler is highly supportive of his larcenous employee. He tells the FBI that Ed was desperate for money to finance an operation for his daughter, who was mangled by a motorboat propeller. After helping to get Ed released from custody on his own recognizance, he finds a surgeon who will perform the operation at no charge.

Keeler is the type of boss who can forgive an employee for both industrial theft and unwitting espionage, and then help solve his legal, medical, and financial problems. He's not the kind of boss you see every day, but you used to see his type much more often on the small screen. For that matter, Hawkeye Pierce isn't your average army surgeon. They're both fantasy characters. It's just that the prevailing fantasies on television have changed drastically over the years.

If television tends to question or even undermine the boss's authority, it rarely demands his outright ouster. The people in charge may be portrayed as insensitive and worthy of ridicule, but TV shows uphold the institution itself more often than they challenge it. This has been true throughout television's history, and it is still true today, to a slightly diminished degree. When scripts broach the topic of either maintaining or reforming an institution, they opt for the status quo about 70 percent of the time. The proportion of status quo-oriented shows has dropped somewhat, from three out of every four before 1965 to two out of three since 1975. Yet the overall trend remains clear. Television may sneer or cluck its tongue at contemporary arrangements, but it rarely issues a rebel yell for change.

The social reform shows are usually well known, and their very visibility may lead conservative critics to overestimate the prevalence of their message. Thus, we recorded a fairly typical exchange between Quincy and his superior, Mr. Astin. Quincy is on one of his weekly crusades, and Astin tries to beg off by claiming that "the bureaucracy is hard to deal with," so change will come slowly. Quincy will have none of this. He responds that "the laws should be changed" and "the bureaucracy held accountable." The issue that week hardly matters for our purposes. This is the show's familiar approach to the institutions of medicine, law, business, and government.

More recently, a 1985 "Cagney & Lacey" episode typifies the many cop shows that pit dedicated mavericks against rigid bureaucrats as well as crooks. Our heroines are assigned to a special narcotics squad aimed at cutting off the flow of cocaine traffic. They are appalled at the number of approvals required to take action and are bedeviled by a police department efficiency expert who proposes even more bureaucratic procedures. After Cagney and Lacey fail to get permission to make some arrests, they go ahead on their own. They succeed in breaking up a cocaine ring but are still reprimanded for not going by the book. They argue that the rules are cumbersome and counterproductive, and their superior finally agrees with them.

If it seems that bureaucracy is a favorite target, it should be remembered that the heroes don't always take on the system. Scripts are often critical of rules or bureaucrats while treating them as something you just have to live with. Otherwise the proportion of reformist shows would be much higher. But there are also many shows that explicitly argue for maintaining the institution's rules or traditions. For every Quincy, there's a Marcus Welby, for every "Mod Squad," an "FBI" and "Dragnet" that regularly uphold the system against its critics.

Our sample included a "Star Trek" episode in which the protagonist places duty and adherence to regulations above the life of his own father. The *Enterprise*'s first officer, Mr. Spock, is preparing to supply the blood his father requires in order to carry out urgently needed surgery. Then the ship's commander, Captain Kirk, is wounded, and Spock must take command. The supremely rational Spock now refuses to carry out the transfusion, citing a list of regulations requiring him to place his duty to the ship above all other concerns. Luckily, Kirk recovers enough to walk to the bridge and relieve Spock before collapsing. Through this subterfuge, the life of Spock's father is saved, but no one ever suggests that the rules should not be followed to the letter. The problem is how to save a life while conforming to regulations, not by breaking them.

A similar message was conveyed in a 1964 episode of "Combat," a World War II drama. After Lieutenant Hawley's patrol is rescued from the Germans by a group of Greek commandos, their leader (a colonel) orders the patrol to join them on a raid. Hawley objects that he has a wounded man who needs treatment, but the colonel reminds him that regulations give him command over both units. Their raid fails, and Hawley again objects. Once again, the Greek colonel asserts his authority and Hawley acquiesces. After a second failure, the colonel orders the men to stay behind while he accomplishes the objective by driving his jeep into an ammunition dump, which explodes.

The unmistakable message is that Hawley must subjugate his personal judgment and concern for his men to a foreign officer's orders because the rules must be obeyed.

No discussion of upholding institutional authority would be complete without an example from "Dragnet." A short vignette will suffice. In a 1968 episode, Sergeant Friday investigates a complaint of police brutality. The officer struck a man in response to his verbal abuse. Friday rips into the decorated veteran: "These are tenuous times; it is fashionable to scream against law and order. Young people fight the system and old people have misplaced values. . . .A lot more was at stake than a man getting hit by a cop. It was a defeat for order and justice." This is a conservative moral that even a liberal could love. The upholders of authority must abide by their own rules, whatever the provocation, so that their authority will be respected. The instrument of social authority is reprimanded in order to preserve the authority of the system.

These examples help to explain how television often upholds institutional authority. Scripts rarely deal directly with abstract issues like the nature of justice, the bureaucratization of the workplace, or the costs and benefits of hierarchical authority structures. Instead, issues like these are raised obliquely through concrete plot developments. A policeman must decide how to subdue a suspect without using excessive force. A doctor tries to help patients within a structure of hospital rules and regulations. A soldier must choose between following his own judgment and that of his superior. In instances like these, broader issues of authority always lurk below the surface. But it is less entertaining (more precisely, it is more difficult to be entertaining) to confront them head-on in dialogue and character development than to develop plot lines that portray conformity or rebellion, adherence or rejection of authority, as unreflective responses to the situation.

When there is no overt discussion of underlying issues, situation and plot become all-important in structuring authority relations. And television usually places even its mavericks and rebels within the system, as members of a larger authority structure. Thus Quincy demonstrated competence and conscience within the medical profession even as he criticizes medical practices. Chris Cagney, Theo Kojak, and Tony Baretta portrayed caring and creative approaches to law enforcement while struggling with a rigid police bureaucracy.

Even at the height of television's "relevance" phase, during the late 1960s and early 1970s, the formula was similar. Would-be "with-it" series like "Mod Squad," "The Interns," and "Storefront Lawyers" put young, hip, socially concerned characters into the standard formats of police shows and medical and courtroom dramas. They were shown as sharper and more committed to social justice than their elders (and superiors) in the department, or the hospital, or the law firm. Yet, their message was that traditional institutions could be renewed and regenerated by putting them in closer touch with "what's happening, baby."

The young rebels were mavericks, but they were nonetheless representatives of social institutions. Hence their good work inevitably carried a double-edged message. They simultaneously criticized traditional procedures and leadership while upholding the viability of the institution itself. As Castleman and Podrazik put it, "Important social problems and contemporary jargon were simply churned into standard television format drama wrapped in love beads. . . . The new breed of hero was the former outsider won over to help the establishment correct its own shortcomings. . . ."[3]

Thus, the social relevance series that peaked around 1970 illustrate how prime time can criticize or ridicule authority figures without directly attacking institutional authority. These shows endorsed social change through the agency of caring professionals who acted as patrons of the oppressed and underprivileged. At the same time, they rejected calls for overthrowing the system. By their very presence, these outsiders on the inside validated the system's claim to adaptability. In short, their essential message was not radical but liberal. Institutions are not hopelessly corrupt or structurally flawed. It's just that the people in charge don't care enough about the human beings they should be serving. The system can work if the designated crusader can break through the barriers erected by pompous bosses, inept supervisors, and faceless bureaucrats. It's a social worker's vision of social problems; the solution is less authority and more humanity.

Work Is Where the Heart Is

Given this backdrop, it is not surprising that television should glorify those who humanize the workplace through their personal involvement with co-workers and clients. What did surprise us was the pervasiveness of this theme. Eighty-eight shows, one out of every seven in the entire sample, carried the message that bosses or professionals should get involved in the personal problems of their workers, clients, or customers. TV entertainment has always taught the lesson that caring professionals can humanize a heartless world by making it their business to reach out to those in need, even when this conflicts with career concerns or normal procedures. We can illustrate the pervasiveness of this view with a few examples from different occupations and time periods.

Long before drug addiction was making headlines, Ben Casey was helping a patient overcome her dependency on morphine. In the episode we coded, a woman is admitted for severe back pain, but Casey discovers that it's her whole life that requires sympathetic treatment. He continues to administer pain-killing narcotics until he can remove the benign tumor causing her back problems. Then he confronts her with the need to break the addiction and put her life in order. Meanwhile Dr. Zorba also discovers the patient's addiction. He reprimands Casey for not withdrawing the medication immediately upon recognizing the condition. Casey responds that he saw no other way to help her. The script suggests that Casey's behavior was technically unethical but probably necessary to his patient's long-term mental and emotional recovery.

A decade later, this holistic approach was applied to law enforcement on "The Streets of San Francisco." Detective Steve Kieller is assigned to guard a prostitute who is being stalked by a murderer. Steve's initial attitude of disapproval gradually turns to sympathy, as he realizes that the woman has been largely a victim of circumstance. He then tries to convince her to turn her life around by helping her to realize that she does have choices and can shape her own existence. After the killer is caught, Steve finds the woman a job as a waitress. The show ends with her working normal hours in a nice restaurant, apparently on her way to a law-abiding and satisfying lifestyle.

Fast-forwarding to the 1980s, we encountered onetime butler Benson in his new capacity as state budget director. He is approached by a seventy-three-year-old gardener who is upset at the prospect of mandatory retirement. At first Benson is reluctant to help, telling the man that the law was set up to help people. Eventually he changes his mind after being convinced that it's wrong to throw away older workers at an arbitrary point in their lives. He then launches an all-out lobbying effort to change the law, throwing his clout as budget director behind a bill in the state legislature.

This theme shows no sign of losing popularity with scriptwriters. For example, a 1988 segment of the critically acclaimed "Frank's Place" focused on a young bartender at Frank's restaurant who gets involved with drugs, shooting cocaine and becoming a low-level drug runner. His employer and fellow workers respond with concern for his welfare, and an older waitress and the head chef finally act as surrogate parents in forcing him to shape up and "get straight." In short, everyone acts like members of a loving family trying to reform a black sheep.

These diverse plots and program formats share the common theme of the caring co-worker whose personal involvement transcends his disapproval of a deviant lifestyle, commitment to professional ethics, or adherence to outmoded legislation. The message is clear and persistent: If only doctors, law enforcers, bureaucrats, and businessmen could get beyond their rules and regulations or narrow occupational interests, if only they would concentrate on helping other people, the world would be a better place. What the workplace needs now is love, sweet love.

The flip side of this call for a humanized workplace is a warning against making a fetish of work. A recurring motif is the danger of workaholism and the emotional cost of subjugating personal to occupational concerns. The conflict between job devotion and human relations was raised twenty-one times among the shows sampled. In 81 percent of these programs, career-minded characters were brought up short by the poverty of their emotional lives. Fewer than one show in five endorsed the single-minded pursuit of occupational goals.

This is an especially common theme on doctor shows. Indeed, workaholism is one of the few vices television associates with the medical profession. A particularly strong version of this refrain was sounded on a 1966 "Ben Casey" episode. Casey is treating a distinguished older doctor with a degenerative nerve disease. In the face of death, he expresses bitterness over how he has lived. He tells Casey that "to be really good at something closes the door to almost everything else . . . .I was quite like you when I started. I made my choice. I married my profession. It was selfish of me to marry."

Later Casey asks the doctor's daughter why her father thought he was selfish to marry. She responds, "He is a very special man. He's a man who can work for years pursuing his dream alone. Martyr, saint, they make fascinating reading in history books, but as human beings they're washouts. I'd rather be the child of a thief, a bully, or a drunkard." Casey says he'd have been proud to have such a father. She replies that she doesn't "mind sharing [my father] with the ages, but I don't even know him." Casey thanks her for this depressing insight into the danger of pursuing a career at all costs. He seems to have learned a lesson and starts considering how to develop a fuller personal life.

Nearly twenty years later, this dilemma was recycled for "Trapper John, M.D." This time it is the hero, Dr. Trapper John McIntyre, who is forced by illness to reflect on his life. Afflicted with Guillain-Barré syndrome, which induces temporary paralysis, he at first refuses help from his family. Eventually his ex-wife begins caring for him. But his son, a resident at the hospital, is reluctant to see his father. When they finally meet, both are ill at ease, since they've never gotten along. Then they begin to talk about old times. They look through the family album and realize that Trapper rarely appears. Later Trapper laments to his ex-wife that he feels he let the family down. He says he should have been there. She replies he had to support the family, and he did love them. Trapper says, "Support means being there. I was a father by proxy." Thus, Trapper realizes his mistake. By the end of the show, he is getting along better with his son and ex-wife. In contrast to the "Ben Casey" episode, it isn't too late for the doctor-turned-patient to make an emotional recovery.

It is not always doctors who must learn this lesson. In fact, they sometimes teach it to other workaholic professionals. Sometimes the results of hard work are even more serious. On a 1981 episode of "One Day At A Time," the career-minded Ann Romano works herself into a heart attack. In an ironic occupational role-reversal, she receives a finger-wagging lecture from her doctor on the virtues of moderation in work. Seven years later Murphy Brown did a stint at the Betty Ford Clinic, after her workaholism had produced stress-related addictions to alcohol, nicotine, and caffeine.

Occasionally television upholds the virtue of devotion to occupational duty, especially in the realm of law enforcement. It's difficult to imagine Joe Friday taking time off from a case to be with his family, because the obsessive pursuit of lawbreakers was so central to his character. Marshal Dillon was also cut from this mold, as a 1969 episode of "Gunsmoke" made clear. While running down some ruthless robbers, he runs into his old girlfriend, Liola, who is now running with the outlaws. When Liola is wounded, Matt takes her into town for medical treatment. While recuperating, she talks to Doc about their happier times. In one scene she asks whether Matt is "still married to his badge." Doc replies that he is, and Liola recalls wistfully that she almost got Matt away from the badge. Doc admits that he was sorry at the time that she failed. But now he believes the job has been good for Matt, keeping him going despite the rigors involved. It is clear that Matt wasn't cut out for domestic life; his life is his work. No one, not even Miss Kitty, laments his lack of a social life or his total devotion to enforcing justice.

Such themes are very much in the minority, however, in a fantasy workplace that values personal relations far more than productivity. In the world of law enforcement, from Marshal Dillon's Dodge City to Sergeant Friday's Los Angeles, the job of protecting law-abiding citizens is usually all-consuming. In most other locales, though, the workplace has become a surrogate family setting. As Janet Maslin writes in the *New York Times*:

> Employment is as central to the pretexts of many current series as happy families were in the late 1950s. . . .All that is

required of a television job is that it not necessitate too much actual labor, at least not in front of the camera. Work is beside the point anyhow, since the television job is usually just a way of getting the characters away from home . . . .When working situations are sufficiently simplified by television, they take on family configurations automatically . . .employees begin behaving as if [the boss] were dad.[4]

We would add one caveat to this comparison. When television portrays family life, parents are usually in control, and they mostly end up in the right as well. Despite the gradual introduction of serious, real life issues in family comedies and dramas, the authority structure of the home has changed hardly at all over the years. By contrast, in the surrogate family of the workplace, father doesn't know best anymore. The decline of authority in television's fantasy workplace is a lasting legacy of programming changes that occurred in the late 1960s. Since then, bosses have been far less likely either to command or deserve their employees' respect.

Ironically, television's new fascination with the workplace has been accompanied by disinterest and even disdain for what goes on there. Little wonder that the scriptwriters often preach a kind of inverted work ethic—don't listen to the boss and don't work too hard, because work isn't where it's at. Thus, on a 1980 episode of "The Jeffersons," Lionel Jefferson is "beeped" from the office on the day of his new daughter's christening party. He races off to work, leaving his sobbing wife and disappointed guests behind. Later his father brings him back to the party with the admonition, "Never put work above spending time with your family." That's standard TV advice to the lovelorn. Except, of course, when the workplace *is* your family.

6

THE WORLD ACCORDING TO J.R.

On television. . .to be in business is to ride a monorail of avarice to disaster and bad sex.

—John Leonard
New York Times

J.R. is unrepentant. He has just fed fraudulent geological surveys to his rival, Cliff Barnes, enticing him to "borrow" corporate funds to gain control of allegedly oil-rich land. After Cliff loses the shareholders' money and his own, he tries to kill himself. But it takes more than a few bankruptcies and a suicide attempt to provoke penitence from J.R. Hauled before a family council, he protests, "It's not my fault if Barnes is so stupid as not to check a deal." Miss Ellie is appalled at her son's callousness, but the audience presumably relishes this moment of malice from the man they love to hate.

As "Dallas" fans know, the cold-blooded maneuver we chanced to code is perfectly in character. Darth Vader may have a last-minute change of heart, but don't expect J.R. Ewing to falter. He's cut from the same mold as Shakespeare's Richard III, a man whose villainy is exceeded only by the pleasure he takes in it. Cutthroat deals, Machiavellian maneuvers, brushing aside legal and moral scruples as so many minor hindrances to personal advancement—they're all in a night's work for the president of Ewing Oil.

That's how business gets done on "Dallas." It's a zero-sum game with no holds barred, and no room for the squeamish in the winner's circle. But is J.R. the exception or the rule for television's portrayal of businessmen? In "The View from Sunset Boulevard", Hollywood writer Ben Stein summed up the charge that businessmen get a bad rap from TV entertainment:

> One of the clearest messages of television is that business-men are bad, evil people, and that big businessmen are the worst of all. . . the murderous, duplicitous, cynical business-man is about the only kind of businessman there is on TV adventure shows, just as the cunning, trickster businessman shares the stage with the pompous, buffoon businessman in situation comedies.[1]

Stein's analysis has not gone unchallenged. First, his book is an impressionistic "snapshot," based on his admittedly unscientific viewing of shows during the late 1970s. Second, he comes from a politically conservative background (he is the son of economist Herbert Stein), which might have influenced his perception of what he watched. On the other hand, Stein's analysis was supported by a content analysis of two hundred prime-time episodes from the 1979-80 season, published by the Media Institute. That study found that only one in four business charac-ters was portrayed positively. As the study's title put it, the majority were shown to be "crooks, conmen and clowns."[2]

THE BIG, THE BAD, AND THE UGLY

How do these charges stack up against the systematic and long-term perspective that our content analysis provides? We found Stein's portrait of the nasty or foolish businessman to be mainly on the mark, especially for the time period he examined. In fact, across the entire three decades of our study, business characters were consistently depicted more negatively than those in other occupations. Only 37 percent of the businessmen we coded played positive roles, compared to 45 percent in negative roles, with the rest neutral. The proportion of bad guy businessmen is almost double that of all other occupations. With businessmen excepted, the positive ratio of all other characters in known occupations is precisely two to one (46 percent positive vs. 23 percent negative).

Moreover, the business category contains more than its share of the really bad apples. Businessmen are over three times more likely to be criminals than are members of other occupations. One in seven business characters commits a crime, compared to one in twenty-three characters in all occupations. This translates into a sizable share of the criminal activity on television. Although businessmen represent 12 percent of all characters in census-coded occupations, they account for 32 percent of the crimes these characters commit. Even this underestimates the venality of TV's businessmen, since their crimes tend to be either violent or sleazy. They commit 40 percent of the murders and 44 percent of vice crimes like drug trafficking and pimping.

The typical exploits of a television business bad guy make the worst robber baron seem a candidate for canonization. For example, we coded a 1979 episode of "The Runaways" about a restaurant owner who runs a drug and prostitution ring for the mob. During the course of the show he kills an underling who tries to do some free-lance drug dealing. And that's just the warm-up. He later attempts to kill his partner, who stands between him and even greater profits. When the father of one of his employees tries to extricate his son from these criminal associations, he manages to get the man arrested. And when one of his prostitutes starts to cause trouble, he personally beats her up to teach her a lesson.

Even this strong-arm artist couldn't hold a candle to a character encountered on a 1972 segment of "The Streets of San Francisco." A well-educated executive, the man is presented as a clean-cut paragon of American business success, who worked his way to the top in Horatio Alger fashion. He's also a deeply religious individual who keeps a wooden cross on his desk to remind him of the need for humility. In his off hours, however, he helps clean up the city's mean streets by murdering prostitutes to save them from themselves. When the police finally track down this buttoned-down Jack the Ripper, they discover that he carved his victims' names on the bottom of his cross, not unlike notches on a gunfighter's pistol.

These characters are more colorful than most, but as business criminals they're strictly run of the mill. In an earlier study of crime on television during the 1981 season, we encountered such evildoers as a bank manager who arranges to have his own bank robbed (on "Lobo"), the head of a worldwide conglomerate who murders a competitor ("Nero Wolfe"), a stockbroker who murders a troublesome member of his call girl ring ("Vegas"), an executive who tries to sell "classified" equipment to an unfriendly country ("The Greatest American Hero"), and a chemical company president who illegally dumps toxic wastes and attempts murder to cover it up ("Walking Tall").[3] We were once inclined to dismiss as hyperbole Stein's comment that "the well-dressed businessman who pays for his kids' orthodontia by selling heroin to teenagers and the manufacturer who has murdered his go-go dancer girlfriend are staples of TV adventure shows."[4] No more. No immoral or illegal act seems too vile—or too unlikely—to be perpetrated by a television businessman.

On the other hand, studies conducted during the past decade tend to show TV businessmen at their worst. There was a time when a business character had almost an even chance of playing a good guy. That was during the early years of television, before anybody was murdering prostitutes or dumping toxic wastes on prime time. In the first decade of our study (1955-1964), negative businessmen barely outnumbered positive ones, by 42 to 39 percent. That's still a long way from the two-to-one positive ratio for other occupations, but it's close to an even split. It's been all downhill since then, though. During the next decade the bad guys extended their plurality by 45 to 39 percent. Since 1975 the margin has grown to 46 percent negative and only 34 percent positive. So businessmen were never television's favorites, but neither were they always so reviled as today.

These differences over time undercut an explanation, sometimes offered by industry spokesmen, that television merely reflects a longstanding antipathy toward business by all forms of popular art. In the words of a Television Information Office press release, "Novels. . .by authors such as Frank Norris, Sinclair Lewis, and Upton Sinclair helped generations ago to popularize the image of the businessman as someone out for his own good. . . .Television doesn't create [this] popular image, it only reflects it."[5] This may help illuminate the general tendency of business characters to fare badly, but it cannot account for the downward trend in their fortunes over the years. Nor does it reflect a more general negative trend. Portrayals of characters in other occupations have remained quite stable for decades. Their 43-to-22 percent positive plurality for 1955-1964 was almost identical to the 44-to-25 percent margin we have recorded since 1975.

A view often heard within the television industry holds that businessmen are favored targets of mass entertainment because they are authority figures in a populist society. Those at the top of the heap have to expect an occasional pie in the face. As NBC Vice President Alfred Schneider puts it in a letter to Media Institute President Leonard Theberge:

> Entertainment programming, dramatic and comedic, relies on conflict: good versus evil. More often than not that portrayal borne out by your statistics involves an individual in a position of authority against whom the underdog, the ordinary man, is played off. This can be a businessman, a father, a professional of some sort, or other like authority figure in our culture.[6]

In the same vein, though in a different vernacular, is the view of sociologist Todd Gitlin:

> In the conflict between the big and the little lies the condensed drama which is the staple of mass culture, especially television. Now in the oligopolistic economy of late twentieth-century corporate capitalism, it is the captains of industry, commerce, and finance along with the top government officials who, more than anyone else, make the deci-

213

sions which set the ground rules for everyone else. . . .These institutions make convincing villains because the predominance of big, impersonal, unbudgeable institutions flies in the face of the value attached to personal liberty in American culture and tradition.[7]

It follows from this line of argument that corporate executives should fare worse than other types of business characters, and small businessmen should fare best. Indeed, as little guys themselves, small businessmen should not look very different from nonbusiness characters, while high level corporate executives should bear the brunt of antibusiness portrayals. To test this explanation, we broke down the portrayals into three broad categories of business characters—big business executives, small businessmen, and all others, including salesmen, realtors, stockbrokers, and so on.

The results of our study do not bear out the reasoning advanced by Schneider and Gitlin. Big businessmen actually fare best of the three groups, with a 44-percent positive and 46-percent negative rating. Small business characters are somewhat more negative than the big guys, with 37-percent positive and 45-percent negative portrayals. Pulling up the rear is the catchall residual category of independent or difficult to classify occupations, with only 31-percent positive and 44-percent negative characters. For a quick comparison, we subtracted the negative from the positive score from each group. That produced a net score of −2 percent for big business, −8 for small business, and −13 for the others. For all non-business occupations, the net score is plus 23 percent.

In short, it doesn't seem that television's attitude toward businessmen can be written off as part of a populist aversion to authority. Instead the data suggest a more general antipathy toward business characters of all stripes, with minor variations that actually favor big business. Nor does the evidence support Schneider's assertion that this negative image extends to educated professionals as the following chapter demonstrates. As for the notion that fathers are tarred from the same brush, imagine a series titled, "J.R. Knows Best."

There is another way to test the argument that television's animus toward business simply reflects America's longstanding populist temper. Consider how differently big and small businessmen have fared at various times throughout television's history. In the first decade studied (1955-1964), the executive suite had by far the better image in prime time. Corporate executives attained a strongly positive margin of 67 to 30 percent, a better than two-to-one ratio. By contrast, small businessmen recorded a plurality of negative portrayals, by 47 to 34 percent.

The 1965-1974 decade saw a dramatic reversal of fortunes for the two groups. Portrayals of corporate executives shifted to a two-to-one negative ratio (59 to 29 percent), a net loss of nearly 30 percent. At the same time, small businessmen made an equally striking revival, attaining a positive plurality of 47 to 37 percent. Thus the two groups switched positions relative to one another in a ten-year span.

After the flip-flop, what could they do for an encore? The only remaining combination was for the two groups to look alike. And that's exactly what happened. In the most recent decade, the 1975 to 1985 seasons, big businessmen remained mainly negative, by a 49- to 39-percent margin. Small businessmen looked even worse, however, with 50-percent negative and only 32-percent positive characters. So it's only in recent years that big and small business are treated the same way—badly.

Thus, the gradual overall decline in the fortunes of TV's businessmen actually masks some sharp variations that produce a more complicated pattern. During television's early years there was no onus attached to big business; quite the contrary. The big bad businessman became an artifact of TV entertainment only during the late 1960s. Small business characters withstood the shift in sentiment until the late 1970s, when they too took on a negative cast. So television's portrayal of businessmen does not reflect a longstanding suspicion of business, especially big business, as part of our national character. Television didn't simply absorb a cultural stereotype of the nasty or foolish businessman. It discovered him midway through its history and has since made him a stock character. The networks didn't merely appropriate today's TV businessman from other media. They helped invent him.

THE ROAD TO "DALLAS"

During the 1950s television rarely showed businessmen at work, except in routine background roles. It was far more common to show them after work, in the context of their family life. That means audiences probably didn't think of such characters as businessmen. Their occupation was like a tag worn inside a garment. It was mainly a plot device that provided a plausible rationale for the middle-class suburban household setting of most stories. Who now remembers that Jim Anderson of "Father Knows Best" was an insurance agent? His real job was to be a warm husband and wise father. How many fans of "Leave It to Beaver" thought of Ward Cleaver as someone who worked in an accounting firm? He was far too busy dispensing sage advice to his two sons. And it seemed positively insulting to picture the suave socialite detective Nick Charles as a businessman. The writers of "The Thin Man" series claimed he was a publisher, but that was an excuse to place him in the high-life settings that provided a backdrop to his sleuthing. Yet all these characters were identified as representatives of the business world, even if their ostensible jobs had little to do with their on-camera activities.

Another unlikely source of good guy businessmen was the Western genre that emerged during the late 1950s to dominate the airwaves. Television's earliest Westerns were kiddie shows featuring fantasy heroes like the Lone Ranger and Hopalong Cassidy. In 1955, however, "Gunsmoke" began the era of adult Westerns that played out relatively realistic dramas of good vs. evil in Old West settings. These shows provided a steady stream of small-town business types, including storekeepers, bankers, owners of saloons and boardinghouses, and the like. Finally, there were ranchers, whose struggles to raise cattle and drive them to market profitably was the moving force behind many a plot. In fact, such characters were often cast as defenders of truth, justice, and the underdog, fighting hand in hand with the local sheriff or marshall to preserve law and order.

"Bonanza"'s Cartwright family certainly fit this bill. Running a spread the size of the thousand-square-mile Ponderosa was not just a business, it was big business. Ben Cartwright and his three sons were often shown pursuing their financial interests, dealing with other ranchers and miners in the area. Throughout a fourteen-year run, including three years as Nielsen's top-rated show, the Cartwright clan acted as good guy precursors of the Ewings, moving through business and romantic entanglements while righting wrongs and upholding the law. The series even spawned imitators like "The Big Valley," which added women to the family and moved the setting from Nevada to California, but otherwise followed the same formula of big-time ranchers upholding the American way. And that was only the beginning.

An updated version of "Bonanza," set in contemporary New Mexico, announced the theme in its title, "Empire." The Garrett ranch housed a financial empire, which included oil, mining, and timber industries, various crops, and animal husbandry. A 1962 segment in our sample is notable for presenting management as good guys. With the Garrett family's support, ranch manager Jim Redigo defends a ranchhand who is wrongly accused of murder. The other workers walk out, refusing to work alongside a murderer, and other businessmen cancel some contracts in protest. In the face of all this pressure, Jim and the Garretts stick to their guns and refuse to fire the man. Eventually he is vindicated and the workers return, the contracts are renewed, and life goes back to normal. But first these businessmen are shown as willing to sacrifice their financial interests to pursue an altruistic goal, defending an innocent man. This "Empire," it seems, is worlds away from "Dynasty."

Business characters were by no means exclusively good guys on Western dramas. Among shows we coded, "Rawhide" featured a rancher who almost destroys a cattle drive through his drinking, laziness, demands for special treatment, and generally selfish behavior. "Bat Masterson" brings to justice another rancher whose opposition to the railroad leads him to kill two detectives investigating his theft of railroad property. And on "High Chapparal," yet another ranching empire, the evil agent of a mining company, hires scalphunters to exterminate an Indian tribe. The Indians went on the warpath against the company after it unscrupulously managed to expropriate their land for its mineral resources.

Largely because of the many series stars who stood for truth and justice, however, business characters were more likely to wear the white hats in Westerns than in other program genres. Across all shows, our study recorded a 44 percent positive rate for businessmen portrayed in Westerns, substantially higher than the 35 percent rate found in situation comedies and 27 percent in law enforcement shows. Even "Gunsmoke"'s Miss Kitty, viewers will recall, was a saloonkeeper with a heart of gold (and nary a hint of hanky-panky with Matt in her off hours at the Longbranch Saloon).

There were even occasional businessmen outside Westerns, in the early days, who stood up for all-American values against the forces of evil. The best known was Herbert Philbrick of "I Led Three Lives," who infiltrated the American Communist party to supply the FBI with information about the party's plans and operations. His three lives were those of a pipe-smoking advertising executive, Communist party worker, and FBI counterspy. This series was released in syndication, where it proved a smash hit. Over a hundred episodes were produced from 1953 through 1956, and they continued to run well into the next decade. A contemporary of the Philbrick hit with similar preoccupations in the international arena was "The Hunter." This CBS series, which ran during 1953 and 1954, featured a wealthy young American whose business interests took him to exotic locales around the globe, where he usually encountered Communist party agents. He regularly thwarted their efforts to undermine the free world, sometimes aided by friends in a European underground organization.

A less politicized but equally benevolent international financier was "Mr. Garlund," the head of Garlund Enterprises, whose exploits were featured on CBS during the 1960-1961 season. In a segment we coded, Frank Garlund is sued by a young artist who claims that his Sea Research Facility is eroding the land under her house. Rather than using his vast financial resources to crush his adversary, Garlund decides to help her. As he gallantly observes, "throwing a battalion of corporate lawyers at one medium-sized artist makes you a bully." So he secretly gives her lawyer a tip that will help her case, rebukes his own overzealous executive who tries to thwart her, and eventually settles amicably out of court. Thus a rich corporate chieftain shows that business instincts can be tempered by compassion and manages to stand up for the little guy against his own company's interests.

By the early 1960s, the righteous or benevolent big businessman was passing from the prime-time scene, aside from a few holdovers in the Westerns. The defense of justice was becoming the province of glamorous private eyes or hard-nosed police detectives, who often uncovered the schemes of unscrupulous business types. On "The Untouchables," special agent Elliot Ness collared numerous mob-connected businessmen when he wasn't tracking down Bugs Moran, Ma Barker, and Mad Dog Coll. On "The Law and Mr. Jones," lawyer Abraham Lincoln Jones handled mostly nonviolent white-collar crime involving fraud, embezzlement, and the like. One episode in our sample dealt with a wealthy real estate developer who buys a contracting company and trades on the former owner's good reputation while using substandard materials and building practices to increase profits. When the previous owner tries to interfere, the developer threatens violence and sends flunkies and thugs after him.

With the advent of action-adventure shows, businessmen were increasingly involved in shady deals and nasty schemes. The trend toward ever-more-serious evildoing accelerated quickly after 1965. Business characters became stock villains in spy shows like "The Man From U.N.C.L.E.," "Mission: Impossible," and "I Spy," along with adventure series like "Hawaii Five-O," "Name of the Game," and "The Wild, Wild West," and crusading lawyer formats like "Storefront Lawyers" and "The Lawyers" (a rotating segment of "The Bold Ones"). A typical villain comes from "Hawaii Five-O," a successful police show whose glorious locales gave it an action-adventure sheen. A 1968 segment in our sample was built around nightclub owner Benny Kalua's efforts to keep some condominiums from being built. He arranges for the murder of the city official who granted the building permit. Then he tries to frame someone else for the crime. When it looks like an accomplice might talk, he tries to murder her as well. He rounds off his hour's work by trying to murder the owner of the construction firm but is killed himself in the ensuing struggle.

219

Thus, by the mid-1960s, the business villain had already become the cliché that Stein documented a decade later. Although viewers may think of J.R. as the archetypal business bad guy, he is actually the exception. Very few prime-time dramatic series have featured continuing characters in starring roles who personify evil in some new way each week. That is the province of soap operas, which made it into the prime-time schedule only in the late 1970s. Before that, the evil TV businessman was a composite of the many one-shot villains who are killed or hauled off to jail by the heroes before the final credits.

In recent years, though, these single-appearance villains have been joined by unscrupulous J.R. clones in a whole series of nighttime soaps that use business as a backdrop. Viewers interested in the sordid world of big business could turn to "Dallas" or "Dynasty" to see dirty work in the oil industry, "Falcon Crest" for the wine business, "Knots Landing" for land developers, "Paper Dolls" for modeling and cosmetics, and "Berrengers" for the retail trade. If this trip proved wearisome, they could relax with the self-explanatory "Hotel." "Yellow Rose" even brought back the world of ranching, perhaps with a sense of déjà vu (although Ben Cartwright would have made short work out of drug traffickers and smugglers of illegal aliens who cropped up in this latter-day Ponderosa). These business people differed from their one-shot predecessors not in their contempt for law and morals, but in their mixture of business and (mostly sexual) pleasure, along with the ability to get away with some of their transgressions. They can't get killed or jailed, after all, without being written out of the series.

Another trend of the 1970s was toward more direct criticism of business practices. The bad guy was no longer just embezzling or murdering to keep control of some generic business. Now he was polluting the local water supply, defrauding the public, or subjecting his employees to dangerous working conditions. The new businessman, whose vices threaten the community at large, was well represented by one Simon Boley on "The D.A." In a 1972 episode we coded, Simon owns a chain of furniture and appliance stores. He uses bait-and-switch sales tactics but is careful to follow procedures that help him avoid prosecution. His real criminal genius lies in selling used appliances as new ones, then repossessing and finally reselling them to start the cycle anew. He begins by selling supposedly new furniture that is actually used or damaged. When the furious buyers refuse to pay, he conspires with the credit company to get default judgments against them. He then buys up the repossessed furniture for a song and resells it. Simon is totally remorseless and driven solely by greed. Luckily for consumers, the D.A. finishes the hour one step ahead of him.

We recorded the last word in sharp business practices on a 1975 episode of "Get Christie Love!" The villain, Maxwell Case, manages a travel agency that arranges European tours. He procures medical histories from participants, supposedly for their own protection while abroad. In reality, he uses the records to select his potential victims—male tourists with weak hearts and no family ties. A female accomplice flirts with the victim and slips him a drug that induces a heart attack. Once the gentleman's status changes from tourist to corpse, the travel agency arranges the burial. But Case surreptitiously leaves the body in Europe while shipping back a casket that is actually filled with heroin. This is entrepreneurship television style—a ploy that assures a booming business in tourism, funerals, and drug smuggling.

Just about the time television drama first branded businessmen a criminal class, situation comedies discovered the appeal of throwing pies in their faces. The bumbling businessman who was too ineffectual to do real harm quickly became a fixture on many successful sitcoms. All his millions didn't do the blustery Thurston Howell III much good once he was stranded on "Gilligan's Island." Equally blustering if ultimately good-hearted was Dobie's father and small-town grocer, Herbert T. Gillis. Much as he kicked up a fuss over his customers' unpaid bills and his son's profligate spending habits, he could usually be counted on to extend credit on both fronts.

As television ventured into the workplace, it often encountered a puffed-up boss who thought he was in control of the business but was really at the mercy of his subordinates. In "The Ann Sothern Show," the hapless manager of the Bartley House Hotel depended on assistant Katy

O'Connor to stay one step ahead of disaster. Following in Miss Sothern's footsteps in 1962 was Lucille Ball, on her own without husband Desi Arnaz in "The Lucy Show." Her comic foil this time was her stuffy boss, bank executive Theodore J. Mooney. Their chemistry proved so popular that actor Gale Gordon was the only cast member to survive a format change in 1968. In the retitled "Here's Lucy," he repeated his role as Lucy's stubborn boss, this time as owner of the Unique Employment Agency.

A slight variation of this formula could be viewed on "The Beverly Hillbillies." There banker Millburn Drysdale was dependent upon the oil-rich Clampett family, his largest depositors. He vacillated among Uriah Heep-like fawning, ludicrous attempts to gentrify the Clampetts, and frantic efforts to manipulate them. In a 1968 episode we watched, Drysdale accompanies the Clampetts to England to visit a castle they own. He wants to go home but dares not leave without them for fear that they might somehow lose their money, leaving his bank high and dry. So he tries to scare them by dressing up as a ghost. He ends up being shot in the backside with a load of buckshot fired by Granny, who doesn't scare easily. Drysdale's single-minded greed and constantly backfiring schemes are rather touching, in the manner of Wile E. Coyote's never-ending but foredoomed efforts to catch the Road Runner.

The blundering sitcom management style was typified by advertising executive Larry Tate, Darren Steven's boss on "Bewitched." When presented with a subordinate's idea for an ad campaign, he responds, "I hate it." Then the client says, "I love it." Larry immediately chimes in, "I love it." One sequence we coded combines the zaniness of the sixties sitcom with television's developing attitude toward business. When the witch Esmerelda accidentally brings George Washington to the twentieth century, Larry decides the father of our country would make a great pitchman for client Hector Jameson's Whirlaway washing machines. But Washington's legendary honesty quickly upsets Jameson. Washington disputes the ad copy claiming that Whirlaway is "America's finest washing machine," and he begins removing various exaggerations from the proposed commercial. Jameson is so upset at this turn of events that he drops his account with Larry's firm.

Thus, the advertising profession is sent up as the province of hucksters who would use our founding father for commercial ends, but whose product can't stand the scrutiny of an honest man. And, of course, the client is portrayed as a man who values puffery over accuracy where his product is concerned. His character is less than sterling in other ways as well. At one point Washington remembers that Jameson's great-great-great-grandfather was kicked out of the Continental Army for cowardice.

Not all sitcom businessmen were bumbling buffoons. For example, "The Flying Nun" featured Carlos Ramirez, the rich and handsome cafe owner who sometimes assisted the convent. In the 1963 episode we coded, Sister Bertrille approaches him to help the Order distribute the grape juice they produce. Initially apprehensive, he ends up spending a great deal of time and money on the project, not because he thinks the project will be profitable, but because he wants to help the church. Similarly, a sampled episode of "Petticoat Junction" concerned a railroad president who plans to shut down the track that keeps the Shady Rest Hotel alive. Then he samples the Bradley family's gracious hospitality. Out of gratitude, he changes his plans and puts their interests ahead of his own.

Such characters are relatively rare, however, and they became even rarer as businessmen in 1970s' sitcoms began to supplement ineptitude with intolerance. On "Bridget Loves Bernie," a newlywed couple was bedeviled by hostility from both Bridget's father, a wealthy Catholic businessman, and Bernie's father, a Jewish delicatessen owner. On "Angie," a poor girl married to the scion of a Main Line Philadelphia family had to face the snobbery of her husband's father, a rich businessman. Waitress "Alice" had to put up with her boss's miserliness and crankiness in equal measure at Mel's Diner. George Jefferson, owner of a string of dry-cleaning stores, was a black Archie Bunker, just as bigoted and opinionated as the original, with the added snobbery that television often associates with business success. Speaking of Archie, he became a small businessman himself, the owner of Archie's Place, where he had ample opportunity to voice his ethnic prejudices among a cast that included a Jewish business partner, a Puerto Rican busboy, and a black housekeeper.

Business ineptitude was mixed with unattractive personal traits in some characters. On "Chico and the Man," garage owner Ed Brown made his young Hispanic assistant Chico the butt of his sarcastic barbs, although Chico was responsible for reviving the business. Ed had redeeming features, but the same can't be said of "9 to 5"'s Franklin Hart, whose lack of business acumen was matched by his overbearing sexism. Station manager Arthur Carlson of "WKRP in Cincinnati" was a bumbling mama's boy. Mama herself was the money-grubbing and overbearing owner of the station. The butt of most jokes on "Flo" was banker Farley Walters. In a 1980 episode we coded, the audience learns how far Farley will go for a new deposit. He arranges to meet someone named Vito ("The Foot") Ragu, who has a quarter of a million dollars in a sack at Al's Weiner Warehouse. When asked if that isn't an unusual spot for a bank transaction, he replies, "I'd go to Titicaca for a quarter of a million." Farley is a classic sitcom businessman, who constantly strives to make an unsavory buck but is just as regularly defeated by his own ineptitude.

Perhaps the single most noxious business buffoon to grace prime time was Louie, the aggressively unlovable dispatcher for the Sunshine Cab Company on "Taxi." Cordially despised by the cabbies, he alternated insults directed at all and sundry with crude attempts to cheat anyone unlucky enough to have financial dealings with him. A 1978 episode in our sample found him in his usual form. When a mechanic named Latka finds $2,000 in his car, Louie lays claim to it, despite universal skepticism from the rest of the cast. Later, frustrated in his efforts, Louie calls Latka a "dumb foreigner." Then Louie insults a woman one of the cabbies is dating. As for his own tastes in female companionship, Louie likes them "homely but hot."

The TV businessmen of the 1980s ranged from the promiscuous bar owner Sam Malone of "Cheers" and the adulterous male chauvinist Hart in "9 to 5," to the drug-dealing and womanizing mob-connected business types who inhabit the pastel world of "Miami Vice." The various vigilante shows in vogue vied to protect the little guy from a wide array of corrupt quick buck artists. "Airwolf," "The Equalizer," "Knight Rider," and "The A-Team" all pitted their stars against businessmen smuggling drugs or illegal aliens, selling government secrets, or (in one case) organizing a private army. Some positive business characters did emerge—mostly "creative" types like advertising executives Michael Steadman and Elliot Weston of "thirtysomething" and Angela Bower of "Who's the Boss," and the interior decorators of "Designing Women."

In a reversion to the 1950s, though, other business good guys in starring roles were seen mainly as crime solvers. Their business interests provided them with the incomes to pursue their true callings. For example, the hero of "Hart to Hart" was Jonathan Hart, a self-made millionaire who headed Hart Industries. Somehow this far-flung conglomerate took care of itself while Jonathan Hart and his wife Jennifer spent their time jet-setting from one adventure to another. The format was obviously borrowed from "The Thin Man," right down to Asta's replacement, their canine companion Freeway. Hart Industries wasn't really a business, but a plot device that justified the glamorous backdrop to their weekly sleuthing. An even more unlikely series star was Matt Houston, who managed off-shore drilling operations for his oil millionaire father. Talk about counterprogramming; it's the oil man as good guy, and an environmentalist's nemesis to boot. It would make J.R. green with envy. Except that the oil business, like Hart Industries, didn't require much personal attention, so Matt followed Jonathan's lead and turned private eye. By the show's second season, in fact, Matt turned over the business to his partner in order to pursue his crime-fighting avocation full time.

When it comes to actually conducting business, many recent shows follow the 1970s' focus on the costs to employees, consumers, and society at large. Consider a few episodes culled from our 1984-86 samples. On "Cagney & Lacey," contractor Harvey Lacey uncovers the use of substandard building materials to pad profits. He works with his policewoman wife to force the offending company to redo the work. "Spenser: For Hire" also exposes the use of substandard materials, that result in the collapse of a housing project. Another "Spenser" segment features a corrupt shipping company owner who uses illegal aliens as dock workers. At the first sign of union organizing, he threatens them with deportation. "Kate & Allie" get involved in a student protest when they discover that a local

225

university has invested in a chemical company charged with violating environmental safety regulations. The heroines eventually go to jail to protest the university's refusal to divest.

These transgressions are all small potatoes compared to a recent "Knight Rider," in which a journalist uncovers health dangers associated with use of an experimental drug. Just as he is about to write an exposé, he is mysteriously killed. Further investigations reveal that the FDA was about to pull the drug off the market. The manufacturer, who needs the profits to stay solvent, murdered the journalist to keep the heat off, while lobbying to forestall FDA action. All in all, the record of recent years leaves little doubt that TV's crooks, conmen, and clowns are alive and well.

WHO'S MINDING THE STORE?

There is one consistent difference between good guys like Jonathan Hart and Matt Houston and the conniving public enemies who are staples of law enforcement and action-adventure shows. The good guy businessman is rarely seen doing business. He has already made enough money to provide him with the lifestyle appropriate to the private or avocational activities he mostly pursues. The sources of legitimate business success remain a mystery far greater than any solved by television's wealthy businessman-detectives. The viewer's only look at working businessmen features the Katzenjammer world of the soaps and the dog-eat-dog world of the action-adventure shows.

This conclusion is borne out by our statistical analysis. When episodes feature only the personal lives of business characters, they enjoy a positive plurality of portrayals, by 44 to 43 percent. When their occupational activities come into play, the proportion of good guys drops all the way to 29 percent, while the bad guys remain at 43 percent of the total. (The rest are shown in a neutral light.) Businessmen at work have consistently received the more critical portrayals throughout the three decades studied.

We did observe one interesting change in recent years. Although working businessmen have always been predominantly negative, portrayals of their private lives were slightly positive until the mid-1970s. It was

226

only in the most recent decade studied that a negative plurality emerged for businessmen at home and at work alike (though the latter are still more negative than the former). On television today, it appears that no business is good business.

What is it about businessmen that television finds repugnant? What personal characteristics distinguish these characters from those in more favored occupations? To find out, we examined the various forces that motivate behavior on the small screen, as well as the methods that people use to get what they want. Businessmen differed significantly from all other groups in only one respect in both their ends and means. They were much more likely than anyone else to be motivated by greed and to use money as means of obtaining their desires. In fact, business characters were over five times as likely as those in other occupations to exhibit greed as a basic character trait. They were over three times as likely as others to rely on money (as opposed to other methods like rational persuasion, or authority) to get what they wanted. Not surprisingly, these attributes were most closely associated with businessmen in recent years. Thus, business characters were three times as greedy as others in the earliest decade studied. In the most recent decade, the 1975 to 1985 seasons, they were ten times as greedy as everyone else. So television has a ready answer to the question, What do businessmen want? They want more. And how do they intend to get it? They buy it.

The association of business with these traits is evident from a profusion of business characters who are virtual avatars of avarice. There is Arnold, a landlord on a 1978 "Mork and Mindy" episode we coded, who tries to harass his tenants into leaving in order to raise the rent. He shuts off their heat in midwinter and tears up the sidewalk in front of the store. Then he stops by and uses the phone to tell an associate to make sure a ninety-year-old man is evicted. He can't go himself because he has to attend a foreclosure. On a "Wild, Wild West" episode, a miserly loan shark named Jeremiah Ratch negotiates with the California government for a $5 million donation to the state treasury in return for clearing his deservedly shady reputation. Meanwhile, he keeps his household expenses down by eating week-old bread that's handed out for free to the poor.

Finally, our "mommie dearest" award goes to the owner of a pizza parlor on a 1976 "Kojak." Early on she's described by another character as someone who would do anything for a dollar. The viewer soon finds out why. To save money she sends her daughter out into a rough neighborhood to make a delivery. When the girl is raped, mom is unsympathetic and calls her a tramp. Then, ever alert to a money-making opportunity, she accepts money from the rapists not to report the crime, but only after bargaining over the price of her silence.

The drift of all this is not terribly subtle. Scripts tend to go to considerable length to illustrate the effects of this particular sin. Television's businessmen are uniquely characterized by an avaricious streak that leaves little room for normal human feeling, much less fair dealing. Not all businessmen act this way on prime time. Nonetheless, this character defect is widespread enough to outpace its occurrence among other occupations to a significant degree, and hence to brand the businessman as its prototypical possessor.

Thus television condemns businessmen as creatures driven by greed, who hurt or ignore other people in their futile efforts to buy happiness. Indeed, this is a leitmotif of television entertainment. This finding provides an intriguing counterpoint to critics on the Left who charge television with glorifying just this mentality. Todd Gitlin's perspective is representative. He writes:

> American television entertainment highlights and upholds
> two values which are central to the legitimacy of corporate
> capitalism: the value of *personal ambition* as the most
> important driving force in an individual life; and the value
> of *consumption* as a social activity. . . . Most shows commend to their viewers a life that equates possession with
> satisfaction [his emphasis].[8]

On the contrary, our study shows that television places clear limits on these values. Scripts repeatedly condemn the ruthless pursuit of power and material gain. Many shows do associate overweening ambition and conspicuous consumption with the representatives of corporate capitalism. But that is why they hold these individuals in such low esteem. One might say that is why they reject the business class, whose hegemony these programs are alleged to uphold.

Television's true attitude was recently made manifest in an episode of "Beauty and the Beast." Catherine (the title's "beauty") falls for a handsome and flamboyant high-flying real estate developer clearly modeled on Donald Trump. He dreams of building a huge office tower of unprecedented size and grandeur. But Catherine gradually realizes that this overweening ambition has spawned a mob operation of harassment and violence against residents of low-rent housing that must be cleared for the project to proceed. Her discovery is particularly painful because her special friend Vincent (the title's "beast") was working to help these unfortunates stave off the effort to displace them. She shouldn't have been surprised; television always champions the Mitch Snyders against the Donald Trumps.

GIVING BUSINESS THE BUSINESS

However one assesses television's social role here, the debate concerns not only business characters but the institution of business. Although it is assessed mainly through the words and actions of businessmen, the nature of business is defined by themes as well as characters. To examine how television portrays the business world, we identified several major themes in prime-time programs. Themes refer to the subject matter of the show, as expressed in plot, character, and dialogue. They express how a program in its entirety deals with business-related issues, regardless of how particular characters are portrayed.

The most common theme was corruption vs. honesty in the business world. This theme was raised in sixty-eight different episodes coded, about one out of every nine shows throughout the entire thirty seasons. Wherever this issue popped up, business fared badly, but its image has gone from bad to worse over the years. Across the entire thirty-year period, 81 percent of the scripts dealing with honesty in business have found this quality lacking. During the years 1955-1964, 63 percent of the episodes coded portrayed business as dishonest or corrupt. Over the next ten years the negative portrayals jumped to 82 percent. In the most recent decade they rose even further, to 89 percent. Moreover, the theme of business corruption occurred more often after 1975 than it had during the preceding two decades combined. So business is being portrayed more negatively than ever, as television steps up the tempo to its drumbeat of criticism.

The earliest examples of sharp business dealings tend to be relatively subtle, compared to what comes later. A 1959 segment of "Alfred Hitchcock Presents" is typical. The show opens in a board meeting. The chairman, Stone, is distressed by their failure to sell burial plots from a piece of land they purchased in order to start a cemetery. They decide they need an occupant to start the ball rolling. So they offer a free plot to a mutual acquaintance named Weems, an old man whose health is failing rapidly. As a sweetener, they offer him a small weekly annuity. When Weems looks at the contract, however, he notes that it "doesn't say anything about what I'm supposed to get." Stone looks closely and replies, with exaggerated surprise, "Oh, that *is* an oversight." Stone corrects the "oversight," since he expects the agreement, like Weems, to be short-lived. He calls it "sort of an insurance policy in reverse, with the death benefits going to the company."

Soon thereafter, Weems unexpectedly begins to recover. Stone grows more and more unhappy at every sign of his good health. When Weems is spotted walking in the park, someone remarks that he has "a right to walk in the sunshine. It may be his only chance." Stone replies, "Not when it's costing us $50 a week, to say nothing of the taxes and upkeep on the property." Eventually we learn that Stone is doubly worried, since he also controls the real estate firm that sold the land for the cemetery, a shady deal he doesn't want to come to light. Finally Stone can stand it no longer and decides to "persuade" Weems to give up the annuity. On his way, he dies of a heart attack, induced by the stairs he must climb to Weems' apartment, but also by the cumulative anxieties of his sweetheart deal turned sour.

Throughout, Stone is portrayed as a cold and unfeeling person whose business concerns override human feeling. The business transactions involved are portrayed as deceptive and sleazy, in addition to treating a man's death as an economic benefit. The appropriately named busi-nessman is hoist on his own petard, however, when his heart of stone is the first to crumble.

This deft early commentary on the heartless bottom-line mentality proved quite tame compared to its successors. Until the mid-1960s, most wrongful or unethical business behavior was portrayed as the product of individual bad apples. By the latter years of that decade, illegality and corruption were related more closely to "normal" economic decisions, like that of an industrialist on "Mission: Impossible" who needed cash to save his company and decided to raise it by selling an atomic bomb to the highest bidder.

By the 1970s, TV let out all the stops and featured corporate activ-ity that encompassed fraudulent advertising, laundering mob money, and international espionage. For example, "The Bionic Woman" battled a businessman whose money-making ventures included threats to launch an ICBM at an American city while jamming air defense radar, unless he received a ransom. Increasingly, such dastardly deeds were committed by a corporation rather than a lone crooked businessman. Thus, the amateur secret agent heroine of "Scarecrow and Mrs. King" helped foil a cosmet-ics and beauty aids firm that used its international distribution network to ship armaments to combatants around the world.

There have been occasional shows that stressed honesty and fair dealing in business relationships. One such episode also illustrated the difference between themes and individual characters. On a segment of "The Law and Mr. Jones," the villain is a crooked real estate developer who abuses the good reputation of a contracting company he buys. His antagonist is Reid, an honest businessman. Reid built the company and is outraged by the abuse of his good name, which the firm still carries. At one point he launches into a defense of his life's work that illustrates the successful entrepreneur's identification with his product:

> I didn't build thousands of homes just to get them up. I
> made a name by building the best I knew how. Homes
> . . . homes that last like this one, and I was proud. I don't

have a wife anymore, or children, just my name. Maybe it's old-fashioned, but I don't want it hurt. I want it back.

It's very rare to see a television businessman make this kind of impassioned plea for old-fashioned craftsmanship and fair dealing. Moreover, the plot signals the program's sympathy for Reid's approach to business. At an emergency meeting, the shareholders remove the crooked developer from the board and invite Reid back to oversee the project. This is more than a matter of balancing a good businessman against a bad one, which is all we could learn from coding the two characters. What's more significant about the show is that a certain approach to business is elaborated by the script and upheld by the plot. Evil businessmen who meet their comeuppance are a dime a dozen in prime time. Much rarer is a show whose theme is that business can be honestly pursued, businessmen can take pride in their work, and their products can give fair value. This show aired in 1960, a year before we encountered magnanimous magnate Frank Garlund helping someone sue his own company in the interest of fairness. That was thirty years ago, and their like has rarely been seen in prime time since.

Instead of providing high-quality products and fair deals, business is likely to be shown trying to throw its weight around. A recurring theme concerns attempts by business to take unfair advantage of its power to influence the public agenda. The coders viewed twenty-one shows dealing with the relationship of business to government. In all but one of these, the theme was that business wields excessive power over the public arena in order to obtain preferential treatment. Like the theme of business corruption, this issue recurs throughout television's history but has intensified in recent years. Since 1975, 62 percent of the shows dealing with business' power over government have been aired.

An early example of Hollywood's concern about the private sector's abuse of power came in a 1956 episode of "The Millionaire." The beneficiary of philanthropist John Beresford Tipton's largess is an idealist named David Trimaine, who uses his million-dollar gift to run for mayor against a political machine. The local political boss is a big land developer who wants the city to develop a parcel owned by his consortium. He offers our hero his support in return for a promise to do just that. When this effort is rebuffed, he sends a female minion to seduce Trimaine and obtain incriminating pictures of their liaison. If that doesn't work, he's ready to bribe one of Trimaine's clients to accuse him of embezzlement. His ace in the hole is a plan to smear the reputation of Trimaine's father. When an associate questions his tactics, he replies that he does play "dirty pool. So what? Don't I always win?" This time, of course, he doesn't. His idealistic opponent triumphs before the final credits.

In recent years the nighttime soaps have provided fertile ground for such shenanigans. When we tuned in to an episode of "Falcon Crest," we had the opportunity to observe ruthless vineyard owner Angela Channing attempting to fix a local election. She's trying to gain control of water rights so she can charge area farmers for the water they need. That requires a favorable ruling from the board of supervisors. First she offers the leading candidate $10,000 if he votes "correctly" on this issue. When he refuses, she tries to discredit him by planting a newspaper story that places him in a bad light. For good measure, she fires the Falcon Crest employees working for his campaign. All this skullduggery ultimately fails, as it usually does on television, and Angela's opponent is elected.

With the decline of the soaps, the newer realist dramas have taken up the same cudgel. On "L.A. Law," for example, Sifuentes handles a suit by a woman whose husband was killed in a building collapse. As Sifuentes builds his case he discovers that company officials bribed building inspectors to look the other way while they weakened the concrete to save on construction costs. Moreover, an influential congressman (heavily backed by the firm's donations) may have used undue influence to win them the contract. In the course of the investigation the local political boss tries to turn the heat down by offering a judgeship to a senior partner in the firm. Through it all, the company's political connections are clearly better cemented than their buildings.

The apotheosis of this evil alliance was attained in an episode of "Quincy, M.E." At the climax, the intrepid pathologist beards "Mr. Big" in his boardroom lair and demands, "You manipulated the law and sent an innocent man to prison. I mean, who do you think you are?" In response, the corrupt corporate chieftain explodes, "Not only will I tell you who we think we are, I'll tell you who we actually are. We're the whole ball of wax, Quincy, the ultimate conglomerate. We and a few other giant corporations control this country. We *are* the government."

These cases are typical of a common pattern of associations that television brings to the business world. Businessmen are greedy for both money and power. They also use their money as a means of influence, often corrupting the public process in order to get still more money. The cycle would be self-perpetuating if it weren't for the idealistic crusaders who stand up to them, fend off their flunkies and thugs, and ensure that justice triumphs. On prime time, big business is a threat, not a promise.

Even small businessmen can emulate this shining example. In a memorable moment from "Taxi," the drivers demand that the company repair their dangerously deteriorated cabs. Louie tries to doctor the books so management won't be held responsible at an upcoming union hearing. When the cabbies protest, he defends himself by telling them, "Every great businessman has done it."

BAITING THE BOSS

If dramatic formats have emphasized the corrupt practices and corrupting influence of business on our society, the comedy formats have provided some relief to its victims. Just as television has increasingly focused on the power and corruption of big business, the business practices of the oafish small business boss have also changed in recent years. Foolish bosses have been a target of comedy since the early days of television. But their employees usually suffered in silence. If the audience ridiculed them, their subordinates did not. Hotel manager James Devery may have been an overbearing bumbler, but he was rarely upbraided by Katy O'Connor. Lucy's manipulations often left Theodore Mooney bobbing helplessly in her wake, but she didn't add insult to injury.

By the early 1970s, however, bosses no longer received such consideration. About that time, television put a new capper on an old blue-

234

collar fantasy. Workers could not only tell the boss to "take this job and shove it," they could kiss off the job and keep it too. Telling off the boss without fear of the consequences became a popular prime-time pastime. And the boss took it, and sometimes gave it right back. Businessmen like George Jefferson, Fred Sanford, Ed Brown, Mel, and Louie either suffered the sting of sharp-tongued employees or traded barbs with them even up. Ridiculing the boss became a popular sport appropriate to the pompous, bigoted, or inconsiderate managers and executives who continued to serve as comic foils.

Once, before prime-time employees discovered confrontation tactics, they took on the boss the old-fashioned way—they worked around him. In fact, they often worked him into position to do the right thing, which he would never do of his own accord. This formula ensured that right would prevail in comedy settings. The sitcom boss's motives may have been as unworthy as his villainous counterpart's in action-adventure shows, but his subordinates acted as his moral guides. Back in the days of "The Beverly Hillbillies," Miss Jane served as the conscience of the greedy Mr. Drysdale. In "Love and Marriage," Stubby Wilson was the buffer for his reactionary boss William Harris. Neither of these underlings had any real power, but their wise counsel usually provided the only real solution. Even the boss could eventually see that. Although the creative Darren Stevens had to labor under fawning and self-serving Larry Tate on "Bewitched," Darren's talent eventually carried the day (with a little magical help from wife Samantha). Just as Ed Brown had Chico Rodriguez to temper his closed-minded attitudes, Alice Hyatt helped teach Mel Sharples the ways of the civilized world, and WKRP's Andy Travis stopped Mrs. Carlson's abuses of the station employees.

Thus the boss usually has his employees right where they want him, although their *de facto* control rarely translates into the actual power they so clearly deserve. Somehow the business muddles through, with the stupid or venal bosses saved from the consequences of their inadequacies by their long-suffering employees.

SILVER LININGS

Is there no aspect of the business world that television shows in a positive light? After all the evidence to the contrary, we did discover one theme that provides a favorable portrait more often than not. When programs addressed the attitude of a business toward its workers or customers, the firm in question was likely to look out for their interest. This issue was raised in thirty-nine programs coded, only about half the number dealing with business corruption or power, but a substantial number nonetheless. When it did come up, business was shown as looking out for the concerns of others 58 percent of the time. The other 42 percent portrayed firms taking advantage of workers or customers in pursuit of the bottom line. Both the occurrence of this theme and its pro-business resolution remained steady throughout the three decades studied.

This result is somewhat surprising, considering the preponderance of greedy or money-grubbing business characters that were coded. One explanation for its divergence from the general pattern of results lies in a formula that pits a good businessman against a bad one, with the good (public-spirited) businessman victorious in the end. This was exemplified by a 1966 segment of "The Monkees." The boys help out an old toy maker named Harper, who has been replaced by a computer installed by Taggart, the heartless general manager. They take advantage of the fact that company president J.B. Guggins is a conscientious and caring person. (Taggart complains, "I'd let Harper go, but J.B. promised him a job for life.") Monkee Mike sabotages Taggart's toy tests designed to show the product's durability, ease of assembly, and so on. After watching the samples self-destruct, Taggart is reduced to arguing that it's advantageous for the toys to break quickly, because the parents will have to buy new ones. But Mike suggests to J.B. that the toys lack the "happiness factor," which no computer can design as well as Harper. J.B. names Harper general manager, and Taggart leaves in disgust. Thus, not only is the bad businessman defeated, but the company is portrayed as caring for both its employees and its customers. J.B. and Harper don't just want to make money, they want to make children happy.

Some pro-business themes popped up in surprising places. A prime example is a 1981 episode of "Lou Grant," a series that featured crusading reporters who exposed social ills. This time around, the staff at the *Los Angeles Tribune* think they're onto a big story. A fire of undetermined origin at the Cal Electronics Company broke out soon after the departure of Sorenson, the former president, amid rumors of financial problems. Sensing a possible cover-up, business-related arson, and who knows what else, the *Trib*'s investigative staff springs into action. When the fire turns out to be the result of a broken gas main, they pursue the change in leadership angle. Then they discover that Sorenson left because he had had a nervous breakdown. The new president, Russell Davidson, protected Sorenson's privacy by announcing that he had left for personal reasons, while keeping him on the payroll on a limited basis. When investigative reporter Joe Rossi asks Sorenson why the company kept his breakdown quiet, he responds, "Because Russell Davidson is a decent man."

Although such pro-business outcomes are in the majority, a substantial minority of shows present a quite different perspective. Over two out of five episodes coded for this theme featured the dark side of business dealings with customers and employees. Typical of these was a 1980 episode of "Freebie and The Bean." The title characters are detectives investigating poorly constructed and ill-managed apartment buildings. A tenant shows them her cracked walls and ceilings, peeling linoleum, and dripping faucets. In the next scene, the foreman on a construction site is telling Stacy, the builder, that the cheap materials they're using won't pass inspection. Stacy tells him not to worry, and adds, "I don't want the building done well, I want it done in five months." Freebie and Bean wonder why anyone would back such a slipshod operation. Then they learn that Stacy hires prostitutes to do "customer relations" work. When the women sleep with potential investors, he makes incriminating videotapes, which he uses to blackmail them into investing. If nothing else, this approach to customer relations is certainly solicitous.

A somewhat more sophisticated criticism of business practices appeared in a 1971 segment of "All in the Family" that shows Archie Bunker as both victim and victimizer. When Archie's hazard insurance is cancelled unexpectedly, he asks his agent, Edith's nephew Wendell, for an explanation. Wendell tells Archie that his policy has been "economically terminated" because he's in a high-risk area. In short, he's a victim of "area displacement," a euphemism for red-lining. Archie complains, "That's discrimination!" Wendell replies, "That's the insurance business."

Soon, however, Archie finds himself adopting Wendell's callous approach in dealing with his own employees. His company decides to reduce the workforce and leaves it up to Archie to fire someone. His choice hinges on ethnic considerations. If he fires a white worker, the other whites will get angry at him. But if he fires a black, the blacks will get just as mad. Then he finds the perfect candidate: "There are [lots of] white guys and black guys at work. He's the only Puerto Rican. He won't be missed." When he talks to the man, Archie tells him he hasn't been fired exactly, he's been "unfortunately terminated." When the worker asks if Archie can't do something for him, Archie replies, "I'm just a little man. These decisions are made by the big men upstairs." But can't Archie talk to someone? "You can't talk to the system, it's not a person. It's. . .it's . . .I don't know what it is. I'd like to help you but I can't."

Like all Norman Lear comedy series, this episode uses humor to carry social commentary. One message is that business will sacrifice its customers or employees to the bottom line. Another is that individuals bear personal responsibility for the "system." Wendell cheerfully terminates his relatives' insurance in accordance with company policy. It never occurs to him that the policy might be wrong, or that he should even consider his involvement in this aspect of doing business. Then Archie similarly makes the decision that's easiest for him, unfairly firing an employee and declining to consider that he might fight the system. Saddest of all, it never occurs to him that he's behaving just like Wendell. So he helps perpetuate the very system that harms him as well. The underlying message is that individuals like Wendell and Archie *are* the system. By their thoughtlessness and moral cowardice they lock themselves into a self-defeating pattern of behavior that lets business take advantage of employees and consumers.

THE BOTTOM LINE

It is not often that scripts go to such lengths to make a point about the behavior of business in American society. "All in the Family" was television's great pioneer of socially conscious comedy, so it is not surprising to see Archie Bunker confront the soullessness of the business world. Most shows that raise business-related themes content themselves with sketches rather than finished portraits—the crooked businessman, the bumbling boss, an exchange of dialogue indicating disapproval of a greedy or malevolent character. These are not universal traits of the TV businessman. As we have seen, there are also idealistic, altruistic, or principled characters who deal fairly with employees or customers. But the latter are in the minority, and that minority has been shrinking in recent years. Our content analysis shows that businessmen have always been pictured more negatively than other characters on prime time, and the gap is widening.

Television's vantage point is not just a populist aversion to bigness. Corporate executives have actually fared better than small or independent businessmen over the years, though all have been held in low esteem recently. Television's aversion to the breed seems to reflect a belief that the personal and social milieu of business is one of unbridled greed, which results in corruption and the abuse of power. All these themes regularly appear on the small screen, driving home the point that business at best serves no useful social function and at worst is a threat to a humane social order. Individual businessmen are sometimes capable of benevolence, but business activities almost never contribute to the social and economic welfare of American life. Viewers rarely witness Horatio Alger stories of business success as the fulfillment of the American dream. Instead, the enterprising spirit of the entrepreneur is often channeled into unsavory or even criminal activities. As Tom Mankiewicz, head writer of "Hart to Hart," puts it, "The businessman—the entrepreneur—is the kind of guy on television that you love to hate."[9]

In real life, of course, entrepreneurs and small businessmen are often objects of popular esteem. But TV reflects the mindset of the Hollywood community, where many writers and producers view themselves as artists at war with crass commercial interests and a venal business culture. In the words of Philip DeGuere, creator of "Simon and Simon":

> When the business community. . .[made] public their griev-
> ance that they were being constantly treated like villains on
> television shows, it hit me like a sledgehammer. I said, "Yes,
> that is exactly what I've been doing personally. . . ." And I'm
> going to do it even more because . . .it makes sense. It's
> something everybody can identify with and consequently is
> probably pretty close to the truth.[10]

DeGuere went on to give an example of how he transformed the "reality" of the business world into fiction in the 1983 adventure series "Whiz Kids." This show pitted a group of precocious teenaged comput- er hackers against a "completely evil" corporation that he named Nascorp, short for Nasty Corporation:

> It was peopled by executives who would go around saying,
> "This project is going to make me a senior vice president and
> nobody's going to get in the way." And as a result of that peo-
> ple would die. I mean it's not exactly unlike the kinds of
> things that are happening with regularity all over the world.[11]

As "Whiz Kids" demonstrated, even a child can understand the exploitative character of the business world. The trick is to know which side you're on. A 1980 episode of "Diff'rent Strokes" shows how easy it is to be seduced by the dark side of the Force. Two young boys go into the business of selling brownies. After accepting an order too big for them to handle, their sister offers to help if they will make her a full part- ner. Although they desperately need her assistance, the boys refuse to include their sister in the partnership. Instead, they offer to pay her a meager salary as their employee. "That's what business is all about," they tell her. "You do the work and we get the profits."

7

THE PROFESSIONALS

Men of feeling and intelligence forced by the harsh realities of a turbulent society to sometimes mask these humane qualities. . . .
—Voice-over introduction to "The Bold Ones"

I f television loves to hate business, its love affair with professionals is more fulfilling. In the world of prime time, TV's businessmen are social parasites, while professional people serve humanity. Businessmen represent grasping and plunder, while professionals stand for sharing and selflessness. Beyond the dedicated lawyers we will meet in chapter 9, the roster of laudable professionals runs through devoted physicians from Casey and Kildare to Marcus Welby, crusading journalists in the Lou Grant mold, and dedicated teachers from Mr. Peepers to Gabe Kotter.

It's not just their business counterparts that professionals outstrip. Among the 922 doctors, lawyers, teachers, social workers, and the like that we coded, 59 percent were positive characters and only 23 percent were negative, a difference of +36. That compared to only 43 percent positive and 26 percent negative among all other census-coded characters, a positive index of only +17. So viewers see about three good guy professionals for every bad guy, a ratio that has remained stable over the years.

Before 1965 their index stood at +34, since 1975 at +33. And from the mid-sixties to the mid-seventies, when the bottom dropped out of businessmen's ratings, the professionals remained TV's quintessential good guys. During television's anti-establishment decade, 62 percent of all educated professionals played good guys and only 17 percent bad guys, for a remarkable +45 index figure. Somebody had to trip up all those crooked businessmen and politicians, not to mention setting a good example to counter the establishment's bad apples.

More generally, the portrayal of professionals shows how television's positive role models have changed over the years. Although television's admiration for professionals has endured for three decades, the context of their activities has shifted from the private to the public realm. Increasingly, members of the helping professions are lauded for their commitment to social as well as personal betterment.

TV's professionals are almost as diverse as their real-life counterparts, ranging from architects to engineers, from social workers to corporate lawyers. In this chapter we take a look at three professions that have provided some of television's most memorable characters and recognizable "types"—doctors, teachers, and journalists. To provide a comparison with a group that gets short shrift from the small screen, we'll also look at the much-less-memorable scientists who have appeared.

HOUSE CALLS

Television's love affair with medicine has lasted longer than most modern marriages. Medical shows have proved an enduring source of human drama and (occasionally) comedy, at least since "The Doctor" premiered on NBC in 1952. Since then the genre has created or popularized such well-known icons of mass entertainment as earnest young intern Richard Kildare, kindly G.P. Marcus Welby, crusading medical examiner Quincy (who, like Paladin, seems too serious to have a first name), and sundry surgeons ranging from brooding Ben Casey to breezy Hawkeye Pierce. All but "M*A*S*H"'s Hawkeye were title characters of hit shows, and all without exception were compassionate, dedicated, highly skilled professionals.

242

These household names are representative of their profession, as far as television is concerned. Doctors have always been prime time's consummate good guys, who dispense healing and wisdom in equal measure. They constitute a substantial group, representing 7 percent of all census-coded characters. That makes them about half as numerous as businessmen, but considerably larger than any other professional group. Their presence is probably magnified by being concentrated in a distinctive program genre.

Finally, prime time doctors are usually a force for good. The positive characters outweigh the negative by nearly a three-to-one margin (57 to 20 percent). Among the 20 percent negative characters, fewer than 2 percent are "pure" negatives, while the rest preserve at least some redeeming trait. By contrast, the business world contains over ten times as many purely negative characters. Also unlike their business counterparts, the positive image of TV's doctors has remained stable over time. For example, the proportion of positive characters went from 55 percent during the earliest decade of the study to 58 percent in the most recent decade. Equally important, doctors are the single most successful profession on television. They succeed in their aims seven times out of eight, an 87 percent success rate. Considering how often their efforts are directed at saving lives or resolving personal crises, this is the sort of image that any profession would envy.

The earliest medical shows portrayed doctors as modern knights-errant locked in combat with the dragons of disease and infirmity. The opening narration to "Medic," the 1950s' most memorable medical drama, said it best: "Guardian of birth, healer of the sick, and comforter of the aged. . . ." This series, which ran from 1954 through 1956, was styled almost as a documentary, with real-life hospital settings and actual doctors and nurses in the cast. "Medic"'s plot lines were based on actual case histories and featured doctors of strong moral fiber struggling to save the lives of their patients.

Beginning in 1959, "Hennesey" portrayed the same type of morally committed, dedicated doctor but handled him with a somewhat lighter touch. Lt. "Chick" Hennesey was a young medical officer who treated military personnel and their families at a navy base. While he set the moral, helpful tone of the show, other characters lightened the atmosphere with typical service comedy antics. In these early series, doctors showed a strong desire to aid the needy or deserving and thwart the arrogant, cruel, or insensitive.

The second era of medical shows began in the early 1960s with "Ben Casey" and "Doctor Kildare." These two shows arrived almost concurrently in 1961. By the time they left the airwaves in 1966, they had established the prevailing character structure that can be found in virtually all subsequent medical shows. It's a straightforward formula. A young intern or resident is ambitious and highly skilled but inexperienced. He works in a hospital setting under an older doctor or division chief who is brilliant and gruff but caring, and who wants his young protégé to succeed. Throw in some less significant doctors and nurses as window dressing and you have a generic medical drama.

"Casey" and "Kildare" differed from other medical series in their intense focus on the trials and tribulations of young doctors. Both tackled some difficult issues or controversial topics like malpractice, drug use, medical ethics, and incurable illnesses. They provided an air of realism and used medical terminology, but without the gritty documentary style of "Medic."

Since these shows followed the lives and learning processes of doctors, they made relatively little dramatic use of patients in their early seasons. Instead they derived their dramatic thrust from the dilemmas doctors faced in treating illnesses. This allowed weighty discussions of the purpose of medicine, the social role of doctors, the proper use of various techniques, and more. These men in white were compassionate and highly moral individuals, but they did not discuss the philosophical or moral dimensions of their professions in the abstract. The issues grew out of their own emerging careers and their education into the profession. Both illness and the medical profession were handled through personal experiences that provided analogues to broader issues.

Drs. Casey and Kildare were committed, energetic, and single-mindedly concerned with healing the sick. Gradually, though, both series developed soap-opera trappings that allowed their stars more of a personal life than "Medic"'s Dr. Konrad Styner ever had time for. The darkly handsome Casey had some romantic involvements, while the earnest Kildare became increasingly involved with the problems of patients and their families.

Another representative of the Casey/Kildare era was "The Nurses," which feminized the format by focusing on a young student nurse and an older head nurse. The show later added a similar pair of doctors and changed its title to "The Doctors and the Nurses." This series was slightly ahead of its time in its emphasis on the problems of patients rather than physicians. "Breaking Point" also marked an increasing focus on patients, this time in a psychiatric outpatient facility. These shows also foreshadowed the changes in "Kildare" and "Casey" of the mid-1960s, when the experiences of patients became more central in their episodes.

In 1969 the debut of "Marcus Welby, M.D." marked the onset of the third phase of medical drama. In this show and its popular contemporary, "Medical Center," the focus was fixed firmly on the patients. Doctors, of course, were always involved in the physical, mental, and moral restoration of their charges. Thus, their cases allowed them to address social as well as somatic ills. Almost every case they encountered required not only healing an illness or injury, but also dealing with such controversial issues as bigotry, antisemitism, the social stigma of cancer, sexism, mainstreaming the handicapped, homosexuality, and the generation gap.

Otherwise these series followed the dramatic formats laid down by their successful predecessors (e.g., conflicts of youth vs. experience). "Marcus Welby" did give us one of the first successful marriages of a starring physician, young Dr. Kiley. TV doctors were not usually allowed to have successful, long-term loving relationships. Most marriages ended either in divorce or the tragic death of a spouse from disease or accident. Romantic interests often had some terminal illness or were married and unavailable.

Unlike Kildare and Casey, kindly Dr. Welby and bold Joe Gannon of "Medical Center" rarely lost a patient. They were saints not only in their personal lives but also in their miraculous success rates. This trend

toward supersuccessful doctors who cure both somatic and social ills continued into the 1970s with "The New Doctors" (a rotating segment of
"The Bold Ones"), "The Psychiatrist," "Matt Lincoln" (another psychiatrist), and "Nurse."

The most recent era of medical shows was ushered in by two
changes that occurred during the mid-1970s. The first was a shift back
to the original focus on the doctors. This can be seen in shows like "Doctors' Hospital," "Doctors' Private Lives," "Cutter to Houston," "Trauma
Center," "Trapper John, M.D.," and "St. Elsewhere." Most of these shows
still dealt with patients' problems, but the primary focus returned to the
lives and learning experiences of the doctors. This has reached the point
where, in some recent shows, doctors or their families are seemingly the
most frequent patients. On various episodes of "Trapper John," Dr. John
McIntyre had a stroke, came down with Guillain-Barré syndrome, and
was hit by a car. On "St. Elsewhere," one doctor lay dying of liver cancer,
and another contracted AIDS. One young female resident at St. Eligius
turned out to be a nymphomaniac and another suffered from bulimia.
One male resident became a rapist and another was himself raped while
providing medical services to a prison population. Finally, a nurse found
it necessary to undergo a radical mastectomy. All this left little time for
either medical or dramatic treatment of patients' illnesses.

In all the above-mentioned shows except "St. Elsewhere," however,
doctors rarely lost patients. They were usually hip, attractive, brilliant medical practitioners who could cure any illness and still find time to engage in
affairs of the heart and other avocational pursuits. Their prevalence may
reflect the rapid failure of two short-lived attempts in 1975 to portray the
negative side of medicine. The more adversarial of these was "Medical
Story," which pointed out the mistakes and foibles of the medical establishment. The other, "The Lazarus Syndrome," was the most appropriately named medical show on TV. The reference to doctors' godlike status as
miracle workers was intended as ironic commentary. Less critical of
medical institutions than the muckraking "Medical Story," "Lazarus" was
still a rather harsh portrayal of doctors as less-than-omnipotent healers.
Tellingly, neither of these shows made it through more than a few months.

The second change in the 1970s was the appearance of medical comedies. Previously, medical shows were almost exclusively serious dramas. The new comedies usually followed one of two standard formats. First, a lead doctor, usually older and often chief of some department, would oppose a blustering self-important hospital administrator or owner. The doctor and the medical staff were usually thorough, competent, and caring professionals, while the administrators or owners were equally rigid, overbearing, and inept. "AfterM*A*S*H," "House Calls," and "Doc" regularly mined this comic lode. A second format could be seen in "E/R," "Little People" (a.k.a. "The Brian Keith Show"), and "The Bob Newhart Show." In these shows a reasonably competent, caring doctor was placed in a crowd of zany characters and somehow had to bring order out of chaos. Here there were no nasty overbearing bosses—just equals and underlings who could easily get carried away with bizarre comic schemes. The doctor still remained a good guy, and the supporting cast members were usually well-intentioned bumblers.

The 1980s have seen fewer medical shows than in earlier years. Only "St. Elsewhere" and "Trapper John" showed any durability. This should be a temporary hiatus, however, because the genre represents a setting rich in dramatic possibilities and a perennial source of heroic characters, a quality that is surprisingly rare on network television. The most recent entries alter the pattern only by shifting to heroines—the short-lived "Kay O'Brien" (a female surgeon), "Heartbeat" (a female-run women's health clinic), and "China Beach" (a surgical head nurse in a Vietnam evacuation hospital).

The highly positive image of doctors is even reflected in television's treatment of the medical establishment. Recurring themes about the institution of medicine deal mainly with questionable medical practices and certain aspects of the doctor-patient relationship. As with business, the issue of unethical, illegal, or simply inept practices gets raised repeatedly. Unlike businessmen, however, doctors are usually exonerated of such charges. These charges are raised much as "The Defenders" used cases of legal ethics and questionable practices, to enlighten the public about the complexities and the dilemmas these dedicated professionals face.

A common ploy is to use charges of malpractice as an opening wedge into broader issues of the difficult decisions doctors face, along with their sometimes competing loyalties to patients, peers, and profession. The malpractice issue cropped up right from the start in both "Ben Casey" and "Doctor Kildare." Thus, in a 1963 episode we coded, Kildare is charged with malpractice after his patient dies from an adverse drug reaction. An older colleague, the appropriately named Dr. Hazard, complains that "there's something in the grainy eye of the public that automatically makes a doctor on trial a charlatan, a killer." The plot revolves around Hazard's reluctance to take risks in treatment after being subjected to a similar suit.

The script's moral is that doctors can't let the threat of suits cow them into "practicing medicine like a turtle," as the sage Dr. Gillespie puts it. On the stand, Gillespie spells out his position: "We doctors live with death hovering over our shoulder. . . . There are always risks, unforeseeable risks, but risks that must be taken. Medicine isn't worth practicing if I have to stop myself because of legal risks. Until I am free to proceed on the basis of my knowledge and skill, I am not a doctor. I am a slave to outmoded laws." In case anyone missed the point, Gillespie drives it home once again after the verdict of innocent comes in. "The real victory was the recognition that the decisions that doctors have to face are unique and difficult and even terrifying. And that those decisions are made not for the doctor's benefit but for the patient's."

In the early series, doctors were never guilty of malpractice. By the late 1960s, though, some television doctors had done questionable things. "Trapper John, M.D." and "St. Elsewhere" have both featured doctors and hospital staff involved in drug-dealing schemes. "Trapper John" also portrayed a doctor doing unnecessary surgery to boost his income. By the 1970s inept doctors were also seen. An episode of "Nurse" that we coded concerns a doctor who is the fourth generation of his family to go into medicine. When he makes a mistake in prescribing a drug, he tries at first to cover it up but eventually comes forward to admit his error. He says he wasn't cut out to be a doctor and always wanted to be an architect. Tradition and family pressures pushed him into medicine.

Malpractice is rarely treated as an institutional problem. It is usually a case of a single careless or inept doctor. In fact, we coded eleven shows that raised explicitly the question of whether hospitals adequately investigated doctors' mistakes or questionable practices. All eleven endorsed the medical profession's efforts to get at the truth; not a single cover-up occurred. In the "Nurse" episode mentioned above, the doctor's error is uncovered by hospital staff. There is some argument over doctors covering for each other, but the whole investigation is handled in-house. Nor is this ever seen as a common problem. In a "Trapper John, M.D." segment where charges of malpractice are made, the doctor's innocence is proven by other doctors. So much for the charge that television is endemically or necessarily anti-authority. As we shall see, it is the source of authority that determines television's response, and medicine is one establishment that scriptwriters trust implicitly.

A notable exception to television's see-no-evil stance occurred in an episode of "St. Elsewhere," when a patient dies after a cardiac operation. The cardiac surgeon worries that he nicked a heart muscle during the operation and that it ripped, causing a heart attack. Then a mortality hearing reveals that residents and doctors alike treated the patient callously. They issued prescriptions without checking other medications, ignored some symptoms while making quick diagnoses, and in general delivered substandard care. The autopsy, however, reveals that she died of a highly unusual condition unknown to her doctors, so that their actions did not cause her death. This is a rare case of institutional neglect. But even here, the script is careful to avoid allegations of malpractice, much less an institutional cover-up.

This wrist slap is an unusual deviation from the long string of vindicated doctors that goes all the way back to "Medic." Appropriately, a 1956 episode of that series contained the earliest instance we encountered of the malpractice theme. Its resolution set the tone for the next three decades. In this show an investigative reporter pursues his doubts about a doctor's treatment of a ballerina who died of cancer. In the course of the show, the woman's primary physician is backed up by a bone specialist, a radiation specialist, and two pathologists. The villain of the piece turns out to be a "doctor of nature" the ballerina consulted in desperation. The script presents his diatribes against the "closed-minded medical establishment" as the self-serving fulminations of a dangerous quack. The show ends with the reporter satisfied that the doctors did the best they could.

Conflict in medical institutions tends to form one of two patterns. In the first, a bright young doctor wants to rush into the use of new or controversial techniques, while his older, more cautious colleague is hesitant. The other format portrays the young doctor as concerned with helping the patient at all costs but forced to confront apparently arbitrary procedures laid down by hospital administrators. In both instances there are few bad guys. Administrators definitely do not reside on the same high moral plane as doctors. Yet even they sometimes have some method to their bureaucratic madness, although they rarely win out in the end. The rigid or insensitive administrator is usually proven wrong or forced to compromise by more sensitive or perceptive doctors.

Medicine is also the most workaholic occupation on television. Doctors seem to be forever on call. They have little or no social lives and their personal lives are often empty. Marriages, if they exist at all, rarely last long. Love affairs are ephemeral at best. A common scene shows one doctor ordering another to go home and get some sleep or see his family. These dedicated professionals normally have to be forced to leave the workplace for their own good.

Medicine comes across as our most sensitive social institution in other respects. The first concerns doctors' commitments to their patients, which transcend all competing concerns and often require involvement in personal as well as physical problems. Television repeatedly tells us that doctors are willing to treat patients without regard to race, politics, or any other nonmedical consideration. We coded eight episodes that presented this theme, without ever seeing it contradicted.

Their dedication even extends to treating enemy soldiers in wartime. In a 1975 episode of "M*A*S*H," Hawkeye Pierce fights to continue treating a North Korean prisoner after Frank Burns demands that the man be shipped to a POW section. Hawkeye bends the rules, puts the POW in his own tent, and surreptitiously gets blood from Burns himself for a needed transfusion. Neither politics nor army regulations can come between him and his dedication to saving lives. More recently, "China Beach" recycled this plot line when the dedicated medical team treats a Vietcong terrorist, even though she had set off a bomb that killed several American soldiers.

This attitude by no means started with the freewheeling postsixties spirit of "M*A*S*H." We found the same message in a segment of "Navy Log," a straight-arrow, flag-waving series from the 1950s. The action takes place aboard a U.S. hospital ship during World War II. When a severely wounded Japanese soldier is brought aboard, the doctor takes him ahead of Americans waiting with less serious problems. The medical corpsmen object, but the doctor tells them that the Japanese is a patient, not the enemy, once he comes through the door. Later the doctor tells a wounded G.I. that he would have been a murderer if he had refused to help the man. He also reminds the G.I. that they will have to live with the Japanese after the war, implying that our military goal was victory over but not extermination of the enemy. The G.I. seems to accept his reasoning. This show is all the more notable for airing in 1957, just twelve years after World War II. That conflict provided a historical resonance that was more immediate then than "M*A*S*H"'s ersatz Korean War setting is now.

Of all the professions seen on television, doctors may be the most likely to become involved in the lives of those they serve. Their involvement goes far beyond mere physical cures. This theme arose often during the closing years of "Ben Casey" and "Doctor Kildare." Casey was even involved romantically with a young woman who had just awakened from a thirteen-year coma. But the real instances of personal involvement came with "Marcus Welby" and "Medical Center." In one segment of the latter, surgeon Joe Gannon helped a Jewish doctor overcome antisemitism and harassment. In another episode, he went into the ghetto to help a black football star. In a third, he helped a man's fiancée deal with both his accident-induced paralysis and his retarded brother-in-law. Yet another time, he helped an exercise instructor get reinstated after cancer surgery. (The company had fired her until Dr. Gannon convinced them that her cancer was not debilitating.)

251

This type of personal involvement is common among recent prime-time physicians. Social or environmental factors are also increasingly dealt with by contemporary TV doctors. For example, "St. Elsewhere" drew attention to the plight of the homeless, and St. Eligius's Dr. Westphall flew to Ethiopia to help care for famine victims. In view of their skill and dedication, it is not surprising that television advises patients to have great faith in their physicians. Indeed, the "trust your doctor" homilies have been a constant on TV. This was a major theme in nine shows coded, three times the number that endorsed questioning the medical establishment. Doctors as omnipotent healers can almost always be trusted. Since the earliest shows, when a patient was lost it was through no fault of the doctor. The illness was simply too great for medicine to conquer.

A segment of "Medic" that we encountered proved typical. A brilliant research chemist needs to have her thyroid removed but fears the risks of surgery. The anesthesiologist explains that newly developed drugs and surgical procedures will assure her safety. Convinced, she places herself completely in the doctors' care, and the operation is successful. Nearly a quarter century later, essentially the same drama was played out in an updated social milieu in "Doctors' Private Lives." This time the patient is Violet, a feminist magazine publisher under the care of a brilliant female cardiovascular surgeon who has developed a new operating procedure that may help Violet's heart condition. The male chief surgeon is opposed to using the experimental procedure. Violet decides to trust the judgment of her primary physician, who then struggles with the hospital bureaucracy to win approval to go ahead. One night Violet has a coronary, and the operation is successfully performed. In this show the addition of feminist trappings and an individual vs. bureaucracy subplot do not alter the perennial moral that doctor knows best.

During the past decade, however, shows like "St. Elsewhere" and "Medical Story" have introduced more tragic elements and downplayed this unmitigated trust in doctors. In addition, the crusading "Quincy, M.E." occasionally found skeletons in the medical establishment's closet. A 1979 episode in our sample contained a rare scathing rebuttal to the notion of faith in doctors. Quincy's curiosity is piqued when he finds severe scars on the face of a woman who committed suicide. He discovers that they were caused by poorly performed plastic surgery. Depressed by her appearance, the woman apparently killed herself. Quincy tries to get the surgeon's license revoked, which enmeshes him in struggles against medical, legal, and government bureaucracies. Midway through an ensuing trial, Quincy rebukes the presiding judge for assuming that a doctor couldn't be a "real" criminal. This episode broadcasts an unmistakable message of "caveat emptor" for potential users of plastic surgery.

Overall, however, doctors in prime time are assumed to be concerned, cautious healers unless they prove themselves otherwise. Their sterling character, professionalism, and high moral standards offer a sharp contrast to the TV businessman, who is presumed guilty of venality or ineptitude until proven innocent. If businessmen bear the mark of Cain, doctors are surpassingly able.

TV's Pets

Although medicine is television's favorite "helping profession," many teachers have edified their students and entertained audiences over the years. In contrast to the steady stream of doctors, teachers have trickled into the prime-time schedule, accounting for only about 2 percent of the census-coded characters. Nonetheless, individual teachers have proven quite popular, and most come out as good guys, if not role models. Their mission is viewed as a noble one, that of instilling knowledge and aiding youngsters mentally and emotionally.

In keeping with this image, teachers tend to be shown as calm, caring, morally concerned individuals who are first and foremost interested in their students' well-being. They are warm and benevolent in their personal lives and dedicated professionals in the context of their work. This persona has changed little over the years, with positive characters consistently outnumbering negative ones by three-to-one margins.

If these trends sound more than vaguely reminiscent of doctors, it is not by accident. They fit television's model of the positive professional, committed to his work but also to the personal betterment of his charges.

On the other hand, there are also major differences in the ways these two occupational groups behave on prime time. Most obvious is the lack of life-or-death conflict situations in the classroom. This atmosphere of heightened drama has always been one of the main attractions of medical settings for entertainment media. Its absence in schoolroom shows is seen in their low-key approach, often mixing comedy and drama in the eternal struggle to mold young minds.

In addition, television's teachers are much less likely than doctors to delve into larger issues about professional ethics, philosophical differences, and the like. They tend to stick to their students, focusing on the concrete problems that confront them every day rather than the ultimate meaning of it all. This day-by-day orientation makes for pleasant characters who may not be memorable but who wear well on the small screen. Indeed, television's first successful schoolroom series featured the most low-key teacher of them all, the mild-mannered "Mr. Peepers." Robinson Peepers taught biology in a small town in the Midwest. His self-effacing manner proved as popular with audiences during the early 1950s as it did with his students at Jefferson High School. Comedian Wally Cox's creation, who combined a small stature with a big heart, seemed to bring out a mothering instinct in viewers similar to that produced by Mary Tyler Moore two decades later. The low-key humor and relatively realistic characters and situations in the series set the tune for many later entrants in this genre.

Another popular favorite of the time was the more extroverted Connie Brooks, the wisecracking English teacher with a heart of gold on "Our Miss Brooks." Her daily travails included a blustery and blundering principal (an enduring comic type) and a handsome biology teacher, Mr. Boynton, whose reticence matched that of Mr. Peepers and thwarted Connie's dreams of married life. This series also provided an early illustration of the audience's tendency to equate actors with their roles. Star Eve Arden not only was a popular speaker at educational functions, but also received several offers to teach English at schools around the country.

Thus television's early views of teaching were generally light-hearted and benign, an impression reinforced by the classroom scenes in

"The Many Loves of Dobie Gillis." It was not until the early 1960s that the dramatic possibilities of the genre were explored on "Mr. Novak." John Novak was a dedicated young English teacher in a Los Angeles high school. The character of the earnest but sometimes brash Novak bore more than a passing resemblance to Dr. James Kildare. Jefferson High principal Albert Vane played the Gillespie role, encouraging but moderating the efforts of his young charge.

The next shift came at the end of the decade, when two new series focused on a more distinctly urban and lower-status teaching milieu than viewers had experienced before. On "The Bill Cosby Show," the star brought his humanistic touch to the comic role of a coach and physical education teacher in a lower-middle-class Los Angeles neighborhood. The real breakthrough, however, came with "Room 222." That was where Pete Dixon, an idealistic black teacher, held forth on American history to an integrated class in a big city high school. During its run from 1969 to 1974, this series focused on real-world youth-oriented issues of the time, such as student rights, racial prejudice, and drug use. It was widely praised and received awards from educational and civil rights organizations.

A 1972 episode we coded illustrates "Room 222"'s willingness to debate educational philosophy, something that rarely came up in earlier series. In this segment, Pete Dixon considers leaving to take a job as principal of another high school. He's attracted by the chance to try new things, particularly a less structured approach. As he puts it, "Teaching is communication. You have to have less structure and formality to achieve that. I might even experiment with no attendance record." Eventually he decides to remain a teacher, because he is unwilling to give up his direct contact with students. His views on structure and learning, however, are the sort of attitudes that endeared him to his students and to real-world groups favoring a more "progressive" approach to education.

After "Room 222," television's teachers became more socially aware and concerned with the wider world, sometimes bordering on social activism. They also began to move away from traditional mainstream subjects like science, history, and English, and into fields like coaching and remedial studies, where they could stick up for students who were the school's outsiders or underdogs. "Lucas Tanner" was something of a transitional figure, a former professional athlete who became an English teacher. Much of this 1974-75 series revolved around Lucas' efforts to relate to the kids with a laid-back style that created conflicts with the stuffy, more traditional teachers.

The new-style teacher took over in the late 1970s in such shows as "Welcome Back, Kotter" and "The White Shadow." Gabe Kotter had returned to his old Brooklyn high school to teach a remedial class of budding juvenile delinquents. His "sweathogs" resembled the ethnic foxholes of World War II films. They included the cool but none-too-bright Italian Vinnie Barbarino, the street-smart black "Boom Boom" Washington, the ambitious but credulous Jewish Puerto Rican Juan Epstein, and the classic class nerd Arnold Horshak. Getting through to this motley crew required considerable patience and bending of the rules. The stand-up humor routines that sold the show to a young audience were punctuated with messages on drug abuse, sex education, and the value of a diploma, usually applied with a light touch. The series gained an air of verisimilitude from being based on the actual experiences of Gabe Kaplan, who portrayed Kotter. Kaplan was himself a student in a remedial class in a Brooklyn high school before becoming a successful comedian.

"The White Shadow" provided a variation on this theme by surrounding a white basketball coach with a losing team of black players from an inner city high school. The coach's goal was to teach them to become winners in both a literal and metaphorical sense, through instilling attributes like discipline and teamwork. After two seasons, the team was good enough to win the city championship. Along the way, they had to deal with topical issues ranging from drug abuse to venereal disease and youth crime. One team member was written out of the show by being hit with a stray bullet from a liquor store holdup.

The cycle of urban ethnic schoolroom shows came to a grand finale with "Fame," a 1982-83 series set in New York's High School for the Performing Arts. The series focused on the aspirations of budding young performers, mostly dancers, singers, musicians, and comedians. Among their many dedicated teachers, the primary focus was on dance instructor

Lydia Grant. Every show featured the performers in song-and-dance routines. A critical hit, "Fame" never really caught on with audiences. It did, however, illustrate one major trend within the genre, a tendency to focus less on the concerns of teachers and more on the activities of students. Kotter's sweathogs, coach Ken Reeves' basketball team, and the talented young artists of "Fame" all played a more central role in their series than had the students of a decade before. Teachers remained important, but the focus shifted toward their interaction with strong student characters. This trend has continued in the most recent shows, such as "Square Pegs" and "Fast Times," which present school life much more from the students' viewpoints. "Square Pegs" in particular provided a panorama of perennial adolescent concerns, ranging from social cliques to new-wave music.

Even as the pendulum swung from teachers to students, the most popular teachers were those who emerged as champions of their students against their common enemy, school administrators. Repeating a theme from medical shows, teachers have always been more sensitive to student needs and problems than administrators. This was especially clear by the 1970s in shows like "Room 222," "Welcome Back, Kotter," and "The White Shadow." Coach Ken Reeves stood as a buffer between his marginal student-athletes and an academically demanding principal. Gabe Kotter shielded his remedial "sweathogs" from the stuffy, slightly malevolent Mr. Woodman. In "Fame," the muses of music and dance had to battle first literature, in the guise of Ms. Sherwood, and then bureaucracy, in the form of vice principal Quentin Morloch. All this took time away from the kids, but not enough to hinder their learning. There is never any mention of corruption in school systems, however, and not much wrongdoing in general. If a teacher is accused of some impropriety, the charge usually proves to be false. If there is any conflict at all, it is between sensitive teachers and officious administrators.

Despite increasing difficulties with superiors and paperwork, the real problem was always how to reach students. At first, the students didn't want to learn or were otherwise preoccupied. Dobie Gillis and his beatnik friend Maynard Krebs were always problem students, and Miss Brooks sometimes despaired of getting through to Walter Denton. By the late 1960s more serious problems began to interfere with learning. There were learning disabilities and family problems including child abuse, alcoholism, drugs, unwanted pregnancy, illegal alien status, and other mental and physical handicaps. From the first, television's teachers have had to struggle to reach their students. As the barriers got higher, the teachers grew even more dedicated.

In dealing with such problems, there was a tendency to make teachers more socially aware and responsive. "Room 222" led the way, but the trend continued with the problems of drugs, crime, and the like in "The White Shadow" and in Ralph Hinkley's efforts to instill some social conscience in his overly complacent students on "The Greatest American Hero." Even "Fame" had teachers of art and music who dealt with intolerance toward the handicapped, racial and religious discrimination, and economic threats to the arts. (All these issues could be handled in an episode and still allow time for a couple of big production numbers.)

More recently, Ed Asner ("Lou Grant") starred as the reform-minded principal of the "Bronx Zoo," a tough New York City high school. This politically conscious drama treated topics like birth control, day care, and racial tensions in a schoolroom setting. Another real-life liberal activist who took his act to the classroom is Howard Hessman. As Charlie Moore of Monroe High School, his (and the show's) lessons often targeted conservative figures and causes. For example, Moore described Ronald Reagan as a president "in whose administration fact and fiction finally came together." And the class science whiz described a William F. Buckley clone as "living proof that the phrase 'conservative thinker' is an oxymoron."

The "progressive" prime-time educator was never a rush-the-barricades radical, but rather a strongly humanitarian, socially sensitive reformer. There hasn't been much demand for such teachers during the current back-to-basics era ("Bronx Zoo" scored better with critics than audiences) and the future of the profession on prime time (as in real life) is up in the air. But there will probably always be some call for the benevolent mentors, officious administrators, and troubled youths who are the staples of the schoolroom scene on the small screen.

THE GOOD, THE BAD, AND THE MAD

Unlike the other occupations we've discussed, scientists are rarely shown and little remembered. Those that we coded accounted for well under 1 percent of the occupational sample, making them only about one-third as populous on prime time as in real life. Nevertheless, they are worth noting for the way they illustrate television's use of occupational stereotypes for entertainment purposes. Science on television is often linked to science fiction, in which scientists are likely to be shaped from molds formed by Jules Verne stories or old horror movies.

A study done for the National Science Foundation found that television highlights the exotic and dangerous aspects of science.[1] The evidence included its association with depictions of violence, natural disasters, distant locales, and fantasies about the future. This research, carried out during the 1970s, also found scientists to be quite rare, as well as less positive and successful than other professionals, although positive portrayals outnumbered the negative.

Our research suggests that this portrait holds throughout television's history. The scientists we coded were positive by almost a five-to-three margin (54 to 34 percent) which places them behind doctors, teachers, and most other professional groups in the prime-time pantheon, but ahead of run-of-the-mill characters (not to mention businessmen). However, they were unusually likely to commit crimes. Almost one in five engaged in criminal activity, a rate exceeding even that of businessmen.

The sources of this mixed portrait lie in the specific dramatic functions of scientific characters. They are rarely the stars of series, and those who attain the mantle of stardom even more rarely enjoy the advantages of long-running hits. A brief survey mainly serves to illustrate their relative anonymity. The late 1950s featured two series built around heroic scientists. In NBC's "The Man and the Challenge," Dr. Glenn Barton was a government scientist who helped test men and equipment in stressful situations. One episode might see him working with explorers to perfect jungle survival techniques, while the next would simulate outer-space conditions for astronaut training.

Meanwhile, over on CBS, Dr. Peter Brady's research on light had the undesired side effect of rendering him invisible. As "The Invisible Man," he became an understandably successful secret agent for British intelligence. (The show originated in England.) This was one of those series in which the protagonist's scientific qualifications served as an explanation for his predicament but otherwise had little bearing on either character or plot. More recent variations on this theme include Prof. John Robinson of "Lost in Space" and Dr. David Banner of "The Incredible Hulk." In fact, Hollywood later offered a reprise of "The Invisible Man" with an anti-establishment twist. In NBC's 1975 version, the scientist destroys his invisibility formula rather than see it fall into the hands of the government, which wants to explore its military applications.

During the past decade scientists have also played sympathetic characters in supporting roles as the hero's sidekick or helper. Thus Dr. Elizabeth Merrill headed a research team that worked with an aquatic superhero, "The Man from Atlantis," to explore undersea life. Their efforts brought them up against various scientific villains like the malevolent Dr. Schubert. Unfortunately, there was no undersea audience to boost the ratings, and the series sank quickly from view in 1978. Slightly more successful was "Buck Rogers in the 25th Century," a 1975 update of the comic book character. During the first season Buck's sidekick was Dr. Huer, the Einstein of his generation. Next season he was replaced by Dr. Goodfellow, a brilliant but somewhat dithering eccentric. There was no third season. More recently, biologist Julie Parrish helped lead the resistance against the Nazi-like aliens in "V."

Because so few scientists have been series regulars, the profession's image is more dependent on characters who make a single appearance. Their roles often fall into one of three hoary stereotypes, dating back to nineteenth-century science fiction, updated for mass audiences by the horror movies of the 1930s and 1940s. The first is the crazed "mad scientist" who uses his intellect to wreak revenge on society or seek world domination. The second is the cloistered genius who is obsessed with his work. He may overlook the dangers of what he is doing, as well as any type of social or family life, as he monomaniacally pursues his research goals. The third type is the guilty genius whose well-intentioned plans go awry, so that he is faced with the error of his ways. He then must help to save humanity from his discovery or invention, no matter what the cost to his career.

The mad scientist pops up in offbeat series like "Alfred Hitchcock Presents," "Twilight Zone," and "The Outer Limits." For example, on "The Six Million Dollar Man" a rejected government scientist uses his research to hold entire cities hostage for ransom. Similarly, one episode of "The Avengers" features a government scientist who discovers how to "broadcast" electricity via sound waves, like a radio signal. He uses charged-up assistants to electrocute other members of the research team, so that only he knows the secret. Then he plans to use his shock troops to take over the country. When he takes on Steed and Mrs. Peel, however, he comes to a shocking end himself.

The cloistered, obsessive scientist appeared in many of the aforementioned shows and also in adventure or spy shows like "Secret Agent." Various research chemists and physicists have been used in this manner. In an episode of "A Man Called Sloane," a scientist creates voracious killer grasshoppers. An evil organization (KARTEL) uses the scientist and his discoveries for its own ends, to corner the world grain market. Its agents eventually kill him when he is no longer needed.

The repentant scientist is really a variation on the second type. These scientists are often so single-minded in their pursuit of knowledge that they don't see the potential for mischief in their research until some disaster occurs. Then they realize that their work poses a danger and they must help the heroes save the world, humanity, or the American way of life. An episode of "The Girl From U.N.C.L.E." gives us a naive scientist working on experiments with light. He develops a bulb that turns everything white. He is approached by the forces of evil who cajole and trick him into turning over his invention to them. They build him a fantastic laboratory and give him cars and money to continue his research. Yet he remains ignorant of their ulterior motives. It is not until late in the show that he discovers their evil intention to bleach all the world's art treasures white. He then regrets his actions and helps the good guys stop the plan.

Similarly, a brilliant scientist on "Star Trek" designs and builds the first thinking computer. Installed aboard the *Enterprise*, it is intended to prove itself in some war games. The computer goes berserk, however, and starts playing for keeps. After the computer disables another ship, killing some of its crew, the scientist is emotionally shattered. The source of his error will be familiar to viewers of the 1956 sci-fi film, *Forbidden Planet*. It emerges that he gave the computer his thoughts and brain waves. The computer possesses all his paranoias and fears, as well as his hatred for the military, with its massive costs and destruction. His invention continues to threaten great destruction until, with the help of its repentant creator, it is destroyed.

In recent years scientists have occasionally been featured in more traditional good-guy roles. The most successful of these is "MacGyver," an American agent who gets himself out of jams by building Rube Goldberg devices that short-circuit the bad guys. Mining this view for a younger audience was "The Wizard," a genius inventor who built toys for children and more sophisticated "toys" for the U.S. government. And "Misfits of Science" featured a team of "superhero" comic book types who are forged into a crime-fighting team by two young scientists at Humanadyne Laboratories.

Presaging this minitrend toward heroic scientists was an episode of "The Bionic Woman" that we coded. The segment was noteworthy for its use of a scientist-hero to score ideological points against nationalism and the arms race.

A brilliant scientist in his declining years decides that he and his profession have done too much to move the world powers toward mutual annihilation. So he uses his massive intelligence to build the ultimate doomsday device. Set up in rugged mountains and surrounded by defense mechanisms, the system will detonate a massive explosion that will destroy the world at the first sign of impending war. He announces to the world that his device is in operation and warns against ever turning to war again. Despite the objections by all governments that it infringes on their sovereign rights, peace reigns. Thus the scientist thinks he has succeeded in ending the threat of war.

Then a small power-hungry nation performs an above-ground nuclear test and starts the device on its countdown toward destruction. The scientist is persuaded to help in an attempt to disarm the device. The efforts fail, however, and he dies of a heart attack. Mankind's only chance for survival is for Jamie Sommers (The Bionic Woman) to go to the facility and disarm the mechanism. She evades all sorts of security measures and gets past the outer barricades. She races to the last door and finally cracks the code to open it, only to find that she is too late. But when the dread moment arrives and the doomsday device is activated, there is no earth-shattering boom or everlasting oblivion. Instead, a recording of the scientist's voice comes on, saying that now they know his secret. He tells them there is no destruction except that which they may bring on themselves. On the side of a cube that rises out of the floor bearing the recording is inscribed the passage from Isaiah (2:4):

> And he shall judge among the nations, and shall rebuke many people: and they shall beat their swords into plowshares, and their spears into pruning hooks: nation shall not lift up sword against nation, neither shall they learn war anymore.

Thus ends the saga of the repentant scientist who tried to bluff the world into peace.

PRIME-TIME PRESSROOMS

Real-life journalists often argue over whether they should be regarded as professionals. Their gritty "get me rewrite" heritage currently clashes with the tremendous rise in education and status they have enjoyed. Television's treatment of their profession reflects this ambiguity. The traditional TV journalist is a tough, hard-edged, street-smart reporter. In the early years they were exclusively male, although women began entering the picture during the 1970s. Journalists are perhaps the most raffish good guys on TV. They drink, they smoke, they pursue the opposite sex, they often lack social graces. They are tough, determined pros who work hard and play hard.

In their initial incarnation in prime time, journalists tended to be crime solvers. They often aided or supplemented the law enforcement establishment with crusades against racketeering or organized crime. They sometimes served as voices of tolerance and fairness who firmly opposed abuses of power. They were establishment-oriented, however, pursuing individual law breakers rather than institutionalized iniquity.

Early viewers could follow the adventures of investigative reporters for the *Illustrated Press* in "Big Town" or the *New York Record* in "Roaring Twenties." They could watch courageous journalists ferret out corruption in "Target: The Corruptors," "Jefferson Drum," and "Man With a Camera." If these urban locales proved boring, they could vicariously pursue adventure with crusading journalists in Hawaii in "Follow the Sun," around the globe on "Wire Service," or back to the Old West on "Tombstone Territory." Those who disdained such escapist fare could turn to documentary-style formats in "The Walter Winchell File" and "The Big Story."

Finally, two series offered unusual portrayals of journalists by adding a dash of political ideology to their activities. In "The Californians," a San Francisco newspaper editor headed a band of vigilantes, which was formed to keep law and order in the face of corrupt courts and police during the California gold rush. "Crusader" gave us Matt Anders, a freelance writer whose sworn goal was to help those under communist or other dictatorial regimes escape. He was spurred on by the memory of his mother, who died in a gulag after resisting the communist takeover in Poland.

In these shows journalists weren't just solving crimes or helping right individual wrongs. They were representatives of the free world who were morally committed to causes of justice and freedom. They went beyond simply exposing criminals so the proper authorities could step in. Instead they were active agents in bringing the struggle against evil to its proper conclusion.

Other series took a less ideological approach. When solving crimes, most journalists were only trying to help friends or honest officials falsely accused or framed by corrupt individuals. They acted less from a commitment to abstract concepts of justice or freedom than from a sense of fair play and a desire to help the upstanding achieve their goals.

One other series from this period is notable for reflecting TV's early tendency to use official records from actual cases. "The Big Story" used plots based on the activities of real-life reporters who uncovered a major story. Some were national stories, others local, but all were factually based. At the end of the show the real-life reporter was awarded $500 cash by the sponsors for his efforts. Never a big hit, this show nevertheless ran for eight years.

Reporters of all types were to remain tough, strong-willed, and somewhat seedy well into the 1970s. They continued to be drinkers and smokers who ate the wrong foods, kept late hours, and knew some of the more undesirable (and entertaining) people in any city. In the early shows journalists had a sense of fair play and a desire to see justice prevail. By the middle- to late-1960s fair play was translated into not letting the powerful get more than their share.

For example, "The Name of the Game" featured a hard-driving investigative reporter who exposed corruption among the rich and powerful for the presciently named *People* magazine (which, however, bore no relation to the later real-life expositor of celebrity journalism). A 1969 episode in the sample featured an unusual statement of environmental themes. At the outset, publisher Glen Howard is knocked unconscious in an auto accident while returning from a conference on the environment. The story segues into an extended dream sequence in which he imagines awakening a century later. In the interim, an environmental catastrophe has driven all life underground, where people live under a repressive dictatorship. Eventually Howard awakens with a renewed dedication to protect the environment.

The Watergate scandal inaugurated a new era for investigative journalism, and television was quick to latch onto the trend. Over the past decade, anti-establishment reporters who fight the powerful or expose injustice have become a fixture of life on the tube. Their targets are usually venal businessmen, chauvinistic generals, and corrupt cops and politicians. "The Insiders" featured hip freelancers who exposed corruption by infiltrating criminal operations to get an insider's viewpoint. Typical segments dealt with a drug operation that involved crooked cops and a car theft ring headed by a big businessman. Similarly, "Fitz and Bones" were the nicknames of a cameraman and an investigative reporter for San Francisco's Newsline 3. They tackled stories involving terrorism and racism in addition to less serious human interest fare. On a more mundane level, "Hill Street Blues" ran a vignette in which a film crew from a local TV station caught officer Renko shopping and running personal errands while on duty.

The most memorable members of the new breed were the staff of the crusading *Los Angeles Tribune*, led by tough but avuncular city editor "Lou Grant." Less well remembered is "Six O'Clock Follies," which offered a unique setting for this genre—the Vietnam War. The heroes were two peacetime journalists, Page and Robinson, who were drafted and sent to work for the Armed Services Network in Saigon. They spent much of their time protecting the interests of the common G.I. against the top brass. In an episode we coded, they are assigned to a story on a general who was awarded a silver star for heroism. They discover the decoration was "pure fiction," and the general wasn't even at the battle for which it was awarded. Instead, he was on a secret mission in Cambodia. If the truth got out, it might widen the war, so they are forced to drop the story.

When not dealing with serious issues like the conflict between freedom of the press and military secrecy, this episode featured standard service comedy devices like the colonel who couldn't clean a rifle without getting his thumb caught in the mechanism. Apparently, the audience wasn't interested in reliving the living room war from this perspective. The series had only a brief run in 1980.

Alongside these hard-charging public tribunes, however, a less savory stereotype has entered the journalistic scene. This is the pushy, obnoxious, sometimes unethical reporter, a dark side of the journalistic persona that television had heretofore largely ignored. These negative newspeople are shown demanding answers to prying questions hurled at grieving relatives during funerals, or springing ambush interviews to produce out of context quotes from their unlucky victims. Such tactics are rarely pursued by series regulars, although investigative reporter Joe Rossi of "Lou Grant" sometimes tested the limits of journalistic ethics. They are usually the province of reporters whose obstreperous activities provide plot complications or make life difficult for a series star.

Typical of this plot device is a TV anchorwoman who appears on a 1985 segment of "Spenser: For Hire." She is taken hostage by a man whose son was killed when a building collapsed on a playground. He demands she do a story investigating political corruption that led to the use of substandard materials in the building. The woman is freed when police kill her abductor, but Spenser asks her to pursue the case anyway. She tells him it's "old news" because they did a story months ago (without pursuing the angle demanded by the grieving father). An angry Spenser replies that he thought she was a journalist, but her attitude explains why he doesn't see any notebooks or typewriters in her dressing room, "just makeup, fancy dresses, and a full-length mirror." She finally agrees to do a story if Spenser can turn up anything new.

As the story progresses, this woman becomes a more positive character, trying to prove her mettle as a true journalist rather than a pretty face for local TV news. At one point she confesses, "I'm thirty-nine years old and only have one, maybe two years left with the station. I'm never going on to the networks. I don't know what I'm going to do. . . . It's the trap of being attractive. You get to a certain age and you can see it start to go. You try and prove there's more there—that you can still cover a story."

And the program isn't yet done with its critique of broadcast news. After Spenser and the reporter have uncovered an alliance between the mob and local politicians, her producer refuses to run the story, telling her that she only reads copy on the air after he has approved it. When she refuses to back down, he replaces her with a young attractive blonde whose newscast consists of fluff like shopping tips and a new diet plan.

It may seem ironic that TV entertainment should criticize TV news for introducing entertainment values into their broadcasts. Perhaps it is a sign of overcompensation that this quintessential medium of mass entertainment so thirsts to be taken seriously that it scolds the news division for the sin of being frivolous. Prime-time criticism of broadcast journalism is seen most often in comedy formats that poke fun at inept, overbearing, or pompous newscasters. The progenitor of this negative stereotype was Ted Baxter, the doltish and narcissistic anchorman at WJM-TV on "The Mary Tyler Moore Show." Ted's recent descendants included the handsome but stupid star of KXLA's "Paul Thurston Show" on "Tabitha" and Les Nesman, the naive news director of "WKRP in Cincinnati." The apotheosis of this character type was "Buffalo Bill" Bittinger, the Archie Bunker of WBFL-TV in Buffalo, N.Y. As host of a talk show, he regularly insulted co-workers, stole credit, shifted blame, and precipitated lawsuits with gaffes he uttered while on the air.

The common thread that runs through these portrayals is that some journalists have grown too big for their britches. The investigative reporter who runs roughshod over standards of civility and the puffed-up preening news personality share an arrogance that TV entertainment loves to deflate. Thus, even as the anti-establishment crusader burst onto the scene as a new type of hero, he was accompanied by new types of villains from within the world of journalism. As a result, this occupation's portrayal became markedly less positive after 1975. Until that time, good guys consistently outnumbered bad guys in the profession by about a three-to-one ratio. The positive margin was 56 to 19 percent prior to 1965 and 52 to 15 percent from 1965 through 1974. Since then, the margin has narrowed to 44 percent positive and 31 percent negative, roughly a four-to-three ratio. Thus journalism's net positive index has dropped from +37 to +13.

So although a plurality of journalists still wear white hats, the proportion of bad guys has more than doubled in the most recent decade. This also means that, for the first time in television's history, the image of journalists is below average when compared to that of all other occupations. Just when the profession's image has improved in the society at large, it seems to have soured in Hollywood. Of course, the new real-life status of journalists may have worked to their disadvantage as fictional characters. The little guys who stood up against the powerful have become big wheels themselves, especially among the high-salaried celebrities of television news. The chain-smoking, whiskey-breathed, rumpled outsiders from "the front page" must now compete with the well-coiffed bubbleheaded pretty faces on the six o'clock news in the pantheon of journalistic stereotypes. As journalists become glamorous insiders, it is perhaps inevitable that they sometimes slip on the same banana peels that trip up bank presidents and bureaucrats.

THOSE WHO SERVE

This whirlwind tour has left no time for stops with the numerous (and sometimes nameless) architects, writers, social workers, and other professional types who populate prime time. But even such a brief visit conveys both their diversity and the common themes that link this group of characters. There are certainly stereotypes geared to specific occupations. The dedicated physician locked in a Sisyphean struggle with disease and death, the caring teacher whose noble mission combines instruction with character formation, the brilliant but unstable or politically naive scientist, the journalist as street-smart public tribune—all these are stock characters who long predate the magic box where we view them today.

Yet their diversity should not obscure certain similarities that bind television's professionals. Most are superior people who stand apart from the crowd. What sets them above their fellows is their dedication to human betterment, as healers or teachers, or seekers of truth and justice. A corollary is their devotion to the ideal of service. Dedication to one's profession is a touchstone. The venal doctor or uncaring teacher is rarely seen. More common are the doctors who work too hard or the teachers who care too much for their own good. By and large, the bad guys they encounter at work are not other professionals but rather managers—rigid administrators or officious bureaucratic types.

Television's professionals have also undergone a common shift of emphasis over the years. Their dedication has never wavered, but it has gradually changed direction. Their ideal of service has opened out from the individual to the larger society. Once they served clients or patients, pausing to solve the personal problems of their charges. Since the mid-1960s, they have become far more socially aware and enmeshed in social problems. A television doctor was always expected to help an impoverished patient get back on his feet financially as well

269

as physically. Today a similar case might involve the physician in the problems of homelessness or famine relief. The teacher who once tried to reach a difficult student would now have to deal with the drug use or sexual abuse that comes between the child and his homework. The journalist who once exposed mobsters now concentrates on the shady business practices that form the backdrop for corruption. Their newly developed social conscience only enhances this group's portrayal as the real benefactors of humanity. Today's good guy professionals represent a socially "enlightened" occupational sector whose representatives display the liberal and cosmopolitan sensibility shared by the Hollywood community as an emblem of their social concern.

This portrait cautions against class-based interpretations of TV's social role that come from both the Left and the Right. This quintessential medium of the masses does not always ridicule the wealthy and powerful, as an expression of the audience's resentment. Neither does it serve the establishment by holding up the upper classes as paragons for the little guy to emulate. The key distinction is one of occupational status rather than economic class. Television differentiates quite clearly between the bad businessman and the good professional, though both may be equally well off. Television generally abhors the former and identifies with the latter.

Indeed, prime time dotes on educated professionals almost as much as it disdains businessmen. They represent all the noble traits television finds lacking in the business world—selflessness, caring for humanity, dedication to a worthy calling. Their common bond is the idea of service to others, which contrasts starkly with the greed that is the touchstone of the prime-time businessman.

Over time, this idea has undergone an important change. Today's TV professionals are more socially aware than their predecessors. They are responsive to social concerns and public issues rather than just individuals and their private problems. So the idea of professional service has been politicized in the broadest sense. Always praised as servants of humanity, they are now prized as its social conscience.

PART
IV

Crime and Punishment

8

PRIME-TIME CRIME

[A] vast wasteland. . .of blood and thunder, mayhem, violence,
sadism, murder. . . .

—Newton Minow, FCC chairman

The debate over TV crime and violence is almost as old as the medium itself. Soon after Newton Minow's 1961 shot heard 'round the industry, congressional hearings zeroed in on the ABC dramatic anthology "Bus Stop." One episode in particular provoked widespread outrage. It featured a young deranged drifter who won acquittal in a murder case by having an affair with the prosecutor's alcoholic wife. He used this to blackmail the D.A. and win his release. Once freed, he killed his own lawyers before finally being done in by the D.A.'s wife. [1]

The sadistic nature of the violence in this episode aroused the ire of Rhode Island Senator John Pastore. The embarrassed president of ABC had to admit to Pastore's committee that he did not let his own children watch such violent programming.[2] Despite the public criticism and political pressure, however, no dramatic changes in programming took place.

Senator Pastore used "Bus Stop" as the best example of TV violence and crime, but he could have turned the dial and found many others. On

Monday night there was "87th Precinct," a show with a fixation for the morbid and bizarre. One episode featured a killer who first tattooed and then poisoned his female victims. At nine o'clock the next evening "The New Breed" presented an equally gruesome picture. In one episode the police were tracking an elusive rapist/killer. They finally discovered that he was a hitchhiker who selected as victims the wives of men who had picked him up on the road. He would find out the men's addresses on the pretense of mailing them payment for the ride and then wait until they were out of town to attack the wives. He often tied up and killed the women after he raped them. In the end, he was fatally shot by police when he returned to murder a woman he failed to finish off in his first attack.

The list of violent crime shows from the early 1960s is a lengthy one. Series like "Cain's Hundred," "Target the Corruptors," "Whispering Smith," and "The Westerner" presented crime and violence with predictable viciousness and frequency. The so-called swinging detective shows like "77 Sunset Strip," "Surfside Six," and "Hawaiian Eye" included fewer crimes and less sadistic forms of violence, but murder was still the most common offense.

This listing suggests that not much has changed in the past quarter century. Graphic depictions of crime and violence have been a prime-time fixture from "The Untouchables" to "The A-Team." Ironically, for all the periodic public furor, television's crime rate has remained more stable than its real-world counterpart. At the same time, there have been changes in both the style and substance of TV's crime wave. Some shifts reflect no more than changing fashions, like the switch from Western gunmen in the 1950s, to secret agents in the 1960s, and hard-boiled cops in the 1970s. Others are rooted in real-world changes. Video cops now read suspects their Miranda rights, and the heroes of "Miami Vice" do battle against designer drugs unknown to Joe Friday.

In fact, the topic of crime offers a rare opportunity to compare television's fictional world with the real world. Statistics compiled by the FBI and other agencies can serve as a benchmark against which television's fascination with crime can be measured. Our picture of crime in the nation was drawn from the FBI's *Uniform Crime Reports:*

Crime in the United States. This annual report offers a statistical picture of crimes reported to the nation's law enforcement agencies. It focuses on seven serious crimes: murder, forcible rape, armed robbery, aggravated assault, burglary, larceny, and motor vehicle theft.[3] The first four offenses are considered violent crimes. The last three are crimes against property. These figures on real-life serious crime provide a benchmark for comparison with television's crime levels. Since many crimes go unreported, we also made use of victimization studies, which identify the victims of crime.[4]

TV'S CRIME WAVE

Our studies show that an evening of prime time puts to shame a night at the station house. Violent crime is far more pervasive on television than in real life, and the disparity widens as the danger increases. For the most serious crime of all, the difference is most dramatic. Since 1955 television characters have been murdered at a rate one thousand times higher than real-world victims. Indeed, television violence has far outstripped reality since the 1950s. In the first decade of our study, there were seven murders for every one hundred characters seen on the screen. This was over 1,400 times the actual murder rate for the United States during the same time period.

Murder was often presented as a means to an end, a method consciously chosen to solve problems. Typical of this was an early "Thin Man" episode in which a restauranteur hired an assassin to kill his partner so that he could take over the whole business. A "Wire Service" episode from 1957 presented an even more convoluted use of murder. In this segment, a lawyer and nightclub owner are being blackmailed over their ties to organized crime. In order to keep their ties to the mob secret, they have the blackmailer killed. Concerned that an anonymous murder would not adequately cover their tracks, they set up a young pianist to take the fall.

This preference for violent crimes was not limited to homicide. Other violent crimes accounted for one crime in eight on TV during the decade 1955 to 1964. Violent crimes short of murder occurred at a rate of forty for every one thousand characters.[5] At that time the real-world rate was only two in every one thousand inhabitants. For example, our sample picked up a 1963 episode of "Arrest and Trial" featuring a virtual crime spree that stopped short of murder. The sequence begins when two bank robbers escape from police custody. The robbers shoot a police officer to make good their escape and then rob a convenience store to get traveling money. To ensure their safe exit they take a young woman and a police detective hostage. One of the robbers almost succeeds in an attempt to rape the young woman before the police catch them.

During the second decade plus of our study, covering 1965 to 1975, crime rose both on TV and in the wider world. In the real world the rate for serious offenses doubled to twenty-five for every one thousand inhabitants, according to FBI statistics. Despite this increase, the television crime rate remained more than five times that of the real world, at 140 crimes per one thousand characters. The FBI-calculated rate for violent crimes also doubled to three incidents per one thousand inhabitants. The TV rate for violent crimes, at one hundred fourteen incidents per one thousand characters, was over thirty times greater than reality. Even the estimates from victimization studies done at the beginning and end of this decade failed to bring television and reality into agreement. The television rate for violent crimes was still fifteen times higher than estimates from victimization surveys.

There were also changes in the quality of violent crimes on TV that weren't reflected in the crime rate figures. These qualitative changes were due largely to the addition of a new type of program, the espionage show. In dramas like "The Avengers," "I Spy," "Mission: Impossible," and "The Man From U.N.C.L.E.," crime became a more complex event. Increasingly murder was presented as a tool to silence informers or eliminate enemies. The psychopathic or deranged criminals seen earlier in "Bus Stop" or "87th Precinct" were replaced by cold-blooded professionals. Violence was less often the action of a single individual and more often the outcome of a criminal conspiracy. While earlier violence was notable for its viciousness, sadism, and irrationality, violence in the second decade was noteworthy for its rationality and premeditation. For instance, in a segment of "Mission: Impossible," members of an organized crime syndicate grow upset with the actions of their leader. After they fail to persuade him to change his plans, they hold a council and order the leader killed. They politely inform him of their decision and dispatch a contract killer to finish him off.

By the early 1970s television featured two patterns of violent crime. The first followed the tradition of "Bus Stop" in presenting brutal, often irrational crimes committed by the mentally unstable. For example, a 1973 segment of "Adam-12" presented a young woman who is being harassed by obscene phone calls. The police, while sympathetic, can do little but suggest she get a new phone number. They are later called back to her apartment after her neighbors hear screams. The police rush in to find that she has been beaten in an attempted rape. They corner the attacker on the roof, where he babbles about it being her fault. He complains that she just kept walking in front of the window while exercising in her leotard. He claims he couldn't take it anymore, and she asked for it.

The other pattern was far more common and took a more cold-blooded approach. In this passionless model, crimes of violence were only a tool. If persuasion and bribery didn't work, then violence was another method to try. Criminal gangs and hired thugs coldly gunned down adversaries. Conspirators were silenced by hitmen who neatly dispatched their targets. These strong-arm types simply did whatever they were told without mercy, conscience, or hesitation. These cold-blooded crimes were common in the new espionage shows and on cop shows like "Mod Squad," "N.Y.P.D.," "Hawaii Five-O," "Ironside," and "The Rookies." The descendants of the 1950s swinging detective shows, like "Mannix," "Cannon," "Longstreet," "Barnaby Jones," and "Banacek" also presented violent criminals as cold and calculating.

All this made the late 1960s and early 1970s a very violent time on TV. This wave of violence and crime led to further criticism of television content. Eventually these complaints led to a change in television standards, which appears to have had some impact on programming. In 1975 the National Association of Broadcasters amended its broadcasting standards to create the Family Viewing Time. All programming in the eight o'clock time slot had to be acceptable for viewing by a general audience. Critics quickly attacked the rule as hypocritical, since the nine- to eleven o'clock period would remain unchanged. The general feeling was that the television content would be little changed.

Our systematic findings present a mixed picture of the almost two decades since 1975. The rate for serious crimes on television fell 3 percent to a "low" of 110 crimes per one thousand characters. The rate for violent crimes also dropped almost 3 percent, to eighty-six incidents in every one thousand characters. The total number of crimes presented by television, however, actually increased 24 percent in the last decade. The bulk of this increase came in nonviolent crimes.[6]

Ironically, while the television crime rate took its first downturn in twenty years, the criminal tide in the country continued to rise. According to the FBI, the rate for all serious crimes rose to fifty for every one thousand inhabitants, or about half the rate found on television. The violent crime rate was only five in every one thousand inhabitants, or about one-tenth the TV rate. If independent victimization study estimates are used, the serious crime rate more than doubles to 110 incidents for every one thousand inhabitants, for the first time equaling the rate seen on TV. The rate for violent crimes rises to eleven for every one thousand inhabitants, which is still only one-eighth the rate seen on television. Thus, television and reality have moved closer in terms of the overall crime rate, but television continues to present far more violent crimes than occur in real life.

Television not only presents a higher rate of violent crime than the real world, it presents a different type of violent crime. TV murders are motivated by very different forces than those that instigate homicide in reality. When Americans kill each other, it is quite often in a burst of anger. Forty percent or more of the murders known to police are found to result from some type of argument.[7] In the malevolent world of television, however, murder is rarely the result of an argument. Television murders are more likely to be what the FBI calls felony murders. These are murders perpetrated during the commission of some other crime like robbery or rape. For example, in a segment of the early Western "The

Rifleman," an embezzler is forced to shoot his partner when his theft is discovered. Unfortunately, a passing traveler sees the murder, so the embezzler tries to kill him before his scheme unravels. In a hip cop show of the 1970s, "Get Christie Love," a travel agency serves as the front for a drug-smuggling operation. The agency offers tour packages to France. From the tourists who wish to go to France, the smugglers search for those with heart conditions or other medical problems and no next of kin. Once the selected American arrives in France, one of the gang gives him or her a drug that induces a heart attack and death. Since there is no next of kin, the travel agency arranges for the return of the body to the U.S. The gang takes the opportunity to have the body buried in France and then ships the casket back full of illegal drugs. During the course of the show, at least three unwitting tourists perish in this scheme. In the real world, only 25 percent of known murders could be classified as such felony-type murders. At least since the late 1950s, nonfelony murders have far outnumbered felony murders in the wider world. On television the reverse has always been true.

The motives of a video murderer are also very different from his real-world counterparts. On television, greed is the most common motive. Of all the arguments that lead to murder in the real world only 3 to 5 percent are about money or property.[8] In the more venal television world, three out of five murders are motivated by greed. Murder on TV is usually a way to acquire someone else's money, possessions, or status. In our sample this was typified by a segment of the early Western, "The Adventures of Champion." An old prospector, after years of searching, finally finds gold. In his enthusiasm, he tells two young men of his find. They decide that jumping his claim would be far easier than staking their own, so they kill him. Then they take his maps and samples into town and claim his find as their own. Thanks to the brilliance of Champion, "the wonder horse," their evil ways are revealed, and they are captured.

Murder is not the only violent crime to receive unusual treatment on television. Rape, although rarely seen in our survey of television, is presented very differently from its real-life counterpart. Rape is the last refuge of the sadistic, irrational criminal on television. In the real world forcible rape is usually an opportunistic and violent act. Victim and rapist are most often unknown to one another, and the rape is a fairly brief assault which usually leaves the victim traumatized but alive.[9]

Rape is also a crime ideally suited to television. It is violent and therefore action packed. The sexual nature of the crime can be emphasized, and it can easily be presented as the act of a violent, mentally unbalanced madman. For instance, in the episode of "The New Breed" mentioned earlier, both violence and a bizarre motive are obvious. The man kills three of the five women he attacks during the show, and several others are said to have died in the same way. When the police catch up with the rapist, they find out his motive. After his parents died he was raised by an older sister. She had a long string of boyfriends and lovers. Eventually she ran off with one and left the young boy to fend for himself. He came to believe that all women were promiscuous and cheated on their husbands. He set out to correct that flaw by killing them.

This was the beginning of a trend that intensified in the early 1970s. Rape on TV became increasingly violent and was often accompanied by other unusual behavior or rituals. In a segment of "Kojak" that we watched, a group of fraternity brothers gang rape a young girl who delivers pizzas. Later they kill her mother in an argument over how much they would have to pay for her silence. In another episode of the same series, two men drag a woman into an alley. The first man rapes her, but the second is unable to complete the act. He becomes enraged to the point of psychosis, prompting him to strangle the woman and then shoot his partner. In an episode of "The Rockford Files," a man harasses his blind psychologist, setting her up to be raped. When he is finally caught, he turns out to have a split personality. One personality is a mob hitman. The other is a diminutive, introverted type who decided to rape in order to prove his strength and virility.

As if that case weren't unusual enough, television has even turned on itself in the search for bizarre crimes. This twist was seen in an episode of the short-lived series "Most Wanted." The segment we watched features a white TV anchorman who has hated Indians ever since his mother ran off with one when he was a child. In order to make

280

Indians look like vicious criminals, he dresses up as an Indian brave and begins to rape and murder white women. He dresses the corpses up as Indian princesses to further the illusion that the crimes have been committed by an Indian.

The 1980s did not see the end of these violent and unusual rapes, and several series tried to add their own gruesome touch. For example, in a segment of "The Equalizer," a woman's life was threatened by the man who had raped her a few years earlier. That rape lasted eight hours and included a beating so severe that it left her permanently blinded. By the 1980s even policewomen weren't safe, as seen in episodes of "Hunter," "Magruder and Loud," "Miami Vice," and "Cagney & Lacey." These series presented policewomen who either had previously been raped or were raped during the show. In all cases the rapes were brutal assaults committed by very disturbed and violent individuals.

Two series from the 1980s added a twist by presenting the first forcible rapes on TV with male victims.[10] The first of these occurred in "Hill Street Blues" when Detective Mick Belker was raped by a gang of thugs in a basement. The second occurred in a "St. Elsewhere" episode when Dr. Morrison and a female resident went to a prison clinic. Prisoners grabbed both doctors, beat them very badly, and then violently raped them.

All this shows how different the TV rape is from its real-world counterpart. Due to the tremendous amount of violence used, the TV rape victim is far less likely to survive the attack than her real-life counterpart. A surprising 5 percent of the murders on TV result from rape. That's over three times the proportion of all real-life murders resulting from rape and all other sex offenses.[11] It is also worth noting that a large number of TV rapists die. In five of the examples mentioned here, the rapist died in the end. Rape is a crime presented in the most terrifying and revolting way on television, and thus its perpetrators deserve the most severe punishment that scriptwriters can mete out. In time-honored Hollywood fashion, the titillating mixture of sex and violence is legitimized by consigning the bad guy to his own violent end.

THE ARMS RACE

On television, as in reality, violent crime often involves gunplay. In the real world about one-quarter of all violent crimes, and a majority of murders, involve the use of a gun.[12] We didn't code the specific type of weapon used in video crime, but even a cursory glance points out the prevalence of firearms. Almost all of television's violent crimes involve the use of some type of gun. More intriguing is television's continuing quest to update its arsenal. In the early days, Matt Dillon's six-gun and Elliot Ness's police special provided enough firepower for the forces of law and order. The criminals they went after were usually similarly armed. There were occasional rifles, and gangsters sometimes carried tommy guns, but such extravagance was unusual. Through the years the choice of weapons on television has broadened, as both the good guys and the bad guys expanded and improved their arsenals. High-powered rifles became more common, and in the 1970s machine guns and other automatic weapons were increasingly evident. By the 1980s a stunning array of weapons was available. There were shotguns, submachine guns, automatic weapons, rocket launchers, laser weapons, hand grenades, and many more.

The early shows that were criticized for their violent content usually presented violence according to a common formula. For example, "The Untouchables" followed a predictable pattern. There would be two shootouts with police, a beating, and a cold-blooded murder in almost every episode. It appeared that crime could only be subdued with a blazing gun. The formula was updated in the cop shows of the 1970s. Shows like "Starsky and Hutch," "Hawaii Five-O," and "S.W.A.T." featured a vast array of violent criminals who had to be stopped by equally violent police. Almost every episode of these shows began with the bad guy perpetrating some violent act on a defenseless citizen. The brilliant and unflagging law enforcers would track down the desperado, and the show would end in a blaze of gunfire that often left the offender dead. This pattern became so entrenched that a viewer could tell how much of the show remained by checking the body count.

The violence, gun worship, and mayhem so central to the plot lines of these action shows has become so prevalent that it recently spawned a parody show called "Sledge Hammer." The premiere episode presented the hero as a police inspector who had been suspended several times for using excessive force. During the course of the episode he shot target practice in his apartment, and on his way to work stopped a rooftop sniper by using a rocket launcher that destroyed the roof and the building underneath it.

Ironically, today's high-powered weapons are less deadly than the six-guns and carbines of yesteryear. In an effort to reduce the severity of the violence shown (and the criticism), many shows no longer present people dying in gunplay. It is now possible for the A-Team to fire off several hundred rounds of submachine gunfire without killing anyone or being killed by returning fire. In "Hunter," Lt. Rick Hunter and his partner may shoot first and ask questions later, but rarely do they kill anyone. This fantasy treatment allows the action and gunplay to go on without its usual ramifications. Unlike "Sledge Hammer," these shows do not treat the violence as comedy; they simply make it noninjurious. Television rarely shows victimless crime, but it's making a specialty of victimless violence.

PROPERTY CRIME

Most Americans who have any contact with crime are victims of a property crime. Nonviolent offenses like burglary, larceny, and motor vehicle theft are the most common real-world crimes. Like violent crimes, these offenses have increased sharply over the years. During the decade 1955-1964, the average rate for serious property crimes was ten incidents for every one thousand inhabitants. For the next decade that rate tripled, and in the most recent decade coded the average rate rose to fifty incidents per one thousand inhabitants. Victimization studies done since 1965 also detect a rise in serious property crime. The rate estimated from these studies was about fifty per one thousand people during the decade following 1965. That figure doubled to roughly one hundred offenses for every one thousand inhabitants in the most recent decade coded.

The prime-time world is oblivious to such changes. The rate for serious property crimes has remained steady at twenty incidents per one thousand characters over the thirty years of our study. This means that only during the first decade of our study did television present property crimes at a higher rate than that known to police. From that point on, the television property crime rate fell well *behind* the FBI-calculated rate and even further behind the rates projected by victim studies.

Television not only presents a lower property crime rate than reality, it presents a very different type of property crime from those seen by the average police officer. Even when a property crime does occur on television, it is often accompanied by a violent crime. For example, an early episode of "Naked City" combined aggravated assault with burglary in a twisted pursuit of the American dream. A character named Mitchell Pierce burglarized apartments in an ingenious way. He assaulted milkmen and stole their uniforms. Pierce then used their route lists to find out which tenants were on vacation. Disguised as a milkman, he entered the selected apartments. All went well until he tried to leave one burglarized apartment, only to discover that the police had found the milkman he assaulted. Pierce shot a policeman to escape and then hid in Belvedere Castle in Central Park. Once in the castle, he took a hostage and had a final shootout before being captured by police.

The property crimes on television do not have the same goals as those found in the real world. According to police records, the average value of property taken in larcenies and burglaries was $650 and for motor vehicle theft $4,500. Burglary or larceny on TV is a very different phenomenon, since television emphasizes high-value thefts. For instance, an episode of "The Greatest American Hero" presented a mercenary group that stole a fighter plane and an experimental bomb sight. They intended to sell the bomb sight to the highest bidder. In a "Knight Rider" episode, a superlative cat burglar stole rare art and expensive jewelry. Television emphasizes rare and high-value property crimes, just as it exaggerates and emphasizes the occurrence of violent crimes.

VIDEO VICE

These are the offenses that occupy most of a real police officer's day. Some are petty, others are more serious, but collectively vice crimes are the criminal activity most often seen by police. These offenses include prostitution and commercialized vice, drug-related crimes, consumer frauds, forgeries, public drunkenness, drunk and disorderly, and a variety of lesser offenses. With the exception of drunkenness many of these offenses have a high-profit motive. In the real world such crimes account for about eight out of every ten arrests.

On television such offenses have accounted for about 60 percent of all crimes committed. During the decade 1955-1964, they made up just over half of the offenses. Over the next two decades the proportion of violent crime dropped 13 percent, while the proportion of other offenses increased to two-thirds of all crimes committed since 1975. The main reasons for this rise in nonindex crime were a fifteenfold increase in prostitution offenses and a tenfold increase in drug-related crimes presented. So TV has not given up flashy crimes, it has simply chosen less violent formats for them.

Vice crimes have become some of the most popular offenses on TV, but it wasn't always so. They accounted for only 3 percent of all televised criminal activity prior to 1964. These early vice crimes were usually drug related and part of a seamy underworld presented as revolting to proper society. Drug dealers and smugglers were nasty people who used every means, including violence, to cover their tracks. A 1957 segment of "The Jane Wyman Show" offered a good example of this type of crime.[13] This episode features a U.S. Customs agent and a Los Angeles Harbor Patrol officer who are trying to intercept a major heroin shipment. The drug smuggler is a crewman on a tuna boat. They almost catch him on the boat, but he assaults a policeman and escapes. He then tracks down a suspected informant and beats her up to teach her a lesson. When finally cornered, he tries to shoot the harbor patrol officer before being shot himself.

As this episode suggests, drugs and vice in general were presented as very repulsive crimes, unconscionable to law-abiding society. Unlike other crimes that could sometimes be justified by circumstances or explained as accidents, drug offenses could only be seen as a profit-seeking venture. No quarter was given to drug smugglers or dealers. Even users received little sympathy.

In the second decade of our study the number of vice crimes more than tripled. Between 1965 and 1974 TV increased the number of vice crimes to the point where prostitution alone was as prevalent as all video vice combined during the previous decade. As television became more permissive in its sexual content, prostitution became a more overt crime. Prostitutes were used to create an even sleazier, more corrupt portrait of the criminal world. Prostitutes were often used as informants, whose trick-turning could be overlooked if the information was good. The number of drug-related crimes also continued to rise, though to a lesser degree than prostitution.

This trend was illustrated in a 1974 segment of "Kojak," in which both drugs and prostitutes were involved. In this episode, two lowlifes named Bert and Spenser run a very profitable vice operation. Spenser is a pimp who keeps a large string of hookers. To recruit new girls and keep them working, he teams up with Bert, who supplies them with drugs. When one of the prostitutes talks to a reporter about the rising price of heroin, Bert kills her. He later kills the reporter as well, to stop him from looking into the drug deals. The police begin to investigate the murders and use the prostitutes as reluctant informants. In one scene Kojak even threatens to arrest one hooker for drug possession unless she cooperates. Once she does, Kojak ignores her drug possession and prostitution offenses, allowing her to remain free. All these efforts eventually bear fruit, and Spenser and Bert are caught.

Beginning in the early 1970s television began to mix and match vice crimes by introducing more large-scale criminal operations. These diversified vice operations offered drugs and prostitutes to affluent clients in a variety of plush settings. Such operations served as vice "supermarkets" where anything was possible. This plot line was delivered with a violent flourish in a 1973 episode of "Police Story." A pimp named Snake is said to be responsible for half the cocaine traffic in the state and one of the largest prostitution operations. The police arrange a sting operation and catch him red-handed. Before being caught, however, he beats up two of the hookers who worked for him. He also has an associate slash his ex-wife's face to stop her from testifying against him in court.

Since 1975, our study found almost double the number of drug-related offenses presented the previous decade, as well as a continued rise in the amount of prostitution. This new wave of vice crimes follows the format established in earlier years. TV's drug dealers are now upscale business types who sell drugs like any other commodity. Drug and prostitution rings continue to be a common plot device for the presentation of vice crimes. Indeed vice lords have become a main focus of attention for TV law enforcers.

For example, an episode of "Joe Forrester" explored the connection between vice and organized crime. In this segment topless dancers are threatened with violence unless they sign with a certain talent agency, a new adult bookstore opens, and a theater owner and his family are coerced into showing porn films. All this angers Joe, who discovers that organized crime wants the vice trade on his beat. While he could tolerate legal topless dancing and massage parlors, Joe can't accept organized crime profiting from it. He ignores the small operators and goes after the big guys, eventually forcing them to give up their takeover efforts.

Despite their new-found prominence, vice crimes have complemented rather than replaced violent crimes. The two types of crime are now rarely far apart. Murder and assault are tools of the trade for television's pushers and pimps. For instance, in a 1979 episode of "Operation Runaways," a retauranteur runs a drug and prostitution ring. His partner supplies the hookers with drugs to keep them working. When one young woman refuses to cooperate, the partner gives her a heroin overdose. He later beats another woman to ensure her silence. Similarly, in a recent episode of the trendy hit "Miami Vice," a major South American drug dealer hires a hit man to kill informants and cops who threaten his smuggling operation.

Over the years the drugs of choice have changed on television. In the early years most drug addicts seen were dirty and desperate, strung out on heroin. Moving through the 1960s, heroin became less obvious as synthetics like amphetamines and hallucinogens became more commonly used. By the early 1970s there was a vast array of drugs. Heroin was common for the grimy streets of slums, while amphetamines and hallucinogens popped up in more fashionable areas. Cocaine and PCP also appeared occasionally in the most crime-ridden cop shows. In the late 1970s and early 1980s heroin dropped into the background, as did old-fashioned "uppers" and hallucinogens. Cocaine, PCP (phenylcyclidine), and a new wave of synthetics or "designer drugs" were the most common types. Designer drugs and cocaine were the drugs commonly seen among the trendy and upper classes. In cop shows such as "Miami Vice," "Hunter," "T.J. Hooker," and "Knight Rider," these become the problem drugs. PCP, heroin, and sometimes cocaine were the drugs of choice in the more realistic cop shows like "Hill Street Blues" and "Cagney & Lacey." "Hill Street" kept its drug activity very current. Episodes in the 1986 season dealt with "crack" (a potent form of cocaine) and "black tar" (a highly potent and cheap form of heroin). Both drugs had only come to the attention of the media during the previous year.

Increasingly in current cop shows, crimes are being committed by people under the influence of serious drugs. PCP users in particular added a violent and terrifying dimension to video crime. Drug sales have continued to be a very profitable part of the criminal underworld on television and they consume a great deal of fictional law-enforcement activity.

BUNCO

This category encompasses crimes of deception or "confidence" games. Specific offenses include fraud, forgery, and embezzlement. Here we will include the crimes of bribery, blackmail, and tax fraud or evasion, since they all involve deception and are treated very similarly on TV. Unfortunately, real-world data on these offenses are very poor. Very few crimes of deception are reported, since victims are often either unaware of the offense or are unwilling to admit to being duped.[14] As a result, no meaningful comparisons can be drawn between fiction and reality. But there have been interesting changes in television's presentation of these crimes over the years.

TV has always been fascinated by crimes of deception. Confidence games and other deceptive crimes are usually seen as clean, white-collar crimes without violent overtones. They can be set in opulent surroundings involving large sums of money, making them very flashy crimes. This type of crime can also be intertwined with other crimes to weave a complex web of criminal activity, a must for the mystery genre. Thus, an early segment of "Man With a Camera" featured a crime boss who used forgery in an attempt to discredit a crusading lawyer and protect his gambling operations. The crime boss hires a photographer to create incriminating fake photos of the lawyer. The photos show the (married) lawyer gambling and going out with other women. The boss and his co-conspirators then try to represent the photos as real to ruin the lawyer's career. The star, Mike Kovac, uncovers their ruse and vindicates the lawyer.

Fraud itself has become more complex over the years. Early frauds were fairly simple schemes, involving few people and designed for the immediate profit of the confidence man. For example, in a 1960 episode of "Maverick," a conman and his associates convinced an English count to send his son to their nonexistent dude ranch. Once the young man arrives in America, they kidnap him and demand a ransom. All seems to be going well until the count refuses to pay and rides to his son's rescue. At that point the fraud falls apart and the criminals are apprehended.

Frauds by the 1970s and 1980s were more elaborate and often included larger institutions. Gradually they became more integrated into routine business practices. For instance, a 1972 episode of the short-lived series "The D.A." created a very elaborate fraud involving a furniture store owner, a finance company, and a furniture distributor. The scheme works by first having the store owner and his salesmen sell new furniture to low-income customers. This is accomplished by helping the customer secure financing through the crooked finance company. When the furniture arrives, the customer discovers broken, dirty, and unusable old furniture instead of the new pieces he saw in the showroom. The angry customer of course refuses to pay for useless furniture, whereupon the finance company repossesses it. The finance company then returns the furniture to the unscrupulous furniture distributor, who in turn ships it back to the stores to be sold again as new.

Frauds were often presented as a method for financially troubled businesses to stay solvent. Fraud thus left the domain of the single con-man and increasingly involved major companies. In fact, businessmen are second only to professional criminals in the commission of frauds and forgeries on television. Characters with business occupations are responsible for a fifth of all the frauds and forgeries, while professional criminals account for about half of these crimes.

Television takes the same approach to embezzlement as does the real world. The crime is rarely reported. More often it is handled internally, with the embezzler making restitution. In a 1971 "Name of the Game" episode, a government bureaucrat's new appointment is threatened by reports that he might have embezzled funds from his previous agency. In an effort to clear himself, he meets with his previous superior. His ex-boss tells him that the agency knew he didn't embezzle the funds, and that the real embezzler made restitution. But the man refuses to come forward with this information since he doesn't want to damage the reputation of the repentant embezzler. The bureaucrat loses his appointment due to the scandal, but the embezzler's identity remains a secret.

Whodunit: TV's Criminals

It is difficult to compare video and real criminals, since official arrest data only describe a small portion of all offenders. Not only do many offenses go unreported, but known crimes often go unsolved. As a result, police figures on arrests could represent as little as 15 to 20 percent of all offenders.[15] Homicide presents a unique case, however, since a large percentage of these offenses are known to police. This fact, coupled with a very high arrest rate for homicide, means that data on arrests are representative of 75 to 90 percent of all murderers.[16] This group will therefore serve to illustrate the differences between television and real-life criminals.

Compared to his real-life counterpart, the television murderer is likely to be a wealthy white mature adult (these traits also hold for perpetrators of other violent video crimes). Actual homicides, however, are committed much more often by juveniles, nonwhites, and low-income groups. Only two characteristics of murderers on television accurately reflect killers in the real world. First, murderers are predominantly male. Second, the murder rate is higher in urban settings. Over the past thirty years, eight in ten of those arrested for murder in the nation have been male. On TV about nine in ten have been male. On television about 60 percent of murders occur in urban settings, while in the U.S. about 70 percent occur in cities. In most other ways, though, the typical TV killer looks very different from real-life murderers.

Age

To begin with, the television murderer is much older than his real-world counterpart. In the real world, increases in the number of young violent offenders have prompted the creation of stricter sentencing laws, new prison programs, and other efforts to deter young offenders. According to the FBI, six out of ten people arrested for murder in the past three decades were under thirty years old. This proportion, while very high, masks the alarming rise of youth involvement in murder seen during just the past ten years. By contrast, television has always made its killers older. Only two in ten video murderers are under thirty, while over three-quarters of TV murderers are between thirty and fifty-nine years old, more than double the actual rate. In real life only 36 percent of arrests for murder are in this age group.

Race

The relationship between race and criminal activity has provoked a long-standing and often angry debate. According to FBI reports over the past thirty years, about forty out of every one hundred of those arrested for murder are white. Over that same time period about forty-

291

seven in every one hundred of those arrested have been black, and fewer than one in one hundred, Asian.[17] Thus blacks seem to be involved in murder about four times as frequently as their distribution in the population. It is often argued that racism by police is responsible for the higher arrest rates for blacks and other minorities. This may be true for earlier time periods, but since 1965 victim surveys have been asking crime victims about offender characteristics like sex, age, and race. These victim surveys reflect a similar distribution of the races involved in violent crimes.[18] It therefore seems unlikely that racism on the part of police departments' accounts for the disproportionate number of murders perpetrated by blacks.

These victim surveys also show that blacks are the victims of violent crime far more often than their distribution in the population. Since blacks make up a disproportionately large percentage of the poor, it follows that blacks would also be the most frequent victims and perpetrators. A more extensive debate of these differential crime rates is beyond the limited scope of this work. Our purpose here is to compare these figures with comparable data from the world of television.

Television has chosen to give most of the murderers it presents a neutral, nondescript, nonethnic background. Over the past thirty years, nine out of ten murders on television were committed by whites. During that period, only three in one hundred murders were committed by blacks, about the same rate we recorded among Asians. But this rough equality of minority murder rates stands in sharp contrast to real life. Blacks on television are about eighteen times less likely to commit homicide than in real life, whereas the Asian homicide rate is three times as high as in the real world.

Of the large group of white murderers, about 70 percent had a generic northern European background. They were not given ethnic names, accents, costumes, or foreign language dialogue that would further specify their ethnic background. TV endowed only about a quarter of its murderers with a distinct ethnic heritage. Of those characters with an identifiable ethnic background, Hispanics were involved in the most crimes, accounting for about 6 percent of all serious crimes. Nine times out of ten these serious crimes were violent offenses. Thus, Hispanics were responsible for 7 percent of all homicides, or nearly double the rate for any other identified ethnic group.[19] Despite the stereotype of the Italian mafioso "rubbing someone out," Italians are involved in only 2 percent of all homicides, just slightly ahead of the English and Irish at the bottom of the list. These ethnic differences are considered in greater depth in chapter 10.

WEALTH

One of the most striking characteristics of the television murderer is his wealth. Almost half the killers with a clear economic status are rich. In two-thirds of the murders we coded, the killer had no clear economic status. Among the remainder, however, the killer was rich nearly half the time. As economic status drops, so does involvement in murder. Middle-class characters were responsible for just under one-quarter of these murders. The working class accounted for another one in six and the poor for only one in seven.

Overall, economic status bears a clear relationship to the commission of violent crimes. Of the violent crimes we coded where the offender had a clear economic status, rich characters committed four out of every ten. The middle class was responsible for another quarter of such offenses. The working class accounted for one in six violent crimes, while the poor were responsible for one in five.

Little is known of the economic status of criminals in the real world, although most of those arrested and in the nation's prisons are from the lower economic classes.[20] From what is known, it appears that only violent offenses are positively linked to economic class.[21] Thus, most of the perpetrators of violent crimes are probably from the lower classes, as are their victims. If this is true, then television turns the world of crime topsy-turvy, presenting a far larger percentage of violent criminals as being rich than is found in reality.

Occupation

The occupations that television gives its criminals are as unlikely as their economic status. We found that a slight majority of all crimes on television were committed by professional criminals. This covers a vast array of hired thugs, contract killers, gang bosses, and the like. But this group was responsible for a much smaller proportion of all the murders committed, only 22 percent.

After professional criminals, business is the occupational group responsible for the largest portion of TV crime. Businessmen carry out one-fifth of all crimes and over one-third of the murders committed by census-coded characters. This high rate of participation in crime belies the fact that characters with business occupations make up 8 percent of all characters in our sample. By comparison, characters with unskilled blue-collar jobs also make up 8 percent of the characters coded. Yet they account for just 8 percent of crimes committed and only 6 percent of the murders. Clearly, the business of TV's businessman is crime. In fact, this is the only occupational group on television that is disproportionately involved in crime.

Some of these businessmen were very violent offenders. Recall the episode of "The Streets of San Francisco," in which a businessman was killing hookers to clean up the streets and save the women from sin. An equally unlikely murder occurred in a "Hawaii Five-O" episode, when a nightclub owner plots to kill the state director of development. But his purpose is not to eliminate obstacles to development. Quite the contrary. He believes the director is allowing too much of Hawaii's natural beauty to be destroyed! Among TV businessmen, even environmentalism leads to crime.

Other criminals committed property crimes to further their business interests. On "Simon & Simon" a fashion designer hired some thugs to steal a competitor's designs, in the hope of sabotaging his fashion show. On "Mission: Impossible" a businessman stole the plans and uranium necessary to build an atomic bomb. After building the bomb, he offered it for sale to unfriendly nations. His sole motivation was to raise several million dollars to keep his company out of bankruptcy.

Other occupations are not nearly so notable for their criminal involvement. Indeed, for most occupations involvement in crime is a rarity. But there are exceptions. For instance, in an episode of "Mannix," a dentist hired an assassin to kill his brother and nephew in order to inherit a large fortune from a distant relative. Such criminal endeavors are unusual for doctors or lawyers. Together these groups commit only 2 percent of video crimes, although they make up 6 percent of the television population. A similar lack of criminal activity can be found among most of television's white- and blue-collar workers.

Not only do businessmen commit a high proportion of crimes, their illegal activities are especially likely to take a violent bent. Almost one of every three (32 percent) crimes committed by a businessman were violent, a proportion surpassed only by professional criminals. All other occupations combined (with twice the number of characters) accounted for only 29 percent of the violent crimes.

For a TV businessman a hostile takeover may mean planning and executing a murder. Many hire contract killers with the same ease their real-life counterparts display in hiring an office manager. The grey flannel suit often represents a very deadly member of the establishment.

THE DRUG CULTURE

Our portrait of criminals has singled out murderers as TV's most visible and violent offenders, and the group that offers the best comparisons with the real world. As this is written, however, public attention is focused on another criminal sector that is sometimes violent and always dangerous—the world of drug abuse. Entertainment media from films to rock videos are criticized for fostering a climate in which illegal drugs are accepted if not sanctioned. So we conclude this discussion with a look at how television has portrayed drug users and traffickers over the years.

Until about 1970 any drug use or sale was viewed as a heinous crime. Drug abuse was portrayed as a terrible calamity that reduced people to sniveling and begging for a fix. This moral opprobrium colors a

1970 "Dragnet" episode we coded. In the opening narration Sergeant Friday informs the audience that "uppers are amphetamine sulphate tablets. A dangerous, personality-destroying drug. It was up to us to stop the flow." A young junkie, brought in for possession of controlled drugs, tells the police he wants to deal. He will tell them where he got his uppers, if they make sure that he receives a light sentence. The tight-lipped officers make no deals, but he gives them the address of his supplier anyway. Sergeants Friday and Gannon check out the pill manufacturing plant, located in a suburban house, only to find it is rented under an assumed name. They press on and arrest a retired radio repairman for manufacture and possession of controlled drugs. The repairman admits to making the drugs but remains unshaken by hard-nosed threats of jail. He knows that, with no previous record, he'll get a light sentence. Still not satisfied that they have the head of the operation, Friday and Gannon dig deeper. Eventually they arrest a wealthy man who is underwriting the operation for its large profits. Thus they cut off the flow of these dangerous drugs into L.A.

About this time, however, other series began to display more sympathetic images of drug users. They often portrayed the user as a person in need of help, whose addiction was explained by a bad environment or childhood deprivation. A 1973 "Streets of San Francisco" segment featured Jack, a scared and troubled drug user, who runs into the law when he tries to feed his addiction. Jack, his brother Spenser, and some friends are robbing a store when the police show up. Jack hits one cop and shoots another as they try to escape. When Spenser fires at a police detective to protect Jack, the detective shoots and kills him. Jack's father then sues the city and the detective over Spenser's death. Slowly the police uncover Jack's addiction to hard drugs, and his father is informed of it. In the climactic scene father and son confront each other. Jack says he needed someone to love him when his mother died, but his dad was too involved in all of Spenser's sports records. Jack explains that Spenser was just trying to help, since his father never cared enough. In the end, Jack enters a drug treatment program. Jack is never seen as a vicious criminal, just a mixed-up kid who got involved with the wrong people and drugs for lack of support at home.

This changing treatment of the drug user does not reflect a change of attitude toward drugs in general. Television rarely embraced the casual acceptance of drug use that marked many feature films of the 1970s. When the shows we coded discuss drug use, they overwhelmingly label it as wrong. The message most often is that drugs destroy people's lives and keep them from reaching their full potential. In the first decade of our study, drug use was always presented as wrong, in the few cases where it was discussed at all. From 1965 to 1974, four-fifths of the discussions of drug use labeled it as wrong.

"Dragnet," with its stark view of right and wrong, offered the clearest example of drugs as a terrible menace. This was especially true in a 1967 segment, focusing on Friday and Gannon's pursuit of marijuana users. In this scenario, Paul and Jean Shipley are a college-educated, middle-class, suburban couple with a young daughter. The police are informed of their suspected drug use by Jean's father, who worries about his granddaughter's well-being. When Friday and Gannon visit the Shipleys, they find them less than cooperative. The couple admit nothing and Jean adds, "It's no more addictive than a drink before dinner and a lot less harmful." Friday warns them that it's the first step toward harder drugs. He tells them they wouldn't be the first experimenters who went too far and spent their lives looking for a fix. A couple of months later, they arrest a man who is high. He tells Friday and Gannon that he got stoned at a party hosted by the Shipleys. The intrepid investigators go to the house and burst in. They find the Shipleys and several other people in a stupor in the living room, and the daughter lying face down in the bathtub. Left unattended by her stoned parents, she accidently drowned. The closing voice-over tells us that Jean Shipley was sentenced to a state mental hospital, while Paul Shipley was found guilty of drug use and involuntary manslaughter and put on probation.

By contrast we encountered a 1969 episode of "The Name of the Game" that presented the use of recreational drugs as acceptable. In this segment, a reporter looks into the death of a well-known talent agent. The agent's main client was a borderline alcoholic blues singer who had a large entourage of groupies. They joke about drug use, and in one scene a record producer pops a handful of pills without any criticism from the script. The overall attitude conveyed is, "if it feels good, do it."

In the most recent decade codoed the number of episodes that debate drug use has increased sharply, doubling the number of cases seen in the previous twenty years. The prevailing attitude of condemnation has remained stable, though, with 85 percent coming out firmly against any drug use. In this decade the antidrug message spreads beyond the police shows, as seen in a 1981 episode of "Nurse." The star, Mary Benjamin, has a son who is enraptured over his new girlfriend. Unfortunately, she develops an addiction to an amphetamine substitute marketed as a diet aid. She relies on the drug to help keep up her hectic schedule as a dancer. Mary suspects the girl's addiction, but her son won't listen. She tries to warn him that the substitute could be as dangerous as real amphetamines, but again he won't believe her. Then the son checks into it and finds out that the diet pills can indeed have the same dangerous side effects as amphetamines. Later his girlfriend passes out and has to be rushed to the hospital, and the danger of these drugs strikes home. The son swears he won't ever touch another pill, and the girl decides to take some time off and put her life together.

In the very few cases where drug use was shown as acceptable, the script's attitude was sympathetic. Characters could understand drug use as a way to escape a depressing life. Drug use was never viewed as the best escape, but in some situations it could be tolerated. Television's portrayal of the drug dealer has also changed over the years. The drug smuggler seen living on the gritty waterfront in "The Jane Wyman Show" gave way to a more clean-cut corporate image. The 1970s' drug dealer resembled a respectable businessman rather than a seedy opportunist who traded on human desperation. The business end of drug dealing became more significant, and drug kingpins more evident. For example, one plot from "The Bold Ones" concerned a lawyer who worked with his gangster clients to smuggle drugs into the country aboard his yacht.

More recently TV has portrayed major drug dealers as more detached from the actual traffic of narcotics. They are often just the managers of a business. Rarely would one of these kingpins sell drugs himself, aside from a seven-figure deal for a major shipment. This is particularly true of current shows like "Hunter" and "Miami Vice," where major drug dealers live in splendor, while rarely dealing directly with their product.

ROGUES' GALLERY

Television has always been fascinated by crime and criminals. From the earliest Westerns to the latest cop shows, crime has been the most common plot device used to pit good against evil. Thus, the fantasy world of prime time is frequently dangerous and violent. Our study of 620 prime-time shows counted 2,228 crimes, an average of 3.6 per episode. Assuming a mix of hour-long and half-hour shows, that comes out to around fifty crimes a night. That total would include about a dozen murders and fifteen to twenty assorted robberies, rapes, assaults, and other acts of mayhem. So television is not just more crime-ridden than real life. It also highlights the most violent and serious crimes. A majority of crimes portrayed involve violence, and nearly one in four (23 percent) are murders. In real life, according to the FBI, violent crimes account for about 5 percent of all arrests. On television they make up 56 percent of all illegal acts.

As these figures suggest, television presents crime in a context that bears little relation to reality. This context suggests that violence flows not from anger or passion, but from premeditated avarice. Crimes are layered on one another to create the scariest combinations. When businessmen commit crimes, they are not the nonviolent white-collar crimes they might commit in reality. Instead they murder for the sake of the company or in the interest of career success. It is not enough for the TV rapist simply to assault his victim; he must brutally murder her as well. In short, video crime is unlike reality in its frequency, severity, and motivation. Moreover, it has become more premeditated and cold-blooded over the years, although the number of crimes committed has remained relatively stable.

Nor do video criminals bear much resemblance to their real-world counterparts. Here too, the discrepancy has only increased over time. On television, it is not lowlifes or desperate characters who commit crimes, but the high-born and well-heeled. Television introduces the viewer to two types of criminals—the professional deviant who lives a life of crime, and the apparent pillar of the community who turns to crime to maintain or better his standard of living. Criminals on prime time are usually middle- or upper-class white males over age thirty. As "mature" adults, they rarely act on impulse. Instead, their lawbreaking is carefully calculated to advance their own interest. The vast majority of television crime is predicated on pure greed. Wealthy characters are far more likely to commit crimes than those identified as poor or middle class. In fact, they make up almost half the murderers with a clear economic status. In particular, a stock criminal type is the businessman whose selfish pursuit of profit leads him into illegal activity. TV businessmen constitute the largest group of murderers aside from professional gangsters. But substantial numbers of criminals are other pillars of the community, including a variety of educated professionals.

Thus TV crime is an establishment activity. Wealth and power corrupt, and gains are likely to prove ill-gotten. In real life, crime and violence may stem from deprivation and desperation. But the mean streets of TV entertainment wind from Park Avenue and Sutton Place to Beverly Hills and Bel Air.

⟫●⟪

9

THE ENFORCERS

There are 8 million stories in the Naked City.

Just the facts, ma'am.

Book 'em, Danno!

These prime-time catchwords could come from only one program genre: the cop show. From television's earliest days, its dramatic series have been fascinated by themes of crime and punishment. Even the most avid viewers would be hard pressed to remember early shows like "Chicagoland Mystery Players" and "Famous Jury Trials." Others, like "The Untouchables" and "Dragnet," live on in syndication, remakes, and the popular imagination.

These shows have featured almost every type of law enforcer. Some were tough, others were sensitive. Some were laconic, others loquacious. Some were men of action and emotion, while still others were cut from the coldly rational mold. Contemporary cop shows draw on all these traditions. Yet, in some ways, today's enforcers have little in common with their early predecessors. The last three decades have witnessed a gradual evolution toward more complex personalities and procedures. Moreover, the evolution of the video law enforcer has run parallel with changes in television's portrayal of the criminal justice system.

This is often seen as the most conservative genre in prime time—a world where clean-cut paragons of decency uphold social moves against deviants and evildoers, where moral and legal standards never diverge, where disorder and ambiguity are dispatched with equal disdain. This stereotype was usually valid when applied to the cop shows and Westerns of the 1950s and early 1960s. But television's criminals and law enforcers have changed far more over the years than those perennial favorites of researchers, crime and violence. These days the cops may screw up the case or even turn out to be criminals themselves. The criminal may get some sympathy, and it's sometimes hard to tell the good guys from the bad guys. And a seriously flawed criminal justice system may rely on mavericks, whistle-blowers, and private citizens to ensure that justice is done. Joe Friday, meet Frank Furillo. Mr. Ness, welcome "Wiseguy" to the profession. This is the story of how modern times caught up with TV's station house.

BAD GUYS WEAR BLACK

Throughout the 1950s and early 1960s the world on television was black and white in every respect. There was a clear line dividing right from wrong, and there was no doubt that wrongdoing would be punished. Contests between good and evil took place in various dramatic formats, but lawmen were most common in Westerns and cop shows. Television had picked up many of these shows from their popular radio beginnings, and their action-packed plot lines were even better suited to a visual medium. Early action series provided a sharp contrast to the musical variety shows, quiz shows, and sitcoms that filled out the prime-time menu.

First horse operas and cop shows had very similar plot lines and characterizations. The story would begin predictably with a grimy desperado breaking the law and terrorizing the populace. Into the fray would ride our hero who, by brilliant deduction and a little luck, tracked down the guilty party. The action moved briskly to its inevitable conclusion, when the lawman captured the criminal in a blaze of gunfire or a flurry of fists.

These shows made clear distinctions between right and wrong. The bad guys were such despicable characters that there was no mistaking them. They threatened helpless widows, accosted women and children, and kicked puppies and kittens. Meanwhile, early law enforcers were exceptionally good. Most didn't drink, had only platonic friendships with "proper" women, and enforced the laws rigorously and evenhandedly.

Most of the early law enforcers were colorless types. Big city police in particular were shown as calm, detached professionals simply doing their job in a routine fashion. The prototype was cool professionals like Lieutenant Muldoon of "Naked City," Sergeant Friday of "Dragnet," and Lieutenant Trask of "Perry Mason."

Soon private detectives cropped up in the gray area of law enforcement just outside official police jurisdiction. Most early P.I.s were square-jawed, hard-boiled men who dealt with the sordid side of life outside polite society. In shows like "Martin Kane, Private Eye," "Man Against Crime," and "Richard Diamond, Private Detective," television presented its knockdown version of Humphrey Bogart's Sam Spade. These stoic investigators rarely had much money. They worked in small, grungy offices for clients who paid commensurately small fees. They were brawlers who solved problems with their fists and without much police assistance. Though well acquainted with their local police departments, these gumshoes were not hindered by the laws and rules that shackled police. Taking advantage of their outsider role, they were able to crack otherwise insoluble cases.

These domestic law enforcers were occasionally joined by secret agents who ranged far and wide to protect the free world against internal and external subversion. In series like "Crusader" and "The Hunter," the stars were motivated by a deep-rooted hatred of international communism. They helped people escape from Marxist villains and thwarted the plans of their Iron Curtain counterparts to spread discord in Europe and America. For example, "Crusader" Matt Anders worked to avenge the death of his mother in a Polish concentration camp at the hands of the communist regime. Other series like "Five Fingers" and "The Invisible Man" featured less-driven heroes, but the communist foe remained a constant. The star of "Five Fingers" was an American counterspy posing as a Soviet agent, while Dr. Peter Brady, "The Invisible Man," worked for British intelligence.

The most memorable of the Cold War spy dramas never appeared on network television at all but proved highly popular in syndication. "I Led Three Lives" was a fact-based melodrama about the exploits of Herbert Philbrick, who (as a voice-over dramatically proclaimed), "for nine frightening years did lead three lives—average citizen, member of the Communist party, and counterspy for the FBI." Each week, advertising executive (and good guy businessman!) Philbrick would enter the shadowy world of spy vs. spy as he battled communist plans to steal government secrets, infiltrate voluntary organizations, or sabotage defense installations. The viewpoint was as Manichean as the nonpolitical cops-and-robbers shows of the period. In one episode a naive young girl was saved from ideological corruption or, as the script put it, "cleansed of her communist infection." Not only did the real Philbrick serve as a technical consultant, but scripts were reviewed by the FBI. During the mid-1950s, 117 episodes were produced, the equivalent of five to six seasons of network programming. Its syndicated run lasted nearly a decade, with reruns airing into the early 1960s.

In the late 1950s, against this backdrop of formula Westerns, Cold War espionage, and gritty cop shows, a new type of law enforcer debuted. In series like "Peter Gunn" and "77 Sunset Strip," the stern, hard-nosed gumshoes of earlier years were replaced by suave, attractive, financially solvent private investigators. These "swinging detective" shows followed plot lines similar to their predecessors. The heroes solved crimes or problems that their clients wanted to keep from police attention.

The settings were more diverse than the story lines in these series. Since many of their clients were wealthy, these investigators circulated in high social circles and often followed the villain to exotic locales. Most of these hip detectives avoided gunplay but were not above using their fists to subdue a culprit. Often the criminal simply surrendered when confronted with their brilliant deductive work. These shows contained fewer crimes than the cop shows, although murder remained the most common crime in both settings. Greed and romantic triangles were the driving forces behind this nightly fare of murder among the beautiful people.

As the 1960s wore on, detective shows became more numerous, replacing all but a few adult Westerns. In all the newer shows P.I.s led exciting lives surrounded by beautiful women. They were brilliant and sophisticated, easily capable of living the "good life" while solving crimes. The glamour of the swinging detective shows carried over into look-alike formats, most notably the espionage show. The spy dramas of the 1950s and early 1960s were usually short-lived. The story lines of many early espionage shows were firmly rooted in Cold War tensions, while others were little more than fictionalized accounts of World War II incidents. With the exception of "I Led Three Lives," none was noteworthy.

Following the popularity of the James Bond movies and books in the early 1960s, television created flashier secret agents. Like the swinging detectives before them, these agents were cultured, well educated, and very hip. The plots featured exotic locales, beautiful girls, and elaborate criminal schemes. "I Spy," "Secret Agent," "The Man From U.N.C.L.E.," and "Amos Burke-Secret Agent" were just a few of the shows that portrayed sophisticated and worldly agents. Like his P.I. cousin, the modern secret agent usually encountered well-heeled criminals. While moving in the circles of the rich and powerful, these young sophisticates repeatedly saved the free world without wrinkling a crease in their custom-tailored suits.

In a shift away from the Cold War format, only a few actually worked for a government agency. The battles they fought were not between the U.S. and the USSR, but between THRUSH and U.N.C.L.E. or CHAOS and CONTROL. The outrageous plot lines of shows like "The Wild, Wild West," "Get Smart," and "The Man from U.N.C.L.E.," involved more parody than peril. Espionage and other threats to the American way could be defeated with style and a laugh line.

MORALISTS AND SOCIAL WORKERS

In the late 1960s two portrayals of law enforcers competed for popularity. In one version, lawmen were crusading moralists who despised
crime, criminals, and everything connected to them. The second type was
the socially conscious law enforcer who could question the "system" and
even empathize with lawbreakers. Shows of both types were successful
well into the 1970s.

The moralist cops first appeared in the 1950s, but they persisted
into the late 1960s and early 1970s. The original "Dragnet," which ran
from 1952 through 1959, portrayed crime and law enforcement in
absolute opposition. Since the plots in this series were based on real cases,
ambiguity was unnecessary. There was no doubt that the offender would
be caught and punished. Reliance on facts eliminated the need for overt
moralizing, but the evil of lawbreaking was emphasized.

In "The Untouchables," which premiered the year "Dragnet" left the
airwaves, the moralist cop was firmly established. Elliot Ness and his
men despised the criminals they fought so tenaciously. Their hallmark of
incorruptibility went hand-in-hand with disgust for would-be corruptors.
They may have used acceptable terms like "suspect" or "known felon"
when referring to offenders in their reports, but in conversation criminals
became thugs, punks, and hoods. Despised for violating social rules,
criminals often compounded the Untouchables' moral outrage by living in
high style. It often appeared at first glance that crime paid very well, but
in the end Ness and his band would destroy the comfortable lifestyle of
the criminal. The more extravagant the crook, the harder he fell under
the law's penalties. This hard line on crime remained as much a trade-
mark as the series' bloody denouements throughout its four-year run.

The 1967 and 1968 seasons marked the revival of the morally driven cop. The rebirth of "Dragnet" and the premiere of "Hawaii Five-
O" once again presented the police officer as moralist. Upon his
return, Sergeant Friday became even more Manichean. Although the
show still dramatized real cases, Friday increasingly delivered moral
judgments against the guilty. There were sermons against drugs, hate

groups, child molesters, and a host of other contemporary evils confronting the police.

In "Hawaii Five-O," Steve McGarrett's relentless pursuit of criminals alternated with personal outrage whenever they were not incarcerated. McGarrett and his men had no sympathy for any wrongdoing. Lawbreakers had to pay for their deeds, and McGarrett made their capture into a mission. Like Elliot Ness, he often referred to criminals as "punks" or "scum." Defendants' rights were observed only grudgingly, particularly when dealing with career criminals.

In the late 1960s, these moralistic crusaders began to face competition from a new kind of cop as television began to reflect the social turmoil and tensions sweeping the country. The world facing the video law enforcer became more unstable, ambiguous, and contradictory. The new TV cop reflected these tensions and social concerns. The colorless police officer of an earlier age was gone, replaced by the lawman with a point of view. If the cop as moralist catered to conservative tastes, viewers seeking a liberal counterpart could turn to the cop as social worker.

In 1969 the opening voiceover from "The Bold Ones" summed up the new type of TV lawman. The narrator told us that law enforcers were "involved public officials encountering challenging issues in today's highly charged, explosive times. Taking strong action that brings them both praise and abuse. Men of feeling and intelligence, forced by the harsh realities of a turbulent society to sometimes mask these humane qualities. The world of the protectors. . .a troubled arena. . .filled with men dedicated to your safety and protection."

The lawmen in "The Protectors," "Mod Squad," and "The Rookies" were part of this new image. They were characterized by greater uncertainty and introspection than TV cops had shown before. They questioned their own motives, the underlying assumptions of the law, and the conduct of their own departments. Social inequity joined individual wrongdoing as targets of their concern. These officers were sensitive to the plight of the underdog, even to the point of empathizing with lawbreakers. They could, for example, understand that desperation might drive a drug addict to commit petty burglaries. They transcended the

307

tasks of merely enforcing the law in order to steer people back onto the right track. When these sensitive lawmen arrested a drug addict, they often worked to see that he received treatment rather than jail.

Despite the uncertainties under which they worked, the new protectors proved very successful at bringing new methods to police work. TV police by the late 1960s were handling their jobs very differently from their predecessors. They were becoming increasingly professional, as new formalized training supplanted the school of hard knocks. Video cops began to use more sophisticated evidence gathering techniques and laboratory methods. Many were college trained or had other technical backgrounds. Officers were increasingly sensitive to defendants' rights as well as community sentiment. This socially aware model of police work became standard in the cop shows of the 1970s and 1980s.

In 1972, "The Streets of San Francisco" introduced a new combination of the character types seen in earlier cop shows. Many of these Bay City police officers were skilled professionals with college training in criminology and law enforcement. They used new technologies in addition to the TV cop's traditional deductive reasoning. Psychological profiles, computers, and forensic science gave detectives more information to work with. Most notable, however, was the way this show combined the moralist cop with the socially conscious cop.

Inspector Mike Stone was the seasoned veteran who worked slowly and sometimes ploddingly through a case to find the guilty party. Like Lieutenant Muldoon of "Naked City," he was civil, efficient, and not without sympathy for those he arrested. Stone stuck to traditional police methods like interviewing witnesses, checking out leads, and questioning suspects. His partner, young Inspector Steve Keller, preferred more up-to-date techniques. A college man, he was more comfortable with modern methods like computers and psychology. At the same time, he was more moralistic than Stone. He railed against prostitution and drug use and was very hard-nosed when dealing with criminals. Keller was often outraged that a criminal could cause so much damage to a victim. His concern for the victim sometimes made him callous and rough with the offender.

"The Streets of San Francisco" set the tone for many of the cop shows that followed. In series like "Baretta," "Kojak," and "Police Story," police officers mixed sensitivity with moralism. They could sympathize with victims or people trapped by circumstance in a bad life, but they still despised crime and criminals. It was not uncommon for one of these cops to pay a call on a grieving widow to express his condolences and in the next scene rough up a pimp to get information.

Like Elliot Ness or Steve McGarrett before them, these cops often called criminals punks, losers, or scum, as street slang became a larger part of their dialogue. Nonetheless, they continued to use technical terms and proper language in their reports. Despite this professionalism, the new video law enforcers could still tighten the screws when they needed information from the criminal underworld. Any compassion toward criminals was shown after the arrest and did not diminish the fervor of the hunt.

While the men in blue battled crime in the streets, a new crop of private investigates handled problems best kept from the public eye. These P.I.s were much like their predecessors, although each had some unique characteristic designed to establish his identity and set him apart from competitors. "Cannon" presented viewers with the corpulent sleuth Frank Cannon, while "Barnaby Jones" gave viewers a geriatric detective. The physically handicapped got a boost from the successful blind investigator in "Longstreet," while "Banacek" took a shot at ethnic stereotypes by presenting a very crafty and successful Polish-American investigator. All these sleuths lived well and enjoyed a leisurely personal life. They moved even further away from the use of violence, since many criminals simply gave up when faced with their well-documented "j'accuse!"

Throughout the 1970s police officers and private detectives changed very little. More women and minorities began to appear, without altering the established forms in any significant way. Women usually emerged in the swinging detective format, while minorities showed up as socially conscious professionals. Moral crusaders were added to the roster in shows like "The Blue Knight," "Joe Forrester," "SWAT," and "Most Wanted," while playboy detectives showed up in such shows as "Switch" and "Vega$."

Two types of private detectives sauntered through the 1980s: playboys and the descendants of Sam Spade. "Magnum, P.I.," "Matt Houston," and "Simon and Simon" pursued evildoers and beautiful women with equal vigor. In "Moonlighting" the dame was built into the cast, but impropriety among the beautiful people was still the focus. Meanwhile, programs like "Spenser: For Hire," "The New Mike Hammer," and "Private Eye" prowled plot lines that had changed little from their 1950s prototypes.

RIGHTS, WRONGS, AND REALISM

In a series of cases arising in the early 1960s, the Supreme Court began to establish specific rights to which suspects and defendants were entitled. These Court decisions forced changes in police procedures and ended some police practices. They also had an effect on fictional police work. Beginning in the late 1960s, suspects' and defendants' rights became a part of TV plot lines. Initially there was no discussion of these rights. They were simply read to suspects upon arrest. In the 1970s the rights of suspects became a greater concern on television. There were debates over their utility and the hindrances they caused. Some shows began to present episodes where suspects were set free because their rights were violated. In other episodes of the late 1970s, whole cases were thrown out due to procedural flaws. By the end of the decade, the concept of legal limitations on police activities was well established in prime time.

Portrayals of suspects' rights became so ubiquitous that they showed up in such unlikely settings as nineteenth-century Dodge City. In a 1971 segment of "Gunsmoke," Matt Dillon runs into an old friend named Murdoch, whom the governor has ordered to hunt down and execute a violent gang of outlaws. When Matt and Murdoch capture some of the gang, two of them turn out to be young boys. Matt urges Murdoch to spare the boys, who are too young to have been with the gang when the execution order was issued. Murdoch refuses, saying they're all guilty of something. Matt argues that you can't hang a man on a John Doe warrant without proof, and scolds Murdoch for talking "a lot about hanging and very little about justice or due process of law." When the weekly victor of "Gunsmoke"'s precredits shootout sequence starts protecting defendants' rights, the winds of change have traveled far.

In the 1980s a string of hard-nosed police detectives arrived to combat crime and carry on the moralist tradition in the new era of limitations. In shows like "Strike Force," "T.J. Hooker," "Miami Vice," "Fortune Dane," "Lady Blue," and "Hunter," police officers found themselves shackled by court decisions and department policies, while facing increasingly violent and despicable criminals. Such plot lines presented a more complex and complete view of police work, making officers a part of a system that limited their actions. Legal technicalities served to frustrate the moral crusade of police officers. Justice was not so swift and sure as it had once been on TV.

To add insult to injury, police officers often found themselves being punished for infractions (like using excessive force) while the criminal walked away. These intrepid enforcers were not hindered for long, however, since they quickly learned to force criminals into shootouts. The bad guys usually lost the shootouts, which permitted no reversal on appeal. Even if they survived, their conviction was certain. These gun battles were a convenient way to avoid reading a suspect his rights or obtaining search warrants. The new tough cops paid a price for circumventing the rules, since they had to face continuous reprimands from superiors. Their high success rate, however, seemed to outweigh any problems that arose. So they continued to win the war against crime and the ratings.

Out of this mix of flashy detectives and shoot-first cops came a new type of cop show in the 1980s. This was the "realist" police drama. The socially conscious cop shows of the late 1960s and the procedurally limited cops of the 1970s paved the way for these series. The ambivalence and ambiguity seen earlier taught audiences to accept the possibility that bad guys didn't always wear black hats and that they sometimes escaped the law. To provide the impression of greater realism, these shows combined a setting of legal complexity and moral ambiguity with new conventions like overlapping dialogue, multiple story lines, and a gritty mise-en-scène. They often rejected the conservative moralism of a Ness or Friday in favor of liberal approaches focusing on the social origins of crime.

In shows like "Cagney & Lacey" and "Hill Street Blues," police officers worked in a very complex world where good and bad were not sharply delineated. A key concern of realist dramas was to show law enforcement at many levels, each with different and competing interests. The chief's office was pressured for results by the mayor's office, while the D.A.'s office voiced complaints about arrest procedures to precinct commanders. Police work was no longer limited to pursuing and capturing criminals. Investigations now involved making deals with suspects, buying information from informants, testifying in court, bargaining with assistant D.A.s, and finishing hours of paperwork. Often these officers had to face the fact that not all criminals were bad people, and that all bad people were not necessarily criminals. Driven by passion or desperation, criminals lacked the premeditated, evil nature seen so often in earlier shows. In other cases very abusive or opportunistic people who deserved arrest were beyond the reach of the law.

The realist format followed in the footsteps of earlier fact-based dramas. Shows like "Dragnet" and "The FBI" had used real cases for story lines. Although the dramas of the 1980s were not based on actual cases, many incidents mirrored current events and issues. There were cases of parents kidnapping children after losing custody battles. One episode of "Cagney & Lacey" dealt with the mercy killing of an old woman. Yet another plot concerned harboring illegal aliens. All these stories dramatized the stuff of recent headlines.

The new realist dramas also set themselves apart by creating less- perfect police officers. The idea of a flawed law enforcer was all but unheard of in the earlier fact-based dramas. By contrast, imperfect cops abound in recent programs. For example, Detective John LaRue had to conquer alcoholism to succeed in "Hill Street Blues." Victor Isbecki stole heroin from junkies to help his dying mother overcome the pain of cancer on "Cagney & Lacey." Christine Cagney faced sexual harassment from a superior, while on "Hill Street Blues" Bobby Hill faced racism from colleagues. Such cases embroiled detectives in difficult social issues that tested their own ethics. The usual result was an unsettling episode in which people didn't always get what they deserved and the system didn't work as well as it ought.

In 1984 the moralist cop enjoyed a recostumed reprise. With the premiere of "Miami Vice" the world became a lush montage where light and dark played over designer suits and beautiful bodies. The emphasis was on the visual, but between the eye-catching pictures and the driving sound track, an old-style hero plied his trade.

In "Miami Vice" and clones such as "Crime Story" and "Heart of the City," cops were moral crusaders who despised their criminal foes. Frustrated by departmental and legal limitations, they often pondered whether it was all worthwhile.

THE COURTROOM CONFESSIONAL

Police officers and private detectives form the front line of law enforcement on TV. From the beginning, however, a second line of enforcement was provided by lawyers and judges. Lawyers, particularly defense lawyers, have been featured in many shows over the years, going back to long-forgotten series like "Justice," "Willy," and "The Public Defender." These early series were dramatizations of courtroom battles or the work of individual lawyers. They went from crime-scene sleuthing to jury summations without presenting the day-to-day routine of the legal profession.

The most successful legal drama in television history, "Perry Mason," ran from 1957 through 1966. This series established the enduring image of the lawyer/sleuth who could personally exonerate his client by brilliant deduction and careful cross-examination. A requisite part of this process was the real culprit's confession in court. The plot lines and structure set down in "Perry Mason" have been used as a model for courtroom dramas ever since. Television lawyers have remained firmly rooted in the lawyer/sleuth tradition. Thoroughly professional, brilliant in their reasoning, they are true champions of justice. Until very recently, in order to win a client's acquittal, most TV lawyers had to find and expose the real culprit.

Only in the late 1980s, in shows like "L.A. Law," "Night Court," and "Foley Square," have cases been solved without courtroom histrionics. Often, in these shows, the real culprit is of little interest. All that matters is protecting the current client.

In 1961, "The Defenders" established an alternative format for legal drama. The courtroom became a forum for discussing major social issues. The defendant and society often sat in the dock together, waiting for the verdict. The father-and-son partners in the firm of Preston & Preston were still part detective, but they did far more than defend the innocent. They raised social and philosophical issues that were often more central to the script than the defendant's guilt or innocence. For example, in an episode cited earlier, a pornography arrest provided the setting for arguments about censorship, morality, and free speech. Other episodes tackled issues ranging from abortion and mercy killing to capital punishment and political blacklisting.

These bold professionals did battle throughout the 1960s, but the golden age for social reform lawyers came in the late 1960s and early 1970s. As social relevance entered into plot lines, lawyers were the standard bearers. In "Judd for the Defense," "The Young Lawyers," "Storefront Lawyers," and "Owen Marshall, Counselor at Law," strongly principled attorneys provided legal aid to those in need. Driven by a sense of justice, they took on one *pro bono* case after another, defending underdogs against the forces of the establishment. Many of the cases explored larger issues of the day. For example, Clinton Judd took cases involving draft evasion and civil rights murders. Meanwhile, the talented team on "The Young Lawyers" handled complaints of police brutality and slumlord abuses.

Perhaps the most remarkable example in our study comes from a 1969 episode of "The Protectors." In this segment a young man deserts from the army. Some of his buddies track him down and kidnap him in order to return him to the base. They take him to a hotel to talk some sense into him. The police catch the kidnappers and charge them with assault, and the deserter is put in the stockade. Despondent and convinced that he has disgraced his family, the young man hangs himself. The district attorney now has no victim, and the only witness to the assault refuses to testify. The D.A. decides to prosecute the soldiers anyway. He argues that when they assaulted the deserter, they committed an offense against all "the people." He points out that the charges are filed in the name of the people of the state and not just the injured man. His

arguments are rejected by the judge and, as the D.A. puts it, justice is not served. The list of controversial issues goes on and on, but none of these shows, with the exception of "Owen Marshall," lasted long. Apparently audiences preferred not to see "the people" defended each week.

During the late 1970s other law dramas came and went. "Kate McShane" featured the first woman lawyer to star in a dramatic series. "Adam's Rib" took a more overt feminist stance, as series star Amanda Bonner mounted crusades for women's rights. Gradually, however, the age of relevance receded and lawyers returned to the role of sleuth. Many lawyers became background characters who rarely held the spotlight.

In the 1980s, some lawyer/sleuths appeared in shows like "The Mississippi" and "Matlock," but starring lawyers were a rarity. Most were single-appearance characters, who were only seen briefly advising a client or reading a will. The 1980s also presented viewers with the first comedies starring lawyers. In "The Associates" and "Night Court" lawyers and their work were treated humorously. Pranks, sarcasm, and bizarre cases supplied the laughs in these comedies.

Two dramas of the 1980s presented a very different view of lawyers that paralleled the new realist approach to police work. In "Hill Street Blues" lawyers were seen as part of the criminal justice system. Some were very good, others barely competent, but none was the supersleuth seen in earlier shows. Gone were the brilliant orations and cagey cross-examinations that could break an alibi or solve a case. There were few courtroom confessions as lawyers struggled just to win the release of their clients. Increasingly, the work of these lawyers was handled through plea bargains, procedural motions, and other routine techniques.

In 1986 the original producer/creator of "Hill Street Blues" brought out a new series, "L.A. Law," which focused on a major law firm. "L.A. Law" had many of the complexities of "Hill Street Blues," but without the latter's gritty, often gloomy portrayal of life on the streets. As in "Hill Street," the characters could simultaneously display virtues and vices without a clear line between the two. "L.A. Law" presented the professional and private lives of lawyers in a mix that allowed for both comedy and tragedy. More than any of its predecessors, this show highlighted the gulf that sometimes exists between justice and the law. Injustices occurred not because of corruption, but because the law and the courts were fallible. The truth could be hidden by legitimate procedural maneuvers, plea bargaining could mask the real severity of a crime, or a host of other obstacles could obstruct justice.

AMATEURS AND AVENGERS

Television has created a wide array of law enforcers based on real-life models. It also reached beyond reality to create freelance enforcers. Whether you call them amateur sleuths or civilian law enforcers, these characters had no real connection to the criminal justice system. Ad hoc enforcers fell into two groups. The first contained the citizen sleuths, who looked and acted much like the swinging detectives discussed earlier but lacked any official status. The second group could be characterized as avenging angels or lonely hunters.

The citizen sleuths were by far the most numerous. Their ranks included journalists, writers, businessmen, cowboys, and even a few clergymen. These amateur detectives usually came into contact with crime through some casual incident or accident. Like their P.I. counterparts, most citizen crime solvers were young, attractive, hip, and successful. They were driven by a strong sense of justice, even more so than their gumshoe cousins. Exonerating the innocent or preserving the integrity of institutions comprised the lion's share of the plot. In a study of six weeks of prime-time programs in 1981, we found that citizen law enforcers were not only portrayed more positively than the police, they were shown as much better crime solvers.[1] From the suave Jonathan Hart ("Hart to Hart") to the hell-raising Duke boys on "Dukes of Hazzard," they put the professionals to shame in stamping out evildoing.

This idealizing of the amateur law enforcer has persisted throughout television's history. The current queen of the genre is Angela Lansbury's Jessica Fletcher, a middle-aged mystery writer who applies her talents to solving real-life murders in "Murder, She Wrote."

Despite their numerous exploits and longevity on TV, the citizen sleuths are not the most noteworthy freelance enforcers on TV. That accolade belongs to the avenging angels. This group is at once the most terrifying and the most comforting. Tough, seemingly invincible, and highly principled, they are the ultimate arbiters of justice in the violent prime-time world. These modern avengers have a strong sense of principle and live by their own code, which guides them as they operate outside the law. This personal code of ethics serves as a platform from which they can make speeches on the law, justice, or human nature.

The mold was set during the 1950s in "Bat Masterson" and "Have Gun, Will Travel." In both shows the star was well educated, peaceful, sophisticated, and deadly. To set them apart from vigilantes, who were motivated by hate or revenge, these men had strong moral codes that guided their actions. They also earned their living by fighting crime and injustice in the Old West. Of these two early shows, "Have Gun, Will Travel" did the most to establish the form.

Paladin the man lived as a gentleman in San Francisco, where he enjoyed fine food and music in the company of beautiful women. Paladin the avenger would ride into town dressed in black under contract to someone who needed a fast gun. Sometimes he was hired to protect a VIP like Oscar Wilde or Samuel Nobel, but more often he helped the weak overcome the strong. Paladin was there to stop injustices and stymie bullies. Driven by principle and his own code of morality, he decided for himself what was right and just, even if it meant turning on those who paid him.

Paladin's true identity as an avenging angel became evident when he caught up with the evildoer. After listing the man's offenses against society, he would demand that he surrender. Inevitably, the criminal would refuse and force Paladin into action. Usually the episode culminated in a showdown between Paladin and his opponent, with the latter gambling that he could beat fate. As the loser lay dying, Paladin would kneel beside him in the dust and deliver a secular last rite. This was the formal pronouncement of the moral lesson the criminal could not learn, but the audience must remember. As the evildoer expired, Paladin showed no joy.

His reaction was never happiness over vanquishing evil, but sadness over his inability to reform a deviant.

The conclusion of one episode we coded illustrates the flavor of these denouements. Paladin has tracked down a robber and misdirected a posse in order to take the man in for a fair trial rather than see him lynched. The outlaw challenges his pursuer to shoot it out. Paladin tries to dissuade him but fails, and they draw and fire. As his opponent lies mortally wounded, Paladin first apologizes for not killing him quickly and painlessly. He then delivers his moral lesson, saying it didn't have to end this way. He tells the outlaw that he chose his path and refused to reform when given a chance. The dying man agrees that he chose his way of life and also his way to die. He says he couldn't face the end of a rope and wanted to die as he had lived—by the gun. He makes Paladin promise to take care of his family and then dies. Moments later the posse arrives, joyful that a violent criminal is dead. But Paladin shows no joy. He tells them to give the reward money and his fee to the man's widow. He warns the posse leader that if the money doesn't reach the widow, he will hunt him down. With that warning he rides off in a cloud of righteousness.

There were many other avengers in early Westerns and even a few private detectives who tried to follow in Paladin's footsteps, but none had the same strength of conviction. Then, two decades after "Have Gun, Will Travel" lost its last showdown with network programmers, there was a resurgence of avenging heroes. Shows like "Knight Rider," "Hardcastle & McCormick," "The A-Team," and "Stingray" all featured freelance enforcers. Two recent shows, "The Outlaws" and "Paradise," reached back to the Old West for their avengers, pitting them against contemporary problems. In "Knightwatch" the heroes were self-styled vigilantes akin to the Guardian Angels.

The real kindred spirit to Paladin, however, is a modern urban variant called "The Equalizer." This series features Robert McCall, a middle-aged ex-spy who uses his expertise to help those in need. As he often puts it, McCall equalizes the odds when the strong prey on the weak. Skilled in deception, surveillance, and killing, he stands ready to face criminals who won't conform to society's rules. Like Paladin before him,

McCall is civil, urbane, and peace-loving. He hates killing but is willing to take a life when necessary. In the tradition of Paladin, McCall also delivers a closing moral lesson, one that often laments the need to kill. Shows like this let the networks have their cake and eat it too. A violent denouement is followed by a moralistic coda that preempts critics by lamenting the violence that has just taken place.

HOLLYWOOD'S HEROES ON TV

This qualitative portrait shows how the flavor of TV law enforcement has changed over the years in ways both subtle and obvious. Our statistical analysis provides a more systematic look at the panorama of police practices and personality types that make up the video justice system. The tale of the computer printouts took some surprising turns. Law enforcers emerged mainly as good guys, but they stressed diligence over derring-do and displayed compassion more often than physical courage. Despite all the violence on TV, they were as likely to catch the crook in a web of deduction as in a hail of bullets. Finally, though still one of Hollywood's favorite heroes, the blue knight's sword of righteousness has lost some of its cutting edge.

Our content analysis identified over a thousand characters who were employed in law enforcement occupations, about one in every seven characters in our sample. And this figure does not include the vast group of citizen crime solvers who do not formally work in that field. The analysis differentiated among six types of law enforcement occupations. Lawyers and judges meted out justice in the courtrooms. Federal agents, police officers, and sheriffs kept peace in the streets. And private detectives helped solve the problems of the rich. Finally, there was a catchall group of security guards and other law enforcers who did not fit into the other categories.

The largest single group was composed of police officers. Half the law enforcers in our sample worked for some type of police department. The majority have been detectives rather than lower-ranked uniformed officers. Lawyers and judges were the next most numerous group, accounting for one in five law enforcers. Federal agents accounted for another one in eight. Despite the high profile of so many individual private investigators, they amounted to just 6 percent of all law enforcers. When they don't take a starring role, private eyes are rarely seen at all.

Always a staple of prime-time life, the ranks of law enforcement have swelled in recent seasons. We coded 250 law enforcers in the first decade of our study, just over one for every program analyzed. By the most recent decade, their number rose to 430, the equivalent of nearly two per program. The biggest increase was in the number of police officers, who were two and one-half times as numerous after 1975 as they had been prior to 1965. The number of private detectives also nearly doubled over that period. (The ranks of federal agents reached their peak between 1965 and 1974, when espionage shows were popular.)

Like the criminals they chase, most video law enforcers have been white males. Only 8 percent have been women, most of whom appeared since 1975, when a wave of hip female detectives hit the streets. Their racial makeup has been equally homogeneous. Nine out of ten law enforcers in our sample were white. Only 7 percent were black, and most of these have appeared since the late 1960s. Hispanic law enforcers have appeared sporadically throughout the three decades we examined, but always in very low numbers, less than 2 percent of the total.

BLUE KNIGHTS AND KNAVES

Nearly two-thirds of the law enforcers in our sample (63 percent) were positive characters. The bulk of these were simply competent, efficient professionals. Surprisingly few performed acts of heroism, aside from the inevitable shootout with the bad guy. "The Lineup," a 1950s series, provides a good illustration of the heroic behavior that is so rare on prime time. In a 1957 segment, Lieutenant Guthrie and his men track down a mad bomber. Guthrie and his men capture the man but learn that he has planted one last bomb. In a psychiatric ward he finally tells the doctors where the bomb is hidden. The police rush to the scene where they find the bomb. There is no time to wait for the bomb squad, so

Guthrie disarms the bomb himself with only seconds to spare. This display of heroism was the exception, not the rule, in an occupation characterized at the time by portrayals of colorless professionals.

If police work on television rarely involves heroism, the long arm of the law often extends a helping hand. Officers frequently go beyond enforcing the law to serve as a counselor to those in need. This type of behavior was typified by Deputy Sheriff Festus Hagen, who helped a mentally handicapped friend in a 1973 "Gunsmoke" segment in our study. Billy is a simple-minded young man who has lived most of his life in a quiet valley performing menial jobs for a few settlers. When the settlers move, Billy finds his friend Festus, who gets him a job at the stable. But Billy emerges as a noble savage whose compassion for animals creates problems in human society. For example, he becomes enraged when a cowboy brings in a horse with deep spur scars. Later, he attacks another cowboy who is torturing a cat by holding it under water. Festus then tries to teach Billy how to deal with the rules of society. This effort falls apart when Festus shoots a deer for dinner and Billy attacks him. A judge orders Billy committed, but Festus can't allow that to happen. He solves the problem by putting Billy in an orphanage where he can help children, but can also be closely watched. Thus, Festus goes beyond the law to help someone in need. Enforcing the law as written is not as important as finding a fair solution for Billy and everyone else concerned.

The majority of positive police officers has consisted of uninvolved professionals who performed their jobs with competent thoroughness. One prototype of this breed was Lt. Dan Muldoon in "Naked City." In a typical 1958 episode, Muldoon is on the trail of a man who attacks milkmen and steals their uniforms. He is puzzled by the robber's behavior until a thorough investigation reveals that the attacks coincided with a string of residential burglaries. Muldoon realizes that the robber used the uniforms to gain entrance to buildings. The milkmen's route lists showed which people were on vacation, which helped the burglar pick his targets. Finally, when Muldoon and his men corner the outlaw, he plans their attack to ensure that no innocent bystanders will be hurt. Careful planning and professional execution result in the man's capture. Muldoon is neither morally outraged by the criminal's actions nor sympathetic to his motivations. He is just a professional doing his job.

Only one law enforcer out of seven was portrayed negatively. Most of these were well-intentioned bumblers whose ineptitude or naivete provided comic results. A good example of the fumbling flatfoot comes from a 1968 segment of "The Flying Nun." In the belief that the nuns are running a gambling operation from the convent, police captain Formento plants one of his relatives there as a spy. Obsessed with catching the nuns red-handed, he remains oblivious to the behavior of his own agent. It seems that there really is a gambling ring, but it's being run by the spy. Formento raids the convent and arrests the nuns, only to find no evidence of their purported gambling. The episode and Formento's dream of glory come to an end when the spy is arrested for bookmaking.

The inept lawman, particularly the bumbling small-town sheriff, has been a common stereotype over the years. Don Knotts won an Emmy as the stammering deputy Barney Fife on "The Andy Griffith Show." Fife was so inept that he had to carry his single bullet in his shirt pocket, lest he shoot himself in the foot. Deputy Fife shouldn't have been a deterrent to crime, but through the magic of television, he always got his man.

An urban variant was provided by officers Toody and Muldoon, the Quixote and Panza of the 53rd precinct on "Car 54, Where Are You?" If their station-house hijinks bore a strange resemblance to Fort Baxter, Kansas, it was no coincidence. Producer Nat Aiken transferred the comic sensibility of "The Phil Silvers Show" (Sergeant Bilko) to the Bronx, and comedian Joe E. Ross switched uniforms from Sergeant Ritzik to Officer Muldoon (absolutely no relation to Lieutenant Muldoon of "Naked City"!).

Only 5 percent of the law enforcers in our sample were real evildoers. Most of these were unscrupulous cops who exploited their official position to make their schemes work. Sometimes these involved comic shenanigans of the Boss Hogg school or stereotypical bad cops seduced by the dark side of the force, like a police captain involved in bribery and drug dealing on a 1981 "B.J. and the Bear." Other portrayals involved recognizable human beings who made the wrong choice and paid the price.

For example, in a 1965 episode of "The Fugitive," a sheriff misuses his authority to secure the reward for capturing the fugitive. When Dr. Kimball comes into town looking for work while fleeing the police, Sheriff Charlie Judd recognizes him from a police bulletin. Assuming a reward is offered, he takes Kimball into custody. Not wanting to share his expected reward, he then conceals Kimball's capture from his deputy and other police officers. Judd has all but spent the reward money when his scheme crumbles. The persistent Lieutenant Girard, who has tracked Kimball all over the country, finds out Judd and Kimball have been seen together. He confronts Judd only to find that Kimball has escaped. Girard files charges against Judd and informs him that there was no reward for Kimball's capture. Judd loses his job and his reputation.

Other motivations have corrupted law enforcers. In a 1976 segment of "Delvecchio," a narcotics cop, Hank Foster, is working with two homicide detectives to solve a murder linked to the drug trade. Foster thinks of drug users and dealers as scum that have to be destroyed. He often physically abuses suspects arrested on drug charges. Foster is unconcerned over the murder of a drug user, which he views as one solution to a major social problem. Detectives Delvecchio and Shaunsky are more concerned with solving the murder than breaking up a drug ring. After Foster abuses several suspects and takes some of the heroin seized as evidence, Delvecchio guesses that Foster is a user himself. Confronted by his accusers, Foster admits that he has been an addict ever since he served in Vietnam. Delvecchio convinces Foster to get help for his problem so that he will be able to continue as a cop. By the closing credits, viewers learn that Foster had sought professional help and that the murderers have been caught.

As these examples suggest, some impurities have crept into the wholesome image enjoyed by TV's men and women in blue. Police are still predominately positive characters, but the bad apples have become easier to spot in recent years. Before 1975, good cops outnumbered bad ones by an overwhelming margin of nearly ten to one. Since then, the gap has narrowed to about three to one. That's still a commanding lead, but it's also a substantial dropoff from the nearly faultless former paragons of virtue. Local sheriffs have undergone an even more dramatic transformation. It's all been downhill from Dodge City to Hazzard County. Before 1975 good guys outnumbered bad guys among this group by about a two-to-one margin (54 to 28 percent). Since then, the ratio has almost reversed itself, with negative characters outnumbering positive ones by 48 to 28 percent.

A similar tendency is revealed by the figures on criminal activity within the law-enforcement ranks. Before 1975 we coded only a trace of corruption on the force. Less than one-half percent of TV's policemen committed crimes, compared to over 6 percent of all other occupational groups. Since 1975, this difference has completely disappeared. During the past decade, cops have committed crimes at the same rate (still 6 percent) as other occupational groups. Once again, sheriffs carry the trend a giant step further. Only 3 percent broke the law prior to 1985. That figure jumped to 14 percent thereafter, or one out of every seven characters.

In contrast to the declining fortunes of uniformed officers, positive portrayals of private eyes have held steady above the 80 percent level throughout the last three decades. Only 3 percent of P.I.s have been portrayed as lawbreakers since 1975, about half the rate of both policemen and other occupational groups. That was a complete reversal of the situation before 1965, when TV's private eyes broke the law as often as any other occupation, and we failed to record a single crime committed by a police officer. Thus, despite the popularity of the brilliant private investigator since Sherlock Holmes' debut almost a century ago, these unconventional law enforcers were not conspicuously superior to their uniformed counterparts during the early years of television. It is only the more critical portrayals of law enforcement regulars in recent years that have opened a gap recalling the gulf between the brilliant Holmes and the dullard Lastrade.

REAL MEN DON'T NEED GUNS

For all the violence we found on the small screen, law enforcers haven't resorted to gunplay as often as might be expected. In fact, they generally emphasize talk over action. Most lawmen rely on persuasion, their legal authority, and trickery before duking it out or drawing a gun.

This choice of methods underscores television's professional image of law enforcement.

Among the law enforcers in our sample, seven in every ten resorted to rational persuasion to accomplish their goals. Persuasion was their main tool during all three of the decades we studied. Legal authority was the next most frequently used method. Over two-thirds (68 percent) relied on their position of authority to question people, search property, take suspects into custody, and so on. Over the course of time, more and more limits were imposed on their authority, but it remained a frequent backdrop for their actions. Such commonplace events as ordering subordinates into action, serving arrest warrants, issuing tickets, controlling traffic, and making arrests were all part of their legal authority. It was persuasion, not violence, that backed up legal authority in most plot lines. Individuals could normally be persuaded to cooperate with legal requests from law enforcers.

If characters resisted persuasion, they could often be tricked into cooperating. Trickery was the third most common method of choice for lawmen. Over one in five resorted to it. Deception was part of a large array of actions, ranging from undercover disguises to tricking suspects into confessions. Trickery was especially common for private eyes and secret agents, who could not fall back on their authority to get things done. Deception became so de rigueur for gumshoes that Jim Rockford ("The Rockford Files") kept a hand-operated printing press in his car to fabricate ID cards for himself.

Violence was reserved for subduing extremely vicious criminals or for coercing assistance from the unwilling. Only one TV lawman in six found in our sample has used violence in the course of his nightly work. Most often violence was a last resort as self-protection against violent criminals. In recent years, some law enforcers have turned to intimidation by threat of force as a way to gain information. But violence on the whole remains reactive and usually occurs in shootouts with the bad guys.

This mixture of methods has changed a bit as the fair sex has increasingly been recruited into crime-fighting roles. Nine out of ten female law enforcers have used persuasion, compared to only two-thirds of their male counterparts. By contrast, over two-thirds of the men in blue utilized their authority to stop crime, compared to just over half the female officers. Perhaps the clearest illustration of the different approaches by male and female law enforcers lies in their use of deception. Only one-fifth of the lawmen in our sample used deception, while almost half (46 percent) of the women relied on deception and trickery. This reflects the way policewomen work on TV. Many of television's policewomen have functioned as undercover agents. Deception has been necessary to maintain their cover and get information from criminals.

Undercover assignments reflect sex role differences in a more direct fashion as well. Women were given assignments relying on their feminine charms, while men assumed the identities of powerful figures. Men took the roles of major drug dealers, businessmen, or military leaders, while women became hookers, strippers, secretaries, or stewardesses. While in these guises, women often used sex appeal and flirtation to achieve their goals. Women were about four times as likely to use these tools as their male counterparts. All this accords with the portrait of TV's women in chapter 3. Even when they make it into TV's roughest, toughest profession, women still fit into traditional feminine roles.

Thus, TV's law enforcers have traditionally relied on the methods that most underline their professionalism. Persuasion and authority were the predominant tools in day-to-day operations. As more undercover work became part of plot lines, the use of deception increased. Despite some memorable exceptions, however, Rambo-style violence has often been too hot for the tube to handle.

THE CREAKY WHEELS OF JUSTICE

If television usually supports the men and women who work for the justice system, it has often criticized the system's failings. Particularly in the past fifteen years, issues like defendants' rights, community opinion, police brutality, racism, and sexism have all come to the fore. TV's law enforcers can no longer operate with carte blanche, since errors in procedure may invalidate an arrest. In the early days, television presented police, lawyers, and the courts as members of a team trying to find the truth. Video cops really did protect and serve, lawyers were knights in grey flannel who championed the rights of individuals, and courts set the mighty on a par with the meek. These good guys battled crime with nary a suggestion of complaint about their behavior.

In the late 1960s television began its first wave of social criticism with a flourish. Characters soared to rhetorical heights as they demanded answers from an often monolithic and sometimes malevolent system. One insoluble problem after another escaped easy answers for these video philosophers. Controversial choices like balancing individual rights with social order were the subject of rhetorical pirouettes.

The age of the social problems soliloquy was short-lived. It proved difficult for viewers to relate to characters who spoke in policy statements. Thus, in the early 1970s, a change in plot structures paved the way for a new type of social criticism. Rather than emerging through flourishes of dialogue, it became a part of the work routine. By including more parts of the justice system in plot lines, criticism and tension were built into the action. Different parts of the system had different goals, rules, and priorities, so criticism emerged naturally. The D.A.'s office could criticize police behavior, police could curse the inactivity of the courts, and the courts could strike down improper procedures by attorneys or police. At the same time, the critic's voice no longer rang out loud and clear against injustice. Instead it sounded weary and frustrated in the face of new limits. The rhetorical leaps and bounds of previous years were largely gone, as the mundane war in the trenches occupied more of the characters' time.

Criticism of law enforcement has focused on both police behavior and the justice system. Many shows presented internal housekeeping as a routine part of police work. For instance, in a 1968 segment of "Dragnet," Sergeants Friday and Gannon look into a citizen complaint of police violence. The citizen, John Meadows, claims that a police officer hit him while breaking up a very loud party. As they press on in their investigation, Friday and Gannon find ample evidence that Officer Hilliard was provoked by the drunken Meadows. Despite this provocation, Hilliard receives a thirty-day suspension. Friday tersely delivers the rationale behind the suspension: "You are a trained professional and when you hit John Meadows, you committed a cardinal sin."

Cops from Kojak to Sonny Crockett have had to face internal investigations when their methods proved controversial. Despite the increasing need to justify their actions, these cops did not view legal limits as excessive. Of the few scripts that paused to consider the limits on police behavior, only one in ten found the restraints too great. Thus television's law enforcers have by and large accepted the new era of limitations without turning to Dirty Harry tactics or rationales.

In addition to individual law enforcers, we examined the way TV has viewed the criminal justice system as a whole. Most shows never questioned the probity of the criminal justice system. Among those that did, four out of five found that the system treated people equally. In the early years of television, equality was assumed as an operating rule of the justice system. A 1961 segment of "Naked City" presented a court that diligently followed procedures even when the accused were two hardened, violent criminals. In this episode two brothers commit a string of armed robberies in New York and then flee to California. When California police capture them, the New York City police demand their return. At their extradition hearing their lawyer tries every procedural motion and appeal he can to block extradition. The judge reviews the evidence and documents before he rules that the brothers must be sent back to New York. Even these two desperate and repulsive criminals are given equal access to procedural defenses in a careful review of the case.

By the 1970s television no longer assumed that police would treat people equally. Criticism began to be voiced, although it was often rebutted. Thus a 1975 episode of "Good Times" addressed complaints of racism against police, but in the end rejected them as unfounded. In this segment young J.J. Evans is arrested as a suspect in a liquor store robbery. The police are calm, professional, and conscientious as they question him. They politely explain the situation to J.J.'s parents, making it clear that they have reasonable grounds to hold him. Despite the courteous behavior of the officers, J.J.'s brother Michael claims that the arrest is outright discrimination. Michael makes protest signs and tries to convince his family to picket the police station. Michael's parents and everyone else involved dismiss his claims, and J.J. is later released when the police catch the real robber.

A more dramatic change has come over television's portrayal of corruption in the judicial system. Before 1975, charges of favoritism or corruption by the police and courts were raised only to be rejected. Nearly 90 percent of the shows in our sample that dealt with this issue ended up exonerating the system. Since 1975, however, TV has shown a much more corrupt system of justice. During the latest decade we studied, precisely half the scripts that looked into shady dealings pronounced the system guilty. Moreover, this theme came up twice as often as it had earlier. Thus, charges of corruption were raised as often in the most recent decade as they were in the two previous decades combined.

Examples abound of TV's newly critical stance. In a 1975 segment of "Baretta," a mobster bought a judge to ensure the success of his operations. On a 1985 "Miami Vice" episode, a powerful drug dealer controlled the entire police force and court system of a small island nation. A 1976 episode of "Kojak" presented a particularly sharp-edged look at favoritism in the legal system. Kojak begins by investigating a death but manages to uncover evidence of a gang rape and finds new information on an old homicide. Pressing further, he finds that a powerful matriarch, who controls a political machine, ordered the rape and homicide covered up. To protect her son, who was involved in both cases, she has the D.A. railroad a conviction, pays off two witnesses, and bribes the investigating officers with promotions. The D.A. cooperates to gain her support for his upcoming run for the governor's mansion. Kojak's diligence unravels the coverup, and the guilty parties are finally punished.

It would be hard to imagine such scenarios in early shows like "Naked City," "Dragnet," or "Gunsmoke." But the past decade has increasingly portrayed a system in need of reform. Fortunately, it is a system capable of being cleansed by the final credits. If a police department is corrupt, it is usually a crusading cop or a lawyer who cleans it up. Outsider whistleblowers like investigative journalists have also played a role in policing the justice system. Particularly in the most recent decade, these outsiders have exposed very complex schemes that had escaped the notice of other officials. What emerges is a system that is increasingly seen as flawed but reparable. This reflects the perspective of the "new realism," whose message is one of liberal reform rather than radical reconstruction or cynical withdrawal. There are few "Chinatowns" in TV law enforcement, but there are also fewer untouchables these days.

THE VERDICT

Law enforcement is one of the major activities of life on television. The men and women who performed this role for years enjoyed an almost revered status. For the better part of two decades they were the virtuous righters of wrongs, living symbols of justice and fairness. They enforced clear-cut moral codes that were either taken for granted or actively championed by these guardians of virtue.

The law enforcement profession itself was incorruptible. Policemen were honest and always got their man. Lawyers protected the rights of the innocent while often finding time to finger the guilty. The justice system worked smoothly, when it was pictured at all. Most often viewers could safely assume that the bad guy being hustled off in handcuffs would get his just desserts. As for those who were carried off under a sheet, they obviously got what was coming to them.

This idealized image began to change during the late 1960s, as TV courtrooms and station houses were increasingly called upon to cope with social turmoil and moral ambiguity. The moralists and cool professionals on the force were joined by social workers in blue who questioned the law and society in their search for justice. By the mid-1970s, the police had lost much of their special status. They could fail in their duties, get caught in red tape, or have their success negated by court decisions. These professional problems were paralleled by new personal and moral failures. These days, TV law enforcers are no longer immune to criticism. They descend into criminality about as often as members of other professions. The justice system itself, all but unseen during TV's early years, is now shown warts and all. In fact, the warts have moved to center stage.

Increasingly, the good guys have to fight the bureaucracy or internal corruption as well as their traditional foes out on the streets.

These changes should not be overstated. Most TV law enforcers still wear white hats, and they have kept up with the times even when confronted by new social problems. Rarely cast as agents of unfair repression, the police instead became trained professionals concerned with social as well as individual justice. On television a more liberal perspective on law enforcement has brought a different sense of mission for law enforcers rather than the rejection of their mission. The heroic cop is now more likely to be an outsider within the system willing to fight stodgy ideas and bureaucratic rigidity to get the job done.

Elliot Ness and Joe Friday would hardly recognize the world of Theo Kojak and Frank Furillo, who had to fight turf battles and red tape as well as punks and hoodlums. And even these evildoers are more likely to receive understanding and even empathy than in the old days of "shoot first and sympathize later." Faced with new demands and complexities, TV's good cops have begun to rely on sensitivity and social work as well as deduction and gunplay.

TV's new era of limits on police work has taken its toll in other ways. Private eyes and citizen sleuths, unburdened by the system's failings and limitations, regularly outshine their uniformed colleagues in crime-solving. The advantage of being an outsider means more today than twenty years ago, when a badge still conferred almost mythic status on prime time. Shackled by new limits and rarely portrayed in the Dick Tracy heroic mold, the police have gradually given ground to the lone outsider in the race to bring evildoers to justice. Today television manages to enforce the law without glorifying the law enforcement establishment. In conjunction with our portrait of prime-time crime, this trend adds a certain irony to television's version of crime and punishment. More and more often on prime time, the insiders break the law and the outsiders enforce it.

PART

V

Public Issues

10

DIFF'RENT STROKES

It takes diff'rent strokes to move the world!
—"Diff'rent Strokes" theme song

W hen Kingfish uttered his last "Holy Mackerel, Andy!" in 1953, it marked the end of television's most controversial depiction of blacks. Ironically, the departure of "Amos 'n' Andy" also signaled the end of a brief period of ethnic diversity that would not reappear in prime time for two decades.

Several of the earliest family sitcoms were transplanted radio shows set in America's black or white ethnic subcultures. "The Gold-bergs" followed the lives of a Jewish immigrant family in New York for twenty years on radio before switching to the new medium in 1949. It featured Gertrude Berg as Molly Goldberg, everyone's favorite Jewish mother. An even more successful series that premiered the same year was "I Remember Mama," which chronicled a Norwegian immigrant family in turn-of-the-century San Francisco. Theme music by Grieg added to the "ethnic" atmosphere, as did accents that made Aunt "Yenny" into a popular character. These white ethnic shows were soon joined by the all-black "Amos 'n' Andy" and "Beulah," which starred the black maid of a white middle-class family.

All these shows relied on stereotypical dialogue and behavior for much of their humor. But social standards were changing, and the new medium created its own demands and perceptions. For example, not only Amos and Andy but even Beulah were portrayed on radio by white males. When the popular radio show "Life with Luigi" made the switch to TV in 1952, Italian-American groups protested its stereotyped portrayal of Italian immigrants. Black groups were equally outraged over "Amos 'n' Andy," which had been an institution on radio since 1929. As the program evolved, it centered on the schemes of George "Kingfish" Stevens, who combined the soul of Sgt. Bilko with the fate of Ralph Kramden. A small-time conman with big plans that never panned out, he became an immensely popular, lovable loser. His schemes usually pulled in the ingenuous cabbie Andy and the slow moving janitor Lightnin'.

From Kingfish's fractured syntax ("I'se regusted") to Lightnin's shuffle and falsetto "yazzuh," the series undoubtedly drew on racial stereotypes. The NAACP blasted the portrayal of blacks as "inferior, lazy, dumb, and dishonest," and urged a boycott of Blatz beer, the sponsor. Nonetheless, some have defended the series. The actor who portrayed Amos pointed out that "many episodes showed the Negro with professions and businesses like attorneys, store owners, and so on, which they never had in TV or movies before."[1] And the authors of *Watching TV* argue that the stereotypes derived more from the program genre than racist putdowns:

> The characters and plots were totally interchangeable with scores of "white" sitcoms that both preceded and postdated "Amos 'n' Andy." . . . As in any screwball comedy, the stories depended on misunderstandings and crazy antics by such tried-and-true stereotypes as a money-hungry bumbler, a slow-witted second banana, a shrewish wife, and a battle-ax mother-in-law. In "Amos 'n' Andy," these familiar comic caricatures just happened to be black. . . . For more

than a decade similar series flourished featuring white performers. In that light, "Amos 'n' Andy" was merely the harbinger of a successful trend, with its black characters no more or less demeaning than their white equivalents.[2]

THE ALL-WHITE WORLD

Whatever the final verdict, this kind of controversy didn't attract sponsors. Although "Amos 'n' Andy" and "Luigi" landed regularly in the Nielsen top twenty, both lost their network slots in 1953. (Reruns of "Amos 'n' Andy" survived in syndication for over a decade.) By the 1954 season "I Remember Mama" was the only survivor of the once-thriving ethnic sitcoms. Thus, by the time our study period began, TV's first era of ethnic humor had already come and gone. The urban ethnic sitcoms were replaced by homogeneous suburban settings. There was nothing Irish about the life of Chester Riley, nothing Scandinavian about Jim and Margaret Anderson. The new family shows were all-American, which meant vaguely northern European and carefully noncontroversial. The few remaining ethnics were mostly relegated to minor roles or single episodes.

Just how homogeneous was this electronic neighborhood? From 1955 through 1964, our coders could identify only one character in ten as anything other than northern European on the basis of name, language, or appearance. Such a small slice of the pie got cut up very quickly, and many groups got only crumbs. Just one character in fifty was Hispanic, fewer than one in a hundred was Asian, one in two hundred was black, and one in seven hundred was Jewish.

While nonwhites were relegated mostly to the role of servants, white ethnics tended to congregate in urban police shows. Ethnic cops, such as Detective Muldoon of "Naked City" and Lieutenant Switkolski of "The Roaring 20s," could sometimes be found in big city station houses. However, not all ethnic characters fared well in these shows. While a few stars were praiseworthy, others were pictured as part of the seedy underside of urban life. For example, Italians were often portrayed as hoods or thugs working for a criminal gang. Ill-mannered, poorly educated, and violent, these characters were among the most negative portrayals of any ethnic group during TV's early years.[3]

Italian-American groups found "The Untouchables" particularly objectionable. At a time when congressional hearings and law enforcement officials were making the Mafia a household word, this series recreated the violent conflict between treasury agent Eliot Ness and the notorious Al Capone gang in 1930s Chicago. Plagued by complaints about reinforcing stereotypes of Italian gangsters, the producers added agent Enrico Rossi to Ness's crew of "untouchables" and expanded their pool of adversaries to include Ma Barker, Dutch Schultz, and Mad Dog Cole.

While white ethnics labored to overcome comic and dramatic stereotypes, other minorities struggled even to be seen. The departure of "Amos 'n' Andy" and "Beulah" all but eliminated black stars. Jack Benny's valet Rochester was one of the few major roles still held by a black in the late 1950s. Black characters didn't even show up in the backgrounds of early shows. Urban settings might feature a black delivery man, porter, or waiter, but black professionals and businessmen were virtually nonexistent. Some Westerns like "Rawhide" and "Have Gun, Will Travel" presented a few black cowboys riding the range with their white counterparts. Aside from such occasional and insignificant roles, black characters were simply not a part of the early prime-time world.

Other groups did little better in this monochromatic world. Hispanics had virtually no starring roles. For most Hispanic characters, life consisted of lounging in the dusty square of a sleepy Latin town, waiting for the stars to come on stage. Occasionally Hispanics would show up as outlaws in the Old West, but even then mostly as members of someone else's gang. Their comic roles were epitomized by Pepino Garcia, a farmhand for "The Real McCoys," who functioned mainly as a target of Grandpa Amos McCoy's tirades.

Like their black colleagues, a few stars stood out in a sea of marginal and insignificant roles. A notable exception was Cuban band leader Ricky Ricardo in "I Love Lucy." As the co-star of one of the most popular shows on TV (and co-owner of Desilu Productions, along with wife

Lucille Ball), Desi Arnaz was a prominent figure. When exasperated by Lucy's schemes and misadventures, Ricky added a comic touch with displays of "Latin" temper and lapses into Spanish. "I Love Lucy" made its mark on television comedy and TV production in general, but it did little for Hispanic characters. The same could be said of another early show with a Hispanic setting, which nonetheless cast Anglos in the major roles. Guy Williams played Don Diego, alias Zorro, the masked champion of the poor and oppressed in old Los Angeles. Their oppressors were evil, greedy Spanish governors and landowners. In one episode Annette Funicello, fresh from the Mickey Mouse Club, showed up as the singing señorita Anita Cabrillo. Despite its "Hispanic" characters, the show was not a generous portrayal of either the people or the culture.

Oriental characters were even rarer during television's early years. When they appeared at all, it was usually as domestic servants. Omnipresent domestics like Hop Sing on "Bonanza," Peter Tong in "Bachelor Father," or Hey Boy in "Have Gun, Will Travel" were the best roles TV offered to Asians. Like other nonwhites, they found that subservient roles were all that kept them from complete oblivion.

THE RETURN OF RACE

In the mid-1960s, the portrayal of ethnic and racial minorities underwent major changes. The proportion of non-northern European roles doubled over the next decade. Before 1965, all racial and ethnic groups to the south or east of England, France, and Germany had scrambled for the one role in ten available to them. Now nonwhite characters alone could count on better than one role in ten. From the first to second decade in our study, the proportion of English characters was cut in half, while Hispanics became half again as numerous and the proportion of Asians doubled. Blacks were the biggest winners, gaining a dramatic fourteenfold increase in what had been virtually an all-white landscape.

Not only did the proportion of black characters jump to 7 percent between 1965 and 1975, but the range and quality of roles expanded even more dramatically. In adventure series like "I Spy" and "Mission:

Impossible," blacks moved into their first starring roles in over a decade. These roles were both more prominent and offered a new style of character. Alexander Scott of "I Spy" and Barney Collier of "Mission: Impossible" were competent, educated professionals. They were highly successful agents whose racial backgrounds were clearly secondary to their bravery and skill. They opened the way for blacks to appear in roles that did not require the actor to be black. There was no more use of poor English, servile shuffling, or pop-eyed double takes for comic effect. Instead, Collier was presented as an electronics expert and Scott a multilingual Rhodes scholar.

The new visibility of blacks quickly moved beyond the secret agent genre. In 1968 the first of television's relevance series managed to convert a negative stereotype into a positive one by casting a young black rebel as a member of the "Mod Squad." Linc Hayes' militant credentials included an afro haircut, aviator sunglasses, and an arrest during the Watts riots. Not to worry, though. This brooding black rebel was working with the good guys on the LAPD's undercover "youth squad," where the dirty dozen met the counterculture every Tuesday at 7:30.

While ABC was co-opting the Black Panthers into the establishment, NBC looked to the black middle class for "Julia," the first black-oriented sitcom in fifteen years. As a dedicated nurse and loving mother in an integrated world, the Julia Baker character looked ahead to "The Cosby Show" rather than backward to "Amos 'n' Andy." She certainly had more in common with Claire Huxtable than with Kingfish's nagging wife Sapphire. Unfortunately, she also lacked the vitality and wit of either Sapphire or future mother figures who would be more firmly rooted in black culture, like Florida Evans of "Good Times."

"Julia" suffered from the dullness of being a prestige series, just as "The Mod Squad" labored under the hype that attended the relevance series. What they had in common with better-written shows like "I Spy" and "Mission Impossible" was a tendency to replace the old negative black stereotypes with new positive ones. The authors of *Watching TV* wrote with a touch of hyperbole: "They were no longer bumbling, easy-going, po' folk like Beulah, but rather articulate neo-philosophers just descended from Olympus, though still spouting streetwise jargon."[4] Having discovered that blacks didn't have to be cast as valets and janitors, white writers turned them into James Bonds and Mary Tyler Moores. Thus, as blacks suddenly began to appear on the tube after a decade's absence, they remained invisible in Ralph Ellison's sense. The frantic search for positive characters smothered individuality with good intentions.

As they worked black characters into a previously all-white world, racial tensions posed a different challenge for scriptwriters. When blackness was raised as an issue now, it was to illustrate bitterness and frustration with the system. Scripts began to crackle with anger at continuing racial injustice, although militancy and violence were invariably condemned. For instance, in a 1966 "I Spy," a black man named Prince Edward plans to create an electrical blackout in Los Angeles that will allow his co-conspirators to go on a crime spree. "Scotty" goes undercover to infiltrate the gang and stop their plot. After Scott has won his confidence, Prince Edward explains his motivation. He says he grew up in Jamaica and can never forget what he learned there. He tells of lying on the dirt floor of his family's shack and looking at the gleaming lights from the white man's house on the hill. Every night he lay there, hearing the music, imagining the dances, knowing that he could never be a part of it. Now it is his turn to show the white man what darkness is like.

Prince Edward almost succeeds, until he is accidentally electrocuted. By contrast, Scott does not share his bitterness and does not see himself as markedly different from his white colleagues. This reflects the series' underlying premise that mutual good will can make race irrelevant to social relations. This episode made manifest a message that was normally latent in the interracial pairing of Scott and Kelly Robinson. Within a few years, such "salt-and-pepper" law-enforcer teams became a prime-time cliché.

Although television disavowed militant solutions, scripts increasingly focused on the corrupting influence of institutional racism. Churches, schools, the courts, and the police had to deal with past and current discrimination as part of their daily operations. Assumptions of equality were no longer enough; institutions had to prove they were egalitarian. Even long-standing procedures faced new tests and challenges.

A few shows took an optimistic view that such problems and conflicts could be solved with a little understanding. In a segment of "Adam-12" in our study, two police officers are ambushed by a black militant group. One of the attackers is wounded, as are both policemen. Officers Reed and Malloy continue to search for the other attackers. Then Reed finds out that the wounded militant is the younger brother of an old schoolmate. Reed and Ken James played football together and became good friends. This incident threatens to destroy the friendship as Ken begins to believe that the police gunned down his brother. The militants continue to accuse the police of committing genocide against young black men. Tensions in the city and the friendship grow as the police come under mounting pressure to resolve the case.

When the police locate the other assailant, he turns out to be a third brother in the same family. In the climax, the police and Ken arrive at his apartment simultaneously. When Reed and Malloy call for the man to surrender he grabs Reed as a hostage, threatening to kill him. Ken realizes that it is not the police who are motivated by racial hatred, but his own brothers. With Ken's help, Reed and Malloy capture the man. With the culprits caught, the city relaxes and Reed and Ken patch up their friendship. Ken realizes he jumped to conclusions rather than believe his own brothers were killers.

Other shows presented more recalcitrant problems in race relations. In a 1971 segment of "Man and the City," a cop is killed in the barrio of a southwestern city. The police department pulls out all the stops to catch the killers. They try to impose a curfew on the barrio and hold suspects incommunicado without legal counsel. All the suspects are Hispanics from the barrio who have little connection to the case. The mayor is forced to intervene and remind the police chief that the city has laws. He demands that all suspects, including minority groups, be given their full rights. The police are reluctant, believing this will impede their investigation. The mayor insists and the police obey his order. They eventually capture a key suspect who helps them catch the killers. There is no indication that racial tensions in the city have ended, merely that one violent episode is over. The groups involved have not learned to like each other; nor are they peacefully coexisting.

One episode of "Star Trek" carried the point even further by creating an alien race of individuals who were each half black and half white. The majority were black on the right side, but a small minority was black on the left side. The majority had labeled their mirror images as evil, rebellious, and decidedly inferior. The crew of the *Enterprise* comes in contact with this race when they pick up a fugitive and the lawman pursuing him. These two are so set upon a course of racial hatred that they have pursued each other across the galaxy for hundreds of years.

Their hatred boils over in the confines of the ship, but the crew can see no difference between the two. When the *Enterprise* and its two unwilling passengers arrive at their home planet, they find a dead world. The racial tensions there exploded into a violent global race war. Even in the face of this devastation, the two survivors continue their chase across the face of their dead planet, rather than tolerate each other. This sharp-edged parable about racial intolerance is not lost on the crew of the *Enterprise*. They breathe a sigh of relief and relax in their own racially integrated society.

Thus, whether delivered as a gentle homily or a searing sermon, television's message about race relations was always the same: Race shouldn't matter. People are all pretty much alike. They need only emphasize their basic similarities over their superficial differences in order to coexist. These lessons of tolerance and sameness were applied across the board to all races and ethnic groups. No group was seen as too different to fit in.

LET A HUNDRED FLOWERS BLOOM

In the early 1970s TV began to broadcast a different message about minorities. The unlikely agent of change was a hard-hat hero who was an equal-opportunity bigot. He excoriated "spics," "jungle bunnies," "chinks," "yids," and every other minority that ever commanded an epithet. Archie Bunker's punishment for such sentiments was to be surrounded by the people he professed to despise. From his black next door neighbors to his wife's archliberal cousin, not to mention his live-in "Polack meathead" son-in-law and a Puerto Rican boarder, Archie was a man besieged by the forces of social change.

It took Norman Lear and Bud Yorkin three years to sell a network on the concept of a bigoted but lovable working-class paterfamilias, borrowed from the British series "Till Death Do Us Part." Then, when "All in the Family" became the top-rated show within five months of its 1971 premier, it attracted a barrage of criticism for making the tube safe for ethnic slurs. The producer of public television's "Black Journal" found it "shocking and racist."[5] Laura Hobson, who wrote "Gentlemen's Agreement," an attack on antisemitism, decried its attempt to sanitize bigotry, "to clean it up, deodorize it, make millions of people more comfy about indulging in it."[6] Of course, the point of the show was to poke fun at Archie and all he stood for, as the script and laugh track tried to make clear. As Christopher Lasch wrote:

> Liberals of Laura Hobson's type, convinced that bigotry can be combatted by propaganda depicting it in the most unattractive light, mistakenly see the Archie Bunker programs as a capitulation to popular prejudices. What the programs really seem to say, however, is that prejudice is a disease and that the only way to overcome it, as in psychotherapy, is to bring to light its irrational origins.[7]

Lear chose to entertain audiences instead of preaching at them. So he created a kind of politicized Ralph Kramden whom audiences could like in spite of his reactionary views, not because of them. He intended that the contrast between Archie's basic decency and his unattractive rantings would prod viewers to reexamine the retrograde ideas they permitted themselves. As he put it, the show "holds up a mirror to our prejudices. . . . We laugh now, swallowing just the littlest bit of truth about ourselves, and it sits there for the unconscious to toss about later."[8]

As a tool for improving race relations, this approach may have been too subtle for its own good. Several studies suggest that liberals watched the show to confirm their disdain for Archie's views, while conservatives identified with him despite his creator's best intentions.[9] But another legacy of the program was to pioneer a more topical and (by television's standards) realistic portrayal of ethnic relations.

An immediate consequence of "All in the Family" was to introduce the first sitcoms populated by black families since "Amos 'n' Andy." A year after demonstrating the audience appeal of a white working-class milieu not portrayed successfully since "The Honeymooners," Lear and Yorkin transferred the setting to a black ghetto in "Sanford and Son." Unlike the integrated middle-class world of TV blacks in the late 1960s, "Sanford and Son" revolved around the foibles of a junk dealer in a poor black section of Los Angeles. "Sanford" proved so popular that it soon trailed only "All in the Family" in the Nielsen ratings.

Meanwhile, in an irony Archie would not have appreciated, "All in the Family" spawned not one but two additional black family sitcoms. "The Jeffersons" featured Archie's one-time neighbor George Jefferson as an upwardly mobile businessman whose snobbishness and inverted racism made him almost a black Archie Bunker. "Good Times" was actually a second generation spinoff. When Archie's liberal nemesis Maude got her own show in 1972, the scriptwriters gave her a quick-witted and tart-tongued black maid named Florida Evans. Two years later the popular Florida got her own show as the matriarch of a family living in a Chicago housing project. This series developed the "Sanford" technique of finding sometimes bitter humor among lower-status characters trying to cope with life in the ghetto while looking for a way out of it. Scripts featured ward healers, loan sharks, abused children, and other facets of life on the edge, in sharp contrast to the comfortable middle-class world of "Julia" or the glamorous and exotic locales of "I Spy."

By this time, other producers, stimulated by Norman Lear's enormous success, were providing sitcoms that drew their characters from minority settings. "What's Happening!" followed the adventures of three big city high school kids. "Diff'rent Strokes" created an unlikely "accidental family" in which a wealthy white man raised two black kids from Harlem in his Park Avenue apartment, without any serious clash of cultures. This trend almost never extended from the ghetto to the barrio. The great exception was "Chico and the Man," a generation gap sitcom that paired an ebullient young Mexican-American with an aging Bunker-ish Anglo garage owner. This odd couple clicked with audiences, but the show's success was cut short by the suicide of comedian Freddy Prinze (Chico) in 1977.

Like the black sitcoms, "Chico" used minority culture as a spark to enliven a middle-class white world that seemed bland or enervated by comparison. Minority characters of the early 1970s prided themselves not on their similarity to mainstream culture, but on their differences from it. Assimilated characters like Alexander Scott, Barney Collier, and Julia Baker gave way to the racial pride of George Jefferson, Fred of "Sanford and Son," and Rooster on "Starsky and Hutch." Where would Fred Sanford or George Jefferson be without their jive talk and street slang? Language was just one way of stressing the differences between racial and ethnic groups.

Minority characters also picked up flaws as they took on more complete roles. Fred Sanford was domineering and could appear foolish. George Jefferson could be as stubborn and narrow-minded as his one-time next door neighbor. By badgering the interracial couple living upstairs and labeling their daughter a "zebra," he left no doubt about his views. But the thrust of the ethnic sitcom was not to ridicule minority cultures; quite the opposite. Instead, racial and ethnic backgrounds were used as an educational tool. The religious, cultural, and other traditions that differentiate minorities from the mainstream were now treated as beneficial rather than problematic. Removed from the confines of the melting pot, these groups offered new approaches to old problems. Television charged them with the task of teaching new ways to the often obstinate world around them. For instance, the Japanese Mrs. Livingston was a frequent source of guidance for young Eddie on "The Courtship of Eddie's Father." Like Hazel or Beulah in earlier times, Mrs. Livingston helped round out family teachings. Her gentle philosophy echoed her Eastern origins and was often presented in the form of ancient proverbs.

The presentation of Eastern philosophy reached its peak in the Western "Kung Fu." The star of this unusual series was Kwai Chang Caine, a Chinese monk born of Chinese and American parents. He was forced to leave China and flee to the U.S., where he roamed the Old West as a fugitive. As a complete outcast from society, he served as a teacher of nonviolence, tolerance, and kindness. Lessons were taught in cryptic Eastern proverbs and driven home with a kung-fu kick.

Blacks and Hispanics also participated in this era of racial and cultural reeducation. It was Chico Rodriguez who taught Ed Brown to relax and be more tolerant on "Chico and the Man." Benson, the sharp-tongued butler, tried to maintain order amidst the chaos of "Soap," while steering his employers onto the right track. In one episode he even saved young Billy from the clutches of a religious cult.

The most spectacularly successful effort to combine education with entertainment was a hybrid of the miniseries and "big event" genres. Indeed, "Roots" became the biggest event in television history. This adaptation of Alex Haley's best-selling novel traced the history of four generations of a black family in America, beginning with Kunta Kinte, an African tribesman sold into slavery. It ran for eight consecutive nights in January 1977. When it was over, 130 million Americans had tuned in, including 80 million who viewed the final episode. Seven of the eight episodes ranked among the all-time top ten at that point in television's history. One study in Cleveland found that over 90 percent of all blacks and 70 percent of whites surveyed had watched some part of the series. "Roots" created a kind of national town meeting comparable to the televised moon landing or the aftermath of President Kennedy's assassination. It was blamed for several racial disturbances but credited for stimulating a productive national debate on the history of American race relations.

The object of all this attention offered some prime roles to such distinguished black actors as Louis Gossett and Cecily Tyson. The writing and the historical perspectives were of a somewhat lower order than the acting and production values. The story featured such titillating elements as rape and nudity, while reducing the story of slavery to a kind of Western, with blacks as the cowboys and whites as the Indians. That made it all the more remarkable that whites as well as blacks gave the series an overwhelmingly positive rating in national polls. But the real secret of "Roots'" audience appeal may be gleaned from its subtitle, "The Triumph of an American Family." The series tapped into a resurgence of ethnic pride and celebration of personal heritage that cut across racial lines. The following week, genealogical inquiries to the National Archives tripled. This surge of ethnic affirmation had many causes, but it was fed by television's own newfound commitment to cultural diversity.

While racial minorities were taking on more complex roles and teaching their contemporaries, white ethnics were also enjoying a renaissance. Many ethnic groups which had disappeared after the early 1960s suddenly reemerged in powerful and popular starring roles. There was the Greek supercop "Kojak," the crafty and shrewd Polish P.I. "Banacek," and the successful Italian attorney "Petrocelli." The comedies of the early 1970s also began to add ethnic characters, until the casts came to resemble UN meetings. In shows like "Calucci's Department," "Rhoda," and "Barney Miller," a mix of racial and ethnic minorities blended in comedy with an implicit message of pluralism and tolerance.

One sitcom even pushed this blending into the bedroom. "Bridget Loves Bernie" became one of TV's more controversial comedies when it presented a Jewish writer married to an Irish Catholic teacher. Typically, the challenge for this couple came not from their own relationship, but from their meddlesome and somewhat intolerant parents. This low-key comedy proved very popular, placing fifth in the year-end Nielsen ratings. But it was plagued by controversy and objections from Jewish groups over its sympathetic portrayal of mixed marriages. It was canceled after one season. Nonetheless the show's concept later received a kind of vindication. In a classic instance of life imitating art, series stars David Birney and Meredith Baxter were later married in real life.

Despite such occasional failures, ethnic comedies became the hottest new programming trend of the 1970s. "All in the Family" was the top-rated show for an unprecedented five straight seasons, surpassing previous megahits "I Love Lucy" and "Gunsmoke." Other top twenty regulars included "Sanford and Son," "The Jeffersons," black comic Flip Wilson's variety show, "Chico and the Man," and "Rhoda," one of the rare series since "The Goldbergs" to feature strong Jewish characters. The ethnic wave crested during the 1974-75 season, when a remarkable six of the top seven rated shows were ethnic sitcoms—"All in the Family," " Sanford," "Chico," "The Jeffersons," "Rhoda," and "Good Times."

If the new decade offered a dazzling array of new roles for minorities, it contained some traps as well. Ethnic characters gained more prominent and desirable roles, but also more unflattering ones. Bumblers, buffoons, and bimbos took their place alongside heroes and sages. For example, Vinnie Barbarino and Juan Epstein were two of the uneducated underachievers on "Welcome Back, Kotter." Barbarino's Italian heritage added ethnic color to his machismo image, while Epstein's ethnic background was contrived for comic effect. He was presented as Buchanan High School's only Puerto Rican Jew.

Louie DiPalma, the pompous, foolish dispatcher on "Taxi," showed that TV's Italians could be nasty even when they weren't criminals. "Good Times" created some negative black characters, such as insensitive building supervisors and abusive politicians. In "What's Happening!" the Thomas family made do without their con man father after he walked out on them. His occasional visits home were usually in search of money for some new scheme. A steady stream of minority characters began to show up as criminals in cop shows like "Kojak," "Baretta," and "Barney Miller."

The late 1970s retained a mix of ethnic heroes and fools in some of the most popular shows of the day. But ethnic characters were beginning to lose their novelty. During the 1979 season, three dramatic series were launched with black leads, but none came close to the ratings necessary for renewal. "Paris" starred James Earl Jones as a supercop who ran the station house during the day and taught criminology at night. "The Lazarus Syndrome" featured Louis Gossett as the chief of cardiology in a large hospital. "Harris and Company" focused on the problems of a single parent raising a family. The twist was that this black family was held together not by a matriarch but a middle-aged widower. Hollywood was certainly trying to create positive role models for black males, but audiences weren't buying.

Integrated casts and ethnic diversity remained common into the 1980s, but heritage became a less central issue. "Roots: The Next Generation" was a ratings success in 1979, but "Palmerstown, U.S.A." never caught on. This series about the friendship between a black and a white family during the Depression was co-produced by Norman Lear and Alex Haley. Neither the historical setting nor the theme of family life proved sufficient to recapture the magic of "Roots."

Overall, the 1980s offered little that was new to racial or ethnic minority portrayals in the wake of TV's ethnic revival. These groups have continued to be presented more or less as they were in the late 1970s. Despite the continuing presence of racial and ethnic diversity, however, racial themes are no longer in vogue. Integration is assumed as a backdrop, as the prime-arrived, but the thrill is gone. The riots are over, the battle has been won, and characters are getting back to their other plot functions.

Among those functions are crime and other wrongdoing. Shows like "Taxi," "The White Shadow," and "WKRP in Cincinnati," continued to present integrated casts, but new roles were often on the dark side of the law. Cops and robber series like "The A-Team," "Knight Rider," "The Master," "Simon & Simon," and "Magnum P.I." began to present Japanese or Chinese gangs in control of vast criminal operations. Close knit, secretive, and deadly, these gangs formed a crime wave in the early 1980s.

Other crime shows like "Miami Vice," "Hill Street Blues," and "Hunter" presented Hispanic drug lords as a major nemesis. Trafficking in human misery made these characters rich enough to own cities and sometimes even small countries. They were among the nastiest criminals on TV in the 1980s. There were also petty Hispanic criminals in the slums of "Hill Street Blues" and "Cagney & Lacey." These small-time hoods, drug addicts, and pimps were less flamboyant than their big-league counterparts, but no less unsavory. Altogether, TV's latest crop of Hispanics included a cruel and vicious group of criminals.

Blacks fared better in the 1980s, largely escaping the criminal portrayals of other minorities. When black characters did turn to crime, they were usually small-time criminals driven by desperation. There were even times when their criminal acts were presented as social commentary. For instance, in an episode of "Hill Street Blues," a black militant occupies a housing project and takes hostages. He threatens to kill them unless the city agrees to keep the project open and fix it up. The man is frustrated and angry that weeks of negotiating led to nothing. The city simply sets a new closing date and moves on. Rage and desperation drive him to act and a tense standoff ensues. In the end, he is mistakenly shot by a police sniper. Everyone is shocked by his desperate act and his tragic death.

Meanwhile, TV has turned out numerous positive black role models, as diverse as Heathcliff Huxtable of "The Cosby Show," Mary Jenkins of "227," Rico Tubbs of "Miami Vice," and Bobby Hill of "Hill Street Blues." These shows suggest the diversity of major roles now available to blacks. "227," "Amen," and the short-lived "Charlie and Co.," continued the sharp-tongued tradition of 1970s sitcoms, without the abrasive or objectionable images that had brought criticism. A product of Norman Lear's old production company, the show is filled with the sarcasm and social commentary he pioneered. But the social lessons and humor are somewhat subtler and less polemical than earlier Lear creations.

Tubbs and Hill both carried on the tradition of salt-and-pepper law enforcement teams. Hill also represented the educative function of minorities by helping to wean his partner Renko, a Southerner, away from residual racist tendencies. (The racist and slow-witted white Southerner is one stereotype Hollywood still accepts.)

"Cosby" further develops the low-key humanistic color-blind approach that Bill Cosby has popularized over two decades as Alexander Scott in "I Spy," high school teacher Chet Kincaid on "The Bill Cosby Show," and later in a black version of "Father Knows Best." The enormous success of his latest venture has led some critics to snipe at Cosby for playing black characters in whiteface to maximize audience appeal. Black psychiatrist Alvin Pouissant, retained by the show to review scripts for racial authenticity, notes that the criticisms come from white reporters more often than black viewers:

Sometimes it seems they want the show to be "culturally black". . . and sometimes it seems they would be happier to see them cussing out white people, a sort of protest sitcom. Some seem to feel that because the family is middle class with no obvious racial problems, that constitutes a denial or dismissal of the black person.[10]

Moreover, such criticism is belied by the top ten ratings obtained by such diverse families as the Sanfords, Jeffersons, and Evans, not to mention Kunta Kinte and his kin. The success of upper- and lower-class, matriarchal and patriarchal black family series suggests that television has gone beyond using black characters as a sign of racial diversity. It has begun to show diversity within the black community as well, at last recognizing both the cultural distinctiveness and the universal humanity of this group of Americans.

A TALE OF TWO MINORITIES

Our content analysis of characters and themes fleshed out the trends noted in this overview. Before 1965, television was a white world populated mainly by generic northern Europeans, save for the occasional black servant, Italian gangster, or Mexican bandito. Soon thereafter, the spectrum widened to embrace an array of ethnic and cultural traditions. However, various minority groups shared unequally in television's new search for ethnic roots. The disparities that still exist can be illustrated by comparing the roles available to blacks and Hispanics.

Both these minority groups have been underrepresented, but three times as many blacks as Hispanics have appeared on the small screen. Perhaps more important, blacks have gradually progressed from invisibility to integration into TV's fantasy world. Since 1975, nearly one in ten characters has been black, while Hispanics have hovered around the 2 percent mark for three decades. (In real life, about 12 percent of Americans are black and 7 percent are Hispanic.)

The two groups have been portrayed as about equally socially disadvantaged. TV's blacks are only about half as likely as whites to have high school diplomas and middle-class incomes. Hispanics hold upper-status occupations less than half as often as whites, and they are half again as likely to portray unskilled laborers. These occupational figures seem to provide ammunition for those who see TV as reinforcing a white power structure. During the past three decades, whites have portrayed 94 percent of the educated professionals and business executives, blacks have played 5 percent, and Hispanics only 1 percent. Ironically, though, these discrepancies stem partly from television's recent efforts toward sympathetic social realism. The tube turned to the ghetto and the barrio in the 1970s to affirm minority cultures, not to disparage their social status.

On television, at least, demography is not destiny. What blacks on TV lack in social status, they make up in starring roles and positive portrayals. Meanwhile, Hispanic characters span a narrow spectrum from villains to second bananas. Before 1965 we didn't code a single black character in a major role. Since then the proportion of blacks in starring roles has nearly equaled that of whites, at a rate double that of Hispanics. More broadly, black characters attain whatever they strive for more often than either whites or Hispanics. In fact, the failure rate among Hispanics is more than double that of blacks.

The same discrepancy shows up in the functions characters play. As we have seen, few people on television appear in a negative light. Out of every ten characters, about four are good guys, three are partly or wholly negative, and another three play neutral background roles. But blacks wear the most white hats and Hispanics the fewest. Forty-four percent of black characters have been portrayed positively, compared to 40 percent of whites and only 32 percent of Hispanics. Conversely, only 24 percent of blacks have been shown in a negative light, compared to 31 percent of whites and 41 percent of Hispanics. To highlight these differences, we subtracted the percentage of negative from positive characters for each group. That yields figures of +20 for blacks, +9 for whites, and -9 for Hispanics. These relative rankings have remained constant across three decades, except that Hispanics moved up to the level of whites (+4) after 1975, still well behind blacks (+14).

Finally, the more villainous the character, the sharper the group differences. Hispanic characters are twice as likely as whites and three times
as likely as blacks to commit a crime. Over one out of every five Hispanic
characters (22 percent) has been a criminal compared to one out of nine
whites (11 percent) and only one out of fourteen blacks (7 percent).

Perusing these figures, it is hard to resist the conclusion that Hollywood has cracked open the door to black concerns while letting Hispanics
serve as window dressing. No wonder a recent *TV Guide* article was titled,
"There's Lt. Castillo, Sifuentes . . .and Little Else."[11] The "Miami Vice"
cop and "L.A. Law" attorney were not only exceptional as continuing
series characters, but also noteworthy simply for being on the right side of
the law. And "Miami Vice" was also one of television's most reliable sup-
pliers of Hispanic criminals. In Ben Stein's pithy phrase, "To viewers of
'Miami Vice,' 'Cuban = Gangster' is the iron law of immigration."[12]

In a widely noted 1982 episode of "Hill Street Blues," Lieutenant
Calletano was chosen by the department as "Hispanic Officer of the
Year." At the award banquet, however, the Colombian Calletano was
identified as a Puerto Rican and Mexican food was served. Angered, he
launched into a denunciation of continuing prejudice among his self-
satisfied co-workers: "I look around this room. . .and the only other Hispanics I see are waiters and busboys." He might have been speaking on
behalf of all Hispanic characters in the television industry. On the tube
today, Steppin' Fetchit is a distant memory, but "Jose Jimenez" is still alive
and well.

All this illustrates the problematic nature of calls for more "realism"
on television, on the one hand, and for positive role models, on the other.
Organized complaints helped doom "Amos 'n' Andy" and its accompany-
ing stereotypes, but another result was to deprive blacks of their only toe-
hold on the tube for a decade. The return of black characters in the late
1960s at first featured saintly or heroic figures with as little sense of place
or heritage as their generic white counterparts. A more general rejection
of TV's never-never land of the sixties, with its idiot sitcoms and glamorous adventure shows, paved the way for grittier social realism and more
topical scripts pioneered by Lear. Yet grounding TV's black experience in

the ghetto inevitably led to the lower status and criminal roles that embarrassed and angered some activists.

Uneducated and unskilled characters trying to overcome their surroundings proved popular partly because they seemed genuine. By the same token, they inspired fears that their very verisimilitude would reinforce perceptions of those surroundings as appropriate or even inevitable. Moreover, all these debates took place under the Damocles sword of the ratings, not to mention the performers' own career interests. Thus "Good Times" was intended as a warm comedy that reaffirmed the importance of a strong black family unit. But comedian Jimmie Walker was more than ready to hitch his star to the rappin', jivin', good time hipster image that made his character J.J. Evans a celebrity, much to the chagrin of Esther Rolle and John Amos (Florida and James Evans).

Our content analysis provides considerable evidence that writers and producers have been sensitive to issues of stereotyping in casting black roles since the mid-1960s. Not only are black characters shown more positively than whites, but they are considerably less likely to commit crimes. In real life, blacks account for half the murders committed in the United States, and nearly half the murder victims. But there is no impetus to carry "realism" in this direction. Lest this point seem unduly harsh, consider the contrast with Hispanics, a group so far unable to get much of a hearing from Hollywood. Over one out of four Hispanics on TV commits a crime, and this proportion has not receded during the tube's era of rising ethnic consciousness. Despite being outnumbered by three to one, Hispanic characters have committed more murders and other violent crimes than blacks. Once TV's roster of Hispanic stereotypes included the grinning bandito criss-crossed with ammunition belts. These days, "any time a Cuban or Colombian crosses the tube, he leaves a good thick trail of cocaine behind," as Ben Stein observed about "Miami Vice."[13]

Compared to the plight of TV's Hispanics, debates over whether the Huxtables are divorced from the black experience may seem a luxury, a sign that a one-time outgroup has reached a mature phase in its relationship with the Hollywood community. In 1979 organized opposition even persuaded Norman Lear to withdraw a new comedy series at the last minute.

"Mister Dugan," a sitcom about a black congressman, was scheduled to premier on CBS a week after Lear arranged a special screening for the Congressional Black Caucus. The screening was a disaster, with Congressman Mickey Leland calling the lead character "a reversion to the Steppin' Fetchit syndrome." Lear promptly pulled the show from the schedule. He commented:

> We have a high social conscience, and we want to get the story right. We do not favor the short-term gain over the long-term public interest. Dropping the show was an exercise in that commitment.[14]

This was an extraordinary episode in a business often excoriated for caring only about the bottom line. When the medium's most successful producer is willing to withdraw a series on the eve of its broadcast, writing off a $700,000 investment, it shows the power of social commitment in television. The only question is the strength and direction of that commitment.

THE LESSONS OF RACE

The story of minorities on television is more than the sum of minority characters. It is embodied equally in the plots and themes that have addressed racial and ethnic issues. Over the years, television has discussed such issues as assimilation, integration, discrimination, and interracial relationships. At first, these themes dealt mainly with white ethnics, but they were gradually applied to all minorities. When dealing with these complex issues, television's perspectives have remained both consistent and simple—some might say simplistic. The basic message is that everyone, regardless of race, creed, or color, deserves an equal chance at the good things in America. With a little understanding and tolerance, all groups can get along and even flourish in American society. Bigotry and intolerance still exist but can be overcome when people learn more about each other.

The one thing that has changed is TV's judgment about whether minorities should melt into the mainstream or be stirred into the mix without losing their individual flavor. The early messages of assimilation have been replaced by paeans to pluralism and ethnic coexistence. Even prior to 1965, three out of five shows that addressed this theme endorsed respect for pluralism rather than assimilation. But then the balance shifted decisively, with over 90 percent of all later episodes celebrating ethnic diversity. Television's interest in the conflict gradually decreased. It was the only race-related theme to appear less and less frequently as time went on—in seventeen shows before 1965, thirteen more shows through 1974, and only eight shows thereafter. As we shall see, scripts began to treat minority conflicts in ways that bypassed or simply ignored the dilemmas of the melting pot.

In its early years television said very little about discrimination or interracial relationships, since so few racial minorities were included among the casts. Scripts did, however, discuss what was proper for white ethnic characters. High on the list of prescriptions was abandoning native ways to follow American traditions and thus fit into the mainstream. For example, in a segment of "The Roaring 20s," reporter Scott Norris is covering a murder trial when he becomes involved with a family of Montenegran immigrants. The prisoner is convicted but later breaks out of jail to return to his family. Then his young bride attempts suicide. Curious, Norris learns that the marriage was arranged while the bride was still in transit to America, as native custom allows. She arrived to find her husband in prison awaiting execution. While she waited to become a widow, she fell in love with another man. Upon learning of her husband's jail break, she chose suicide rather than face his anger.

While she recuperates in the hospital, Norris tries to find a solution to her problems. He urges her to become more American and buys her new clothes. He encourages her to go out and see New York City with her boyfriend, telling her it is her life to do with as she pleases. All this causes trouble with her family, which is outraged by this break with tradition. The reporter tries to explain that they are in America now, and that means new habits. They insist that their traditional ways are best. Norris continues his efforts on the woman's behalf, but the family remains opposed to divorce and new lifestyles.

The situation comes to a head when the husband returns in a rage, prepared to kill his wife's suitor and anyone else who gets in his way. His rival tells him that he can go on killing for every insult, or he can start living by their new country's rules. The enraged husband finds that Norris has won over the rest of the family to this new attitude. The fugitive refuses to give up his traditions and rushes out into a hail of police gunfire.

Thus assimilation was at first endorsed by television as a central part of the immigrant experience. By the late 1960s, however, calls for assimilation were sounded much less often during prime time. An occasional show still explored traditional folkways and concluded they just weren't right for modern America. This occurred in an episode of "Sanford and Son" in which Lamont tries to recapture his African heritage. Outfitted in a dashiki and a new name, he is ready to be a native African. His father Fred dismisses this as silliness, since their family has been in the U.S. for as long as anyone remembers. Undeterred, Lamont continues to explore African traditions. But this becomes increasingly difficult as he realizes the limitations traditions put on personal choice. Eventually he decides that traditional ways are fine, but they just don't fit into modern America. He agrees with his father that they are more American than African.

Lamont's about-face was unusual, since shows of this period usually extolled other cultures as worthy of admiration or emulation. Since the early 1970s, the prime-time world has been based on pluralism, where minority cultures add vitality and novelty to story lines. Ethnic foods, native costumes, and ethnic festivals have been depicted as celebrations of America's freedom and diversity. In "Taxi," for example, cabbie Latka Gravas's indeterminate East European ethnicity supplied both laughs and interesting story lines. A 1981 segment featured Latka's marriage to a woman from his native land. The proposal is delivered by an intermediary who acts out an elaborate dance and makes a very formal speech that requires predetermined responses from the woman. Once she accepts, the wedding plans begin and they turn out to be as ritualized as the proposal. All of this ritual and nonsensical recitation is observed with great interest and enthusiasm by the cabbies. Despite Latka's own reservations, these traditions are celebrated for their diversity.

Television championed pluralism above assimilation (though to a lesser degree) even in the homogeneous prime-time world of the 1950s. The form was very different from the 1970s version, but the underlying message was always one of acceptance and tolerance for other traditions. We encountered an early example in a 1956 episode of the Western series "Broken Arrow." It featured Tom Jeffords, an army scout assigned to get the U.S. mail through hostile Apache territory. Instead of relying on brute force, he learns Apache ways and negotiates a truce with Cochise. Meanwhile he falls in love with an Indian maiden. Cochise helps to arrange the marriage, and harmony reigns in both domestic and intercultural affairs. Then an evil Indian-hater tries to kill Tom and Cochise. Tom's bride is killed before they can fend off the bushwhackers. In a final gesture of fair play, the noble Cochise stops the furious Tom from killing the only survivor among the renegade whites who attacked them. By the program's end, Tom is appointed commissioner of Indian affairs and a lasting peace is achieved.

This series foreshadowed a standard theme of later shows—different peoples can coexist in harmony if only mindless bigotry is overcome. Throughout the episode, the Apaches are portrayed as decent, fair, ethical people whose traditions happen to differ from those of whites. As Tom puts it, "They live well together and hold their heads high." Tom succeeds through humanity and honesty where others failed through violence and perfidy. This revisionist Western thus presaged television's currently pervasive theme that harmony will spring from heterogeneity. It is a sentiment best proclaimed by the theme song of "Angie," a 1979 sitcom about the marriage of a working-class Italian-American and a Philadelphia Main Liner: "We come to each other from different worlds. . . .We give to each other from our different worlds."

How did television get from the necessary anguish of immigrants learning new ways of life to the cheerful celebration of pluralism without pain? This neat trick was achieved by redefining the problem out of existence. It wasn't necessary to choose between one's personal heritage and the common culture, the tube increasingly proclaimed, because all groups have basically the same makeup and motivations. Any differences that do exist on the basis of ethnic or racial heritage can be worked out with a little good will and mutual understanding. As a corollary to this reassuring portrait, the only real problems in ethnic or race relations are caused by bigotry and ill will. By beating back the occasional outburst of bigotry and demanding equal rights, all minorities can intermingle harmoniously.

The theme of similarities vs. differences among minorities is more easily expressed and far more common than that of assimilation vs. pluralism. It occurred 182 times in the shows studied, and the frequency nearly doubled after 1965. When this issue was raised, similarities between groups were emphasized about three times out of four. When differences were stressed, they were almost always treated as minor obstacles. The tally: 74 percent of shows presented minorities as basically the same, 24 percent said their differences could be worked out, and only 2 percent concluded that group differences were insuperable.

Pluralism Without Pain

Sometimes the message of similarity within ethnic diversity was presented as a human relations lesson. In a 1959 episode of "Father Knows Best," the Andersons' Mexican-American gardener, Frank Smith, is chosen to represent the town by giving a gift to the governor. A committee picked Frank sight unseen because they liked the sound of his "good solid American name." When they discover his Hispanic origins, the town fathers try to dissuade him from making the presentation. The Andersons tell Frank that he is as good an American as anyone and should go through with it. Finally, Frank decides to make the presentation. But he gives the governor a tree instead of the gift selected by the town. He explains that he likes trees, since the different types will all grow next to each other. They grow side by side, and no tree tells another it's not good enough to grow there. This meets with applause from the audience and hearty thanks from the governor.

Common as this sentiment was in the 1950s, it has intensified since the ethnic revival of the mid-1970s. Before 1975, shows stressed similarities over differences two times out of three. Since then it's jumped to seven out of eight. That means the proportion of shows probing ethnically based differences dropped from 32 percent to only 14 percent during the last decade. The trend has been especially strong in shows dealing with black and Hispanic cultures. From the mid-1960s to the mid-1970s, one show in four emphasized their cultural differences from the mainstream. Since 1975 we coded thirty-three shows that pointed up their commonality with other groups and not a single show that stressed their distinctiveness.

As this message became woven into the very premise of many series, the point was often made obliquely. Typical of this approach was the 1970s' sitcom "Chico and the Man," which showed how the young and enterprising Chico Rodriguez and the older mock-cynical Ed Brown could make a success of Ed's garage business (and, by extension, Anglo-Hispanic relations). After actor Freddy Prinze's suicide, the "Chico" character was replaced by Raul Garcia, a young orphan who hides in Ed's car trunk to get from Tiajuana to the United States. The series established a linkage to Chico's enterprising spirit early on. Raul refuses to return because he wants "to become a millionaire in the United States." When Ed tells Raul he can become rich in Mexico, he responds that he wants to be a millionaire "in a stable economy." The show treats this sentiment as a lovable expression of the American dream, and it's clear that Raul will take over where Chico left off in Ed's affections.

When television isn't assuring us that we're all alike underneath our surface differences, it's reassuring us that those differences needn't come between us. In a segment of "All in the Family," a doting Jewish mother is appalled to learn that her son is dating a gentile woman. In a self-dramatizing outburst, she threatens to "drop dead" if the relationship goes too far. Then the voice of reason enters in the form of a mutual friend who reveals that she and her husband, both Christians, are guardians of a young Jewish girl. How is it working out? On television, their answer could only be, "we all love each other."

We found a more exotic expression of the same theme on an episode of "Lou Grant." An Armenian couple complains to Lou that the *Tribune* caused great pain by printing the wedding announcement of their niece and her Turkish fiance. To crusty old Lou, though, Turks and Armenians can work out their differences just like anybody else. If the next generation doesn't act to heal old wounds, he tells them, the world will always be at war.

Once again, television's wisdom on race relations can be summed up in a theme song. (It is tempting to assume that television's wisdom on any topic is summed up in some theme song.) "Diff'rent Strokes" centered around two young black boys from Harlem who were adopted by a rich white man after their mother's death. The song said it all, without apologies to Thoreau: "The world don't move to the beat of just one drum. What might be right for you may not be right for some. . . .It takes diff'rent strokes to move the world."

In light of this development, it comes as no surprise that television has vastly expanded its portrayals of friendship and romance among different ethnic and racial groups. Before 1965, such relationships occurred only about once in every five shows. During the next decade, they were seen in nearly one show in three. Since 1975, they have appeared in almost half of all shows. Overall, we coded 206 such relationships, only one of which was viewed as unacceptable.

Equally dramatic is the increase in interracial personal relations. Before 1965, blacks figured in none of the intergroup relations we coded. From 1965 to 1974, they accounted for 35 percent, and after 1975 for 42 percent. Audiences have watched blacks and whites work and play side by side as equals in schoolrooms from "Welcome Back, Kotter" to "Fame," in hospitals on "Trapper John, M.D." to "St. Elsewhere," in sitcom settings as diverse as "Silver Spoons," "Soap," and "The Love Boat," and in station houses and squad rooms on cop shows of every type, from "Barney Miller" to "Miami Vice." Interracial friendship is now securely woven into the fabric of television entertainment. It is fitting that Bill Cosby recently headed up TV's top-rated show, as we celebrate another anniversary of the unprecedented gamble of "I Spy"—that a black and a white could share the small screen as friends and equals.

Even as television has embraced pluralism, however, it has done so by ignoring its conflicts and dilemmas. In this fantasy of ethnic and racial equality, traditions don't collide and cultures don't clash. People of every

creed and color naturally get along together, aside from the odd burst of
mindless bigotry or misplaced nationalism. Only one out of four relationships among ethnic or racial groups has created problems, and they
have diminished over time, dropping from one out of three before 1975
to one in six thereafter. When there are problems, they are almost always
imposed from the outside. In only 4 percent of all such encounters has
either of the parties created difficulties. Five times as often, any problems
have been partly or wholly the fault of outsiders, social pressures, or
national differences. Relations between blacks and whites are especially
idyllic. Eighty-five percent of these interracial relationships have gone
smoothly, and we never encountered a single case of racial tension that
didn't stem from external pressures.

Not for the tube the tense human drama of blacks and whites confronting their differences in films like "The Defiant Ones." Instead, television blames it on outside agitators or national stereotypes. The comical
Jewish mother who shrinks from a gentile daughter-in-law never gets to
address the problems of preserving one's religious heritage in a mixed
marriage. Nor does George Jefferson discuss the identity problems faced
by children of interracial marriages when he opposes Lionel's marriage to
Jenny Willis. His opposition is presented as simply irrational. He calls
her "the zebra out there," the child of a white father and a black mother.
Similarly, the racially mixed basketball team on "The White Shadow" has
misgivings about hosting a visiting team from the USSR, but everyone
gets along fine. The Soviets give the Americans tee-shirts labeled "peace,"
and their hosts introduce them to native delicacies like twinkies.

As often as not, even the sitcom villains admit to their folly in the
end. Thus "M*A*S*H"'s narrow-minded Boston Brahmin, Major Winchester, tries to prevent his sister's marriage to an Italian-American,
which he sees as the mating of "a fine thoroughbred with Tony the Pony."
Colonel Potter responds angrily that "this is America," and refuses to
grant him leave. But Winchester has a change of heart when he learns
that his sister's prospective in-laws terminated the engagement on religious grounds. Duly chastened, he apologizes to his sister for his own
"narrowness of mind."

Even in Hollywood, racial consciousness can't always be raised this easily. Sixty-eight shows in our sample, about one in nine, dealt with discrimination against minorities, ranging from verbal harassment to murder. Like most other racial and ethnic themes, charges of discrimination heated up after 1965. Previously they occurred only about once in every thirteen shows. Since then, they have shown up in one out of eight shows. Such charges were proved correct three times out of four, a ratio that has remained stable throughout the past three decades. Thus, in a 1971 episode of "All in the Family," Archie Bunker supplemented his usual ethnic epithets with outright job discrimination. Told by his boss to fire someone, Archie has to choose among Stretch (a white), Elmo (a black), and Emmanuel (a Hispanic). In Archie's exchanges with his daughter Gloria and her husband Mike, the script goes to great lengths to puncture Archie's unconvincing denials of bias. First Mike reminds Archie that he said Stretch had an IQ of one. Archie responds wanly that it's improving. When Archie complains that he can't depend on Elmo, Gloria reminds him that Elmo hasn't missed a day of work. Archie, getting flustered, replies, "I can't depend on him keeping it up." As for Emmanuel, "he don't speak no good English, and how can you depend on a guy that don't speak no good English?" Finally, Archie admits that he wants to keep Stretch to avoid irritating his white co-workers—"ya don't know what Stretch means to them." Mike's rejoinder: "Yes I do. White power." Archie eventually fires Emmanuel, who warns him that Stretch's bad work habits will set the job back. The final scene bears this out, as a harried Archie has to live with the consequences of his decision to discriminate.

Although this script made it abundantly clear that Archie's behavior was reprehensible, the Norman Lear approach was basically to humanize bigotry in order to poke fun at it. Many dramatic series used a more hard-hitting approach that bluntly condemned discrimination as inhuman. On the Western "High Chapparal," for instance, a mining company agent put out a bounty on Indian scalps to make the territory safe for development. The plot involved getting the local whites to understand that Apaches are people too. Equally despicable was the villain on a 1971 "Dragnet" who tried to blow up a school rather than see it integrated. He allows that "Hitler had the right idea to keep the races pure. No minorities to cause trouble." Such rantings provoke a characteristically deadpan response from an outraged Sergeant Friday: "You put your walnut-sized brain to work on this. You keep harping about minorities. Well, mister, you're a psycho, and they're a minority too." You don't put over a racist ideology on Joe Friday.

TV has been more willing to condemn racism than to urge specific actions to eliminate it. This is not surprising, since identifying the disease is less controversial than finding the cure. But we did code twelve shows that dealt with appropriate means of redress. Nine of them urged aggressive action, while only three condoned caution. So writers and producers who are willing to step into this minefield at all usually hit it at full stride.

One common means of deflecting controversy was an exotic or historical setting that kept the story from hitting too close to home, though the relevance was always clear. For example, a 1982 episode of "Voyagers" took time-travelers Jeffrey and Phineas back to 1847 Missouri, where they help to free Harriet Tubman from slavery. They enlist the aid of a young boy named Sam Clemens. He is reluctant to help at first, since "the preacher, teacher, and government all say [slavery is] OK." (Young Sam's daring use of future slang suggests his potential as a creative writer.) Then Jeffrey convinces him that the evils of slavery justify opposition to contemporary laws and morals. In a productive day's work, the time-travelers give a boost to both the underground railway and the writing of *Huckleberry Finn*.

Similarly, "The Men from Shiloh" (a.k.a. "The Virginian") adapted modern jurisprudence to 1890s' Wyoming. Ah Sing, the Grainger family's cook, is prevented from opening his restaurant by a bigoted justice of the peace who conjures up images of Tong warfare and opium dens. The cook asks rhetorically, "Does law say no license to anyone with pigtail? . . . Does law say no license to man with last name first or first name last? No, law say give license to anyone willing to work." Spurred by their sense of injustice, the Graingers back Ah Sing's legal battle all the way to the Supreme Court, where their lawyer argues eloquently (if somewhat dubiously), "Your honors, it is unlawful to deny a man the right to work because of the accident of his birth. The end being unlawful, it is equally unlawful to use any means to accomplish that unlawful end. . . . Something that is morally wrong can never be legally right." The court rules that a man cannot be prevented from practicing his profession because of his race, thereby transporting a twentieth-century legal victory back into the Old West.

Perhaps the most unlikely blow against inequality was struck by the Impossible Mission Force. In one episode, the high-tech heroes are called upon to free a black rebel from a repressive white government very reminiscent of South Africa, complete with racial purity guidelines and pass laws. The prisoner was captured when he stole a gold shipment from the government to finance a revolution. The government is portrayed as so despicable that there is never any question about the appropriateness of helping the revolutionaries. The I.M. Force sets up an especially nasty army officer to take the fall for the theft by first convincing him that he has black ancestors, then giving him a drug to turn him black, and finally incriminating him as an agent of the rebellion. Then they spirit the real black leader away before the government or the audience can sort out the confusion.

Labored as such plots may be, they were clearly intended to strike a blow against racism during a period of domestic racial strife and controversy. The blows may have been cushioned by the need to distance the settings from contemporary controversies such as busing and affirmative action, but they seem nonetheless heartfelt. Moreover, the stories were in keeping with television's optimistic perspective that only clear-cut bigotry stands in the way of a pluralistic paradise. This suggests the secret of television's vision of pluralism without pain. It's a throwback to the 1950s liberal view that cultures and traditions should be respected, even celebrated, as a kind of exotic or colorful backdrop to life, but they shouldn't interfere with the abstract "humanity" that we all share. The only threat to racial and cultural harmony comes from the prejudice or narrow- mindedness that would deny this humanity to minorities or other outgroups.

Scripts almost never treat racial and ethnic tensions as an inevitable outgrowth of a multiracial society, not merely a product of foolish misunderstanding or blind hatred. Of course, television has never purported to represent real life. On the set of a recent TV movie purporting to recreate the immigrant experience, one actor commented on the difference between life and popular art:

> My character marries an Irish Catholic woman, loves an aristocratic American Jewess, becomes good friends with a black man and an Irishman, and strikes up a working relationship with an aristocratic Frenchman. . . .My grandfather, on the other hand, set up his family in a Greek community. . .and pretty much socialized with other Greeks.

Critic Martha Bayles observed wryly, "Thus do the TV networks rewrite history to look as much as possible like a beer commercial."[15]

Perhaps TV's wisdom on race relations was best summed up in a 1980 episode of "Mork and Mindy." This series used the familiar device of an alien visitor to get audiences to look at themselves through different eyes. When Mork, who knows nothing of racial prejudice, encounters a hate group modeled after the Ku Klux Klan, Mindy gives him (and us) an extensive lecture on the evils of discrimination. "We're all created equal," she explains. "It's easier to put down someone who is different than understand him." Mork is sufficiently impressed that he waxes eloquent to his Orkan superior on the virtues of pluralism: "When you mix all earthlings together, you get this incredible rainbow. Everyone has his pot of gold."

———◦◦◦———

11

THE ESTABLISHMENT

Just two good ol' boys
Wouldn't change if they could
Fightin' the system like two
Modern day Robin Hoods

        —"Dukes of Hazzard" theme song

D oes television serve the establishment or subvert it? Critics on the Left have long held that TV entertainment is at best a tool and at worst a handmaiden of the power elite. Sociologist Muriel Cantor speaks for many of her colleagues in labelling TV as "one of the most conservative of media—an instrument of social control. . . ."[1] In this version, prime-time shows uphold the status quo by reinforcing the hegemony of conservative groups and institutions. On the other side are conservatives who see the world of prime time as a corrosive agent stripping away the legitimacy of traditional values and leaders. In Ben Stein's words:

> Groups that. . .have leadership or power roles—business-
> men, bankers, government leaders, military men, religious
> figures—are treated as bad or irrelevant, while underdog
> groups—the poor and criminals—are treated as deeply
> sympathetic.[2]

On the evidence from earlier chapters, both sides seem overstated. No agent of social control in a capitalist society would attack business or ridicule bosses as regularly and gleefully as TV entertainment does. On the other hand, we found few echoes of "Bonnie and Clyde" on prime time. Scriptwriters are less likely to vilify criminals than in Jack Webb's heyday, but they rarely convey deep sympathy or otherwise idealize their behavior. And, of course, these are only two of many dimensions of ideological division. So the question remains open. Apart from treating business as a *bête noir*, how does television portray other traditional powerholders and institutions? In this chapter we will consider three pillars of the establishment—government, the military, and religion. In each case we will examine how both individuals and institutions are portrayed.

POLITICS AS USUAL

Imagine the *Variety* headline: "Picked-on Pols Protest!" Over the years every minority group from homosexuals to fundamentalist Christians has complained about its ill-treatment by TV entertainment. It was only a matter of time before politicians would jump on the bandwagon. In a 1985 article in *TV Guide*, U.S. Senators (and occasional novelists) Gary Hart and William Cohen complained that the tube portrays *homo politicus* as someone "made up in equal parts of stupidity and cupidity."

Where's the beef? For Hart and Cohen, it's that "lawmakers are depicted wheeling and dealing. . .or going to parties where a Carrington or a Ewing slips them a few thousand for the campaign."[3] To counteract this canard, they invited writers and producers to come to Washington, where they could meet the "diligent, hard-working and conscientious" public officials the authors say they work with every day.

Good luck, fellows. Maybe your next spy thriller will catch some producer's eye and give us a TV portrait of the "real" Washington. Or maybe ex-Senator Hart will script his own life story as a miniseries, now that his typical day turns out to have been more interesting than he made it seem in *TV Guide*. Until then, Hollywood is likely to continue its time-honored tradition of pol-bashing. Our study found that politicians have the worst image of any occupational group on television. They're the only group to contain a majority of bad guys. On the other hand, there have been quite a few concerned or crusading politicians as well. We counted 40 percent positive pols among this group, compared to 51 percent who played negative roles. So, it's not all politicians who wear black hats, just a much higher proportion than the prime-time norm. Subtracting the percentage of negative from positive portrayals yields a -11 figure, the only occupation other than business to land in the negative column.

This didn't start with Boss Hogg. Our elected representatives were treated just as badly thirty years ago as they are today. For the decade 1955-1964, political characters rated a -15 total; since 1975 they've been cruising at -14. These negative bookends surround a brief positive period for government officials and aspirants. From 1965 through 1974 they actually enjoyed a positive plurality of +6, as Hollywood brought some crusading outsiders into the political system to solve the social maladies scriptwriters had suddenly discovered.

Throughout these three decades, television's ballot featured a ticket of wheeler-dealers, corrupt evildoers, and honest crusaders. The types haven't changed much over the years. Only the mix has varied. The early 1960s featured a host of hard-nosed manipulators who reveled in the exercise of power. Sometimes their frenetic machinations served constituents or noble causes. More often they were either Machiavellian empire builders or the lackeys of shadowy power brokers. Various corrupt pols and influence peddlers were regular targets of crusading reporters on "Target: The Corruptors" and "Saints & Sinners"; likewise the crusading lawyers of "Cain's Hundred" and "The Defenders."

As early as 1955 our sample picked up a corrupt politician on the "Schlitz Playhouse of Stars." The plot concerns a young man who is framed for the murder of a woman. The man behind the frame-up turns out to be Art Healy, a ward boss in the local machine. It seems that Healy was romantically involved with the dead woman. When her father objected to the relationship, Healy had him killed. He covered up the murder by committing another old man to a nursing home in the father's name. When the woman attempted to blackmail Healy with this information, he had her killed too. Then he set up the young man to take the fall. One thing does lead to another in politics.

The politician as wheeler-dealer was typified by an unusual segment of "The Adventures of Jim Bowie." This 1957 historical adventure managed to present politicians as corrupt manipulators while endowing them with a rather winning raffish quality. The plot involves Bowie's efforts to gain power and influence by securing a racehorse for President Andrew Jackson. As the story opens, Bowie is telling one Senator Holcomb about the campaigning he did for both Holcomb and Jackson. Holcomb responds that "such loyalty should not go unrewarded." He tells Bowie that Jackson has "a very deep sense of gratitude. So deep, in fact, that his enemies label his devotion to his friends as the spoils system." He then offers Bowie the office of Collector for the Port of New Orleans in exchange for procuring a favorite racehorse for the president. Holcomb's pitch presses all the right buttons. "Think of the prestige, my boy, not to mention the fortune for a man of your talents." This last is accompanied by a knowing look.

Bowie is hooked and sets off to buy the horse. When the owner turns out to be a Whig, Bowie smoothly gets around his own suddenly inconvenient campaign record. "You must be confusing me with my brother," he lies, "the black sheep of the family—has funny ideas about politics." To get the money he needs, Bowie casts his lot with his friend Sam Houston, who is portrayed here as a local politician. In the end, however, Houston double crosses him, steals the horse, and rides off to give it to the president himself. The upshot is that Bowie is a novice at politics who is outmaneuvered by a real pro. It's not exactly a tale for the civics texts.

But even then, video politicians could sometimes be good guys. For example, the 1962 season featured Fess Parker in the TV version of "Mr. Smith Goes to Washington." The hero, Senator Eugene Smith, charmed the sophisticated capital with his homespun homilies and aw-shucks rustic good nature. Unfortunately, the series lacked the bite of the Capra original, to put it mildly. It better resembled "Davy Crockett Goes to Congress," complete with Smith's guitar-picking Uncle Cooter in the Buddy Ebsen sidekick role.

More typical of TV's crusading politician was the 1964 series "Slattery's People." James Slattery was the idealistic and reform-minded minority leader of a state legislature. In an episode we coded, he jeopardizes his reelection chances by defending an old friend accused of past communist associations. This early prototype of the politician as progressive crusader really blossomed during the early 1970s. Two series were built around idealistic political leaders who regularly locked horns with the establishment in their efforts to serve the public. One was "The Senator," played by Hal Holbrook, before he became Deep Throat in "All the President's Men." Senator Hayes Stowe was for a better world, a cleaner environment, better consumer protection, and any other vaguely progressive cause that wouldn't prove too controversial for NBC executives. He was against entrenched interests (usually represented by business lobbyists) and the dread specter of politics as usual.

While Holbrook was cleaning up Washington, Mayor Thomas Jefferson Alcala was protecting his constituents from machine politicians and an unfeeling bureaucracy in a thriving Southwest metropolis. (The series, "The Man and the City," was filmed in Albuquerque.) Anthony Quinn played Alcala as a kind of Zorba the Hispanic, exuding charismatic vitality from every pore as he rushed around governing and empathizing. A 1971 episode in our sample was typical. A distraught mother asks Tom to help her son, who was picked up by the police after two officers were shot in an ambush. When Tom discovers the boy is being held incommunicado, he demands that they release him. When his acting police chief objects, Tom replies, "You can't suspend the law," and more heatedly, "In my city we go by the rules."

Meanwhile Tom has to deal with a city council that wants to crack down on unrest in the Hispanic community. He reluctantly interviews their preferred candidate for police chief, a man named Wheeler (as in wheeler-dealer). This establishment candidate favors "aggressive police work, some preventive measures, and curfews for troublesome areas" (by implication, high-crime minority areas). This leads to an exchange that further establishes Tom's liberal credentials:

373

Tom: "Doesn't the curfew restrain freedom?"
Wheeler: "It's for the good of the community."
Tom: "Do they willingly give up the freedom and really
        have a choice?"
Wheeler: "The curfew is inconvenient but necessary."
Tom: "Isn't law and order without justice meaningless?"

Eventually Tom manages to help catch the killers without succumbing to the arguments of the law-and-order crowd. Unlike the backbiting pols on the city council, he's willing to take unpopular stands to preserve individual rights. And in the end his judgment is vindicated. Like "The Senator," though, this mayor is a quintessential maverick. His character is defined in opposition to the traditional, self-serving politicians who surround him. He embodies not politics as usual but politics as it might be carried on by men of courage and principle.

Counterbalancing the politics of principle are the politics of corruption practiced by many a villain on dramatic series. For example, a 1968 episode of "Bonanza" involved system-wide corruption in the Bureau of Indian Affairs. The Cartwrights protect a witness against the eight top men in the bureau, who are all involved in land fraud. Their efforts to stop his testimony range from a $50,000 bribe attempt to kidnapping and attempted murder. In fact, a subplot concerns the Cartwrights' efforts to win the witness's trust. He's been sold out so many times by government officials that he assumes they're on the take as well.

This dark side of political life increasingly captured Hollywood's attention after the mid-1970s. More than ever, cop shows featured venal or unethical politicians involved in various conflicts of interest, bribery schemes, and sexual shenanigans. The typical script pitted a maverick cop against a scheming pol allied with business or criminal interests. By the 1980s, evil politicians were de rigueur on the prime-time soaps. "Flamingo Road" featured the highly sexed Fielding Carlyle, while "Knots Landing" offered mob-connected Gregory Sumner. Neither bore much resemblance to the civics book model of a state legislator. Even NBC's short-lived "Grandpa Goes to Washington," a variation of the old "Mr. Smith" maverick politician theme, presented corruption as the norm. Retired professor Joe Kelley was the unlikely victor in a Senate race where both major party candidates were exposed as crooks. Kelley's platform was honesty in government, which the series treated as a scarce commodity.

The other recent trend has been toward foolish or bumbling politicians in comic roles. Thus "Benson" took charge of his well-meaning but inept boss Governor James Gatling. "Hail to the Chief" presented a White House so sex-crazed that TV critic Tom Shales commented, "After watching it, one may feel the compulsion to disinfect the television set with Lysol."[4] The champion of this lightweight clan was Boss Hogg, the blustery county commissioner and political boss of Hazzard County on "The Dukes of Hazzard." Hogg's weekly schemes and fulminations against the Duke boys were like Wile E. Coyote's futile efforts to catch the Road Runner. In a 1980 episode we viewed, Hogg's plan to foreclose on an automotive show depends on his keeping the Dukes from competing. So he orders his dimwitted minion, county sheriff Roscoe Coltrane, to get rid of their car "any way you can, legal or otherwise." After Roscoe impounds the car on trumped-up charges, Hogg sends it to the crusher. When the Dukes rescue it in the nick of time, he orders their arrest for grand theft, auto. When all else fails, Hogg tells Roscoe to stop the show by arresting someone. On what charge? "Invent one."

Beyond looking at particular politicians, we asked how television was portraying the political system. One recurring theme was that politics is a selfish business. Political decisions stem from either narrow self-interest or shameless pandering to special interest groups. Twenty-one shows presented some version of this theme, with the majority appearing since 1975. Not a single show rebutted it. (The crusading politicians were invariably cast as mavericks or outsiders who had to battle politics-as-usual to protect the public.) Politics per se is never credited with serving the public interest. For example, a 1981 segment of "Lou Grant" revolved around the Los Angeles pollution control board. One member tries to end the board's practices of giving waivers to any company that will aid the city's economic development. The other board members outmaneuver him, however, and his fight for clean air falls victim to the cozy partnership between business and government regulators.

Although television condemns political selfishness, it isn't quite ready to write off the whole system as corrupt. Of thirty-eight shows that raised the issue of honesty versus corruption, 58 percent portrayed the system as fundamentally honest. The picture has darkened, however, in recent years. Prior to 1975, the episodes we watched endorsed the system's honesty by a two-to-one ratio. Since then, visions of honest and corrupt politics have been shown in precisely equal numbers. This shift reflects the disappearance of political crusader shows after the early 1970s and the sharper focus on dirty politics since then.

Even when television affirms the system, it's not without a struggle. Back in 1961, "Target: The Corruptors" devoted an episode to lobbyists. The opening narration set the tone:

> The business of making laws by which the citizen is bound is almost an impossible task at best. At worst it can be a criminal activity of shocking proportions—when controlled by lobbyists who exceed their legal limitations. . . . Fortunately most state legislatures are comprised of men of high caliber. . .honest men the corruptors haven't been able to buy. But where money proves useless, those forces of evil that can't afford to have honest obstacles stand in their way have other means of chasing these paths.

Following this portentous voice-over, the audience sees two thugs enter a state senator's office, knock him out, and throw him out the window to his death. Politics seems to be a tough game. Then that crusader for all seasons, an investigative reporter, discovers that the murder was orchestrated by a powerful lobbyist with ties to organized crime. It turns out that the mob wants the legislature to keep the state "dry" to preserve their control over the illegal liquor trade. The lobbyist is arrested and honest politics prevails, but only after a muckraking attack on the power of lobbyists. This is typical of television's treatment of "special interests" as a blight on the political landscape rather than a legitimate facet of representative government. At best they are a necessary evil, at worst a corrosive agent attacking the democratic system. Good-guy politicians are often allied with vaguely defined reformist forces locked in battle with the special interests.

The problem of corrupt government and politicians became even more pronounced in the 1970s and 1980s. In the early years, corruption was often mob connected. By the 1970s corruption tended to be either for personal gain or political power. There was also an element of international intrigue. An episode of "Airwolf," a mid-1980s action-adventure series, highlighted this idea. The villains were a congressman and an industrialist who conspired to build an attack helicopter. The payoff? They both stood to make a fortune through the illegal sale of the weapon abroad.

There was also increased attention to the work of special interests in government. Major corporations or powerful individuals were seen manipulating politicians, undercutting political opponents, and so on. All this stripped away what little luster remained from the role of public servant. The results were clear in a "Scarecrow and Mrs. King" episode we viewed. The story was inspired by a real-world struggle over industrial pollution that threatened marine life in the Chesapeake Bay off the coast of Maryland. A politician has received financial backing from a major fishing company. In return, he must block any bills restricting the company's operations on the bay. The politician can't keep his promise in good conscience. He begins working with other lobbyists who want to "Save the Bay" (a popular environmentalist bumper sticker in real life). When all else fails, the company has the politician killed rather than lose its profitable position.

Perhaps the most pointed commentary on politics that we came across was from "Good Times," a Norman Lear comedy set in a black ghetto. In an episode we coded, the local alderman threatens to evict the Evans family from a public housing project if J.J. doesn't make a reelection speech for him. The entire episode is peppered with bitter jokes about politicians who break the faith. Sample: A new dress is billed as "the election special." Why? "It's cut real low, making all kinds of promises you know you're not going to keep." As the episode progresses, alderman Davis keeps the pressure on by sending prospective tenants to look at the Evans' apartment. When Thelma Evans complains that there must be laws against this, her mother answers that it's politicians like Davis who make the laws. In the end, the threat evaporates, but the family matriarch Florida Evans directs one final aside to the audience: "That's the sad thing. As long as there are aldermen like Fred Davis, people like us will always live here in the ghetto." The unmistakable message is that wretched housing conditions in the slums are the product of political corruption.

In recent years the good-guy politician has virtually disappeared from the screen. In fact, politicians are rarely found as continuing characters anymore, aside from the occasional schemer who provides subplots on the evening soaps. This undoubtedly reflects the conspicuously low ratings of shows that star political figures. Political series have rarely lasted longer than a single season. Those that enjoy longer runs are usually domestic comedies with political backdrops.

This trend goes back to "The Farmer's Daughter" in the mid-1960s. It was the story of Katrin Holstrum, a simple farm girl who became governess to widowed Congressman Glen Morley. Her lack of pretension and common sense were intended as a welcome contrast to the stuffiness of official Washington. But the series was only peripherally concerned with Glen's political causes and career. The real question was whether wedding bells would ring for Glen and "Katy." They finally chimed in the show's third season, but the Nielsen voters declined to bring back Mr. and Mrs. Morley for a fourth term.

A few years later "The Governor and J.J." tried a generation gap variant on this domestic format. J.J. was the governor's young daughter, who presided as first lady. When the show seemed in danger of actually addressing political issues, it could always cut to cute animal stories, courtesy of J.J.'s regular job as a zoo curator. Among recent offerings, there is only "Benson," who earned his bona fides as a butler before assuming a functionally similar backstage role to Governor Gatling as budget director and majordomo. And it is Benson, not the governor, around whom the series revolves.

Several other recent series built around government officeholders have quickly disappeared. "Fortune Dane" was a standard cop show with a twist. The rough, tough Dane reported directly to hard-nosed Mayor Amanda Harding, who was always concerned with the practical politics of law enforcement. The show addressed current legal/political topics, like the sanctuary movement, during its brief run in 1986. Another short-lived effort from the same season was "He's the Mayor," a comedy about a young black mayor who lived with his father, a maintenance man at city hall. Then there was Norman Lear's stillborn effort at a comedy about a bumbling black congressman. As we noted in chapter 10, the Congressional Black Caucus started a recall campaign and the project was stillborn. On television, it seems that politics, like satire, is what closes on Saturday night.

B*A*S*HING THE BRASS

Television's service record started strongly. In the beginning there was Bilko. Master Sergeant Ernest Bilko was the quintessential fast- talking conman. His hopeless victims usually recognized too late the warning signals implicit in his name and explicit in his manner. He regularly ran circles around his bumbling army superiors, especially dim-witted Colonel Hall, the ostensible commanding officer at Fort Baxter. Bilko's frenetic efforts to score with some scam inevitably ran afoul of both the brass and the bureaucracy, in the grand tradition of service comedy. By transferring Borscht Belt vaudeville routines to a Kansas army base, comedian Phil Silvers created one of TV's golden age comic icons, a worthy rival to Lucy and Ralph Kramden.

It may seem surprising that no one in this copycat industry raced to clone Bilko. But "The Phil Silvers Show" (a.k.a. "You'll Never Get Rich" and "Sgt. Bilko") was one of those nostalgic favorites that never really hit its stride with audiences until it went into syndication. During its run from 1955 through 1959, it never made the year-end Nielsen top twenty. In fact, it was often beaten in its own time slot by competitors like "Cheyenne" and Bob Hope (although "Bilko" did knock

Milton Berle right off television). So there was no immediate rush to copy the Bilko formula.

The short-term singularity of "Sgt. Bilko" was significant. It ensured that TV's main military images would come from dramatic series. And these images were 180 degrees removed from Silvers' service send-ups. The earliest military dramas provided quasi-documentary portraits of realistic people and real-life situations. Few viewers remember CBS's original lead-in to "Bilko," an adventure series called "Navy Log." Yet it lasted three full seasons, only one less than the more celebrated master sergeant. "Navy Log" was an anthology whose scripts were based on actual incidents from official navy files. The producers worked in cooperation with the Navy Department. One memorable segment, on the sinking of PT-109, featured Senator John Kennedy as a special guest. "Navy Log"'s counterpart on dry land had an even more impressive official pedigree. "West Point Story" was produced with the help of the Defense Department, the U.S. army, and the U.S. Military Academy. Once again, stories were drawn from actual incidents in the lives of West Point cadets throughout the academy's history.

These shows focused on intimate human drama within the context of a military setting. They were not flag-waving paeans to military engagement, but they did uphold the military's traditions and authority structure. Indeed, they usually took such things for granted while focusing on individual conflicts that conveyed themes about the need for teamwork, the nature of courage, and the like. For example, we coded a 1955 "Navy Log" about Lt. "Robbie" Robinson, a very cautious photo interpretation officer aboard an aircraft carrier during World War II. Some of the pilots, a gung ho group, suspect that his caution in planning operations stems from personal cowardice. As a cruel joke, they convince him that he's been reassigned to the underwater demolition team, a high-risk activity. To everyone's surprise, Robbie calmly accepts the idea. The embarrassed pilots admit their prank to the captain, who dresses them down. Then he salvages the situation by telling Robbie that he's past the age limit and won't be allowed to take on the mission. The episode's moral is contained in the captain's reprimand to Robbie's abashed tormentors:

Don't think for one minute that Rob's caution is for himself. It's for the benefit of all of us. His caution reflects on the success we've been having in our [air] strikes. . . . Rob has courage since he knew his best work was here, but in the final analysis he put aside his usual caution and his personal fear to volunteer for a mission we all know would have been unwise. . . . Caution and courage always average out in our favor. Reckless courage? Well, I wonder.

The message is that courage shouldn't be identified with bravado, and quiet courage should be recognized and respected. The social context is also important—the success of the military's mission depends upon the "Robbies" as well as the Audie Murphys and Sergeant Yorks. Finally, note that the military authority structure is reaffirmed. Not only does Robbie accept his presumed mission, regardless of personal risk, but the commanding officer sorts out the problems and delivers the moral to the story. There are no fast-talking sergeants and dithering colonels in this squadron.

The low-key intimacy of these early dramas soon gave way to a cycle of more glamorous action-adventure series with World War II settings. The first and most successful of the foxhole dramas was "Combat!" which premiered in 1962 and lasted until 1967. It was straight wartime adventure, pitting a U.S. army platoon against the Germans after D-Day. Unusual touches of realism included actual battle footage and a week of genuine boot camp training for the cast. Cut from the same mud-spattered mold was "The Gallant Men," which concerned an infantry division fighting in Italy about the same time. Unfortunately, the Italian campaign was abbreviated by the series' cancelation after a single season.

The setting moved to the wild blue yonder in "12 O'clock High," which detailed the exploits of American bomber crews based in England. This series was notable for presenting general officers as heroic figures. Most of television's wartime dramas have concentrated on enlisted men and junior grade officers in the field, relegating the top brass to headquarters off screen. But square-jawed General Frank Savage personally piloted a bomber on high-risk raids over German territory. Indeed, the risks proved so high that he was killed in action during the series' second season.

Ironically the fierce Marine Corps tradition was represented only by "The Lieutenant," which focused on the peacetime activities of a newly minted officer at Camp Pendleton. This series was notable for the relationship between the young lieutenant, Bill Rice, and his immediate superior, Captain Ray Rambridge. Rambridge rode the young lieutenant hard and sometimes made his life miserable. His purpose, however, was a noble one—to force his subordinate to learn the skills and discipline to become a good officer.

The military adventure series was a phenomenon of the early 1960s. "Rat Patrol," set in the North African campaign, was the only member of the genre to be launched successfully after 1964. "Combat!" and "12 O'clock High" were canceled in 1967, and "Rat Patrol" bit the Saharan dust a year later. In their place came a steady stream of service comedies that proved a prime-time staple, without ever really dominating the airwaves.

The comic invasion was led by "McHale's Navy," a seaborne version of "Bilko." Ernest Borgnine played the Phil Silvers role of lovable con-man caught in the military bureaucracy. Although Lt. Commander McHale ranked higher than his master sergeant predecessor, he commanded a similar crew of cutups who carried on get-rich-quick schemes under the nose of a bumbling superior. "McHale" appeared in 1962, three years after "Bilko"'s demise, and lasted until 1966. By that time a spate of service comedy settings had run the gamut from Old West cavalry troops ("F Troop") to modern-day astronauts ("I Dream of Jeannie"). Other nautical formats included "Ensign O'Toole" and "Broadside," which featured a company of navy WAVES. The punning title gives some indication of that series' comic style, which might itself be delicately described as broad.

"F Troop" took the formula to the Western outpost of Fort Courage, where the inept Captain Parmenter was constantly outwitted by Sergeant O'Rourke, another lovable conman. O'Rourke signed his own treaty with the local Indians, which gave him the franchise to market their artifacts to the tourist trade. The tribe featured such unlikely guest warriors as Wise

Owl (Milton Berle) and Bald Eagle (Don Rickles), who wandered in from the Catskill reservation. "Hogan's Heroes" altered the Bilko formula slightly by using a German POW camp commandant as the incompetent authority figure. Needless to say, the American prisoners ran circles around the bumbling Colonel Klink, whose resemblance to Erich von Stroheim's archetypal POW commandant in "Grand Illusion" ended with their mutual monocle.

Other comic formats were also well represented. "Gomer Pyle" relied on the stereotype of the good-hearted foul-up whose naivete both charms and frustrates his superiors. The foil for Private Gomer Pyle's well-intentioned misdeeds was Sergeant Carter, whose own stereotype was the hard-nosed but soft-hearted Marine drill sergeant. This series was a spinoff from "The Andy Griffith Show." Ironically, the Gomer character picked up the man-child yokel role that first brought Griffith stardom as a private first class in "No Time for Sergeants." Meanwhile, "I Dream of Jeannie" provided an Air Force setting for a fractured relationship between astronaut Tony Nelson and a curvaceous and somewhat scatterbrained genie. At the time, the series made the two-thousand-year-old genie (Barbara Eden) into a minor sex symbol. In retrospect it serves as a cautionary parable that the all-American Captain Nelson (Larry Hagman) could undergo his own magical transformation into the evil J.R. Ewing.

These service comedies were popular throughout the later 1960s. But the spirit of the sixties was most fully realized within the military format in a show that premiered in 1972, gradually picked up popularity, and rolled right into the 1980s, when its finale became the most widely viewed series episode of all time. "M*A*S*H" was spawned by a 1970 antiwar film comedy set in a Korean War medical unit. Despite the Korean setting, the sensibility and situations were straight out of the Vietnam experience, right down to the actors' hairstyles (including Elliot Gould's fashionably rebellious Fu Manchu mustache). The movie pushed service comedy conventions to new limits, using them to subvert the notion of military authority rather than gently poking fun at it. For example, the "regular army" authority figure was not just the usual blustering bumbler and comic

foil. Instead, Major Frank Burns was a supercilious fanatic who eventually went over the edge into a well-deserved psychotic breakdown.

The TV version softened the corrosive spirit of the original without
losing its antiwar and anti-establishment edge. TV's "M*A*S*H" began
as a hybrid of the original Robert Altman black comedy and the old Bilko
conventions. Its lighthearted and sybaritic heroes, Capts. Hawkeye
Pierce and Trapper John McIntyre, flouted military discipline and ran the
usual rings around their nominal superior, Lt. Col. Henry Blake, while
pursuing nurses, liquid nourishment, and good times. But the series soon
moved from the traditional sitcom format to an innovative comedy-
drama structure that allowed for character development, multiple plot
lines, and Hawkeye's musings on the futility and immorality of war.

This was something new—a service comedy about draftees who
questioned and, when possible, subverted the military system. All the
while they performed their own jobs with professional effectiveness.
Their status as military doctors allowed them to carry on their work of
saving lives while criticizing the military's mission of taking lives. As the
series developed, casting and scripting changes turned some of the card-
board comic foils into more credible and complex characters. The inept
Colonel Blake was replaced by Colonel Potter, who was not only more
competent but occasionally even exercised discipline. The dithering and
ineffectual Father Mulcahy became a more rounded character whose very
earnestness leavened his bromides.

Through all the changes, however, the show never lost its antimilitary viewpoint. The good guys knew that army regulations were made to
be broken. The Frank Burns character remained a laughable (but no
longer evil) Colonel Blimp. In 1977 the Burns role was replaced by Major
Charles Emerson Winchester, a stuffy Boston brahmin who substituted
aristocratic arrogance for Burns' bureaucratic rigidity. Nonetheless, the
TV version softened the visceral and somewhat sour anti-authority tone
of the Altman original to attain a more complex, and occasionally even
moving, portrait of unwilling soldiers joking to keep death at bay.

The show's appeal was so universal that its fans included the likes of
former General (and Secretary of State) Alexander Haig and conservative

columnist James Kilpatrick, who admitted to a special fondness for Frank Burns.[5]   Ironically, one avowed nonfan was retired Marine surgeon Richard Hornberger, who wrote the book on which "M*A*S*H" was based. Amidst the kudos attending the show's final episode in 1983, the real-life "Hawkeye" disavowed the Hollywood version. He complained that his work was "only antiwar in the minds of a lot of flaky people. . .and I know more about war than a bunch of undereducated actors who go around blathering those sanctimonious, self-righteous noises."[6]

Television's second wave of service comedies followed on the heels of "M*A*S*H"'s rise in the Nielsen ratings. Their middling success, however, only confirmed the singularity of the original. Some of the new entries tried to milk the military format with the ethnic humor that pervaded 1970s' sitcoms. "Roll Out" chronicled a WWII army transport unit made up mostly of blacks and headed by Captain Rocco Calvelli. Their success in getting supplies to the front lines usually depended on their inventiveness in breaking the rules to get things done. "C.P.O. Sharkey" featured comic Don Rickles as a navy chief petty officer. Rickles's specialty of insult humor was channeled into ethnic jokes about his motley crew of new recruits like Kowalski, Mignone, Apodaca, and Rodriguez. Of course, Sharkey's tough exterior housed a heart of gold. The real heavy (naturally) was his blustering superior Lieutenant Whipple.

Other entrants tried to follow "M*A*S*H"'s example by imitating successful feature films. Like "Mr. Roberts" before them, however, "Operation Petticoat" and "Private Benjamin" perished from a fatal lack of star power, not to mention scripts that relied on jokes about buxom nurses in small submarines and the like. The series that came closest to "M*A*S*H"'s anti-establishment ethos was "Baa, Baa Black Sheep." This was a comic turn on the "Dirty Dozen" movie formula of putting foul-ups and misfits together for a dangerous mission. The "black sheep" were a WWII squadron of Marine Corps fliers who were reprieved from court martials in order to scramble against the Japanese in the South Pacific. Like the surgeons of "M*A*S*H," they combined womanizing, practical jokes, drinking, and gambling with highly professional behavior when needed. The unit's Hawkeye was Major

"Pappy" Boyington, and the resident incompetent authority figure was the aptly named Colonel Lard.

Apart from "M*A*S*H," none of these second-wave service sitcoms established a firm identity or foothold in the ratings. The cycle died a natural and perhaps merciful death with the quick failure of "At Ease," a self-conscious attempt to revive the "Bilko" formula. This sitcom featured not one but two negative authority figures. Colonel Clapp took the bumbling Colonel Hall role, while Major Hawkins was a security chief cut from the Frank Burns martinet mold. Like "Operation Petticoat" without Cary Grant, however, "Bilko" without Phil Silvers quickly went bust.

In the early 1980s it was inevitable that military characters would find their way into the popular nighttime soap format. Far less predictable was a series built around a sympathetic portrait of a career air force officer. But that's exactly what "Call to Glory" provided in a drama about a fighter pilot, Col. Raynor Sarnac, and his family during the early 1960s. Though the series never really caught on, it won plaudits from conservatives for its endorsement of patriotic virtues.

Elsewhere it was business as usual, with the brass wearing the black hats. "For Love and Honor," set on a contemporary army base, revolved around the bigoted commander of an airborne unit and his alcoholic and adulterous wife. "Emerald Point N.A.S." added that old standby, the unscrupulous big businessman, to the usual stew of steam and schemes at a naval air station. Brooks and Marsh call it "the usual mix of maneuvering for power, sleeping around, and horrible revelations about flawed characters with hidden pasts, along with the intrigue added by the military setting."[7]

By the late 1980s the new vogue for "realistic" drama merged with renewed interest in the Vietnam War to produce the first combat-oriented prime-time shows since the early 1960s. "Tour of Duty" follows an infantry platoon through its daily grind of fear and frustration. "China Beach" focuses on an evacuation hospital and recreation center. More naturalistic and graphic than their predecessors, these series sometimes tread a fine line between criticizing the war's rationale and upholding the integrity of the common soldier. The military is no joke here, as it often was in "M*A*S*H." But military authority is upheld more often than it is respected. For example, "Tour" followed the misadventures of an overzealous colonel whose Cold War mentality and thirst for glory cost the unit many lives, including his own. And one episode of "China Beach" concerned an unearned medal that the brass thrusts on an unwilling recipient. It's part of a coverup for a failed secret mission that led to his squad killing civilians in Cambodia. The army cynically covers its mistakes by creating a "hero" rather than disclosing the squalid truth.

It is too early to tell whether these shows represent a new phase of television's own "tour of duty." But it's a long way from "Navy Log" to "China Beach." This progression also flavored our statistical portrait of TV's soldiers. The content analysis shows how the military has slipped from its once secure beachhead in prime time. The number of military personnel held steady at about 9 percent of all characters with census-coded occupations until 1975. Thereafter, however, it tumbled to only 4 percent. When the question turns from how often to how well they were portrayed, the key change came much earlier. In the early years, TV lauded soldiers of all stripes. After 1965, it began to distinguish sharply between the virtues of enlisted men and officers.

In the first decade of the study, dominated by military dramas, positive portrayals outnumbered negative ones by roughly two-to-one margins for both groups (47 to 21 percent for enlisted men, 49 to 26 percent for officers, with the remainder playing neutral roles). Then came television's social relevance decade and the first wave of service sitcoms. Both groups suffered as the military's image went into eclipse, but officers bore the brunt of the decline. From 1965 through 1974, enlisted men managed a slightly positive overall portrayal (36 to 26 percent), while a majority of officers were shown in a negative light (51 percent negative and only 37 percent positive). Since 1975, the enlisted men have rebounded back to the levels of their glory days, with 44 percent positive and only 14 percent negative characters. The officers have remained in television's doghouse, with only 29 percent attracting positive portrayals and 44 percent cast in negative roles.

Across the entire three decades, that leaves enlisted men with a two-to-one advantage in positive over negative characters (42 to 21 percent), while officers have been evenly split between good and bad guys at 39 percent apiece. Even that standoff draws heavily on the reservoir of goodness the brass built up during television's early promilitary years. Since 1965, military officers have taken their place in the prime-time rogues' gallery, along with business executives, local sheriffs, and politicians.

This grouping is somewhat misleading, since the military characters were far less likely than the others to commit crimes or lack redeeming characteristics. Unlike the murderous businessman or the corrupt politician, TV's military officer was usually no worse than an inept bumbler or a blustering Colonel Blimp. It was not even officer status per se that disqualified most characters from virtue. The kiss of death was to have a higher rank than the series star. The real enemy in most military shows was army regulations or a military mindset. These vices were inevitably embodied by a comic foil who outranked the hero. Thus Trapper John and Hawkeye, both captains, managed to work around Major Burns and later Major Winchester. Lt. Commander Quinton McHale maneuvered around the hapless Captain Binghamton. And Capt. "Pappy" Boyington continually outsmarted Colonel Lard. By the same token, noncoms from Sgt. Bilko to CPO Sharkey made life miserable for their superior officers.

The common theme in these shows is one that caught on later in TV's white-collar workplace—ridiculing the boss. Our content analyses found that whenever military scripts commented on backtalk, they heartily endorsed the practice. Of course, ridiculing authority was never an option in the dramatic treatments of military life. It was only the comedies that took this theme and ran with it. For instance, midway through a 1966 episode of "McHale's Navy," a besieged Captain Binghamton asks rhetorically, "How do I get myself into these things?" Ensign Parker immediately answers matter-of-factly, "Well, I think it's because you're so stupid." When McHale acts disturbed by this remark, Binghamton puts his arm around Parker and says, "Don't worry about it! What are a few insults when my whole life is at stake?"

The early dramas naturally conveyed a very different tone. A common theme was that the roles and traditions of the institution should be upheld. When the system's authority or legitimacy was brought into question, the status quo was upheld 85 percent of the time. A vivid instance of this lesson came in a 1956 "West Point Story" we coded. When a star halfback on the football team breaks a minor regulation, Major Nielson puts him on report, and he's sentenced to extra guard duty. Unfortunately, this will make him unavailable for the big game against navy. Nielson's wife thinks it's silly not to overlook the infraction in view of the game's importance. Nielson explains that it's part of the tradition of equality for all cadets: "The essence of West Point discipline is equality, and equality is the key to the character of the academy. . . .

"There are no favorites at West Point; regulations apply to everyone. Even [superintendents] don't tamper with them. If they did, equality would disappear and the whole system would fall apart."

That's not exactly the image of the system that "Emerald Point" or "M*A*S*H" conveyed. In fact, virtually all the pro-status quo episodes we coded aired before 1970. This illustrates the more general point that television's version of the military has changed markedly over the years. In fact, its portrayal has probably undergone as sharp a change as any sector of society. In the mid-1960s, a dramatic genre that fostered conservative moral lessons about authority, tradition, and discipline gave way to a sitcom format that satirized and lampooned those very traits. In principle the two formats could coexist, as "Bilko" did with "West Point Story" in the 1950s. But recent forays into the soaps notwithstanding, the traditional military drama has shown no sign of life for nearly two decades. It will take more than a "M*A*S*H" unit to revive it.

THE GOSPEL ACCORDING TO HOLLYWOOD

On television religion is relegated mostly to Sunday mornings and televangelists. Clergy are a rarity on prime time, and religious themes are rarer still. Just over one in every hundred census-coded characters have had religious vocations, and their number has dipped below the 1 percent mark since 1975. When they do appear, however, the clergy are portrayed as the establishment's human face. Unlike executives, politicos, and military brass, they have always been one of television's good-guy professions.

Throughout the three decades of our study, the proportion of positive clergy has always exceeded 80 percent. Yet this consistently positive portrait actually reflects significant changes in the way television presents both clergy and churches. Over the years, TV's religious figures have held onto their halos by changing their tunes.

There is no prime-time genre of religious themes along the lines of cop shows, doctor dramas, or service sitcoms. Television has never found a living room-sized equivalent for the big-screen biblical epics of Cecil B. DeMille. Nor have small scale cinematic approaches like "The Nun's Story" or "Song of Bernadette" attracted much attention from the networks. As a result, most religious themes and characters have played in single episodes of series that otherwise featured strictly secular fare.

There have been a few series built around the religious life. A notable early entrant was "Crossroads," an anthology series that aired from 1955 to 1957. Each episode dealt with the personal or professional problems of a clergyman. A wide variety of faiths was represented, and the various ministers were usually portrayed as sensitive, caring, and very human. A 1955 episode in our sample concerns a young minister who is duped into letting a con artist become a church fundraiser. The man absconds with the money but is caught and sent to jail. The minister later supports him at his unsuccessful parole hearing. Though the church elders reprimand him, he argues for the Christian principle of forgiveness. Later the minister learns that the man has had a religious conversion. Despite his qualms that it might be a ruse, he again speaks for him at a parole hearing, this time successfully. The one-time conman's conversion turns out to be genuine, and the minister's faith and charity are redeemed.

This episode was typical of the period in its portrayal of clergy as compassionate and humanitarian, as well as in placing their behavior in the context of traditional religious settings. A similar atmosphere marked TV's early 1960s' version of the film classic "Going My Way." It featured Gene Kelly in the Bing Crosby role of an idealistic young priest in a working class New York City parish. Series in which clergy appeared in a single episode featured similarly positive portrayals. For example, we coded a "Combat!" episode about a German military chaplain who saves the life of a wounded American soldier during World War II. He not only prevents a German officer from killing the man, but eventually sacrifices his own life by throwing himself onto a live grenade. The American is deeply impressed at how dedication and religious devotion can transcend the hatred bred by war.

Other shows from the 1950s and early 1960s dealt directly with religious themes by portraying a transcendent God whose ways surpass human understanding but whose laws must be obeyed. For example, a 1956 episode of "Noah's Ark" chronicles the successful efforts of two veterinarians to save a fawn shot by hunters. When the fawn recovers, they plan to release it. Their receptionist asks why they bothered to save it, since they're sending it out to be shot again. Sam, the old and wise Dr. Gillespie character, tells her that their skills were only a small part of what saved the deer. God saved it, he continues, as part of His plan. The fawn may be shot again or die of disease, or it may live to a ripe old age. They can only do their job without knowing what God intends.

Divine law was no more to be transgressed than divine intention was to be guessed. For example, a "Gunsmoke" segment in our sample follows the efforts by a group of nuns to care for a wounded outlaw and turn him to the path of righteousness. They even protect him from Marshal Dillon while he heals. When one sister worries that they are breaking the law by harboring a criminal, the Reverend Mother replies, "We answer to a higher authority, and whatever we do must be right in His eyes." Her faith is rewarded when the ex-robber turns himself in and helps the marshal capture the rest of the gang.

The last successful series to portray clergy in a traditional fashion was "The Flying Nun." Of course, a nun who flies when the wind catches her starched cornette can hardly be called traditional in all respects. But this was a gimmick typical of 1960s "idiot sitcoms," that featured such bizarre leading characters as a Martian, a witch, and a talking horse. In this programming atmosphere, the most surprising thing about the aerodynamic Sister Betrille was that the writers didn't give her wings. Aside from this soupçon of silliness, the series followed the "Going My Way" formula by pitting a spunky but impulsive young nun against an older superior who was more conservative but fundamentally good-hearted. There were problems with hierarchy and rules, but Mother Superior was portrayed as reasonable and often justified in her efforts to rein in her charges. She was genuinely interested in their welfare and the dignity of Holy Orders. And the convent setting rooted the characters' behavior in its institutional context. The series was even commended by real-life religious orders for humanizing the work of nuns.[8]

Despite Sister Betrille's hijinks, the old-school tradition of religious portrayals began to change in the late 1960s. Until then clergy were almost invariably shown as representatives of religious institutions whose legitimacy was taken for granted. They questioned neither their own faith nor their church superiors. On the eve of television's social relevance phase, however, religious characters began to ask such questions.

The new trend was epitomized by a 1967 episode of "The Fugitive" that we coded. In this segment Dr. Kimball (the fugitive) turns to his old friend Sister Veronica for help. The antithesis of the cloistered clergy, this socially concerned nun runs a school for troubled girls. Years ago, we learn, Kimball dissuaded her from renouncing her vows, because she felt out of touch with the people she wanted to help. Kimball suggested she get a new assignment rather than leave the order. Now Kimball asks her to help him find the one-armed man who killed his wife. But Sister Veronica first tries to find a runaway from her school. Unfortunately, she not only fails to find the girl but also loses the chance to help Kimball. This brings on another personal crisis, as she questions her abilities and vocation. Then the runaway returns, and a sympathetic priest convinces her that she is doing God's work, even though she failed her old friend.

Sister Veronica was like many of her TV contemporaries—socially aware, reform oriented, driven to make the world better. The moral and ethical teachings of their churches began to take a back seat to more narrowly personal virtues. The goal now was to be a moral person, but not a moralist. For these clergy morality meant compassion, humanitarianism, and sacrifice. Soon the message took on anti-establishment overtones. Tradition, standard procedures, and even the law should be challenged if they impinged on an individual unfairly. The clergy of the late 1960s and early 1970s were great proponents of individual conscience in opposition to social authority.

Clergy in shows like "The Bold Ones," "Sarge," "Storefront Lawyers," and even "Kung Fu" were often shown as impassioned reformers demanding that justice or propriety be defined in new terms. In an episode of "The Bold Ones" in our sample, a radical Catholic priest is harboring Vietnam draft evaders and deserters. Two soldiers come into his church, beat him up, and take one deserter back to camp. The police investigate the assault and kidnapping despite objections from both the military and the church. The priest's superior, Bishop Martinez, sanctimoniously tells the D.A., "Now that Father Hayes cannot speak for himself, the Church must speak for him. I am anxious that the Church's voice be heard reassuring the community, acting to unite rather than divide. I don't want tirades against the armed forces from the pulpit." The D.A. observes that "The Church has often needed the army," to which Martinez replies, "The army has often needed God. . . .This is a time for caution and common sense. A realistic appraisal of what is best for the whole community, rather than just a few who would fragment it." These sentiments are intended to appear self-righteous and hypocritical. The church hierarchy is presented as the heavy in opposition to the idealistic young priest. Eventually the injured priest announces his disgust with the whole system. He blames everyone, including himself, for the violence that occurred. The show tells us that the Church is lucky to have such idealistic rebels to counterbalance its repressive tendencies.

One series presented such a character in the lead role. The star of "Sarge" was a Catholic priest who used to be a police detective and, before that, a Marine Corps first sergeant. Father Cavanaugh was a tough fighter for the underdog. A giant of a man, he was as likely to use his fists as his position of authority. In the episode we viewed, Cavanaugh is asked to fill in for the Catholic chaplain at a Marine base. Once there, he meets a young Marine recruit who is being harassed by his first sergeant. When the recruit disappears, Cavanaugh becomes worried. The other chaplain on the base tells him the young recruit is lazy and unworthy of his concern. Undeterred, Cavanaugh presses on, forcing a reluctant base commander to open files that reveal a string of abuses. Eventually Cavanaugh discovers that the first sergeant hates anyone who comes from his area of Appalachia, so he forces them out of the unit. Cavanaugh eventually rescues the recruit and pushes the military into punitive action against the offending sergeant. An interesting sidelight is the complete callousness shown by the "establishment" chaplain. He has never met the recruit but, on the basis of hearsay, labels him lazy and worthless.

By the mid-1970s the radical priests were gone and clergy in general dropped out of sight. With the exception of "M*A*S*H"'s Father Mulcahy, most of those who remained were background characters. They could still be seen at weddings, funerals, and occasionally in neighborhood centers. During this period, a short-lived 1978 sitcom called "In the Beginning" indicated how far TV's religious milieu had moved from the "Going My Way" model. This series featured the same mix of an older conservative and a young progressive cleric, but there the similarity ended. The basic conflict was between a young, with-it, Hispanic nun and an old, fogey, Irish priest. The story was set in an inner-city storefront mission among bookies and winos. The mossback priest, Father Cleary, was a pompous bore played by McLean Stevenson (previously "M*A*S*H"'s bumbling authority figure Colonel Blake). He referred to his young antagonist, the street-wise Sister Agnes, as "Attila the Nun."

In recent years the few clergy who play substantive roles are often either social activists or questioners of church authority. In 1986, for example, "Cagney & Lacey" work with a radical priest to help an illegal alien avoid deportation. The priest, who is involved in the Sanctuary movement, explains that many aliens face persecution in their home countries. His mission is to help them stay one step ahead of the Immigration and Naturalization Service. Impressed, the dynamic duo help one alien evade an INS agent who discovers the Sanctuary safehouse.

That same year, "Spenser: For Hire" featured a muckraking plot recalling the feature film *And Justice for All*. The story begins with a young novitiate who decides against taking her vows and instead dedicates herself to fighting slumlords. When she unexpectedly commits suicide, Spenser investigates. Her former lover, a public interest lawyer she

394

worked with, tells him she received some unknown piece of shocking news the day she killed herself. Eventually Spenser uncovers the truth. She had discovered that the landlord she was fighting was the Catholic church. It seems the church secretly swapped land parcels with a shady land developer. The deal enriched church coffers by making it one of Boston's biggest slumlords.

In the course of Spenser's investigation, the developer and an influential monsignor try to cover up the deal. When the monsignor fails to stop the investigation, the developer has the lawyer killed and tries to murder Spenser as well. After Spenser threatens to make the whole story public, the church agrees to make major repairs and transfer the priests who authorized the deal. The church is treated throughout as a powerful interest group pursuing political and financial goals, with nary a hint of more elevated purposes.

The only religious figure to star in a recent series manages to bypass institutional hierarchies altogether. On "Highway to Heaven," Michael Landon plays an itinerant angel named Jonathon who helps the troubled and needy. His travels take him to the sides of a Vietnamese refugee facing prejudice from American townspeople, elderly pensioners whose housing is about to be razed by the inevitable greedy businessman, and so forth. In the 1984 premier, he comes to the aid of an uptight former cop who's wallowing in self-pity and booze. Jonathon's rescue mission involves helping the man get in touch with his feelings. The ex-cop finally develops the self-confidence to express his gratitude by hugging Jonathon and confiding, "I couldn't have done that before I met you."

Washington Post reviewer Tom Shales commented on this touching scene, "It's always so bemusing when Hollywood 'discovers' traditional values and then parrots them back as hot-tub theology and beach-blanket nonthink."[9] Hollywood has had its share of angels, from Claude Raines' redoubtable Mr. Jordan to James Stewart's unlikely guardian Clarence in *It's a Wonderful Life*. But they lacked the social consciousness and angelic coiffure of the character industry insiders call "Jesus of Malibu."

Jonathon's approach is typical of prime time in one other respect. He relies mainly on gentle persuasion rather than the miraculous powers available to him. Television has never been big on miracles or similar demonstrations of a supreme being's work, despite its fascination with paranormal or occult phenomena. In our study one show in every twelve contained some apparently extrasensory occurrence. Almost one-third of these (31 percent) were ultimately shown to have a natural or scientific explanation. Another one in three turned out to be the product of genuine psychic phenomena, in the familiar manner of sci-fi series like the "Twilight Zone" and "The Outer Limits." By contrast, only 6 percent were attributed to the work of God or the possibility of divinely inspired miracles. (The remainder were either unclear or attributed to comic book "superheroes" like the Incredible Hulk.)

Like the role of clergy on television, the treatment of paranormal activity has changed markedly since the mid-1960s. Before that time, miracles accounted for nearly one paranormal event in five (18 percent). Since then, only 3 percent of these phenomena were treated as manifestations of God's work on earth. By the same token, the popularity of normal explanations for apparent miracles has risen steadily. Before 1965, 18 percent of the scripts eventually explained paranormal occurrences in normal terms. During the next decade, the proportion grew to 27 percent. After 1975 it rose to 40 percent, more than double the proportion of normal explanations offered two decades earlier. Thus, as television grew older, it ceased to believe in miracles.

It's been so long since television celebrated miracles that it's worth recalling some examples of that bygone era, to recapture a milieu that grows dimmer every season. One such story in our sample was a 1962 episode of "The Lloyd Bridges Show," a dramatic anthology. The setting is mid-nineteenth-century Mexico. Two men, David and Tac, steal some gold and hide it in a statue. Tac is caught and jailed, but David tracks the statue to a small town, where it stands in the local church. Soon after the statue arrived, apparent miracles began to happen, and the villagers attribute them to the statue. Instead of stealing the statue, David settles into the village. Then Tac arrives, anxious to recover the gold. He ridicules what he calls a "stupid native superstition" about the miracles. But David replies, "The statue has helped the monks bring faith to the people. Before they came, the villagers were half pagan, and it's helped them to have something to believe in." The incredulous Tac decides to make off with the statue, and David tries to stop him. A villager shoots at Tac but hits David by mistake. As David lies dying, he beseeches Tac to leave the statue in the village, telling him it belongs there. Tac promises and, as David dies, the rain starts to fall, ending a long drought that threatened the village. Standing in the rain, Tac finds the faith to believe in miracles.

If this episode affirmed the virtue of faith, a 1956 "Navy Log" set aboard an aircraft carrier emphasized the power of prayer. As the pilots prepare for their mission, the ship's chaplain prays for their success and safe return. The cocksure Lieutenant Hawkins tells the chaplain to pray for the other pilots, since he prefers to place his trust in "my orders, my training, and my equipment." The mission is a success, but trouble develops on the way back. The rendezvous point is covered with clouds and fog, and the planes are forced to circle while looking for a break in the weather. As their fuel supplies dwindle, the situation grows desperate, and they prepare to ditch in the ocean. Meanwhile the chaplain prays for "these men of war [who] work to save the peace for their children." Various pilots are also shown praying, and one asks God to watch over his family if he should die.

In the climactic scene, the once-skeptical Hawkins speaks to the chaplain over the radio. He asks for help and says he doesn't know a prayer. The chaplain reminds him of one he learned at flight school. Hawkins then prays for God to protect those who fly in times of peril. Suddenly the bridge reports that they've spotted a patch of clear sky. The captain cancels the order to ditch and tells the pilots to "come on home."

Afterward, Hawkins tells the chaplain that he asked the weatherman how the fog happened to clear around the carrier just when they needed it. The chaplain asks what the response was. Hawkins replies that the weatherman, along with the rest of the pilots, "want[s] you to thank God for it tonight in your prayers." Hawkins pauses and then asks the chaplain to include him among those offering their gratitude. In those days, there were no atheists in cockpits, at least not in prime time.

Over the past twenty years, we didn't encounter a single script to match these early paeans to the importance of faith, the power of prayer, and the possibility of miracles. These traditional religious messages were replaced by television's social gospel and cautionary tales about the need to question religious authority. In addition to criticizing church hierarchies, television has also begun to warn against the intolerance of the Religious Right. Recall the story line, cited in chapter 2, in which radio station "WKRP in Cincinnati" was forced to fend off censorship efforts by a fundamentalist minister who bore a strong physical resemblance to Jerry Falwell. A similar message recently appeared in the form of a fable on the updated "Twilight Zone." In this segment, a young trucker joins an older one in driving a mysterious cargo down a barren, deserted road. He is unaware of the cargo or destination until they arrive. Once at the dark, forbidding complex, he finds out that they haul the dead to hell. He is shocked by this, but his partner tells him to enjoy the money and ignore the problems. Increasingly, however, he hears of problems in hell and of cases where innocents are put there. On his second trip, many people beg him for mercy and help.

Shortly thereafter, the trucker meets with the man in charge of assigning people to heaven or hell. He is a self-righteous, book-burning type who decrees damnation for anyone who did something he finds offensive. Mortal sins now include homosexuality, drug addiction, writing suggestive books, and much more. There is no mercy or compassion, and God no longer makes the decisions. The man explains that God finally had to delegate authority. He is thrilled with his new authority, because it allows him to "make heaven even better." He and his colleagues have proudly used a very rigid moral code to send most of humanity to hell. One sin now suffices; neither overall goodness nor repentance bring redemption.

The trucker pretends to go along with all this. On his next trip, however, he stops in a remote area and asks the damned why they are there. He frees basically good people who are victims of the sanctimonious, including a homosexual, a drug addict, and a librarian who stocked allegedly "lewd and dirty" books. The closing narration leads the viewer to think that the trucker will continue to let some go and point them toward heaven. The moral is that going to hell is now a bureaucratic procedure controlled by self-righteous prudes. There is no consideration of individual cases, just strict enforcement of a rigid code of conduct. It is hard to miss the attack on the New Right as a purveyor of hell on earth. According to this script, hell is where they enforce the old morality.

UP (HOLDING) THE SYSTEM?

When all is said and done, where does television stand—alongside the establishment or up against it? The answer is not as clearcut as critics on either the Left or Right sometimes assert. None of the three institutions reviewed in this chapter was panned as badly as business was. Government got burned the worst, but television objects less to the business of governing than to the practice of politics as usual. Prime time has presented model statesmen and legislative crusaders as well as sleazy or selfish pols. Ironically, TV's muckraking social relevance period proved to be the finest hour for prime-time politicians. For once they were the white knights who cleaned up business and other corruption. Otherwise, the pols have been mostly the targets of TV's clean-up campaigns. But the goal has usually been to make government work better, not to get it off our backs. If political leaders would just work for the public interest instead of feathering their nests, television tells us, the world could be a better place.

TV's politicians don't serve competing, but equally legitimate interests. They either serve the people or the special interests. Indeed, politics per se does not serve the public interest, and the public is not protected by the political system. At best, it is protected *from* the system by the occasional reformer who takes on the smoke-filled-room crowd. When it comes to politics as usual, television always votes "no."

An equally sharp dichotomy appeared in military settings. Just as television praises statesmen and condemns politicians, so it applauds the grunt and boos the brass. In the political arena, the distinguishing factor is idealism. The good politician is one who has it. In the military, it is a matter of authority. The good soldier is one who rejects it. Although GIs rate better treatment than officers, the secret of military success is to rank lower than the show's top-ranking character. In prime time, command corrupts. It wasn't always like this. Of all professions, the military's image took the greatest nosedive after the mid-1960s. During TV's social relevance phase, enlisted men and officers were tarred with the same brush. During the past decade, the G.I.s recovered, but the brass remained tarnished. On TV today, military leadership is a force to be ridiculed rather than reckoned with. The real crime is not so much officer status as a regular army mentality that takes regulations and service rah-rah seriously. As usual, it's the mavericks who prevail over the organization man. But that's the exact opposite of TV's military bearing a generation ago.

Of the various establishment groups, only the clergy have always commanded television's respect. Apart from the occasional church corruption uncovered in one of TV's liberal activist dramas, religious characters are rarely more negative than "M*A*S*H"'s ineffectual but endearing Father Mulcahy. On the other hand, rarity has become a defining characteristic of television's clergy. Rarer still are church settings. TV's clergy were made "relevant" during the late 1960s by stripping them of their religious settings. They became social workers or social critics, when they weren't grappling with crises of faith in a secular society. After this social gospel fell out of vogue, religious characters retreated to the sidelines, except when scripts called for marriages and funerals. So today's TV clergy mark life transitions and otherwise mark time. They usually get written into scripts that air during the Christmas holidays, which religious historian Martin Marty calls TV's "be kind to God week."

All this illustrates both television's skepticism toward establishment figures and its reluctance to take on the institutions themselves. This is a distinction often emphasized by critics on the political Left. TV criticizes politicians but not the political system. It ridicules military authority but not the military's mission. It ignores religion but refrains from attacking it. It is hardly surprising, however, that our most popular form of commercial entertainment fails to mount an attack on some of America's central social institutions. More interesting is its increasing unwillingness to uphold the traditional missions of those institutions actively.

Until the mid-1960s television did endorse the traditional roles of religion and the military. Since then it has praised the mavericks while criticizing the established hierarchies. The good guys are no longer the typical representatives or upholders of institutions. Today the internal critic, the breezy skeptic, or the outraged whistleblower has become the hero. This is the flip side of the Left's criticism. TV lauds the crusading politician while presenting politics as either selfish or corrupt. It laughs at military authority and discipline. It praises priests and ministers for their humanity but shrinks from endorsing the essence of their vocation—to represent God to man. In this way, prime-time entertainment remolds the representatives of traditional institutions so they fit into more contemporary modes of exemplary behavior. TV's favorite soldiers expose the idiocy of military authority and bureaucracy, its heroic politicians stand above politics, and its occasional fighting young priests challenge church hierarchies and outmoded traditions. Always excepting business, television doesn't need to take on the establishment these days. It just redefines it out of existence.

———⟶⟵———

12

CONCLUSION:
CALIFORNIA DREAMIN'

*In the vernacular of "Star Wars," television (is) "The Force" of
today.*

—Lawrence Grossman
Past President, NBC and PBS

he medium isn't the only message. The sheer fact of television—its
pervasive physical and cultural presence—has excited endless com-
mentaries about the meaning and import of this new medium of communication. It's the perfect vehicle for armchair philosophy—a subject
you can actually observe from your armchair. Certainly the very existence
of television has changed the way we see the world and each other. But
our lives are not reshaped by a black screen sitting in the living room. The
tube is an empty vessel until it is filled with sounds and images. And in
some ways, television's content is the most accessible aspect of this radi-
cally new entertainment medium. Yet there has been a striking disparity
between the sweeping speculation that goes on about life on television
and the narrow focus of most scientific inquiry.

Sometimes the message is the message. Television tells stories, just
as novels and plays and movies do. Indeed, it demands stories, on a fixed
schedule, day in and day out. The endless flow of plots and characters,

403

always available at the flick of a switch, is what differentiates this from all other forms of mass entertainment. It creates an alternate reality that is effortlessly accessible to the rich and poor, the attentive and passive, the learned and illiterate alike.

The world of prime time is preeminently a social world rooted in the interactions and institutions of American society. Even shows set in the Old West or outer space bear the marks of contemporary America in their plots, characters, and dialogues. And the changing schedules and program genres, from the squeaky clean suburban sitcoms of the 1950s to the steamy miniseries of the 1990s, have carried changing messages about personal relations, occupational roles, moral values, and social structures. To some degree these changes reflect parallel developments in American society. But they also show an internal consistency that can be at odds with external reality. Our anthropology of TV's alternate reality has uncovered the following long-term plot lines:

PRIVATE LIVES

Sex. Its status has gone from prohibited to pervasive since the mid-1970s. Previously taboo topics ranging from homosexuality to incest no longer raise an eyebrow among the network censors. Less obvious but equally far-reaching is a change in attitudes toward sexual activity. Sexual frankness and expressiveness are presented as positive goals, and sexual repression and prudery are condemned as barriers to human fulfillment. Before 1970 extramarital sex had to be justified by a loving relationship, if it was justified at all. During the next two decades, recreational sex was presented as acceptable about six times as often as it was rejected. In the 1990s, hardly anyone ever argues against having sex for any reason.

Characters who were once ignored or condemned, such as homosexuals and prostitutes, are now treated sympathetically, as social victims whose needs or circumstances require understanding and good will. Television doesn't present controversial expressions of sexuality like adultery or prostitution or pornography as desirable. Instead it upholds a non-judgmental stance and warns against the dangers of imposing the majority's restrictive sexual morality on these practices. The villains in TV's moralist plays are not deviants and libertines but Puritans and prudes.

Women. If television's treatment of sex has changed markedly over time, its messages about women have always been mixed. The female of the species has been presented as man's better half but not his equal. In the aggregate, female characters have been portrayed in a more positive light than males and as more likely to succeed in their aims. But their accomplishments have been circumscribed by their traditional roles as zany comediennes, warm mother figures, or practitioners of "women's work."

Female characters have been less likely than males to portray mature adults and to hold high-status jobs or advanced educational credentials. For example, women have accounted for fewer than one in ten educated professionals on TV. Women's activities and motivations tend to represent the private realm of home, personal relations, and sexuality, while men have represented the public realm of work, social relations, and ideology. These portrayals have altered somewhat in recent years, as female writers and producers have begun putting a feminist stamp on prime-time programming.

On the other hand, television adopts a far more feminist perspective toward women in general than it does toward particular women. Whereas female characters often appear in traditional roles, story themes and plot lines frequently argue for women's rights or sexual equality. This advocacy of equal rights for women goes back to the medium's earliest days, but it has intensified in recent years, with male chauvinists often serving as the butt of jokes. Overall, the medium's vision of women has shifted gradually along the spectrum from Lucy toward Lacey. But some tension between feminist scripts and traditional characters still exists.

Family. TV's family life had been more stable and traditional than either its sex life or its depiction of sex roles. From Jim Anderson to Cliff Huxtable, parents (if not father) have usually known what was best for their children, and scripts have rarely undermined parental authority. This is not to say that the tube teaches children unquestioning obedience or justifies authoritarian child-rearing methods. The genius of TV's parents had been to accommodate their children's needs and quirks without losing control over them. Thus television favors a relatively egalitarian family in which parental wisdom lies in appeals to reason and fairness rather than demands for obedience. Youthful rebellion is treated as a legitimate phase that children go through on their way to becoming adults. The generation gap can eventually be bridged by keeping the channels of communication open.

If parent-child relations have remained stable, important changes have occurred in the structures of families and the problems they must confront. The family comedies of the 1950s featured pleasant settings and relatively trivial problems. Not until the 1970s did the wider world break into the family circle, bringing increasingly difficult and controversial problems like teen-aged sex, drug and alcohol abuse, and family violence and sexual abuse. Meanwhile, TV families have had to operate in a social environment that increasingly includes poverty, racism, and a host of other social ills that are often debated or worked out with reference to their effects on the family. So the political world has entered into family life, even if the politics of the family remain unchanged. Finally, TV's traditional family unit has gone the way of the Western. The typical household is now likely to include single-parents or "accidental families" that bring together unlikely demographic and psychological combinations.

THE WORKING WORLD

The Workplace. Television discovered sex and work about the same time. Over the years plots have focused on domestic workers, office workers, businessmen, and professional of all sorts, leaving factory workers as odd men out. Before about 1970, however, TV's work force rarely resided in ordinary offices. The place of families was in the home, adventure was often home on the range, and the workaday world was relegated to glamorized genre settings like cop shows and medical dramas. Then Mary Tyler Moore showed that the office could house an alternative family of co-workers, and the cameras began to go to work.

Even as life on TV changed to include the work world, the ambience of the workplace shifted. Until the mid-1960s, bosses were in charge and workers carried out orders. Since then the lines of authority have broken down. Subordinates not only began to ridicule their bosses, they usually prevailed when push came to shove. Bosses grew less authoritative, while underlings began to run the show from below. By the mid-1970s, the workplace functioned best when morally superior mavericks could work around inept or obtuse higher-ups.

Today television gives us a social worker's vision of the workplace—the solution is less authority and more humanity. The heroes are caring individuals who humanize a heartless world by getting involved in the personal problems of their co-workers, clients, or customers. The villains are the workaholics who put the job ahead of people and bureaucrats who put rules and regulations ahead of common sense. On TV, fortunately, there need be no conflict between personal relations and productivity. So long as everyone gets along in the surrogate family at work, the job somehow gets done. In this family setting, though, father doesn't know best anymore.

Business. Given this vision of the workplace, it is not surprising that businessmen have become Hollywood's favorite heavies. Indeed, it may surprise current viewers to learn that prime time's corporate suites aren't always populated by J.R. Ewing clones. Before 1965 two-thirds of the executives shown on TV were good guys. Since then that figure has been cut in half. Overall, TV's businessmen were not only portrayed twice as negatively as characters in other occupations, they were three times as likely to commit crimes and five times as likely to be motivated by pure greed. It wasn't just big bucks and boardrooms that drew TV's ire; the bumbling small businessman was as common a caricature as the scheming CEO.

In recent years, the image of business has gone from bad to worse as scripts began to take on the institution of business. Commentary on business corruption has become commonplace as writers race to condemn the acquisitive mentality that drives out humane values. If business has any redeeming social values, they rarely turn up on prime time, although low-level entrepreneurs sometimes behave decently. Frequently, though, business characters are cast as selfish social parasites whose avarice leads to villainous and often criminal behavior. In TV's version of the executive suite, crime is the bottom line. According to Hollywood, what is good for business is not likely to be good for America.

Professionals. TV dotes on educated professionals almost as much as it disdains businessmen. Doctors, lawyers, teachers, and the like represent all the noble traits television finds lacking in the business world—selflessness, caring for humanity, dedication to a worthy calling. Their common bond is the ideal of service to others, which contrasts starkly with the greed that is the touchstone of the prime-time businessman.

Over time, this ideal has undergone an important change. Today's TV professionals are more socially aware than their predecessors. They are responsive to social concerns and public issues rather than just individuals and their private problems. The ideal of professional service has been politicized in the broadest sense. The doctor who might once have been content to help an impoverished patient must now get involved in famine relief. A teacher whose work was once confined to the classroom today confronts the problems of racism, drugs, or sexual abuse in a student's home environment. Always praised as servants of humanity, professionals are now prized as its social conscience.

CRIME AND PUNISHMENT

Crime. For all the concern about violence on television, research has rarely focused on the criminal behavior that forms the social context of most violent acts. Video crime is more frequent, more severe, and more premeditated that its real-life counterpart. Our study counted about fifty crimes, including a dozen murders, in every evening of prime time. TV's crime rate has remained fairly steady across three decades, though crime has become even more premeditated and cold-blooded in recent years. But the typical prime-time criminals are neither the vicious muggers and desperate drug addicts who imperil urban life nor the faceless psychopaths who populate theater screens in "slasher" films.

Television tells us to fear the apparent pillar of the community whose well-heeled lifestyle is funded by shady dealings and malicious behavior. Criminal violence is committed most often by upscale mature white males who stop at nothing to improve their already enviable standard of living. The wealthy are far more likely to commit crimes than the poor. A stock character is the greedy businessman whose gains prove ill-gotten. Businessmen make up the largest group of TV murderers apart form professional gangsters. If real-life crime often stems from deprivation and desperation, TV crime is an establishment activity.

Crime Fighters. It takes a horde of heroes to subdue all these heavies. TV's law enforcers range from uniformed cops and Western marshals to private eyes and private citizens who stumble into weekly opportunities for sleuthing. In recent years, the cops 'n' robbers genre has been livelier than ever. The proportion of police has doubled over the course of our study. Despite their beefed-up forces, however, the armor on TV's blue knights has been losing its shine of late.

Until the mid-1970s, law enforcers were clean-cut exemplars of virtue and fighters of evil. Throughout the real-world turmoil of the 1960s, TV's police continued to pursue their quarries within a clear-cut moral universe and a smoothly functioning system of justice, but these were becoming frayed around the edges. During the past decade, this Manichean world has begun to unravel, as scripts have questioned police behavior, their legal and moral assumptions, and the justice system itself. Prior to 1975, good-guy cops outnumbered bad guys by ten to one, and police almost never got involved in crime. Since then, the good-to-bad ratio has declined to three to one, and police are now as likely to commit crimes as any other prime-time occupation. Among all law enforcers, the crime rate tripled after 1975.

Meanwhile, the police increasingly deal with criminals who are portrayed more sympathetically and a justice system that is not. The old-school moralist mentality now shares the stage with the sociological perspective of individuals driven to their illegal activities by conditions beyond their control. Even when they finish their newly complicated task of sorting out good and evil, law enforcers may discover that the bad guys either go free or are in cahoots with a corrupt criminal justice system. Before 1975, nine out of ten shows affirmed the system's honor. Since then, fully half have portrayed it as corrupt. Moreover, the issue has been raised twice as often since TV began to cast a more jaundiced eye on the system. Today the good guys have to fight the bureaucracy or internal corruption as well as the killers and vice lords who populate TV's mean streets.

As the cops have been encumbered by new constraints, much of the slack has been picked up by private eyes and citizen sleuths, who are exempt from the system's failings. Unlike their official counterparts, these outsiders are as heroic and effective as ever. Thus television continues to enforce the law without glorifying the law enforcement system. The need for mavericks and outsiders to catch up with establishment evildoers makes for a major role reversal. More than ever on prime time, insiders break the law and outsiders enforce it.

THE PUBLIC SQUARE

Race and Ethnicity. Burned by protests over early shows like "Amos 'n' Andy," the networks created a homogeneous world of generic Northern European characters that lasted until the late 1960s. Then black characters established a foothold in the prime-time fantasy world, and during the following decade ethnic comedies became a programming staple. All-black sitcoms and ethnic melting pot premises both proved popular, and the heroes of cop shows began to take on an ethnic flavor. During 1965-75, the proportion of identifiable ethnics doubled over the preceding decade's total.

Equally important, television began to celebrate cultural diversity. Whereas a common early theme concerned the need for immigrants to cast off their old-country ways, the newer shows pointed out the virtues of pluralism. TV presents a pluralism without pain, in which groups of all sorts could get along with a little understanding, and the only real roadblock to harmony was the occasional ignorant bigot. Deep-rooted cultural differences were rarely recognized and never legitimized. Any differences that existed on the basis of racial or ethnic heritage could be worked out with a dose of good will. Accordingly, television began to feature a vast array of friendly relations among people of diverse backgrounds, which ran smoothly aside from external pressures caused by ignorance or intolerance. Paradoxically, television celebrated cultural diversity by focusing on the abstract "humanity" we all share. Universal good will was denied only by the prejudiced and narrow-minded, who were the villains in this morality play.

Notwithstanding this idyllic vision, not all groups fare equally well in television's multiethnic society. Once virtually excluded from prime time, blacks are now favored with relatively positive or upbeat portrayals, although critics still complain about enduring racial stereotypes. By contrast, Hispanics have always been portrayed as criminals and low-lifes. For example, over one in five Hispanic characters commits a crime, twice the rate among whites and three times that of blacks. Despite all the rhetoric in scripts praising pluralism, Hollywood has cracked the door open wider for some minorities than for others.

Politics. Politics runs neck and neck with business in the competition for TV's least-liked occupation. A majority of politicians wear black hats, and this was true even in TV's early years, when the medium was generally kinder to the establishment. Television's ticket has been split between Machiavellian wheeler-dealers and corrupt power-brokers, on the one hand, and the occasional crusading maverick or idealistic outsider, on the other. The latter, the good-guy politicians, dominated during television's relevancy period during the late 1960s and early 1970s. They tended to stand for Good Things like the public interest, honesty and accountability, civil rights, and environmentalism. But the Mr. Smiths who came to Washington were quickly swept out of office, leaving behind a motley crew of bumbling Boss Hoggs and backroom schemers on the soaps.

The tube takes a dim view of the whole political process. Political decisions are pictured as the outcome of narrow self-interest or the unseemly influence of special interest groups, often representing big business. If anything, this view has taken a change for the worse in recent years, with the political process portrayed as corrupt half the time in shows since 1975. On television, politics per se does not serve the public interest, and the public is not protected by the political system. At best, it is protected *from* the system by the occasional reformer who takes on the smoke-filled room crowd. When it comes to politics as usual, television always votes "no."

The Military. While TV has been down on politics from the beginning, it was once upbeat on the military. Since the mid-1960s, though, the armed services' image too has gone downhill. In fact, the military's prime-time profile has endured the greatest fall from grace of any social institution.

During the first decade of our study, soldiers appeared in action dramas set in World War II and anthology series that upheld the military's mission and traditions in a relatively low-key fashion. In this early phase, positive portrayals of soldiers outweighed negative ones by a two-to-one margin. Even then, flag-waving shows were rarities. The focus was on human drama within the context of a military setting whose legitimacy was taken for granted.

Since the late 1960s, the dominant genre has been the service sitcom, which has followed in the footsteps of "Sgt. Bilko." These series followed the formula of quick-witted subordinates fast-talking their way around bumbling brass hats and rigid regulations. The genre found its apotheosis in "M*A*S*H," which added a sharper edge to the antimilitary jokes and eventually developed into a unique comedy-drama format with an antiwar message.

In recent years, the military's presence on TV has receded sharply, with officers still cast largely in the Colonel Blimp mold. The real crime is not so much officer status as a regular army mentality that takes regulations and service rah-rah seriously. As usual, it's the mavericks who prevail over the organization man. But that's the exact opposite of TV's military bearing a generation ago.

Religion. This is the one establishment institution that television has rarely criticized. But here, too, much has changed over the years. Religious themes and figures have always been a rarity on prime time, although the clergy who do appear are usually positive characters. Early on, their activities were placed in the context of traditional religious settings and church institutions. Beginning in the late 1960s, this traditional image disappeared as television's clergy became more socially aware and reform oriented.

Television's social gospel soon took on anti-establishment overtones, and its model religious figures came to resemble Scott Sloane, the trendy "fighting young priest" from "Doonesbury." In the full bloom of the relevance era, radical priests took on the church hierarchy to demand changes in an outmoded system. In recent years, religion has remained on the sidelines, aside from the occasional proponent of social justice or parody of New Right fundamentalism.

As one indication of the decline of traditional religious material, we found that paranormal events were portrayed as divinely inspired six times as often before 1965 as thereafter. As television has grown older, it has ceased to believe in miracles. Today, religion is neither reviled nor venerated in prime time. Mostly, it's regarded as irrelevant.

Box Populi

These changes in the prime-time dreamscape are all of a piece. They show how this fantasy world has become more concerned with social relevance, political commentary, and cultural criticism. Escapism has given way to engagement, and entertainment meshes ever more seamlessly with advocacy. Hollywood's version of America has changed as much as America itself has, but not always in the same direction.

Thirty years ago television's content reflected a more traditional social order, more conservative assumptions about how society works, and more restrictive standards about the propriety of program material. This distant world was dominated by the private lives of traditional families and the protection of society by high-minded law enforcers. It was a world in which social institutions worked, and political concerns rarely intruded into the private lives of the populace. The military assured our national security, and the churches looked after our spiritual values. Moral codes were clear cut and transgressors were punished. Business executives were good guys, and even when bumbling bosses offered amusement, backtalk from workers was a rarity. In general, life's problems were manageable, and the people in charge could usually be trusted to manage them pretty well.

This world began to disappear in the middle 1960s, as television discovered political issues, social conflict, and populist appeals. By decade's end some characters were calling for social change, others were confronting newly hostile authority, and still others were posing moral dilemmas in the sphere of sexual behavior, race relations, and professional conduct. Within a few years, pointed social and political commentary had become as integral a feature of successful sitcoms as wacky redheads and slightly precocious kids once were. The gangsters and low-lifes who were once the main threat to law and order were joined by a phalanx of evil executives and crooked cops. The establishment became a villain, and the good guys had to fight the system in order to make it work. Private life was laden with conflict, as families had to face a new range of social problems and workers and bosses exchanged sarcastic barbs. As surcease from this increasingly conflicted world, television offered its characters new opportunities for sexual gratification. But even the current epidemic of heavy breathing is punctuated by debates over the boundaries of normal behavior and the appropriateness of moral standards.

This, then, is the world that survives in the current prime-time schedule—sarcastic, sometimes cynical, and apt to cast a jaundiced eye on the very standards and sensibilities the medium embraced so enthusiastically a mere generation ago. To call this a less conservative or more liberal version of reality contains some truth but probably carries more weight than these unwieldy labels can safely bear. Some of the change is best characterized as populist—an anti-establishment upsurge of resentment against the rich and powerful. But populism itself has partisan variants, which were expressed in the rise of both a "New Left" and a "New Right" on the recent political landscape.[1]

The New Left's anti-establishment flavor was directed against institutions like business, the military, and religion. Government, in the guise of "old politics," was depicted as a tool of the military-industrial complex and derided for its failure to control economic powers or to protect civil liberties. New Left populism scorned traditional moral restrictions and endorsed "alternative life-styles," including sexual experimentation, feminism, and more egalitarian family groupings. It castigated the "system" as an instrument of upper-status white males that oppressed blacks, women, homosexuals, and other minorities outside the charmed circle of wealth and power. It embraced the banner of society's victims and endorsed strong government action to make politics more open (the "New Politics") and society more egalitarian and pluralistic.

The New Right was equally anti-establishment, but its goals and villains were quite different. Its target was the liberal Eastern establishment, comprised of government do-gooders, activist judges, woolly-headed intellectuals, and an adversary media. This populism mistrusted government not as the handmaiden of repressive capitalism but as an intrusive tax collector on a quixotic mission of economic redistribution and social leveling. It embraced "traditional values," including a patriarchal family and more restrictive standards of sexual morality. It condemned the coddling of criminals and catering to minority "special interests" at the expense of hard-working, God-fearing middle Americans. It called for a return to old-fashioned virtues like free enterprise, personal responsibility, patriotism, and religious faith.

These competing strands of populism diverge sharply in the values they uphold and the "establishments" they oppose. Both arose as self-conscious movements in the 1960s, although the populist Right attracted little media attention except in its incarnation as a "silent majority" until the Reagan years, when it became very vocal indeed. Meanwhile, the contemporaneous rise of populistic material in television entertainment clearly drew upon the left-wing variant far more than the right-wing. The changes in television's social agenda—increasing criticism of business, the police, and the military; endorsement of sexual diversity and experimentation; women's rights, racial and cultural pluralism—have paralleled the development of Left populism.

This is not to say that TV entertainment has followed this agenda unreservedly or has engaged in anything like a radical critique of American society. As we have seen, the "politics" of TV entertainment are mainly a matter of either legitimizing or criticizing social norms and modes of conduct. But beginning from a relatively apolitical and traditional perspective on the social order, TV has meandered and lurched uncertainly along paths forged by the politics of the populist Left.

We can demonstrate this point more systematically with regard to social institutions. To illustrate TV's changing view of the establishment, we combined all 139 shows that addressed the theme of honesty vs. corruption in business, politics, and the justice system. Before 1975, 47 percent of these shows indicted the system and 53 percent exonerated it. After 1975, 70 percent condemned the institution as corrupt, and only 30 percent upheld its honor. Moreover, nearly as many shows (sixty-nine) raised this issue in the study's last decade as in the first two decades combined (seventy). So establishment corruption has become a much more common theme of TV entertainment in both relative and absolute terms since 1975.

Although the direction of change is evident, the extent of change varies from one topic to another. For example, television is still relatively traditional in the roles it assigns to female characters but aggressively feminist in the plots that directly address the status of women. Similarly, shows rarely cast such traditional authority figures as clergy or policemen as bad guys, but scripts are increasingly likely to attack religious intolerance or corruption in the criminal justice system.

These examples illustrate more than that the politics of TV entertainment is a mixed bag. They also reveal something about the nature of the mix. The conservative side of television appears mainly in the aspects of life it takes for granted. Few would argue that writers and producers are consciously trying to keep women in their "place" by casting decisions that place them in traditional roles. They are simply populating the screen in terms of social arrangements and interactions that they take for granted, at least until activist groups protest.

This is one complaint of critics on the Left, who argue that television reinforces the status quo by portraying it without criticism. As Donald Lazere puts it, the messages of TV entertainment (and other mass media) "assure us that there are no irreconcilable conflicts within the present social order and that those presently in power are capable of resolving every social problem if we just trust them."[2] Similarly, Larry Gross of the Annenberg School of Communications argues that "the basic reality of the television world is the reality of the American middle-class establishment; its morality is the conventional and rigid Sunday-school morality of the middle class; its heroes and villains are those of the great silent majority."[3] Just by presenting the world as it is without criticizing it, the argument goes, mass entertainment legitimizes its imperfections and thereby helps to perpetuate them.

There is still some truth in this criticism, but it applies far more to the program schedule of a generation ago than to today's prime-time world. Some series, especially traditional family comedies like "Full House," represent holdovers from the early years. But they are not pervasive enough to reverse the trends that began in the late 1960s and have continued unabated since then, as our statistical analysis shows. In fact, the absence of any measurable "Reagan reaction" during the 1980s belies the assertion that television follows the election returns. The internal dynamic of social trends on prime time remained impervious to conservative trends in public discourse on the other coast. If anything, the ascendance of conservative politics in Washington may have accelerated television's leftward tendencies by alarming and mobilizing the predominantly liberal Hollywood community (see below).

Similarly, the networks' much-ballyhooed sensitivity to outside pressure has undoubtedly acted as a brake on the engines of change, but it cannot shift them into reverse. For some pressure groups have been more successful than others. It is difficult to imagine producers submitting their scripts to the fundamentalist Coalition for Better Television for prior review, as they have done for the Gay Media Task Force. Hollywood's response to special interest complaints is dictated not only by the amount of pressure these pressure groups generate, but also by the perceived righteousness of their cause.

Television's America may once have looked like Los Angeles' Orange County writ large—WASPish, businesslike, religious, patriotic, and middle American. Today it better resembles San Francisco's Marin

County—trendy, self-expressive, culturally diverse, and cosmopolitan. Some aspects of this world, like the casual acceptance of recreational sex, turn the Left's argument on its head. One could just as easily argue that television is reflecting controversial social changes and, by presenting them as legitimate, accelerating their acceptance across the country.

In many other areas of life, moreover, television offers a picture of life that clearly does not reflect the status quo. One example is the workplace, where workers tell off bosses and warm personal relationships are infinitely more important than economic productivity. Another is ethnic relations. In prime time's pluralistic paradise all racial and ethnic groups live and work together harmoniously, threatened only by the occasional bigot, who is either defeated or sees the error of his ways. Perhaps the clearest divergence from reality is in television's portrayal of criminals, which inverts the real-world portrait of FBI crime statistics. In real-life violent crimes are committed disproportionately by blacks, youths, and low-income groups. In prime time violent criminals are mainly wealthy white, mature adults, especially businessmen.

Equally important, this whole line of argument ignores a critical aspect of TV entertainment. Television does not just portray a social landscape, it tells stories that infuse that landscape with meaning. Yet virtually all scientific research has focused on TV's social arrangements and interactions rather than its stories. The result is a static portrayal that ignores the narrative flow and treats programs as data banks rather than popular entertainment. We know far more about what TV shows than what it tells. As Muriel Cantor writes, "Content analysis usually takes sequences, characters, and events as the unit of analysis and aggregates these into sum totals, outside the context of plots and themes in which they are embedded."[4]

This missing dimension, it turns out, is critical to understanding the nature of life on television. For it is the plots and themes that carry overtly political messages, and they are most likely to convey the concerns of left populism. If TV is most conservative in what it takes for granted, it is most liberal when it tries to make explicit statements about social issues. And this aspect of TV entertainment has become far more pro-

418

nounced since social commentary became a regular feature of Lear-style sitcoms, realist dramas, and TV movies during the 1970s.

As a sign of the changing times, *Washington Post* columnist Jonathan Yardley complained in 1984 that:

> . . .television, which claims to have "grown up," has now arrogated unto itself the business of telling the nation what *life is really like* [his emphasis], up close and personal. . . . The moguls of the medium and their "creative" geniuses, freed by this new maturity, have abandoned the timidity of the past—no more leaving it to Beaver, by golly!—and have taken on what Ed Sullivan would have called the rilly big subjects, the rilly rilly *rilly* big ones: nuclear war, incest, homosexuality, adultery, killer dogs. They love nothing more than the chance to be "relevant" and "bold," to show us the real world "like it is."[5]

Thus, the portrayal of women, minorities, occupations, and the like may constitute the latent politics of prime time. But TV's overt politics can be found every night in shows that tackle themes of feminism, racial justice, and business corruption. To record the former without the latter is like turning off the program at the first commercial break. You see how the scene is set, but not how the story turns out.

Moreover, critics imbue even the demographics of life in prime time with dubious political significance. For example, many studies have shown that women appear on the tube less frequently than men. Further, they usually show up in traditional home and hearth settings or in low-status jobs, such as nursing and clerical work. To feminist critics, these facts carry a sinister political significance. In the words of sociologist Gaye Tuchman, "television proclaims that women don't count for much. They are underrepresented in television's fictional life—they are 'symbolically annihilated.'"[6] This interpretation follows the Annenberg School's conceptual framework, in which the mere presence or absence of a group on television carries political weight. Its "representation in the fictional world" symbolizes "social existence," whereas its "absence means symbolic annihilation."[7]

Although grounded in factual data, such pronouncements on television's "symbolic politics" range far afield in their interpretations of the facts. Is it really fair to conclude that a group is "symbolically annihilated" just because it is statistically underrepresented or shown in socially dependent roles? Or is this a loaded term that expresses the researchers' own outrage without adding to our understanding? As communications theorist Joshua Meyrowitz notes wryly, "It is ironic that many observers of the sexist content of television express horror over the power of television to impose 'second-class citizenship' on young girls, and yet they do not ask why it is that during the same period in which this powerful sexist medium spread through America women advanced in record numbers into the work force and then demanded equal rights and roles."[8]

Similar difficulties await those critics who find conservative implications in the casting of women and minorities as victims of violence by white males. The leading proponents of this view are George Gerbner and his colleagues at the Annenberg School. They regard violence as a symbolic indicator of power. The perpetrators of violence are seen as more powerful than its victims. The audience allegedly internalizes this image of power relations. This interpretive framework underlies their contention that television reinforces the status quo. The perpetrators of violence on television tend to be white males, while victims tend to be female and nonwhite. By presenting women and minorities in such a dependent position, they claim "the prime-time pecking order . . . socializes people for their role in an unequal power structure."[9] That is, this picture of life allegedly strengthens the existing power structure of a sexist and racist society. In short, Gerbner argues, "the violent, sexy, and sexist world of television reinforces prevailing inequalities in the American culture."[10]

Of course, as we have demonstrated throughout this book, the point of these programs is almost always to create sympathy for the victims and anger at their oppressors, who are just as invariably defeated before the closing credits. Once again, the critics can't see the dramatic forest for the demographic trees. Beyond this, it is difficult to see why portrayals of underdog groups as victims necessarily reinforce their

420

dependent position. According to this logic, *The Grapes of Wrath* becomes a conservative book, and the famous Odessa Steps sequence in Sergei Eisenstein's film classic *Potemkin*, in which czarist troops fire on unarmed protesters, takes on a profoundly conservative coloration. That interpretation might have surprised the film's Bolshevik director. The same logic applies to Norman Lear's socially conscious sitcoms, which sympathetically portray minority and working-class women and young people. In Gerbner's framework, Maude Findlay challenges the status quo, while Florida Evans reinforces it.

In evaluating such interpretations, we might also ask what would happen if the tables were turned. What if most prime-time violence were perpetrated by blacks and women on helpless white males? Would feminist and civil rights leaders welcome the change as politically progressive or liberating, because it portrays their constituents as socially dominant? Or would they decry the negative portrayals of criminal blacks and aggressive women as a racist and sexist reinforcement of establishment thinking?

More in line with our findings are the observations of Richard Levinson and William Link, the highly regarded team who wrote such socially conscious TV movies as "That Certain Summer" on homosexuality, "My Sweet Charlie" on interracial romance, and "The Gun," a plea for gun control. They take exception to Gerbner's view that:

> . . . there's a reinforcement of racist, and elitist, and anti-feminist, and anti-age, a reinforcement of totally establishment values as opposed to more radical and theoretically humane values.[11]

Instead, these practitioners of relevancy programming argued:

> TV advocacy usually reflects liberal attitudes. . .many controversial television films—including ours—are manifestations of a liberal (one might more accurately say "humanistic") philosophy.[12]

The View from Sunset Boulevard

Levinson and Link's assessment harks back to our argument that the social values expressed on prime time reflect the personal perspectives of television's creators. But readers needn't take our word for this linkage. It is borne out by a systematic survey of the creative community. Our poll of Hollywood's most influential television writers, producers, and executives uncovered a political profile corresponding to the left populist themes of recent TV entertainment.[13]

The 104 individuals who were interviewed represent the cream of television's creative community. The sample includes fifteen presidents of independent production companies, eighteen executive producers, forty-three additional producers, twenty-six of whom are also writers, and ten network vice-presidents responsible for program development and selection. Many have been honored with Emmy awards, and some are household names. Most important, this group has had a major role in shaping the shows whose themes and stars have become staples of our popular culture.

We found that television's creative leadership represents an urban and cosmopolitan sector of society. Very few have roots in middle America; instead, they were raised in big cities on the East and West coasts. Seventy-three percent hail from either California or the Boston-Washington corridor, with more than one in three coming from New York State alone. Eighty-two percent grew up in large metropolitan areas, leaving fewer than one in five who made the fabled journey from small-town America to Hollywood.

In other ways, however, television's top creators have traveled far from the world of their youth. For example, they have moved toward a markedly secular orientation. Ninety-three percent had some sort of religious upbringing, the majority of them (59 percent) in Jewish households. Currently, however, 45 percent claim no religious affiliation whatsoever, greater than the proportion who profess to any particular religion. Only 38 percent now call themselves Jews, 12 percent remain Protestant, and 5 percent Catholic. Moreover, most of those affiliations appear to be purely nominal—93 percent say they seldom or never attend religious services.

Conclusion: California Dreamin'

Politically, a large majority considers itself liberal and regularly votes for Democrats. Seventy-five percent describe themselves as left of center politically, compared to only 14 percent who place themselves to the right of center. (This contrasts sharply with the national picture. In response to similar questions in national polls over the past quarter century, liberals have never accounted for as many as one-third of those questioned.) In presidential elections, they have supported Democrats over Republicans by margins that ranged between three-to-one and five-to-one. No Republican presidential candidate ever received more than 25 percent of this group's votes. For example, 82 percent supported George McGovern in 1972, while Ronald Reagan polled only 20 percent in 1980.

The creative community's liberal self-image and presidential selections are consistent with its attitudes on social and political issues. Seven out of ten believe that the government should substantially reduce the income gap between the rich and the poor, and 44 percent think the government should guarantee employment of anyone who wants a job. Yet most support the private enterprise system that has been so good to them. Fewer than one in five believe big corporations should be taken out of private ownership, while two out of three believe that private enterprise is fair to workers.

They are far more skeptical about our social and political institutions. In fact, more than two in five (43 percent) endorse a "complete restructuring" of America's "basic institutions." Three out of four say our legal system favors the wealthy, and nearly two-thirds believe that the very structure of American society causes people to become alienated from it. They are just as critical of those in positions of authority. Two out of three agree that public officials are not interested in the average citizen, and over 80 percent reject the notion that people in positions of authority usually know best. In short, their acceptance of the economic system contrasts with substantial alienation from the social and political system.

If the creative community's political alienation contrasts sharply with its moderate economic views, it is consistent with its social liberalism. These people express strong support for the social advancement of women and blacks, and they picture society as unfair to racial minorities

423

and the poor, whose underprivileged position is seen as no fault of their own. Nearly three out of four (73 percent) attribute black poverty to a lack of educational opportunities. Only one-fourth as many (18 percent) see the problem as a lack of motivation. Only 3 percent believe that black gains have come at white expense, and 43 percent endorse "special preference in hiring" for blacks.

With regard to women's rights, only 8 percent believe women would be better off staying at home and raising families than having outside careers, while three out of four strongly disagree with this patriarchal view. However, they are less likely to support preferential hiring of women; only 28 percent endorse this policy. Finally, in their broader expression of sentiment toward social disadvantage, a majority (51 percent) agree that the poor are victims of circumstance rather than their own lack of effort.

This group's social liberalism is most evident in its views on sex and morality. On such issues as abortion, homosexual rights, and extramarital sex, they overwhelmingly reject traditional restrictions. Ninety-seven percent believe that "a woman has the right to decide for herself" whether to have an abortion, and 91 percent say they "agree strongly" with this pro-choice position. Four out of five do not regard homosexual relations as wrong. Only 5 percent agree strongly that homosexuality is wrong, compared to 49 percent who disagree strongly. Moreover, 86 percent support the rights of homosexuals to teach in public schools. Finally, a majority of 51 percent do not regard adultery as wrong. Only 17 percent strongly agree that extramarital affairs are wrong. From this evidence, it would be difficult to overestimate the clash of values when television's creative community confronts conservative critics like fundamentalist Christian groups.

These findings suggest that the Hollywood community's political alienation is rooted in social rather than economic issues. In fact, it is their social liberalism that most clearly distinguishes it from the general public. When the general population was asked the exact same questions during the same time period as our survey, they almost always expressed much more conservative opinions than the Hollywood sample.[14]

TV's leading lights seek new directors as well as new directions for American society. We asked them to rate ten leadership groups in terms of the influence each wields over American life. Then we asked them to rate the same groups according to the amount of influence each *should* have. They perceived America's power structure as dominated by the media and business, who finish in a virtual tie at the top of the heap, followed by government agencies, labor, and the military. Blacks and feminists are at the bottom. When this group was asked for its preferences, the picture changed dramatically. American society should be influenced most by consumer groups and intellectuals, followed by blacks and feminists. Business and the media fall from the top to the middle of the pack. Lowest in the pecking order would be government, religion, and the military.

Finally, we asked these leaders of the creative community about the social implications of their work. Their answers suggested they believed they had a role to play in changing American society. Thus, they rejected the notion that television was too critical of traditional values by an eight-to-one margin. They also indicated a personal preference for realism over escapist fantasy. Three out of four believed that TV should portray society realistically. Most significantly, two out of three agreed that TV entertainment should "play a major role in promoting social reform." This response linked their political attitudes directly to their work. According to television's creators, they are not just in it for the money. They also seek to move the audience toward their own vision of the good society.

These results demonstrate scientifically what members of this community are perfectly willing to concede on the basis of their own intuition or experience. In Levinson and Link's words, "As we sometimes say, there aren't any shows putting down welfare on television. There is a liberal cast. We might say that there is a liberal cast because it is the right attitude that anyone enlightened would have."[15] That is, it is the predominant attitude of the successful writers, producers, and industry executives with whom Levinson and Link work and play. In a separate survey, we found almost identical attitudes among writers and directors of top-grossing feature films.[16] Little wonder that the Hollywood liberal has become as popular a stereotype as the country club conservative. Liberal journalist Sidney Blumenthal suggests that "a generational shift" has made this community more politically homogeneous in recent years, to the point where, "in this Hollywood, the dominance of liberalism has never been in doubt . . . conservativism is barely audible."[17]

Insofar as it is reflected in program content, however, this generational change probably involves a new sense of social mission as much as changing attitudes. This explanation is supported by evidence from sociologist Muriel Cantor's interviews with television producers in 1967 and 1970.[18] She divided producers into groups she called the filmmakers, the writer-producers, and the old-line producers. All three groups were mainly liberal, but their attitude toward TV entertainment differed markedly. The filmmakers were young producers who viewed television as a training experience to help them move into feature films. The old-line producers, the oldest group, viewed their programs as pure entertainment intended to sell products, not politics.

That left the writer-producers, in their late thirties and forties, who aspired to make what Cantor called:

> more "meaningful" television films, that is, films with social messages. . . . They thought television should function as an instrument of social change. . . . One of their main complaints is that instead of leading public opinion and social change, the networks follow social conditions after they have begun to change.[19]

What has happened in the years since Cantor collected her data? It requires no great inferential leap to suggest that, as the filmmakers left the medium and the old-line producers began to retire on their residuals, the politically oriented writer-producers formed the dominant perspective in the community.

For example, a friendly *New York Times* profile of "M*A*S*H" creator Larry Gelbart identifies his creative motivation as "a political anger that laughter helps mask. . . just as 'M*A*S*H' combined humor with anger at a system that created the Vietnam War." The *Times* comes close to an operating definition of "limousine liberal" when it observes, "It may at first seem surprising that a man with four homes can be angry about anything, but he cannot help taking a dim view of those he feels are undermining this country."[20] Among these are numbered Ronald Reagan, the late CIA Director William Casey, and Oliver North. Gelbart himself describes "M*A*S*H" protagonist Hawkeye Pierce as "an idealized me" who "was saying what I felt. . . .He's often frustrated by whatever particular system he finds himself bumping up against."[21]

Once entrenched, this perspective became self-perpetuating. Thus, today's producers treat politicized television matter-of-factly, almost as a professional "perk." In the words of Linda Bloodworth-Thomason, creator of "Designing Women," "It's 23 minutes of prime-time television. . . to address any topic I want. I'd be lying if I didn't say I put my personal opinions in. I do get my own propaganda in." [22]

The increased influence of this mindset is reflected in the way contemporary and controversial material filters into scripts much more rapidly than in the past. For example, producer Irv Wilson got the idea for a TV movie about toxic chemicals in the food supply from a *Los Angeles Times* series entitled "The Poisoning of America." He tried to sell the idea to NBC but got only a lukewarm response. So he waited several months until a *Time* cover story appeared with the same title. Then, Wilson recounts, "I showed it to [NBC Entertainment President] Brandon Tartikoff, and he says, 'All right, write the script.'"[23] The result was a muckraking 1981 film called "Bitter Harvest."

The same principle operates in episodic television, with writers scanning the headlines for materials that can be incorporated into a series script. Quinn Martin describes the approach he took with "The Streets of San Francisco":

> . . .right out of the newspaper, thematically, you deal every day
> with the mores of society. Art should reflect life, and you
> should be right up to date. It's almost journalistic reporting,
> whether it be the Zebra killer or the fact that women's groups
> are forming to combat the attitude about rape—whatever you
> read in *Time* magazine. I try to be as up to date as possible,

reflecting the mores of society told through the two guys on the show.[24]

This is a major change for what was once the most cautious of the entertainment media. Thirty years ago television did avoid controversy, and its content lagged far behind social trends. Today its eagerness to tackle the very latest controversy has made TV entertainment an integral part of the trend-making machine that entwines both news and entertainment media. Norman Lear makes the case succinctly: "The exciting thing in television is to pick up a headline one day and have a story about it three months later on the air for a vast audience. . ."[25]

The references to newspaper headlines and news magazines suggest the specific role television plays in this process. It takes issues and ideas that have filtered into the national news media and further simplifies and dramatizes them for distribution to the viewing audience. Television thus stands at the end of a long chain of popularization that begins with the creation of ideas and issues in universities, think tanks, "public interest" groups, and the like. The process continues with their entry into what Gans calls "upper middle" popular culture via the prestige press and "quality" magazines like *Atlantic* and *The New Yorker*. The most simplified version reaches the mass public in TV movies, "realist" dramatic series, and socially conscious sitcoms.[26] In Dwight MacDonald's terminology, television now carries ideas along the final passage from midcult to masscult.

What this means on a practical level was perhaps best formulated by former CBS executive Bob Wolf, who presided over such wildly successful socially conscious comedies as "All in the Family" and "M*A*S*H": "It just seemed to me that if there was a parade going by, you couldn't be content to sit on a rocking chair on your porch and watch it, you had to get into the parade, and you had to elbow your way to the front of the parade."[27] Todd Gitlin calls this "the ideal network strategy: locate the cultural avant-garde and follow it one step ahead of the rest of the public parade, pulling it along."[28] Thus are the emerging causes and conflicts of American society filtered through the cultural and political preoccupations of New York and Los Angeles and then packaged as entertainment and distributed to the hinterlands.

THE CHICKEN OR THE EGG?

The impact of this process in the popular consciousness is easy to see but difficult to measure. On the one hand, there is a tendency to grant television almost mythic status as the primal shaper of modern life. When former network president Lawrence Grossman compared the medium to "The Force," he was not shy about staking out his claim:

> It is the frame in which we view the dimensions of our society. It reflects the quality of our culture and the character of our priorities. It is a determining influence on our politics, our economics, our ethics, our aesthetics, as well as our psychological and social perceptions.[29]

Unfortunately, precisely because television is so pervasive, and so enmeshed in transmitting cultural images and values, it has proven nearly impossible to sort out its independent influence on attitudes and behavior. Scientists like to look for causes and effects by comparing a group that is exposed to some influence with another control group that is not. Where do you find such a control group in a society in which more homes have televisions than refrigerators or telephones? So, researchers design laboratory experiments whose results may or may not reflect real life. In a typical study on TV violence, after seeing a TV film of an adult attacking a large doll, children engaged in more aggressive play than those who did not view the film.[30] Or they use national surveys to compare the social attitudes of people who say they watch only a little television every day with those who watch a lot. On this basis, George Gerbner concluded that heavy viewers have slightly more socially conservative and economically liberal attitudes than light viewers.[31] But he also reported that heavy viewing is more strongly associated with low levels of income and education, a demographic profile associated with "hard-hat" liberal attitudes. So television viewing may not be the chicken but the egg in this instance.

The real question is not what TV watchers believe but how their beliefs change from exposure to TV programs. Ideally that involves studies done over lengthy time periods that sort out particular viewing patterns as well as the social content of programs viewed, and measures their impact on relevant attitudes. Even if such ambitious research is ever done, don't expect an end to the controversy. After nearly two decades and hundreds of studies on television violence, the National Institutes of Health could conclude only that "the evidence for a causal relationship between excessive violence viewing and aggression goes well beyond the preliminary level."[32] Even this less than earthshaking conclusion is still disputed, especially by researchers at the networks.

One difficulty is that any effects are likely to be cumulative over long periods of time. Heavily publicized special events like "The Day After" (about a nuclear war and its aftermath) and "Amerika" (about a Soviet takeover of the U.S.) produced no measurable change in public attitudes.[33] Such big events can, however, focus public and elite attention on a particular topic by generating interest and discussion through tie-ins with news broadcasts. In each case, issue activists seized the opportunity to mobilize support, and current and former high-level officials actively joined the debate. The programs may not have changed any minds, but they succeeded in dominating the public agenda.

When it comes to more permanent alterations of the public consciousness, though, Levinson and Link are probably closer to the mark in speculating on the effect of their own work:

> We do a show saying homosexuals have a right to conduct themselves the way they choose. We don't know that people are suddenly going to say, "My God, we've seen this show and let's change. We're going to be kinder to homosexuals." Or "My Sweet Charlie" and "We're going to be kind to blacks.". . .We think all of it together, night after night, year after year, may have a little bit of effect.[34]

The potential cumulative impact of such messages should not be underestimated. Scholars know that news media coverage of social issues can gradually alter public opinion very substantially, even when the coverage diverges from expert opinion or objective indicators of reality.[35] Even those who downplay the media's ability to reshape attitudes concede its power in reinforcing existing beliefs and forging new ones on unfamiliar topics. All the barriers of selective perception cannot entirely funnel the flow of information into familiar channels. These considerations led George Comstock to conclude from his survey of the existing evidence in his text *Television and America*, "given the continuing exposure of viewers to unfamiliar experiences and the inculcation of new generations that grow up with television, its influence in a liberalizing direction has probably been profound."[36]

Research on the news media may provide clues to the impact of TV entertainment in another respect. Public attention focused on the impact of TV news during the turbulent 1960s. Social scientists were at first reluctant to credit these impressions because they were unable to measure much effect on public attitudes. It is only in recent years that new research techniques have begun to validate scientifically the massive impact that the public had long taken for granted.[37]

Aside from the violence studies, most TV entertainment content and effects research dates only from the 1970s. The tools are still being developed, as are our abilities to get the best use out of them. We don't always know what to look for or how to interpret what we find. For example, Gerbner reports that heavy television viewers are more critical of business than light viewers. Intuitively this accords well with TV's portrait of executives as villains, but it is subject to the same limitations as Gerbner's other use of survey data to infer causation from correlation.

Herbert London, a dean at New York University, reaches a less obvious but equally interesting (and disturbing) conclusion. On the basis of focus group interviews with New York City high school students, he believes young people learn from television that villainy is necessary to business success. Moreover, this is a price they would willingly pay:

> Insinuating itself into our conversations was the extent to
> which nighttime soap-opera characters serve as models to

431

be emulated. . . . Do the ends justify the means?. . . Yes, say students who watch television regularly.[38]

Interestingly, this mirrors Ben Stein's conclusions from his own interviews with California students:

> Television makes people want to be business people, but it also tells them that to be a business executive you have to be an unscrupulous creep. . . . The mores you see now (in the insider trading scandals on Wall Street) are the mores on "Dallas" and "Dynasty." It's not just coincidence.[39]

This provocative (if unproven) hypothesis carries implications far transcending the portrayal of businessmen. It should give pause to those who seek to send social meanings to the public via TV entertainment without realizing that the message may get garbled in transmission. Our own research recently provided a similar example of unexpected effects. A survey of an ethnically mixed high school revealed that most students gave positive ratings to such flawed or mixed characters as "Taxi"'s half-pint tyrant Louie DiPalma, "Falcon Crest"'s scheming Melissa Agretti, and George Jefferson, the black Archie Bunker. Majorities also regarded the former two as "typical" of Italian-Americans and the latter of blacks.[40] This seems to support not only London's fears but those of Norman Lear's liberal critics that television's power to legitimize characters and behavior can override both the writer's intentions and the laugh track's signals.

Who can predict what other unexpected findings await future researchers in this uncharted terrain? In order to know what to ask about television's effects, much less how to measure them, we need to know more about the changing pictures of American life that the medium brings us. That is why we have sought to illuminate the history of television's fantasy world, as it has both mirrored the real world and cast its own reflection back onto it. This is only a first step, but a necessary one, toward mastering the mysteries of the magic box. We may never fully comprehend the force of its impact on everyday life. Yet, the more our

432

understanding grows, the more we reduce its subtle power to shape our lives behind our backs and under our noses every day. As Comstock writes, "what is most striking about television is that its power is exercised almost beyond the control of anyone—viewer, writer, producer, actor, or network executive."[41]

The uneasiness many people feel about television stems from the sense that the medium is changing our lives in ways we cannot measure and may not even notice. In the brief span of little more than a single generation, television has become the great American dream machine, the source of an alternate reality whose profound impact is widely assumed but little understood. Life on this parallel planet can seem baffling or contradictory, because it is the product of both Hollywood's fantasies and America's. Like Oscar and Felix, they are an odd couple, but an inseparable one.

<hr />

ENDNOTES

PROLOGUE

1. Leonard Goldberg, quoted in Horace Newcomb and Robert S. Alley, *The Producer's Medium* (New York: Oxford University Press, 1983), 73.

2. Quinn Martin, ibid., 72.

3. David Victor, ibid., 91.

4. Earl Hamner, ibid., 169.

5. Garry Marshall, ibid., 249.

6. Todd Gitlin, *Inside Prime Time* (New York: Pantheon, 1983), 269.

7. Herbert Gans, *Popular Culture and High Culture* (New York: Basic Books, 1974), 138.

8. Quotations from Muriel Cantor, *The Hollywood TV Producer* (New York: Basic Books, 1971), 171-172.

9. Earl Hamner, *The Producer's Medium*, 172.

10. Herbert Gans, ibid., 103.

11. Ben Stein, "Miami Vice: It's So Hip You'll Want to Kill Yourself," *Public Opinion*, October/November 1985, 43.

12. George Comstock, *Television in America* (Beverly Hills: Sage, 1980), 123.

13. Ben Stein, *The View From Sunset Boulevard* (Garden City, N.Y.: Anchor Books, 1980), 87, 103.

14. Todd Gitlin, *Inside Prime Time*, 269.

15. Tom Englehart, "Children's Television," in: Todd Gitlin, ed., *Watching Television* (New York: Pantheon, 1986), 87.

CHAPTER 1

1. *Washington Post*, 9 September 1992, G6.

2. *USA Today*, 1 July 1993, 2A.

3. Newton Minow, *How Vast the Wasteland Now?* (New York: Gannett Foundation Media Center, 1991), 24.

4. Times Mirror poll, 3 March 1993; *Electronic Media* poll, 2 August 1993.

5. Times Mirror poll, press release, 10 December 1993.

6. Scripps Howard poll, 22 December 1993.

7. *Electronic Media*, 13 December 1993, 3.

8. Ibid.

9. *TV Guide*, 1 May 1993, 20.

10. In recent years the use of focus groups and other audience research techniques has increased the networks' role in tailoring shows and shaping their development.

11. *TV Guide* cover on David Caruso (Lieutenant Kelly), 8 January 1994.

12. Barry Sopolsky and Joseph Tabarlet, "Sex in Primetime Television," *Journal of Broadcasting & Electronic Media* (Fall 1991).

13. *TV Guide*, 14 August 1993, 9.

14. Ibid., 10.

15. *New York Times*, 25 September 1991, C1.

16. Tom Wolfe, *The Right Stuff* (New York: Farmer Straus Giroux, 1979).

17. *TV Guide*, 30 November 1991, 34.

18. *New York Times*, 23 May 1992, H1.

19. Dorothy Rabinowitz, "Stepping Back into Yesterday," *Wall St. Journal*, 23 September 1991.

20. The data from Nielsen season-to-date ratings reported in *Electronic Media*, 13 December 1993, 30.

21. The data from Nielsen ratings for October 25-31, 1993, reported in "TV's Battle of the Sexes," *Satellite Orbit* press release, 10 December 1993, Vienna, VA, 1.

22. Linda Lichter, Robert Lichter, and Stanley Rothman, "Hollywood and America," *Public Opinion*, December/January 1983, 55.

23. David Prindle and James Enderby, "Hollywood Liberalism," *Social Science Quarterly* 74, 1 (March 1993), 147-148.

24. "Special Report: Black Television Viewing 1992/93," *BBDO Special Markets*, 15 March 1993.

25. *Newsweek*, 6 December 1993, 59.

26. Ibid, 60.

27. William Raspberry, "Thanks, Coz," *Washington Post*, 17 April 1992.

28. Sut Jhally and Justin Lewis, *Enlightened Racism* (Boulder, CO: Westview Press, 1992), 73, 139.

29. See Ellis Cose, "Breaking the Code of Silence," *Newsweek*, 10 January 1994, 22-23.

30. *TV Guide*, 12 September 1992, 39.

31. Leonard Theberge, ed., *Crooks, Conmen and Clowns: Businessmen in TV Entertainment*, Washington, D.C.: Media Institute, 1981.

32. S. Robert Lichter, Daniel Amundson, and Linda Lichter, "Does Hollywood Hate Business or Money?" *Journal of Communication*, in press.

33. *TV Guide*, 14 August 1993, 11.

34. Megan Rosenfeld, "TV Preview," *Washington Post*, 5 April 1993, D6.

CHAPTER 2

1. *New York Times*, January 27, 1988.

2. National Institutes of Mental Health, *Television and Behavior* (Rockville, MD: 1982), Vol. I, p. 56.

3. Joyce Sprafkin and Theresa Silverman, "Update: Physically Intimate and Sexual Behavior on Prime-Time Television, 1978-1979," *Journal of Communication*, Winter 1981, 37.

4. The above quotations are from "Titillating Talk Tests the Limits," *USA Today*, November 18, 1986, D-1.

5. Sprafkin and Silverman, op. cit.

6. Michael Robinson, "Prime Time Chic," *Public Opinion*, March- May 1979, 43.

7. Richard Levine, "How the Gay Lobby has Changed Television," *TV Guide*, May 30, 1981, 6, 3.

8. *Washington Post*, October 7, 1982, D12.

9. Quoted in Gitlin, 261.

10. Robinson, 46.

11. *Washington Post*, October 7, 1982.

12. "Is Prime Time Ready for Its First Lesbian?" *People*, May 1988.

13. Gitlin, 261.

14. *TV Guide*, May 6, 1989, 49.

15. *New York Times*, March 5, 1989, C18.

16. Quoted in *New York Times*, April 4, 1987.

17. Ibid., H29.

18. Ibid., H29.

19. Quoted in *Washington Post*, August 30, 1987, G1.

20. Marlo Thomas and Susan Dworkin, "Sex, the Single Woman, and TV," *TV Guide*, May 7, 1983, 8.

21. Terry Louise Fisher, quoted in *New York Times*, March 8, 1987, H29.

CHAPTER 3

1. *New York Times*, September 16, 1984, H-29.

2. Quoted in Judy Fireman, ed., *TV Book* (New York: Workman, 1977), 48.

3. Harry Castleman and Walter Podrazik, *Watching TV* (New York: McGraw-Hill), 131.

4. Ibid., 225.

5. National Institutes of Mental Health, *Television and Behavior: Volume 2* (Washington: Dept. of Health and Human Services, 1982), 181-183. Among the many studies cited therein, the most thorough are probably found in George Gerbner and Nancy Signorielli, *Women and Minorities in Television Drama 1969-1978* (Philadelphia: Report of the Annenberg School of Communications, October 1979); and Bradley Greenberg, *Life on Television* (Norwood, NJ: Ablex, 1980).

6. Gaye Tuchman, "The Symbolic Annihilation of Women by the Mass Media," in G. Tuchman, A.K. Daniels, and J. Benet, eds., *Hearth and Home: Images of Women in the Mass Media* (New York: Oxford University Press, 1978), 3-38.

7. Quoted in Tim Brooks and Earl Marsh, *The Complete Directory to Prime Time Network TV Shows* (New York: Ballantine Books, 1985), 136.

8. *New York Times*, September 16, 1984, H-29.

9. "Networking Women," *Newsweek*, March 13, 1989, 48-52.

10. Ibid.

11. Ben Stein, "You've Come a Long Way Since Harriet Nelson, Baby" *World & I*, March 1987, 244.

CHAPTER 4

1. From Harry Castleman and Walter Podrazik, *Watching TV* (New York: McGraw Hill, 1982), 263.

2. Quoted in *Washington Times*, November 10, 1987.

3. Thomas Juster and Frank Stafford, *Time, Goods and Well-being* (Ann Arbor: University of Michigan, 1985).

4. Martha Bayles, "At Last, a Family of Mortals," *Wall Street Journal*, June 15, 1987.

Chapter 5

1. Even that ratio includes "mixed" characters with both positive and negative traits among the bad guys. Since such characters tend not to be what sociologists call positive role models, we combined these categories for the sake of simplicity and convenience.

2. Union Media Monitoring Project, "Television: Corporate America's Game" (New York: International Association of Machinists and Aerospace Workers, 1981), 2.

3. Citation noted.

4. Janet Maslin, "In Prime Time, the Workplace Is Where the Heart Is," *New York Times*, February 10, 1980, D1.

Chapter 6

1. Ben Stein, *The View from Sunset Boulevard* (New York: Basic Books, 1979), 12, 15.

2. Media Institute, *Crooks, Conmen and Clowns* (Washington, D.C.: Media Institute, 1981).

3. Linda S. Lichter and S. Robert Lichter, *Prime Time Crime* (Washington, DC: Media Institute, 1983) 25.

4. Stein, 15.

5. TIO press release, June 25, 1981, 1.

6. Letter dated May 1, 1981.

7. Todd Gitlin, "On Business and the Mass Media." Paper presented at the University of Pennsylvania conference on business and the media, Philadelphia, November 4-5, 1981.

8. Gitlin, 5.

9. From an interview on "Hollywood's Favorite Heavy," a PBS documentary that aired on WETA-TV, Washington, D.C., on March 25, 1987.

10. Ibid.

11. Ibid.

CHAPTER 7

1. George Gerbner, Larry Gross, Michael Morgan, and Nancy Signorelli, "Television's Contribution to Public Understanding of Science: A Pilot Study" (Philadelphia: Annenberg School of Communications, 1980).

CHAPTER 8

1. Walter J. Podrazik and Harry Castleman, *Watching T.V.: Four Decades of American Television* (New York: McGraw-Hill Book Co., 1982) 152.

2. Tim Brooks and Earle Marsh, *The Complete Directory of Prime Time Network Television Shows 1946-present*, 3rd ed. (New York: Ballantine Books, 1985) 129.

3. Since 1979, the FBI has collected statistics on arson as an index crime. Previously, it was only reported in sporadic fashion as a Part II offense. Because of this unavailability of rates for earlier time periods, arson has been excluded from our tabulations of the television crime rate and FBI statistics have been retabulated to exclude arson.

4. For instance, the actual rate of forcible rape may be two to three times higher than reported to police. Only half of the aggravated assaults may ever be reported to police. As few as one in three burglaries may be known to police. Philip H. Ennis, *Field Surveys II, Criminal Victimization in the United States: A Report of a National Survey* (Washington, D.C.: Government Printing Office, 1967); U.S. Department of Justice, *Criminal Victimization in the United States* (Washington, D.C: Government Printing Office) reports from 1973-1979. Rather than relying on official police records to indicate crime, these studies select random samples from the population and question those people about their victimization by criminal activities. The first victimization study was done in 1965 by the National Opinion Research Center. Subsequent studies were begun in the early 1970s by the Census Bureau under the auspices of the Law Enforcement Assistance Administration and are collectively referred to as the National Crime Survey. The methodologies and sample composition of these studies diverge from each other and the FBI reports, so direct comparisons are not possible.

5. Violent crimes are the offenses of forcible rape, aggravated assault, and robbery. Rape was a very rare crime in our sample and was less than 1 percent of all crimes committed during this decade.

6. The ratio of comedy programs to dramatic programs was not significantly altered by the implementation of Family Viewing Time, since family-ori-

ented dramas could be used in the early time slots. The decision did reduce the number of time slots open to traditional cop shows, private eye shows, and other crime-ridden program types by almost 4 percent.

7. U.S. Department of Justice, Federal Bureau of Investigation, *Uniform Crime Reports: Crime in the United States* (Washington, D.C.: Government Printing Office), reports from 1955-1984.

8. Ibid.

9. FBI data and National Crime Survey findings indicate that in two-thirds to three-quarters of all rapes, victim and attacker are strangers to each other. U.S. Department of Justice, Federal Bureau of Investigation, *Uniform Crime Reports: Crime in the United States* (Washington, D.C.: Government Printing Office) reports from 1955-1984; U.S. Department of Justice, Bureau of Justice Statistics, *Criminal Victimization in the United States* (Washington, D.C.: Government Printing Office), reports from 1973 to 1979.

10. It should be mentioned here that according to FBI definitions and most criminal statutes only a female can be forcibly raped. When such sexual assaults occur on males they are usually categorized as sodomy or some other form of sexual assault.

11. The FBI Uniform Crime Reports group rape, prostitution, commercialized vice, and other sex offenses, so specific percentages for rape are unavailable. Since prostitution and commercialized vice are far more common than rape, it would appear that rapes resulting in murder are even less frequent than this 1.5 percent figure would indicate. The percentages for TV are based solely on rape.

12. U.S. Department of Justice, Federal Bureau of Investigation, *Uniform Crime Reports: Crime in the United States* (Washington, D.C.: Government Printing Office), reports from 1955-1984.

13. This show was known as "Fireside Theatre" until 1956 when its title was changed.

14. For a more extensive discussion of these crimes and the perpetrators, see; Robert C. Prus and C.R.D. Sharper, *Road Hustler* (Lexington, Mass: Lexington Books, D.C. Heath and Co. 1977); Edwin M. Lemert, *Human Deviance, Social Problems and Social Control* (Englewood Cliffs, N.J.: Prentice-Hall, Inc. 1967); Don C. Gibbons, *Society, Crime and Criminal Careers* (Englewood Cliffs, N.J.: Prentice-Hall, Inc. 1973); Donald Cressey *Other People's Money* (New York: Free Press 1953); David Maurer, *The American Confidence Man* (Springfield, Ill: Charles C. Thomas 1974); M. David

Ermann and Richard J. Lundman, *Corporate Deviance* (New York: Holt, Rinehart and Winston 1982); and President's Commission on Law Enforcement and the Administration of Justice, *Task Force Report: Crime and its Impact, An Assessment* (Washington, D.C : Government Printing Office 1967) 49-51.

15. Approximately 48 percent of the violent index crimes (other than homicide) known to police over the past twenty years were cleared. The clearance rate for index property offenses has averaged about half the rate for violent offenses. These low clearance rates, combined with the low reporting rate illustrated by the victim surveys, make any description of these offenders very sketchy.

16. Clearance rates for murder between 1955 and 1964 averaged 90 percent. During the next decade, that rate drops so that only 85 percent of known homicides are cleared. In the most recent decade only 75 percent of known homicides are cleared.

17. U.S. Department of Justice, Federal Bureau of Investigation, *Uniform Crime Reports: Crime in the United States* (Washington, D.C.: Government Printing Office), reports from 1955 to 1984.

18. U.S. Department of Justice, Bureau of Justice Statistics, *Criminal Victimization in the United States* (Washington, D.C.: Government Printing Office reports from 1973 to 1979). While these surveys do not include data on murder, they do ask about offenders in other violent crimes.

19. Before 1980 the FBI did not report data from arrests on ethnic backgrounds, and since that time only Hispanics have been reported as a separate group. All of this makes it impossible to draw any comparisons between TV and reality.

20. For further discussion of just some of the forces that help to determine arrest, see; David H. Bayley and Harold Mendelsohn, *Minorities and Police* (New York: The Free Press, 1969); Paul Chevigney, *Police Power: Police Abuses in New York City* (New York: Pantheon Books, 1969); Jerome Skolnick, *Justice Without Trial*; James Q. Wilson, *The Varieties of Police Behavior*.

21. Even when accounting for nonreported offenses it seems unlikely that the upper classes are more frequently victimized than the lower classes. Gresham M. Sykes, *Criminology* (New York: Harcourt, Brace, Jovanovich, 1978) pp. 159-161.; for specific figures see *Criminal Victimization in the United States; A National Crime Panel Report* (Washington: U.S. Dept. of Justice, November 1974-1979) vol. 1, 5. It should be mentioned that murder occurs at all economic levels without a clear pattern.

CHAPTER 9

1. Linda and Robert Lichter, *Prime Time Crime* (Washington, D.C.: Media Institute, 1983).

CHAPTER 10

1. Quoted in Tim Brooks & Earl Marsh, *The Complete Directory to Prime Time Network TV Shows* (New York: Ballantine Books, 1985), 40.

2. Henry Castleman & Walter Podrazik, *Watching TV* (New York: McGraw-Hill, 1982), 59.

3. Apparently the intervening decades have brought little change to this image. In an intensive study of 263 prime-time programs during the 1980-81 season, we found that Italian-American characters were portrayed as gangsters or criminals more frequently than as executives, managers, and educated professionals. Not only did most of those characters hold low-status jobs, a majority were unable even to speak proper English. See S. Robert Lichter and Linda Lichter, *Italian-American Characters in Television Entertainment* (New York: Commission for Social Justice, 1982).

4. *Watching TV*, 208.

5. Ibid., 226.

6. Laura Z. Hobson, quoted in Christopher Lasch, "Archie Bunker and the Liberal Mind," *Channels*, October/November 1981, 34.

7. Lasch, 35.

8. Quoted in *Watching TV*, 227.

9. See Richard Adler, ed., *All in the Family: A Critical Appraisal* (New York: Praeger, 1980).

10. Quoted in William Raspberry, "Cosby Show: Black or White?", 1980 *Washington Post*, November 5, 1984.

11. Geraldo Rivera, "There's Lt. Castillo, Sifuentes...and Little Else, " *TV Guide*, April 18, 1987, 40-43.

12. Ben Stein, "Miami Vice: It's So Hip You'll Want to Kill Yourself," *Public Opinion*, October/November 1985, 42.

13. Ibid.

14. Quoted in *Time*, March 19, 1979, 85.

15.   *Wall Street Journal*, June 12, 1986, 27.

CHAPTER 11

1.   Quoted in Michael Robinson, "Prime Time Chic," *Public Opinion*, March/April 1979, 43.

2.   Ben Stein, *The View from Sunset Boulevard* (Garden City, NY: Anchor Books, 1980), 105.

3.   William Cohen and Gary Hart, "TV's Treatment of Washington—It's Capitol Punishment," *TV Guide*, August 24, 1985, 5, 7.

4.   *Washington Post*, April 9, 1985.

5.   "The Fans; Farewell," *Washington Post*, February 28, 1983, B11.

6.   "The TV Column," *Washington Post*, February 28, 1983.

7.   Tim Brooks and Earl Marsh, *The Complete Directory to Prime Time Network TV Shows* (New York: Ballantine Books, 1985), 252.

8.   Ibid., 289.

9.   *Washington Post*, September 19, 1984, B9.

CHAPTER 12

1.   See William Schneider, "The New Shape of American Politics," *Atlantic*, January 1987, 50ff.

2.   From Donald Lazere, ed., *American Media and Mass Culture: Left Perspectives* (Berkeley: University of California Press, 1987), 235.

3.   Larry Gross, "The 'Real' World of Television," *Today's Education* 63 (Jan-Feb 1974), 86.

4.   Muriel Cantor, *Prime-Time Television* (Beverly Hills: Sage Publications, 1980), 41.

5.   *Washington Post*, January 9, 1984, B2.

6.   Gaye Tuchman, ed., *Hearth and Home* (New York: Oxford University Press, 1978), 10.

7.   Gerbner, 1972a, 4 (cited by Tuchman).

8.   Joshua Meyrowitz, *No Sense of Place* (New York: Oxford, 1985), 213.

9. *Washington Post*, October 6, 1984.

10. Ibid.

11. Levinson and Link, quoted in *The Producer's Medium* (New York: Oxford University Press, 1983), 151.

12. Levinson and Link, *Stay Tuned* (New York: St. Martin's Press, 1981), 106.

13. For a detailed description of the sampling techniques and findings, see Linda S. Lichter, S. Robert Lichter, and Stanley Rothman, "Hollywood and America: The Odd Couple," *Public Opinion* (December/January 1983), 54-58.

14. The survey by Prindle and Enderby, cited in chapter 1 (op. cit.) shows large differences between the political commitments of Hollywood opinion leaders and the American public on a wide range of issues. For example, members of the general public were two to three times as likely as the Hollywood group to identify themselves as religious, conservative, or anticommunist. Conversely, the Hollywood group was about five times as likely as the national sample to support gay rights and oppose school prayer.

15. Levinson and Link, quoted in *Producer's Medium*, 152.

16. Stanley Rothman and S. Robert Lichter, "What Are Moviemakers Made Of?" *Public Opinion*, December/January 1984, 14-18.

17. Sidney Blumenthal, "Hollywood Women's Clout," *Washington Post*, October 21, 1987, D4.

18. Muriel Cantor, *The Hollywood TV Producer* (New York, Basic Books, 1971).

19. Ibid, 75, 136.

20. Merwyn Rothstein, "Is There Life After 'M*A*S*H'?" *New York Times Magazine*, October 8, 1989, 53-54.

21. Ibid. 91.

22. Quoted in *TV etc.*, Media Research Center, August-September 1989, 8.

23. Quoted in Todd Gitlin, *Inside Prime Time* (New York: Pantheon, 1983), 171.

24. Quinn Martin, quoted in *Producer's Medium*, 63.

25. Norman Lear, op. cit., 185.

26. Herbert Gans, *Popular Culture and High Culture* (New York: Basic Books,

1974), chapter 2.

27. Quoted in Gitlin, 21.

28. Ibid.

29. Quoted in Barry Cole, ed., *Television Today* (New York: Oxford University Press, 1981), v.

30. Albert Bandura, *Aggression: A Social Learning Analysis* (Englewood Cliffs, N.J.: Prentice-Hall, 1973).

31. George Gerbner, "Political Functions of Television Viewing," in Gabrielle Melischek, K. Rosengarten, and J. Stappers, eds., *Cultural Indicators: An International Symposium* (Vienna: Austrian Academy of Sciences, 1984), 329-343. For a critical analysis of Gerbner's approach and conclusions, see Paul Hirsch, "The 'Scary World' of the Nonviewer and Other Anomalies," *Communication Research* 7 (October 1980), 403-456; and "On Not Learning from One's Own Mistakes," *Communication Research* 8 (January 1981), 3-37.

32. National Institutes of Mental Health, *Television and Behavior*, Vol. I (Rockville, MD.: NIMH, 1982), 2.

33. William C. Adams, et al., "Before and After 'The Day After,'" *Political Communication and Persuasion* 3 (Spring 1986), 191-213; Adams, "ABC's 'Amerika'—The Impact of a Televised Drama," paper presented at the annual conference of the American Association for Public Opinion Research, May 16, 1987, Hershey, Pennsylvania.

34. Levinson and Link, *Producer's Medium*, 152-153.

35. S. Robert Lichter, Stanley Rothman, and Linda Lichter, *The Media Elite* (Washington, D.C.: Adler & Adler, 1986); Elizabeth Noelle-Neimann, *The Spiral of Silence* (Chicago: University of Chicago Press, 1984); Hans M. Kepplinger and Herbert Roth, "Creating a Crisis: German Mass Media and the Oil Supply in 1973-74," *Public Opinion Quarterly* 43 (Fall 1974), 285-296.

36. George Comstock, *Television in America* (Beverly Hills: Sage, 1980), 141. The specific reference is to race and ethnicity, even after taking account of studies showing viewers' selection perception of shows like "All in the Family."

37. See, e.g., Benjamin Page, Robert Shapiro, and Glenn Dempsey, "What Moves Public Opinion?" *American Political Science Review* 81 (March 1987), 23-43; Michael Robinson, "Public Affairs Television and the

Growth of Political Malaise," *American Political Science Review* 70 (1976), 409-432; Shanto Iyengar, Mark Peters, and Donald Kinder, "Experimental Demonstrations of the 'Not-So-Minimal' Consequences of Television New Programs," *American Political Science Review* 76 (1982), 848-858.

38. Herbert London, "What TV Drama Is Teaching Our Children," *New York Times*, August 23, 1987.

39. Ben Stein, "The View from Hollywood and Stein," *Television and Families*, Spring 1987, p. 7.

40. Linda Lichter and S. Robert Lichter, "Adolescents' Racial and Ethnic Images: Television vs. Reality" (New York: American Jewish Committee, 1987).

41. Comstock, *Television in America*, 123.

APPENDIX

Because this book is aimed at a general audience, we have refrained from lengthy and esoteric discussions of our research methods. However, it is the use of social scientific procedures that sets this book apart from more casual and impressionistic surveys of television entertainment. Therefore, we have included this appendix for readers interested in a more extensive discussion of our research methods.

The study relied on the technique of *scientific content analysis*. This method is defined as the objective and systematic description of communicative material. Objectivity involves following explicit rules and procedures that define analytic categories and criteria to minimize a researcher's subjective predispositions. It implies reliability—additional researchers applying the same procedures to the data should reach the same conclusions. Reliability checks and measurements are an integral part of the research. A systematic approach requires that media content

and analytic categories be included or excluded according to consistently applied rules.

Content analysis is a specialized method of scientific measurement.
Because it is both systematic and reliable, it permits the researcher to
transcend the realm of impressionistic generalizations, which are prone to
individual preferences and prejudices.

For this study, we began by conducting what is called an *emergent* or
qualitative analysis. This procedure has more in common with literary
analysis than the tightly defined categories of studies that count the number of minority characters or acts of violence in an episode. It involves
examining a diverse sample of shows and taking extensive notes on all
topics that may later be subjected to formal content analysis. The idea is
to develop an intuitive "feel" for the material so that the formal categories
reflect the essence of the stories and characters, rather than being imposed
on them artificially. In practice, this meant charting a sufficient number
of themes, plots, and character traits, to gain a sense of the way television
tells its stories and the substance of the tales themselves.

For this first phase, we reviewed two hundred programs from the
1977-78 season (four episodes from each of that year's fifty series),
along with one episode from each of fifty different series that aired
between 1963 and 1966(on file at New York City's Museum of Broadcasting) to get a sense of how earlier programs were structured. This
information became the basis of a formal content analysis system that
examined each character for fifty different traits and each program for
over one hundred themes. The character traits ranged from age, race,
and sex, to more complicated factors like motivation and plot function. The themes ran the gamut from timely controversies like abortion and drug use to timeless issues like authority relations and generational rebellion. Each character trait and thematic treatment was
identified on a standardized coding sheet, and college students were
trained to scan the people and plots in each program to see how the
analytic categories were applied. Only then did we begin the systematic analysis that provided the material for our conclusions about life
on television.

Appendix

The procedures for the final phase of the content analysis are described in chapter 1. We catalogued the plots, themes, and character from 620 programs aired over three decades of prime time. This represents roughly one-half of 1 percent of the relevant series episodes broadcast during that period. The techniques of random sampling permit us to generalize about the twenty thousand programs catalogued at the Library of Congress, from which these episodes were selected.

An additional two hundred randomly selected episodes were used to test and refine the content analysis system. Working seperately and independently, two viewers would analyze the same program material until they reached the same conclusions about the themes and character traits on display. If consistent agreement proved impossible on some theme or trait, it was dropped from the analysis. More often, though, initial disagreements were resolved by refining the rules according to which coders based their decisions. Eighty percent agreement was the minimum allowed, and it was usually much higher..

Following these rules was critical to the study's scientific objectivity, because it insured that the coders weren't making subjective judgements based on their own inclinations. For example, is Archie Bunker portrayed as a good guy or a bad guy? In our study, it depends on what he does in the particular episode you watch, how the other characters react to him, what reactions the laugh track signals, etc. It does not depend on what the coder thinks of Archie from previous viewings.

Equally important, each such interpretation is guided by a set of standardized rules and procedures designed to insure that different viewers will assign the same meaning to Archie's behavior. In making such judgements, coders are following rules rather than expressing personal opinions. The resulting high levels of agreement in coding decisions, or *intercoder reliability*, indicate how well the rules worked in minimizing individual subjectivity.

Thus, content analysis is as removed from causal viewing as scientific polling is from "man in the street" interviews. It is not a panacea, in the sense of providing perfectly objective or absolutely definitive results. As in polling, the success of the enterprise depends to some degree on the skill and sensitivity of the investigator, and there is always some margin of error to the findings. In principle, however, this approach can help to structure the vast diversity of entertainment programming by assigning material to discrete categories that facilitate valid, reliable, and quantifiable judgements.

INDEX